2/94

# Cooperative Learning in the Early Childhood Classroom

**NEA**
**EARLY CHILDHOOD**
**EDUCATION SERIES**

# Cooperative Learning in the Early Childhood Classroom

Harvey C. Foyle
Lawrence Lyman
Sandra Alexander Thies

A NATIONAL EDUCATION ASSOCIATION
P U B L I C A T I O N

Printing History
  First Printing: September 1991
  Second Printing: September 1992

**Note**

The opinions expressed in this publication should not be construed as representing the policy or position of the National Education Association. Materials published by the NEA Professional Library are intended to be discussion documents for educators who are concerned with specialized interests of the profession.

**Library of Congress Cataloging-in-Publication Data**

Foyle, Harvey Charles.
    Cooperative learning in the early childhood classroom / Harvey C.
Foyle, Lawrence Lyman, Sandra Alexander Thies.
        p.   cm. — (NEA Early childhood education series.)
    Includes bibliographical references.
    ISBN 0–8106–0361–6
    1. Group work in education—Handbooks, manuals, etc.   2. Early
childhood   education—United   States—Handbooks,   manuals,   etc.
3. Teaching—Aids and devices—Handbooks, manuals, etc.   4. Activity
programs in education—United States—Handbooks, manuals, etc.
I. Lyman, Lawrence.   II. Thies, Sandra Alexander.   III. Title.
IV. Series: Early childhood education series.
LB1032.F69   1991
372.13—dc20                                                    91–24721
                                                                CIP

# CONTENTS

## The Authors

Harvey C. Foyle is Assistant Professor of Education, Emporia State University, Kansas. He is a coauthor of *Cooperative Grouping for Interactive Learning*, published by NEA.

Lawrence Lyman is Associate Professor, The Teachers College, Emporia State University, Kansas. He is a coauthor of *Cooperative Grouping for Interactive Learning*.

Sandra Alexander Thies is Assistant Professor of Early Childhood Education, The Teachers College, Emporia State University, Kansas.

## The Advisory Panel

Peter C. Cross, Kindergarten Teacher, Spencer Borden School, Fall River, Massachusetts

Ruth I. Foster, Instructor/Supervisor of Elementary Student Teachers, Iowa State University, Ames

Patricia D. Freeman, Education Specialist, North Metro Technical Institute, Cartersville Lab, Cartersville, Georgia

Faith L. Garrold, Director of Curriculum, MSAD #56, Searsport, Maine

# PREFACE

This book combines two topics that are not usually linked—early childhood education and Cooperative Learning. Birth through age eight (approximately third grade) is the age span that defines early childhood, according to the National Association for the Education of Young Children (Bredekamp 1987). As a matter of convention, the words "Cooperative Learning" will be capitalized throughout this book. Since there are several approaches to the topic, the authors wish to refer to the whole methodology of Cooperative Learning, rather than to any one particular approach—thus, the capitalization. As we reviewed information on both topics, we found that some Cooperative Learning researchers do not adapt their materials below grade two; others indicate that grade four may be the lower grade limit for their approach; still others believe that their approach works at all grade levels. We noted a lack of coherent information about Cooperative Learning that is aimed specifically at the early childhood level, although one researcher holds workshops specifically for that level.

We hope that early childhood educators and Cooperative Learning practitioners will be able to combine these two areas on the basis of our understanding about Cooperative Learning as it applies to the young learner.

Who are the authors, and why do they have anything to say on the subject?

Harvey C. Foyle taught in public schools for 18 years and has been at Emporia State University for 4 years. Since 1981, he has used a variety of Cooperative Learning approaches in his classes, both in public schools and at the university. He has extensively researched the topic of Cooperative Learning and has conducted classroom field experiments in elementary schools. He is currently a curriculum and instruction faculty member.

Lawrence Lyman taught elementary classes and was an elementary school principal for 13 years prior to joining the Emporia State University faculty 5 years ago. He has used Cooperative Learning both in the public schools and at the university. In addition, his specific knowledge of kindergarten through sixth grade learners has lent invaluable continuity to our understanding of Cooperative Learning. He is currently an elementary education faculty member.

Sandra Alexander Thies came to Emporia State University in 1990. Prior to accepting her current faculty position, she taught in the public schools for 15 years. She taught regular and special education, preschool through sixth grade, spending the greatest amount of time at the kindergarten level. She also served as a Cooperative Learning team facilitator for a staff development consortium of 24 public school districts. Currently, she is a member of the early childhood faculty.

All of the authors use Cooperative Learning in their classes, teach courses about Cooperative Learning, and conduct in-service workshops about Cooperative Learning.

Many teachers contributed to this volume. The authors wish to thank all those teachers who have helped develop the ideas presented in this material. In particular, the following early childhood educators who use Cooperative Learning have provided lessons to us. These lessons vary in content and style due to the many ways in which these educators have developed and presented them. In every case, however, each lesson attempts to point out at least one key feature of Cooperative Learning as it applies to a particular chapter topic.

Many thanks to all of these hard-working educators:

Robert L. Bull, Oklahoma State University Tech, Okmulgee, Oklahoma

Jody Drake, Mission Trail Elementary School, Leawood, Kansas

Julia Ferguson, Lincoln Elementary School, Junction City, Kansas

Mildred Hackler, Lincoln Elementary School, Junction City, Kansas

Dr. Dorothy G. Hamilton, Hamilton Associates: Consultants in Education, Columbia, Maryland

Dr. Mary McDonnell Harris, Center for Teaching and Learning, University of North Dakota, Grand Forks, North Dakota

Verlene Kling, McEowen Elementary School, Harrisonville, Missouri

Carol Ann Lewis, Rising Sun Elementary School, Elkton, Maryland

Vicky Lorentz, Buhler Grade School, Buhler, Kansas

Susan B. Lyman, Office of Professional Education Services, Emporia State University, Emporia, Kansas

Jan Morehead, Walnut Elementary School, Emporia, Kansas

Linda Post, Mill City Elementary School, Dalton, Pennsylvania

Barbara Shafer, Nickerson Elementary School, Nickerson, Kansas

Lori A. Skolnick, Rosemary Hills Primary School, Silver Spring, Maryland

Melanie Smith, Highland Park South Elementary School, Topeka, Kansas

Dr. Bill Stinson, Division of Health, Physical Education, Recreation, and Athletics, Emporia State University, Emporia, Kansas

Dr. Britt Vasquez, Sierra Children's College, Roseville, California

Sandra Williams, Carmichael Elementary School, Sierra Vista, Arizona

We would like to especially recognize the following people for their collegiality and support: Daryl Berry, Joanne Foyle, Susan Lyman, Mike Morehead, Jack Skillett, Wayne Thies, and Gene Werner.

# Chapter 1

# A RATIONALE FOR COOPERATIVE LEARNING WITH YOUNG CHILDREN

*Children are the living messages we send into a
future we shall never see.*
*—Betty Siegel*

Around the globe, presidents and premiers proclaim the critical importance of quality care and education for young citizens. President Bush, in his State of the Union message in January 1990, announced six national goals for education. The first was "that by the year 2000 all children in America will start to school ready to learn." Initially, concerned leaders prioritized good nutrition and health care for mothers and infants. But, increasingly, attention is being focused on the importance of early learning experiences.

Evidence indicates that an investment in the complex task of providing appropriate educational environments for young children will reap generous returns (Weikert 1989). However, the definition of appropriate education is the subject of continuing controversy. Despite consensus among preschool, kindergarten, and primary teachers that the focus of curricular decisions must be on "best practice," the recommendations for appropriate programs fall along a broad continuum from highly structured, cognitively oriented, and teacher-directed programs to open-structured models that employ teacher-child cooperatively initiated activities along with individualized, teacher-structured experiences. At the far end of the continuum are the unstructured, child-initiated models. Amidst the diversity of early childhood programs and the debate over appropriate practice, some common threads emerge—rapid growth and uncertainty (Day 1988).

In the face of rapid expansion and the increasing complexity of providing appropriate experiences for young children, early childhood teachers must reflectively contemplate what the best practice is. Rejecting the easy answers, educators must seek what Boyer (1987) calls the "elegance of understanding." Optimal growth and development for every child must be at the heart of this quest. The fulfillment of the potential of young children depends on orchestrating environments that meet their needs.

## APPROPRIATE LEARNING ENVIRONMENTS

The National Association for the Education of Young Children (NAEYC) has a position statement on developmentally appropriate practice in early childhood programs (Bredekamp 1987), which opposes the recent trend toward increased formal, teacher-directed drill and practice on isolated academic skills. In addition, Bredekamp presents emerging research, which affirms that the most effective learning occurs through a child-directed concrete, play-oriented approach. The push for early academics is at odds with the basic developmental needs of children and is diametrically opposed to what we know about how children learn.

Young children learn best in an environment in which an integrated approach is used to facilitate all areas of development: physical, emotional, social, and cognitive. An appropriate curriculum, based on teacher observations of children's interests and abilities, includes activities that are concrete, real, and relevant to children's lives. Appropriate environments provide opportunities for children to communicate in small groups and to work individually. The emphasis is on learning as an active exploration process embedded in interactions with adults, peers,

14

and materials. As children choose from a variety of activities, adults assist and guide them, based on what is individually appropriate for each child (Bredekamp and Shepard 1989).

For decades, educators have acknowledged that basic self-concept needs—a sense of identity, trust, belonging, and acceptance by others—are prerequisite to learning. Children must feel valued for who they are and what they are as individuals (Glasser 1986, Katz, 1988). With this foundation in place, children can build communication and social skills and develop the self-confidence to explore, solve problems, and resolve conflicts as they negotiate human relationships and investigate their world.

Addressing these needs and establishing an environment conducive to the development of capable individuals require that the curriculum be flexible and dynamic—not static. Rigid programs with the inappropriate expectation that children must be "ready" or be "screened out" are based on misconceptions about how children learn. Learning experiences must be shaped by children's developmental needs, not represent a mold to which children must conform.

Weikert (1989) reported the results of a ten-year follow-up study, which suggests that children in "developmentally appropriate and child-initiated programs—who plan, who have responsibility of their own making and who initiate their own work—develop the capacity to work independently of adults" (p. 28). They maintained their own goals and organized their own futures into adolescence and will probably continue to do so into adulthood.

This same study suggested that children who learn by working within rigidly defined limits, who pursue fixed objectives predetermined by adults, and who develop little personal investment in these activities develop a sense of separation from school. This appears in adolescence as alienation from society and in high delinquency rates. Cooperative Learning is one methodology that offers a cooperative-interactive

15

approach to meeting children's needs within an appropriate learning environment.

## THE ROLE OF COOPERATIVE LEARNING

Peer collaboration as a vehicle for social and cognitive skill development is *not* a new concept. Children working together on a common task with a singular goal has long been recognized as a beneficial strategy (Dewey 1966). Since the inception of early childhood education, cooperative efforts have been integral to the development of the whole child. Cooperative activity occurs spontaneously with young children, and collaboration seems to be a natural phenomenon. However, these efforts often do not work out well, and much of what looks like cooperation really is not (Tudge & Caruso 1988). In order to develop the skills to learn cooperatively, young children need appropriate experiences, adequate time, and opportunities to process those experiences. Although a positive learning climate is supportive of peer-interactive learning, specific structure and process must be provided. The teacher must construct methods and frameworks for group functioning. Only then will group interactions result in Cooperative Learning: "Cooperative learning is a teaching strategy involving children's participation in small group learning activities that promote positive interaction" (Lyman & Foyle, *Cooperative Learning Strategies*, 1988).

Several hundred classroom studies over the past 20 years have repeatedly confirmed the positive cognitive and social benefits of Cooperative Learning. Students experiencing Cooperative Learning consistently achieve at higher levels than do students learning by other methods. The former are motivated, are interested, and like the content better when cooperative group work is a major strategy in learning activities. Socially, students feel accepted and included by peers. The cooperative group identity translates into positive social values and behaviors (Lyman & Foyle 1990). Groups of researchers involved in these

16

studies include the Johnsons in Minnesota; Slavin, DeVries, and Frank Lyman in Maryland; Aronson and Kagan in California; and Sharan in Israel.

The relationship between Cooperative Learning and early childhood education is this: the process of peer interaction within a group-interdependent structure (Cooperative Learning) provides several of the components critical for effective learning in young children (early childhood education). Cooperative Learning includes several basic principles. *Positive interdependence* in a *heterogeneous group* promotes acceptance, inclusion, and caring for others. Children with diverse ideas collaborate on a task that no one member could achieve alone. *Group interaction* develops communication skills (speaking and listening) and social skills, which become the primary tools for task accomplishment and success as a group. Active involvement within a small group or pair offers opportunities for self-direction, problem solving, and conflict resolution. *Individual accountability* requires personal investment and builds individual responsibility for learning. Each child's contribution to *group success* is acknowledged through *group rewards*, processing and evaluating group performance on the task and in cooperative behaviors. (See Figure 1.)

# Figure 1
## Cooperative Learning Components
## and Learning Needs of Young Children

| | |
|---|---|
| HETEROGENEOUS GROUPS<br>"max mix" | Sense of identity<br>Sense of acceptance/inclusion<br>Sense of belonging to group |
| POSITIVE INTERDEPENDENCE<br>"pulling together" | Trust building<br>Child directed<br>Motivation<br>Learner responsibility |
| GROUP INTERACTION<br>"Let's do it!" | Communication skills<br>Social skills<br>Problem solving/conflict resolution<br>Active involvement |
| GROUP REWARD<br>"We did it!" | Task completion/pride<br>Bonding to group<br>Motivation |
| INDIVIDUAL ACCOUNTABILITY<br>"I did my part!" | Value to group/belonging<br>Learner responsibility<br>Individual progress check |
| SUCCESS<br>"We did it WELL!!!" | Group processing/evaluation<br>Planning/self-direction<br>Motivation |

## THE ROLE OF THE TEACHER

The teacher's role is critical to the success of Cooperative Learning. Selecting children for pairs or small groups; designating "roles" in the task; monitoring, observing, and intervening during group interactions; and providing for individual accountability and group rewards are all vital elements of the process. Cooperative Learning is often viewed as an easily understood concept, but, in reality, it is extremely complex in implementation. "Think big . . . start small!" is wise advice in embracing any new teaching strategy—especially this one!

Young children from three and one-half to five years of age work best in pairs. First and second graders with good social skills can operate in teams of three or four. To begin with, though, coupling children into "partners," "pairs," or "buddies" is a productive choice, even up through third grade. Pairs can always work together for a while and then compare notes with another pair in a group of four (Lyman 1981).

Partners may not change for several days or weeks in primary grades. These long-term pairs can work together on such academics as spelling word activities, can become reading buddies who read to one another, or can cooperatively write or edit stories each has written. Younger pairs might cooperate in dressing tasks, such as buttoning a paint smock or putting on clothing for outdoor play. Other cooperative activities might include blocks, puzzles, art projects, cooking, and puppet plays that require more than one set of hands. The important components are the positive interdependence and individual accountability to self and the group for its success. The lesson "Help Dress the Person for Winter" is an example of a cooperative partner activity that encourages positive interdependence with shared materials.

## Help Dress the Person for Winter
### (Winter Clothing Activity)
*Dorothy Hamilton*

*Objective:* Students will share materials promoting positive interdependence.

*Group Structure:* Partners.

*Procedure:*
1. The teacher shows the children a hat that is obviously used in warm weather (e.g., visor used in golf, large-brimmed sun hat). The children are asked to relate the uses of the hat and the materials from which it is made to the kind of weather in which it would be used.
2. A second hat—one that is heavy, is perhaps knitted, and pulls down over the ears—is compared and contrasted with the first hat.
3. Items of clothing that would be worn with the heavy winter hat are displayed by the teacher (e.g., boots, mittens, coat, scarf).
4. Each child is given one drawing of a winter hat that has a numeral on it. There are matching numerals on two drawings. Partners are formed as each child finds the person with the matching numeral.
5. Each set of partners is given one large sheet of paper (18" x 24") and one box of crayons. The children next
   a. Draw one large picture of a person dressed warmly for winter.
   b. Write the partners' names on the back of the paper.
6. The children are asked to bring their pictures to the large-group meeting place. The teacher collects the pictures. Each child is asked to tell the part(s) of the picture that his partner drew. Students are encouraged to name the parts by the kind of winter clothing that the partner drew.

*Comments:*

1. The cooperative drawing activity may be applied to any topic.
2. As children become more proficient in working with partners, the task can be done in groups of four. If groups of four work together, larger papers are usually needed. "Butcher" paper, which is often used for murals, can be used.

3. This activity is a good "group builder." If the teacher observes that one child dominates the activity, the teacher might want to build in the sharing of the drawing by using one of the following techniques:
   a. Indicate a time to switch to the other partner by ringing a bell.
   b. Assign selected crayon colors to each partner; only that partner may draw with those colors.
4. Intermittent use of this activity is one way to assess/evaluate the cooperative skills of young children.
5. At times when there is a large-group discussion, the Think-Pair-Share approach (Lyman 1981, 1987) may be used.

---

For any age level, cooperatively planning the day, planning a project, and brainstorming solutions to a classroom/playground problem are all worthwhile and productive activities. Young children can understand cooperation as they see it in their daily lives, especially since "helpers" are commonly assigned in centers and schools. The concept of *positive interdependence*, the heart of Cooperative Learning, is a tricky one. The idea that "I can't do this alone, but we can do it together" can be illustrated on the playground with the teeter-totter or merry-go-round. Ask a child how long she would have to sit on the teeter-totter by herself in order to go up and down. What is missing? Of course! Another person has to sit on the other end and cooperate! With older children in primary grades the example of team sports serves well to illustrate positive interdependence. One player cannot win the game alone, but if the players work together as a team, with each player fulfilling a role/responsibility, the team can score! Celebration is important when a game is played well. Celebration should be a part of learning and working well together in the classroom. At least silent cheers would be appropriate!

The following two-part lesson, "The Three Little Pigs," is a language development activity for preschool-kindergarten. This approach could be adapted for ESL students. Note the components of Cooperative Learning evident in the lesson.

21

The Three Little Pigs
*Britt Vasquez*

PART 1

*Grade Level:* Preschool.

*Subject Area:* Language.

*Procedure:*

1. Select a lesson: "The Three Little Pigs." Part 1 on concept/vocabulary readiness precedes Part 2.
2. Make the following decisions:
   a. Group size: Pairs, then a large group of eight.
   b. Assignment to groups: Teacher assigns one more language proficient child as a buddy with one less language proficient child.
   c. Room arrangement: First, children sit on carpeted area, then move to sit/stand next to their buddies around a round table.
   d. Materials: Each pair will need a bucket. In each bucket is a baggie of straw, a baggie of sticks, a baggie with chunks of brick in it, a small toy pig, and a small toy wolf. (If toys cannot be obtained, use pictures.)
   e. Assigning roles: Bucket Person—holds the bucket; Picker—takes items out of the bucket/puts items back into the bucket.
3. Set the lesson task: State the following in language your students understand.

Boys and girls, today we are going to learn some new words and use the words to play a game. You will work with a buddy. [Read the names of buddies and have them sit on the rug.] Hold your buddy's hand up in the air so I can see who your buddy is. [Monitor.]

One of you will be the Bucket Person. The Bucket Person holds the bucket when I hand it out. What does the Bucket Person do? [Elicit response: *holds the bucket.*] One of you will be the Picker. The Picker takes items out of the bucket and puts items back into the bucket. What does the Picker do? [*Takes things out of the bucket and puts them back.*]

[Pass out the buckets.]

Leave everything in the bucket. Watch me. I have something long and yellow and soft. [Show a handful of straw.] It's called

22

straw. Say "straw." [*Straw.*] Very good. What color is straw? [*Yellow.*] What do you think straw is used for? [Elicit responses. *Straw is used to make beds for animals, and sometimes for people. Sometimes animals eat straw.*] What do you think happens to straw when you squish it with your hand? [*It mashes up.*] Pickers, in your bucket is a bag of straw. Take it out of the bucket. Open the bag, and you and your buddy touch the straw. Squish it and smell it. Do you think you'd like to eat it? [*No way!*] What do you think would happen if you made a house out of straw? [*It would fall down.*] Let's put the straw back in the baggies and put the baggies back in the bucket.

[Repeat the process for the sticks and for the bricks. Modify the process for the pig and the wolf as follows.] Have you ever seen a real pig? What color is it? How does it smell? What does it say? What does it eat? Does it wear clothes? Where does a pig live? [*In a barn or in a sty.*]

[Collect the buckets.]

You've learned some interesting words. [Hold up each item, one at a time.] Let's see what you've learned. What do we call this? [*Straw.* Repeat for each item.]

Let's play a game with these words. Hold your buddy's hand and walk to the game table. . . . Now let's look at our game board. [See Figure 2.] You and your buddy will be a team. Each team gets to select a token. If you are the Bucket Person, you get to select the token. [Let each Bucket Person select a token and put it on "Go."] Your token is trying to get to the Brick House (at the end). But it can only move when it is your team's turn. When can you move your token? [*When it is our turn.*] To move you must draw a card and say the name of what is on the card. [The cards have pictures of straw, sticks, bricks, a pig, and a wolf on them.]

You may move three spaces each time one of your team can tell us what is on the card. [To ensure each child practices the words, have the children alternate, so that the person who did *not* give an answer during the previous round must give the answer this time.] It is all right for buddies to help/tell each other as long as the person whose turn it is actually says the word. If you cannot say the word, you can get help from the rest of the teams. If the other teams help you say the word, you may move two spaces. When you get to the Brick House, you may trade your token in for two stickers, one for you and one for your buddy.

While we play the game, you must take turns. What does take turns mean? [*First you, then me. Or if there are several children, first one, then the next, then the next, until it gets back to me so everyone gets a chance to play.*] Can we take turns today? [Play the game going round-robin around the table.]

    a. *Variation:* Have a game cloth on the floor. One of the buddies is the token and gets to move from space to space by jumping, hopping, or walking.

    b. *Positive interdependence:* Goal interdependence—Each one must say the new word in order to move the token. Buddies may help each other identify and say the correct word. Role interdependence—The Bucket Person holds the bucket, and the Picker removes and replaces items.

    c. *Individual accountability:* Each person must take a turn saying the word.

    d. *Criteria for success:* To be successful, each child must stay with her buddy, take turns, feel the new things in the bucket, and guess words during the game.

    e. *Social behaviors expected:* Taking turns. First one, then the other. Or, if there are several children, first one, then the next, then the next, until it gets back to the first child, so everyone gets a chance to play.

4. Monitor and evaluate:

    a. *Evidence of expected behaviors (appropriate actions):* The teacher will stay with the group of eight during the game time and monitor continuously.

    b. *Observation form:* None.
       *Observer:* None.

    c. *Plans for evaluation/feedback:* When a team reaches the Brick House, the teacher will say, "Tell me about one time you and your buddy took turns."

5. Evaluate student outcomes:

| | Poorly | | Adequately | | Completely | |
|---|---|---|---|---|---|---|
| a. How well did students achieve their task? | 1 | 2 | 3 | 4 | 5 | 6 |
| b. How well did groups function? | 1 | 2 | 3 | 4 | 5 | 6 |
| c. How well did individual students function? | 1 | 2 | 3 | 4 | 5 | 6 |

6. Evaluate lesson outcomes:
   a. Task achievement
   b. Group function
   c. Notes on individuals
   d. What went well?
   e. What would you do differently next time?

Figure 2
Gameboard for
"The Three Little Pigs" Lesson

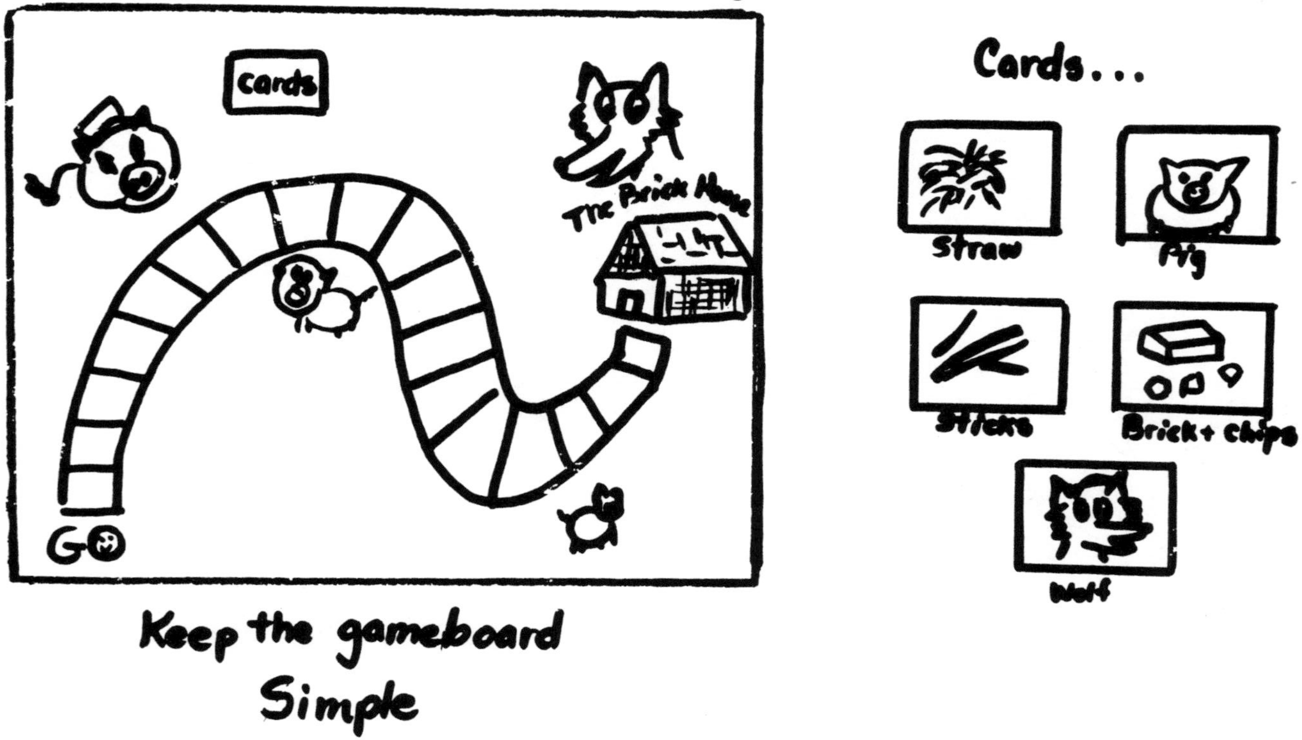

*Grade Level:* Preschool.

*Subject Area:* Language.

*Procedure:*

1. Select a lesson: "The Three Little Pigs," Part 2 on remembering.
2. Make the following decisions:
   a. Group size: Children will work in pairs.
   b. Assignment to groups: Teacher assigns pairs of children, one more language proficient and the other less language proficient, as buddies.
   c. Room arrangement: Pairs work together, side by side, at small tables.
   d. Materials: One set of two uncolored sequencing cards of "The Three Little Pigs" (6" x 8"), one "mat" (a large sheet of construction paper 17" x 22") with the letter *L* printed on the left side of the sheet, and one red necklace.
   e. Assigning roles: Story Teller—tells the story; Card Placer—places the story cards in order.
3. Set the lesson task: State the following in language your students understand:

[The task follows at least one lesson where the teacher reads a story, shows two sequencing picture cards about the story he has just read, describes what is happening in each picture card, and then models sequencing from left to right, using a mat as described below.]

Today, we are going to listen to a story. It's about pigs. Can anyone guess what the name of the story is? [Entertain guesses.] That's right, it's The Three Little Pigs!

First, I will read the story to you. Then you will work with a buddy. You and your buddy will be given two picture cards. The cards *show* the story of "The Three Little Pigs." You and your buddy may look at the cards and decide what each card *shows* about the story. It will help you to listen carefully to the story.

Then you and your buddy will decide which picture happened *first* in the story and which picture happened *last* in the story.

[Read the story to the children. Since they will be working with their buddies at the tables to do the sequencing, allow them to sit or lie comfortably on a carpeted area to hear the story.]

27

Now we will work with our picture cards. Look at what interesting pictures we have today. [Hold up each picture for the children to see. If the children are not very verbal, discuss what is in each picture. Then read the names of buddies and have them sit at their tables.]

Hold your buddy's hand up in the air so I can see who your buddy is. [Monitor.]

Terrific! Everyone has a buddy to work with today.

One buddy will decide which picture happened *first* in the story and which picture happened *last* in the story.

Now I will tell you what to do. One of you will be the Story Teller. The Story Teller will tell me the story of "The Three Little Pigs." The Story Teller will have a red necklace to wear today. [Place a red necklace around the neck of each child who will be the Story Teller. The first time the Story Teller should be the most verbal child.] Who will tell me the story today? [*The Story Teller.*]

Terrific! Next, if you are *not* the Story Teller, you will be the Card Placer. Your job will be to put the story cards in order, from left to right. Only the Card Placer may touch the story cards. Who will touch the story cards? [*The Card Placer.*] That's right, the Card Placer.

Look at your mats. Where is "left"? [Children should point to the letter *L* on the left side of their mats.] Wonderful, that *is* left. It is the left side of the mat. You know that because the *L* is there to remind us.

Card Placers, I will give you the cards. Show each card to your buddy. Together talk about what the card shows. Ask your buddy, "What's in the picture?"

Now, you and your buddy will decide which picture happened *first* in the story and which picture happened *last* in the story. Ask your buddy, "Which happened first?" [Give them time.] All right, Card Placers, take the picture that happened *first* and place it on the left side of your mat next to the *L*. [Monitor to see that everyone gets it correct. If incorrect, ask the Story Teller if she agrees with which card was placed. Discuss. Repeat for the last card.]

Wonderful. You've done such a great job! Let's color our Three Pigs story cards. I will put a basket of crayons on each table. You and your buddy may each color one picture. You may share the crayons. What does "share" mean? [Elicit responses. *"Share" means sometimes I get to use it, and sometimes you get to use it.*

*We both get to use it.*] Will everybody share? [Look for nods from every child.]

While you are coloring, I will come around and ask the Story Teller to tell me the story of the three pigs. If you are the Story Teller's buddy, you may help out telling the story. It's all right to practice telling the story to your buddy before I get to your table.

[Go to each table and have the Story Teller tell the story. You may ask questions of each child. For language-delayed or ESL students, you may first ask the question of the more verbally proficient child and then repeat the question for the less verbally proficient child so the child only has to repeat the correct response. You may want to prompt the correct response as follows: What did the Big Bad Wolf do to the Pig's house? The bad wolf huffed . . . and puffed . . . and blew the house down. Julio, what did the bad wolf do? Say it with me (or say with your buddy): "huffed . . . and puffed . . . and blew the house down." Terrific.]

Boys and girls, you've done a wonderful job. Everyone told me the story of The Three Little Pigs. Everyone had their story cards in order. Everyone colored their story cards. What do you get to do? [*Give my buddy a prize.*] Give your buddy a pat on the back and thank your buddy for her help, and I'll be around with the prize box so you may select a prize for your buddy.

   a. *Positive interdependence:* Goal interdependence—Each pair of buddies must arrange the cards in order, tell the teacher the story of The Three Little Pigs, and color their story cards. Materials interdependence—Each pair of buddies will have one set of story cards, one work mat, and one set of crayons to share. Role interdependence—One student in each pair is the Story Teller. The Story Teller will tell the teacher the story. The other student is the Card Placer. Only the Card Placer can place the cards in order. The Card Placer may give ideas to the Story Teller to help him tell the story. Reward interdependence—If the students put their cards in order, tell the teacher the story, and color their cards, each one may select a prize for her buddy.

   b. *Individual accountability:* The teacher will visit each group to see that only the Card Placer is putting the cards in order and to listen to the Story Teller.

   c. *Criteria for success:* To do a good job, the Story Teller must tell the teacher the story of The Three Little Pigs, and the Card

Figure 3

He huffed...and he puffed...
and he blew the house in!

—R.Bull

Figure 4

# The wolf came down the chimney...

Placer must place the cards in order. Both students must color their cards.

d. *Social behaviors expected:* Sharing. Sometimes one buddy gets to use it, and sometimes the other gets to use it. They both get to use it when they share.

4. Monitor and evaluate:

a. *Evidence of expected behaviors (appropriate actions):* The teacher will monitor each pair for sharing behavior.

b. *Observation form:* None.
*Observer:* None.

c. *Plans for evaluation/feedback:* The teacher will ask the children:
   - "Raise your hands if your Card Placer placed the cards in the right order. . . ."
   - "Raise your hands if your Story Teller told me the story. . . ."
   - "Raise your hands if you colored your cards. . . ."

5. Evaluate student outcomes:

|  | Poorly | | Adequately | | Completely | |
|---|---|---|---|---|---|---|
| a. How well did students achieve their task? | 1 | 2 | 3 | 4 | 5 | 6 |
| b. How well did groups function? | 1 | 2 | 3 | 4 | 5 | 6 |
| c. How well did individual students function? | 1 | 2 | 3 | 4 | 5 | 6 |

6. Evaluate lesson outcomes:
   a. Task achievement
   b. Group function
   c. Notes on individuals
   d. What went well?
   e. What would you do differently next time?

## CONCLUSION

Cooperative Learning *does* provide an approach that fosters acceptance and inclusion, communication skills, and learner responsibility within a peer-interactive, group-interdependent structure. The developmental needs of young children can be met as they experience the Cooperative Learning process.

Chapter 2

# GROUP BUILDING FOR COOPERATION

*Group building is the process of creating a cohesive group that functions positively and productively to accomplish tasks.*

—Lawrence Lyman and Harvey Foyle

One of the basic tasks of the early childhood teacher is to help children develop the social skills necessary for positive interaction with others. Because children come to the teacher with a variety of cultural backgrounds, social experiences, and skill levels, activities to build the classroom group are needed.

## THE NEED FOR GROUP BUILDING

Young children are preoccupied with themselves. The primary goal of group building (Lyman & Foyle 1990), therefore, is to help each child become aware of others in a positive way. Group building also helps the child affirm his own special talents and abilities, while developing an appreciation for the talents and abilities of other children.

Two kinds of group building are needed in the early childhood classroom. *Whole class* group-building activities are used to build class morale, develop team spirit, and promote awareness of others in the class. *Paired* group-building activities are designed to bring students together in pairs to develop awareness of others, build communication skills, foster trust, and provide practice in interacting successfully with others.

# ELEMENTS OF GROUP-BUILDING ACTIVITIES

Lyman and Foyle (1990) define five essential elements of group-building activities. Group-building activities involve heterogeneous grouping, bringing together students who would not necessarily have chosen to work together. Group-building activities promote positive interdependence, while maintaining the individual accountability of each student for participation in the group. Group-building activities should have a high probability of student success, and group reward should be used, as appropriate, to assure that the child's early experiences with cooperation are positive.

*Heterogeneous grouping* involves pairing students with other students. The teacher does this with the goal that all students in the classroom will have the opportunity to work together in a pair at some time. Heterogeneous grouping permits children to encounter peers who may look or act differently or who have different ideas and viewpoints. Positive situations are designed to build appreciation and liking.

*Positive interdependence* is a key element of any Cooperative Learning activity. Positive interdependence means that each member of the group must be actively involved if the task is to be successful. In whole class group-building activities, every child must have an important role in the group task and must honestly feel that her participation is essential to the group's success.

In paired group-building activities, care must be taken that one child does not do all of the task. This can be accomplished by assigning each child specific responsibilities or roles related to the task. If the teacher distributes materials to a pair, for example, one student could be the "counter," who makes sure the pair has the correct number of items, and the other student could be the "sorter," who makes sure the items are arranged or sequenced appropriately.

Positive interdependence in whole class and in paired group-building activities results in *individual accountability*; that is, each individual is actively participating in the activity and contributing to the group effort. In whole class group building, the teacher monitors to make sure all children are participating in the activity.

Participation can be encouraged by grouping reluctant students near students with whom they feel confident. Having more confident students demonstrate the task before the whole group does the task may also relieve anxiety. Competition between students should be discouraged because competition increases anxiety among some students and causes them to withdraw. Competition with last year's group or a previous personal performance may be more appropriate.

In paired group-building activities, the teacher monitors to make sure each student is participating according to the directions given. If specific responsibilities or roles have been assigned, the teacher checks to see that each child is doing what he has been assigned to do. If one child is dominating the activity, the teacher can refer to the assigned roles to clarify each child's responsibility.

Success is perhaps the most crucial factor in group-building activities. These activities need to be designed so that children experience success in their early efforts to cooperate with others. When children experience success, their desire to participate in other cooperative activities is enhanced. For this reason, teachers should avoid comparing or grading perform-ances during group-building activities. All children who partici-pate should be rewarded for their effort and involvement in the activity.

Group reward is provided for successful participation in group-building activities. If the activity is fun, no other reward may be needed since intrinsic rewards are most fulfilling. However, early childhood teachers may choose to use verbal praise, food rewards, singing of a favorite song, an art activity, free play time, or other suitable rewards for a job well done. Many younger children like to see themselves on videotape, so some activities may be taped as a reward. The use of appropriate rewards shows the children that the teacher values cooperation and appreciates their efforts to work together cooperatively.

## GROUP EVALUATION

Johnson, Johnson, and Holubec (Johnson & Johnson 1990) identify the importance of group processing in Cooperative Learning. Group processing is the component that involves Cooperative Learning participants in discussing their success: how well they have worked together, how well they have achieved their goals, and how they could improve their work next time. With young children, such processing is limited somewhat by the level of communication skills; but, teachers can help the children recognize and articulate positive feelings about cooperating, benefits of working together, and positive attitudes about other children gained from cooperative activities.

Group-building activities provide opportunities for group processing. At the conclusion of a whole class group-building activity or a paired group-building activity, the teacher can ask questions to facilitate the discussion of how well cooperation has taken place during the activity. Questions that can encourage groups to evaluate their work together can be adapted to the ages and abilities of the children. The "Questions to Encourage Group Evaluation" listed in Figure 5 might be useful for group processing.

Figure 5
Questions to Encourage Group Evaluation

1. Why is it important for us to work together?
2. In the last activity, how did we work together?
3. Why were you glad to have others to help you in the activity we just did?
4. Why was each person important in the last activity?
5. What could have happened if you hadn't worked together so

well in the last activity?

6. How did you have fun working together?
7. How did you help your group?
8. Who did a particularly good job of helping?
9. (After a paired activity) Tell the whole group one thing you learned about your partner.
10. (After a paired activity) Tell your partner one thing you enjoyed about working with her.

Group evaluation, as in sports where videotapes help teams review what was done well or not so well, can also be encouraged by using photographs or videotapes of cooperative activities. As children are working together, the teacher can take pictures or videotape the groups. While looking at the pictures or videotape, the children can be asked to identify ways they see people working together, how people are helping each other, and why it is important to work together. Photographs can also be displayed on a cooperative bulletin board to remind students of the importance of working cooperatively.

## WHOLE CLASS GROUP-BUILDING ACTIVITIES

One of the most challenging tasks facing the early childhood teacher is molding the diverse individuals in a class into a cohesive group that works cooperatively by showing consideration, respecting others, sharing, and listening to others. Whole class group-building activities help the teacher meet this challenge by providing opportunities for the children to work together successfully and positively. The lessons "We're Connected!" "Cooperative Weaving," and "Just Like Me!" illustrate whole class group-building activities.

## We're Connected!
### (Movement Exploration)

*Objective:* Students will review parts of the body while working cooperatively with others.

*Procedure:* To begin the activity, students work in pairs. Each pair of students is given a long balloon. The teacher will have one pair of children model how the others will "connect" with each other. The pair chosen to model will support the balloon between their noses. Each pair will then practice supporting the balloon between their noses. The teacher will then give other directions for supporting the balloons:

1. Connect the balloon between your knees. (One knee of each partner supports the balloon.)
2. Connect the balloon between your elbows. (One elbow of each partner supports the balloon.)
3. Connect the balloon between your hands. (One hand of each partner supports the balloon.)
4. Connect the balloon between your backs.
5. Connect the balloon between your feet. (One foot of each partner supports the balloon.)

The teacher will then provide additional balloons. Each pair will again support the balloon between their noses (or backs). New balloons will be used to join each pair with another pair. (Any appropriate part of the body is acceptable.) By continuing this process, all members of the class can be joined together by balloon connectors.

*Group Evaluation:* After the activity, the teacher can ask the children to tell what they enjoyed about the activity. The children can also share why everybody had to work together to make the activity succeed.

# Cooperative Weaving
## (Art)
### *Julia Ferguson*

*Objective:* Students will create a group weaving project.

*Procedure:* Students will paint with watercolors on two large sheets of white butcher paper (4' x 8' sheets work well). Primary colors can be used, or colors can be adapted to the season of the year: pastel colors for spring, bright colors for summer, colors mixed with white and black paint to produce tints and shades of color for winter. One of the completed sheets is folded lengthwise and cut into one-inch strips. These strips will serve as the weft for the weaving project. The other sheet is folded in half and cut at one-inch intervals from the fold up to two inches from the open edge. When the paper is opened, it will serve as the warp for weaving. Students then work together to weave the strips. Because of the size of the project, students should work together on the floor. The final result is an attractive group project.

*Group Evaluation:* Children can look at the completed project and identify their own strips of color and the areas of the project they helped with.

---

# Just Like Me!
## (Classification)

*Objective:* Students will recognize characteristics they share with other students by forming teacher-directed groups.

*Procedure:* The teacher will select common characteristics that are observable in the class. Students will be instructed to form "Just Like Me!" groups with other students who have the same characteristics. Examples:

- white shoes, brown shoes, other colored shoes
- black hair, brown hair, blond hair, red hair
- names that start with the same letter
- names that have the same number of letters
- Students who like white milk, chocolate milk, no milk

(Allow students to suggest other groupings if the age and ability of the class permit.)

*Group Evaluation:* The teacher can ask students to remember who was in one of their groups or have them draw a picture of the group for display.

---

## PAIRED GROUP-BUILDING ACTIVITIES

Pairs provide an excellent structure for children's first experiences with Cooperative Learning. The goal of paired group-building activities is to have children encounter as many others in the class as possible. Paired group-building activities provide awareness of the similarities and differences of other children in the class. Success in these experiences builds trust in others, as well as enhancing communication and other social skills. The lessons "Getting to Know You," "Matching Game," and "What's in the Bag?" illustrate paired group-building activities.

## Getting to Know You
### (Visual and Auditory Discrimination)

*Objective:* Working in pairs, students will respond accurately to spoken directions.

*Procedure:* Students will work together in pairs selected by the teacher. Their task is to listen carefully and do what the teacher says.

A. Visual discrimination: Tell students to stand up if their partner is wearing
   1. something red
   2. something blue
   3. something green
   4. something yellow
   5. shoes with white on them
   6. a shirt with a picture on it
   7. a shirt with buttons on it
   8. something in her hair

B. Interaction: Tell students they will need to ask their partner to find out whether or not to stand up for each of the questions. Tell them to stand if their partner
   1. has a dog
   2. has a cat
   3. has a brother
   4. has a sister
   5. had cereal for breakfast
   6. watched TV before school this morning
   7. walked to school this morning
   8. likes chocolate milk
   9. likes to play outside
   10. likes to come to school

*Group Evaluation:* The teacher can ask students to share one or more things they found out about their partner with the whole group.

# Matching Game
## (Communication Skills)

*Objective:* Through cooperative discussion, students will identify similar likes and preferences.

*Procedure:* Children work in pairs. The teacher reads items from the list below, one at a time. Students are given a minute to identify as many matches as they can. A match could be made, for example, if both find they like chocolate ice cream (example 1). After each example, students share one of their matches with the whole group. Students should take turns sharing for their pair (one student shares for example 1, the other for example 2, and so on).

1. Find foods you and your partner both like.
2. Find things you and your partner both like to do.
3. Find things you and your partner both like about school.
4. Find things you and your partner both are wearing.
5. Find colors you and your partner both like.
6. Find television shows you and your partner both watch.
7. Find holidays you and your partner both like.
8. Find things you and your partner both know how to do.

*Group Evaluation:* Lists can be made of the favorite foods, television shows, etc., of the whole class, using information from the activity. These lists can be displayed in the classroom.

---

## What's in the Bag?
## (Problem Solving)

*Objective:* Given a brown bag with an unknown object in it, pairs of students will work together to identify the object.

*Procedure:* A number of items with different textures are placed in paper bags. There should be enough bags so every two students can have one. Objects that work well are sponges, tennis balls, combs, crayons, straws, wadded-up pieces of paper, spoons, chalk, chalkboard erasers, and lids from plastic containers. Each pair is given a bag. The teacher cautions that students may not look into the bag or shake the bag. The teacher plays music while pairs exchange bags. (One member of each pair can be designated as the "exchanger" to avoid confusion.) When the music stops, the pair tries to identify what is in the bag they now have. Each child must reach into the bag, and both must agree on what the object is. After a short time, the teacher goes around to each pair and asks them to identify what they think is in their bag. The bag is then opened to check if the group identified the object correctly. The bags can be passed around again as desired.

*Group Evaluation:* Students can be asked to tell their partners one thing they enjoyed about the activity. Responses can be shared with the whole group, if desired.

## CONCLUSION

Early childhood students are often inexperienced in cooperating with others. Group-building activities help these children practice cooperating in pleasant activities with a high probability of success for each child. Whole class group-building activities can help to make the class more cohesive and positive by providing opportunities for the group to work together. Paired group builders allow children to practice communication and other social skills with a variety of different children. Group building is an essential preface to success in other cooperative activities.

## SELECTED RESOURCES FOR GROUP BUILDERS

Canfield, J., and H. C. Wells, 1976. *100 Ways to Enhance Self-Concept in the Classroom*. Prentice-Hall, Englewood Cliffs, NJ 07632.

Chase, L. 1975. *The Other Side of the Report Card: A How-to-Do-It Program for Affective Education*. Scott, Foresman and Company, 1900 E. Lake Ave., Glenview, IL 60025.

*Childhood Education*. Journal of the Association for Childhood Education International, 11141 Georgia Ave., Suite 200, Wheaton, MD 20902. (See "Idea Sparkers," a continuing feature, for group-building ideas.)

Cihak, M. K., and B. H. Jackson. 1980. *Games Children Should Play: Sequential Lessons for Teaching Communication Skills in Grades K–6*. Scott, Foresman and Company, 1900 E. Lake Ave., Glenview, IL 60025.

Feldscher, S., with S. Lieberman. 1990. *The Kidfun Activity Book for Ages 2-1/2 to 8*. Harper & Row Publishers, 10 E. 53d St., New York, NY 10022.

Fry-Miller, K., and J. Myers-Walls. 1988. *Young Peacemakers Project Book*. Brethren Press, 1451 Dundee Ave., Elgin, IL 60120.

Gibbs, J. 1987. *Tribes: A Process for Social Development and Cooperative Learning*. Center Source Publications, 305 Tesconi Circle, Santa Rosa, CA 95401.

Jenkins, P. 1989. *The Joyful Child: A Sourcebook of Activities for Releasing Children's Natural Joy.* Joyful Child, Inc., P. O. Box 82236, Phoenix, AZ 85071.

Johnson, R., and D. Johnson. 1985. *Cooperative Learning: Warm-Ups, Grouping Strategies, and Group Activities.* Interaction Book Company, 7208 Cornelia Dr., Edina, MN 55435.

Kriedler, W. J. 1984. *Creative Conflict Resolution: More Than 200 Activities for Keeping Peace in the Classroom.* Scott, Foresman and Company, 1900 E. Lake Ave., Glenview, IL 60025.

*Lollipops.* Good Apple, Inc., Box 299, Carthage, IL 62321. (Activities for reproduction, some of which are good possibilities for group-building activities, are starred in the table of contents.)

Lyman, L., and H. C. Foyle. 1990. *Cooperative Grouping for Interactive Learning: Students, Teachers, and Administrators.* National Education Association, P. O. Box 509, West Haven, CT 06156.

*The Mailbox.* The Education Center, Inc., P. O. Box 9753, Greensboro, NC 27429. (Preschool/kindergarten and primary editions are available. Both contain many activities that are ideal for group building.)

Schniedewin, N., and E. Davidson. 1987. *Cooperative Learning, Cooperative Lives: A Sourcebook of Activities for Building a Peaceful World.* Circle Books, 30 Walnut St., Somerville, MA 02143.

*Teaching Pre-K–8.* Early Years, Inc., 40 Richards Ave., Norwalk, CT 06584. (Monthly calendar and "Green Pages" are sources for group-building activities.)

Vernon, A. 1989. *Thinking, Feeling, Behaving: An Emotional Education Curriculum for Children.* Research Press, 2612 N. Mattis Ave., Champaign, IL 61821.

Weinstein, M., and J. Goodman. 1980. *Playfair: Everybody's Guide to Noncompetitive Play.* Impact Publishers, Inc., P. O. Box 1094, San Luis Obispo, CA 93406.

# Chapter 3

# NURTURING SELF-ESTEEM

*Learning to love yourself is the greatest love of all.*

*—George Benson*

Building positive self-esteem in children is one of the major goals of the early childhood teacher. Student self-esteem has been positively correlated with increased academic achievement, greater enthusiasm for learning, better mental health and emotional stability, and the ability to interact positively with others. Children with high self-esteem can be identified by five major factors:

1. They feel safe and secure in the class.
2. They experience success in school tasks.
3. They identify areas of personal talent and interest.
4. They feel accepted by other children and adults.
5. They contribute to the success of the class and view themselves as an important part of the class.

Cooperative Learning strategies can assist the teacher in promoting the self-esteem of children. Since self-esteem is directly influenced by the child's perceptions of how others view him, positive interaction in cooperative settings enhances self-esteem and encourages the child to view himself and others more positively.

## SAFETY AND SECURITY

Models of effective schools have defined a safe and orderly environment as a basic criterion of school effectiveness.

Children cannot learn and grow when they feel emotionally or physically threatened. While the teacher has primary responsibility for maintaining safety in the early childhood classroom, helping children become aware of the feelings and needs of other students can also help them become more considerate of each other.

In a safe and secure environment, the child is able to express herself without fear of ridicule or embarrassment. The child is able to take risks by doing things that are difficult for her. The child is also concerned about the feelings of others and reacts empathetically to fellow students. Literature is an excellent vehicle for encouraging discussion about the feelings and needs of others. The lesson "We All Have Bad Days" is an example of a Cooperative Learning lesson that deals with feelings.

---

### We All Have Bad Days

*Objective:* Children will recognize that all children have bad days and that bad feelings are not unique to them.

*Procedure:* The teacher reads the book *Alexander and the Terrible, Horrible, No Good, Very Bad Day* by Judith Viorst (Aladdin Books, Macmillan Publishing Company, 1972) to the class. The book tells of all the things that go wrong for Alexander on a very bad day. The teacher encourages students to share personal feelings about what might make a bad day.

Students are then grouped in pairs. Each pair thinks of five things that could make a bad day and writes them down or draws them. Both partners should agree on the five things that would make a bad day for them.

*Group Processing:* Partners share their ideas with the whole group.

*Follow-Up:* Partners make lists of things that would make a good day and share them with the class.

---

# SUCCESS IN SCHOOL TASKS

Success in the academic, social, and physical tasks that the child undertakes is a crucial factor contributing to or detracting from the child's self-esteem. Whole group and paired group-building activities, when structured to result in student success, help promote these feelings of success. As the student experiences positive feelings in working with the class or a partner, self-esteem grows.

Other students can help the student feel successful. In some cooperative structures, the role of encourager is assigned to one student in the group. This student is responsible for saying positive things to others about their ideas, contributions, or efforts in the group. Group processing can also be designed to reinforce the success of each student in a completed activity. The lesson "We Can Do It!" is an example of building the feeling of success in children.

---

### We Can Do It!

*Objective:* Children will identify skills and competencies that they already have.

*Procedure:* The teacher chooses one child who says, "I can . . . ," describing some action he or she can do, such as "tie my shoes," "bounce a ball," "smile at my friend," "zip up my jacket," etc. The child then demonstrates the action named. (With younger children, the teacher may need to suggest the actions that most can do and choose a child to perform each one.) Other students then do the action or raise their hands if they think they can do the action. The teacher should emphasize that everyone does not have to be able to do all of the actions.

*Group Processing:* Each student tells one thing he was able to do.

*Individual Accountability:* Each student draws a picture of something she is able to do well for a class bulletin board, booklet, or display.

---

# IDENTIFYING AREAS OF PERSONAL STRENGTH AND INTEREST

Perhaps the greatest gift a teacher can give a child is the knowledge of a particular individual characteristic or skill that is an area of personal competency for the student. It is an irrefutable fact that some students possess talents and skills that are more numerous and easily identified than those of others, but every student has strengths that need to be nurtured and encouraged.

One of the premises of Cooperative Learning is that the combined talents and skills of group members are stronger than those of an individual. When talents and skills are merged into a group effort, the final group product is better than the individual product would be. In order for this assumption to work, each child must feel that he brings needed talents and skills to the group. Helping students identify such talents and skills is, therefore, necessary if each child is to be a successful member of a group. In the lesson "What's Your Talent?" students identify their individual talents.

---

### What's Your Talent?

*Objective:* Students will identify individual talents or skills that they have.

*Procedure:* The teacher reads the book *Frederick* by Leo Lionni (Knopf 1967) to the class. Frederick is a mouse who appears to be lazy, but makes important contributions to his family through his poetry. After the story, the class is asked to identify the special talent Frederick had. The teacher then brainstorms a "talent list" with the whole group, listing all the different talents and skills the children can have.

Students are then placed in pairs. Each pair lists or draws one or more talents each believes her partner has.

*Group Processing:* Each pair shares the partners' talents with the whole group.

---

# GROUP ACCEPTANCE

Glasser (1986) and many others have defined children's needs for belonging and acceptance as basic to their self-esteem. Beyond feeling merely safe and secure in the group, each child must also come to feel that she is accepted and cared for by other group members.

Children's early experiences with others color their future social relationships. This is a basic reason why early childhood classrooms need to be safe and caring places for young children to be. These early social contacts with others also help to shape each child's perception of who he is, how to get positive (or negative) attention from others, and how to contribute to the success of the group. The lesson "Student of the Day" helps promote the acceptance of children in the early childhood classroom.

---

### Student of the Day
*Carol Ann Lewis*

*Objective:* Students will receive positive recognition from other class members.

*Procedure:* A student is selected by random draw or alphabetical order. The teacher then asks peers to dictate some information they know about the student (likes pizza, likes football, etc.) or a positive remark about the student (good colorer, helpful). The teacher records the statements on a large chart for all to read.

Working in pairs, each pair of students writes a friendly letter to the star student, including why they like or admire the person. The letter is accompanied by a picture. While the other students are working, the "Student of the Day" decorates a folder in which the letters and pictures can be saved.

*Group Processing:* Students share their letters and pictures with the Student of the Day.

---

# CONTRIBUTING TO CLASS SUCCESS

The need for belonging and group acceptance also depends on the extent to which the child feels that he is an important part of the group. Too often, children bring "baggage" from past experiences in which parents, siblings, or neighborhood acquaintances have devalued their importance. The school setting provides an opportunity for all children, regardless of past experiences, to learn that they have important things to offer a group and that they are important.

Cooperative interaction in group activities provides the child with a chance to contribute to something bigger than herself. The opportunity to have ownership of a class project that is valued by the student and by her peers is an important self-esteem builder. The lesson "Class-a-Pede" is a class project that builds self-esteem.

---

### Class-a-Pede

*Objective:* Working in pairs, students will construct part of a class art project.

*Procedure:* Students are grouped in pairs. The teacher distributes one copy of the Class-a-Pede body pattern (see Figure 6) to each student. Each student designs the feet and legs, including such features as toes, socks, and shoes as desired. Students then exchange Class-a-Pedes with their partners. Each student decorates the body of the Class-a-Pede that his partner has worked on. The decoration can be a design of the student's choice, a colorful design using the partner's name, drawings of what the partner likes to do, or a seasonal subject chosen by the teacher.

When completed, the partners' body parts are linked together with tape. The Class-a-Pede head can be designed by the teacher, or by a pair of students.

*Group Processing:* Each pair of body parts is connected to the head, and the final project is displayed. Students can discuss which parts they feel turned out especially well, or pairs can tell the whole group about the parts they designed.

---

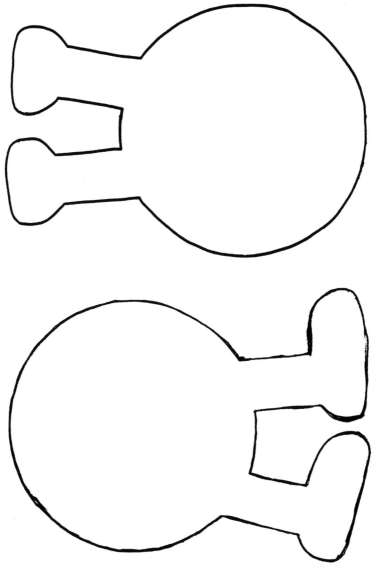

Figure 6
Head and Body Part Pattern for Class-a-Pede

55

# CONCLUSION

Individual self-esteem is a vital factor in mental health and in social relationships. Children with positive self-esteem are more likely to do well in school and to have enthusiasm for what they do. They are also more likely to relate well to peers and to adults.

Many children come to school having had limited or unhealthy opportunities for interaction with others. For some, this lack of opportunity and/or success makes the teacher's task even more difficult. As children come to see themselves as safe and secure in the classroom, they can begin to experience success in school activities. These successes can be used to help the children identify areas of personal interest and strength. As each child begins to feel successful and important, feelings of group acceptance and of contributing to the class are nurtured.

Cooperative Learning experiences provide positive opportunities for teachers to build student self-esteem developmentally. Many activities currently used by early childhood teachers can be easily adapted to Cooperative Learning and can be used to build the positive student self-esteem so necessary to future school success.

# Chapter 4

# SOCIAL SKILLS AND COOPERATIVE INTERACTION

*There is nothing more basic than using one's knowledge in cooperative interaction with others.*

*—Roger Johnson and David Johnson*

Developing a strong, positive sense of identity and the social skills needed to interact productively with others are reciprocal components in growth toward social competence. Katz (1988) defines social competence as the ability to develop and maintain satisfying relationships with others.

Relationships with peers can provide young children with opportunities to learn about themselves and get along with others. The foundation for this development of social skills is *trust.* Certain aspects of trust are apparent: trust develops over time through continuous interactions with people, and trust of others is based on others' abilities to meet one's needs in predictable and sensitive ways.

Friendships play an important role in trust building and social confidence. Young children who may have poor communication skills or are lacking in social skills may be rejected or ignored by their peers. Socially successful preschoolers interact with peers in cooperative ways. They initiate and respond to others in positive ways and receive, in turn, positive feedback in eye contact, smiles, and touching.

Children who are socially dysfunctional need assistance to break the recurring cycle of negative behaviors triggering the peer rejection that reinforces those negative behaviors. The years of early childhood are "prime time" for intervening in this cycle and helping these children develop positive, appropriate social behaviors (Katz 1988).

Children who are unable to identify and follow the rules of the social group not only disrupt interactions, but also are apt to be judged socially *and* intellectually incompetent. The consequences of low peer acceptance may be more severe and far-reaching than the consequences of low achievement (Spodek, Saracho & Lee 1984). Early social adjustment in the primary grades seems to predict adult adjustment. Children who are socially isolated seem more prone to maladjustment, delinquency, and poor mental health.

As early childhood teachers face the diverse ethnic, social, and cultural backgrounds of our children, it is vitally important that they orchestrate experiences that promote positive social interactions. Learning to get along with a variety of peers, to experience mutual respect, and to value differences is imperative.

Early childhood teachers need to help children bridge their home-school experiences and assist them in accepting, in a positive way, others who are different because of race, culture, sex, language, handicapping conditions, family organization, and/or cognitive style. Valuing and supporting diversity must be a continual thread in the tapestry of an inclusive environment. When children feel valued for who they are, and when they are included as productive group members, trust and communication are enhanced. Cooperative, equal-status interaction among heterogeneous group members generates positive acceptance of similarities and differences (Slavin 1991).

## COOPERATIVE INTERACTION

A number of research studies have found that Cooperative Learning fosters positive social attitudes and behavior. By celebrating the unique characteristics and valuing the contribution of each child in the group, early childhood educators can build a positive sense of identity and the mutual trust necessary to engage in productive cooperative interactions.

The following lesson, "Cooperative Interview," can be used at the beginning of the school year. It provides opportunities for positive identity building, uses communication skills (speaking, listening), and serves as a trust-building process as well.

---

### Cooperative Interview
*Barbara Shafer*

*Objective:* Students will find out information about their partners and be able to introduce their partners to the whole class.

*Group Size:* Partners.

*Reward:* Make a new friend.

*Procedure:* The teacher tells the children the following:

1. We are going to "interview" and introduce our partners.
2. Choose a place where you and your partner can sit and talk together.
3. Decide first who will get one piece of paper and one pencil.
4. Together make up five questions to ask about each other, and write the questions on your paper.
5. Each of you will "interview" the other by taking turns with your questions and writing your partner's answers on your paper.
6. I will observe and monitor as you work.
7. When you finish and *both* are ready to introduce your partner, sign your names on your piece of paper.
8. Introduce your partner to the class when the signal is given to stop interviewing each other.
9. Answer these questions together:
   a. What did we do well to get this job done?
   b. What could we do better next time?
10. Shake hands and say "thanks" to your partner.

---

Young children need to become more sensitive to others' feelings and learn that others do not always share their viewpoints. Consideration of an alternative perspective requires a "decentering" process. The child moves from an egocentric posture to a decentric one in which the child views herself in relationship to others (Kamii & DeVries 1980; Spodek, Saracho & Davis 1991).

Cooperation demands decentering. As children have multiple opportunities to express ideas, negotiate with peers, and problem solve within a positive interactive structure, they will develop the self-confidence and peer trust necessary to acknowledge other perspectives.

Members of cooperative groups or pairs should be carefully selected to include a mixture of races, genders, cultures, learning styles, personalities, and handicapping conditions. After groups or pairs are selected, early childhood educators need to plan interdependent activities with high success rates and minimal adult supervision. Children are much more likely to disagree, air views, and negotiate when an adult is *not* an active force in the group. This is an opportune time for teachers to practice observational and monitoring/intervening skills, while resisting the temptation to be *too* helpful.

As communication skills and self-confidence build, children will gain understanding of the perspectives of others in their group. Expression, explanations, and conflict resolution by *all* members of the group should be encouraged. It may be necessary to "walk" children through the problem-solving process: identifying the problem, listening to suggestions from all members, considering all options offered, and agreeing on a solution together (see Figure 7). This takes time, but the dividends are well worth it. Working toward a common goal with a heterogeneous group of peers with minimal adult intervention is a socially and intellectually empowering experience for young children. It also creates a climate of mutual respect and inclusion. "I CAN" becomes "WE CAN."

Figure 7

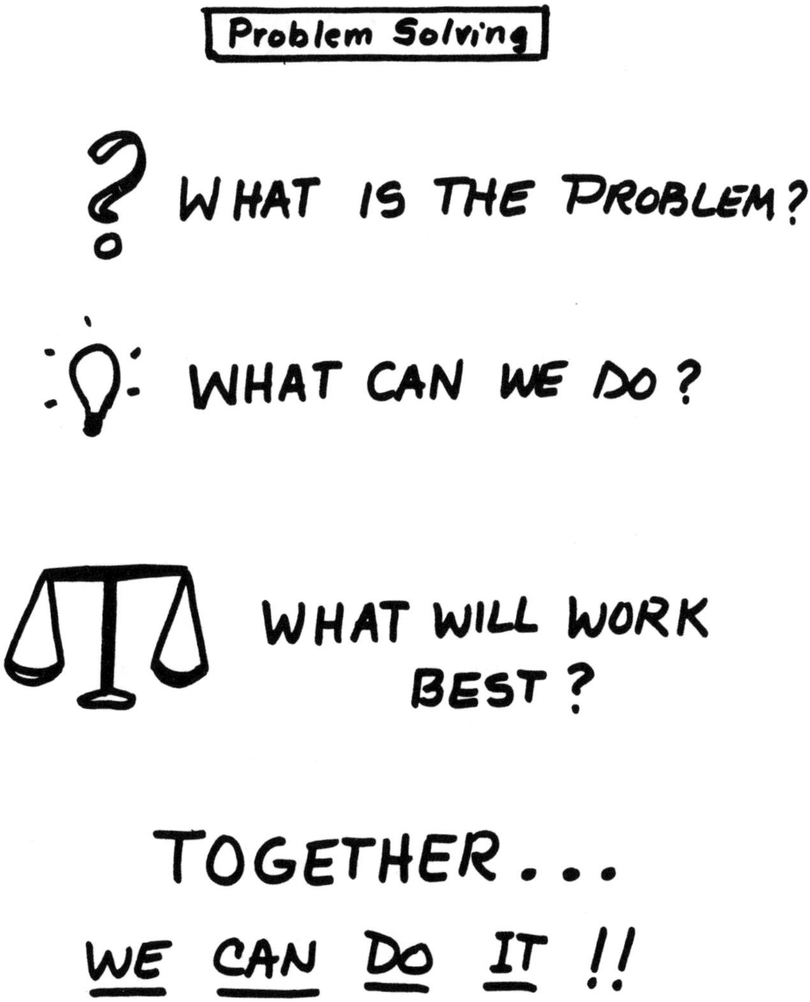

**Problem Solving**

? **WHAT IS THE PROBLEM?**

💡 **WHAT CAN WE DO?**

⚖ **WHAT WILL WORK BEST?**

**TOGETHER...**
**WE CAN DO IT !!**

The following lesson—"Cooperative Cooking with Reading and Math Is Fun!"—is an example of an activity that has proved to be successful in a primary-level resource room populated with special needs children. Note that the teacher structured the team members' roles and the task sequence, but clearly gave full responsibility to the teams.

---

## Cooperative Cooking with Reading and Math Is Fun!
### Vicky Lorentz

*Objective:* Students will finish a sequenced task with a minimum of teacher involvement.

*Group Size:* Three.

Procedure:

1. The teacher places a Group Chart where the children can see it. The chart has team names with three numbered student names below each team name. For example:

### GROUP CHART

| Shining Chefs | Best Bakers | Cool Cooks | Delicious Dudes |
|---|---|---|---|
| 1. George | 1. Tom | 1. John | 1. Jim |
| 2. Betty | 2. Ann | 2. Nancy | 2. Jennifer |
| 3. Lisa | 3. Chris | 3. Nathan | 3. Thad |

2. The teacher gives the following directions:
   a. Look at the Group Chart before you start.
   b. Look at your number.
   c. Do the jobs by your number in order, and put a check mark on the line in front of your number when the step is completed.
   d. Encourage others as they do their jobs.
   e. When you are finished complete the Cooperative Cooking Worksheet.
3. Hand each group a copy of the Jobs list as follows:

## JOBS

____1. Spray the pans with nonsticking substance.
____2. Check to make sure the oven is on, and pick up your supplies at the supply area (cake mix, bowl, spoon, measuring cups/spoons, water, oil, eggs, and vanilla).
____3. Open box and dump cake mix into bowl.

____1. Pour one cup of water into the bowl.
____2. Pour in 1/3 cup of oil.
____3. Crack three eggs into a cup—one at a time. Check the eggs to make sure they are fresh. Pour into bowl.

____1. Mix 100 times using a spoon. (Members 2 and 3 count.)
____2. Mix 100 times using a spoon. (Members 1 and 3 count.)
____3. Mix 100 times using a spoon. (Members 1 and 2 count.)

____1. Add 1 tablespoon of vanilla—the secret ingredient.
____2. Ask the teacher to check your batter.
____3. Pour the batter into the pans.

____1. Take the batter to the baking area. Place the cake pans into the oven, and monitor the time. *You are responsible for watching the cake bake and taking it out when it is done!*
____2. Spray tables and chairs with a cleaner.
____3. Wipe tables and chairs off with a cloth.

____1. Get a towel, sponge, and soap. Take your dishes to the health room to wash.
____1/2/3. Now complete the Cooperative Cooking Worksheet.
____1/2/3. When you have completed your, jobs sit down quietly at your desk and read.

## COOPERATIVE COOKING WORKSHEET

Date _____ Group Name _____

Please complete the following questions as a group. Pick the person who is oldest to be the writer. *All* group members must be able to answer all the questions before signing at the end.

1. What is the name of the cake mix?_____
2. What was the price of the cake mix? _____
3. What is the flavor of the cake mix?_____
4. How many ounces (oz.) are in the cake mix?_____
5. What did you add to the cake mix? List the items and prices below:

| *Item* | *Price* |
|--------|---------|
| _____ | _____ |
| _____ | _____ |
| _____ | _____ |
| _____ | _____ |
| _____ | _____ |

6. Now total all the prices. The total is _____
7. What is the total number of products used?_____
8. Write three ingredients in the cake mix:
   1._____ 2._____ 3._____
9. How many calories are in one serving of the cake? _____
10. How much would five cake mixes cost? _____
11. What did your group do well? _____
   _____
12. What can your group do better next time?_____
   _____
13. Group members sign below when *everyone* in the group can individually answer *all* of the questions above.
14. Ask the teacher to quiz you on the answers.

   1. _____
   2. _____
   3. _____

### CONGRATULATIONS TEAMMATES!

Beyond carefully selecting heterogeneous group members, planning interdependent activities, and reducing adult control to a minimum, early childhood educators need to provide structured opportunities for learning social skills. Role-playing alternative actions in social situations and considering the consequences of those alternatives comprise an appropriate technique. Discussion and problem solving throughout the day in various interactive situations will provide adult-guided experiences as models for children.

Young children construct social values in the same way they construct knowledge. As they engage in repeated interactions with others, they internalize bits and pieces of those experiences and formulate relationships. Through social imitation and modeling, young children learn how to get along in society. Children's new knowledge about how others interact develops by their active modification of what they already know. This is a fluid and dynamic process, not a cumulative one such as laying bricks (Kamii & DeVries 1980).

However, the mere presence of children in a group does not guarantee cooperative interaction. It takes systematic, guided interaction to begin. Many experiences and the gradual reduction of adult intervention are needed as social skills develop. An example of this is found in the lesson "Cooperative Shapes."

---

## Cooperative Shapes
*Linda Post*

This kindergarten lesson illustrates teacher-guided social skills development.

My first attempt at Cooperative Learning involved setting up three social guidelines: (1) use quiet voices, (2) share and take turns, and (3) no put-downs.

Since the children did not know what "put downs" were, I role-played a few situations for them, and then they, in their own words, decided that it meant to "make fun of someone." (I thought that was pretty perceptive for five- and six-year-olds!) I role-played a pair working together, with another teacher, so the children had a concrete model. (Appropriate behavior and roles need to be modeled for young children.)

In this first cooperative activity, I decided to review the shapes we had covered so far. On large sheets of paper, I drew either a square, a triangle, a circle, or an ellipse in the center. Each group of three children had one paper, with a shape in the center, and one set of markers. Groups were randomly chosen, but I attempted to mix boys/girls and outgoing/shy in each group. The assignment was to turn each shape into a picture of something.

Prior to this assignment, during "circle time," I read a book about turning shapes into real "things" like a triangle into a clown hat.

As they began, I reminded the children again about the social skills I would be looking for, especially no put-downs. At first, the children sat shyly in their groups without interacting at all. (I wondered if I had forgotten something!) I approached one group and stimulated them by asking them what they thought they could make. I reminded them to think of the book I had read. One of the boys in the group offered that he could make the triangle into a truck. "That's a wonderful idea, Bobbie! What part of the truck could you make?" I asked. "I could put some wheels on," he answered.

"That's great! What part could Janie make?"

"Janie could put the road on."

"Janie, would you like to do that?"

"Okay."

As I was intervening with this group, I was aware of the other groups watching intently, so I "played it to the hilt." Now, the first group was taking the first tentative steps toward creating the project. It was not long before members of each group were talking about what they could create with their shape. I gave them sufficient time to finish their projects, collected the drawings, and then called each group to tell which part of the drawing each member had contributed (individual accountability).

---

## SPECIAL NEEDS CHILDREN

Young handicapped children especially need to develop positive social behaviors. They may display a range of problem behaviors from shy, withdrawn isolation from peers to hostile aggression toward them. Underdeveloped social skills and behavioral deficits lead to frustration, which triggers more negative behaviors (Spodek, Saracho & Lee 1984).

Special needs children can increase their social skills development by observing and interacting with regular needs children. *All* children become more sensitive to individual differences by developing early relationships with special needs children (Souweine, Crimmins & Mazel, 1981).

Cooperative Learning interactions help young children develop a positive group identity and a feeling of belonging, assist them in decentering and considering other perspectives, and foster acceptance of others who are different. As many positive experiences occur, children construct values and continually modify those values based on repeated experiences. Early childhood educators can provide the structure for these positive interactions in order to attain the goal of an inclusive social environment.

## CONCLUSION

Young children can acquire social skills through modeling and teacher-guided experiences in cooperative groups. Repeated encounters with peers, in a positive interactive process, provide opportunities to grow toward decentering and the acceptance of others and their views. At the same time, self-confidence, group identity, and inclusion develop the trust necessary to continue growth in collaborative skills.

# Chapter 5

# COMMUNICATING EFFECTIVELY

*Speech is a mirror of the soul: as a man speaks,*
*so is he.*

—*Publilius Syrus*

Communicating effectively with others is a lifelong skill that begins at birth and is nurtured through the early childhood years. One of the social skills that Cooperative Learning enhances is that of communication. The child is self-centered and speaks of "I," "my," and "me." Through Cooperative Learning activities, the child can be helped to shift from this individual focus to group intercommunication.

Cooperative Learning builds communication skills in five ways:

1. Children have opportunities to listen to other children's ideas. (Listening skills are developed.)
2. Children have opportunities to share their ideas with others. (Speaking skills are developed or cultivated.)
3. Children learn to build on their own ideas by using the ideas of others.
4. Children learn to solve problems by communicating with others.
5. Children learn to use communication skills to evaluate the usefulness of ideas.

The child needs a structure that will not only allow personal thinking, but also encourage him to express that thinking in "I" comments, and then in "we" comments. In order to communicate effectively, children need to be able to express themselves personally *and* to make that expression understandable to others without negative feedback. Sometimes, however, negative feedback will occur, regardless of the effectiveness of the communication. The emphasis should be on understanding others and being understood by them. The statement "I want this block!" with a simultaneous grabbing for the block is an example of the "me"-centered type of communication. On the other hand, "I want this block so that we can build a tower!" is a statement about oneself, but it also relates that self to others. In the early childhood years, the need is present to move the child from "me" to "we" communication skills.

## UNFINISHED STORIES

The unfinished story is one technique that can be modified to enhance communication in a cooperative manner. Children are given stories without endings. Then individual children complete the story according to their own thinking. Cooperative Learning is a group activity, so this strategy must be adapted.

However, when a young child is individually confronted with an unfinished story, she may become frustrated, seeking the "best" ending, or she may become mentally "blank," not knowing what to put. The child seeking the "best" ending may have to choose between several endings and, thus, constantly seek the help of the teacher. "Teacher, which (ending) is better?" The teacher sometimes attempts to have the children think it through alone and come to a solution. A child who is "blank" may look around or listen to others to get an idea for an ending. As a consequence, whatever is written bears strong resemblance to another child's ending. In both cases, Cooperative Learning could assist the teacher.

Using Think-Pair-Share (Lyman 1981, 1987), two children can work as a pair on the unfinished story. They read the story out loud together. Speaking words aloud often generates thoughts and ideas that reading silently does not. Then the pair discusses what might be a "good" ending for the story. After they have both verbalized their thinking, both children write out the ending of the story in their own individual words. Thus, the skills of reading, communicating, and writing are enhanced through the technique of two children working together. Partner editing would be a natural extension of the story writing. An example of an unfinished story lesson is the following one about "Abraham Lincoln and the Correct Change Incident."

---

### Abraham Lincoln and the Correct Change Incident (Unfinished Story)

*Objective:* The children will communicate their ideas to one another and then complete the story.

*Grouping:* Pairs.

*Procedure:* The teacher reads the unfinished story to the class. The children in their Think-Pair-Share groups discuss endings to the story. The children then explain or write their own endings. The teacher then tells the children what really happened.

*The Story:* Abe Lincoln, who once was a president of the United States, was well known for being an honest person. When he was growing up, he worked in a store. A customer bought something from Mr. Lincoln and left the store. Mr. Lincoln discovered that the customer had given him too much money for the purchase. What should Mr. Lincoln have done with the extra money that he had received from the customer?

After the children have finished the unfinished story, the children should be told that Mr. Lincoln walked a long way to the person's home and gave the person the correct change.

---

## ORAL LANGUAGE DEVELOPMENT

In numerous classrooms today, children come to school with little or no ability to speak English. However, in order to communicate effectively, either the English-speaking child must learn the non-English language or the non-English-speaking child must learn English. This simple statement is surrounded by social, economic, and political ramifications. However, communicating effectively is a key point here.

Children can be paired together—one child who speaks English with a child who is a non-English speaker. Where the number of English-speaking or non-English-speaking children is limited, the pairs can be shifted from content lesson to content lesson throughout the day.

During the activity, each child repeats what is said in the other child's language. For example, the teacher directs the children to pick up the pencil. In each pair, the English-speaking child says "pick up the pencil" and then picks up the pencil. The non-English-speaking child then picks up the pencil and says the same thing in his other language. The English-speaking child then picks up the pencil and repeats the other language. If the teacher is using a language other than English and the majority of the children are non-English speakers, the process would be reversed. The lesson "Help Mr. Peanut Solve the Problems" illustrates this approach.

## Help Mr. Peanut Solve the Problems
*Melanie Smith*

During classroom activities, children would proceed through the lesson activities. In a lesson on addition by single digits up to 18 in the first grade, the teacher hands out the Mr. Peanut addition practice sheet, which has addition problems within a peanut shape. (See Figure 8.) The teacher states, "Help Mr. Peanut solve the problems." The children repeat this title/direction in both English and the other language. The teacher states, "Pick up your pencil." The children repeat the teacher's words in both languages, while picking up their pencils. The teacher then states, "Place your pencil point on the first peanut." This is repeated by the children. The teacher states, "Seven plus six equals what number?" This is repeated by the children. The pairs of children decide on the solution together. Then the individual children write the solution on their individual practice papers. Next the children state the number in both English and the other language.

During the course of this exchange, pairs of children are assisting each other in mathematics, but they are also learning another language at the same time, thus learning to communicate more effectively.

Figure 8
Help Mr. Peanut Solve the Problems

Name _____

$7 + 6$

$8 + 8$

$4 + 9$

$9 + 8$

$9 + 9$

$6 + 8$

$8 + 7$

$6 + 6$

$8 + 9$

$7 + 8$

$7 + 7$

Young children often have difficulty with spatial relationships. What does it mean to be "above," "below," or "on"? The lesson "Feed the Turkey," in addition to practicing counting and learning about spatial relationships, has young children orally rehearsing their concepts of spatial relationships and developing their repertoire of words. Direction following is important to this lesson as well, but will be treated in the next section.

---

### Feed the Turkey

*Objective:* Children will practice counting skills in pairs. Children will practice spatial relationship vocabulary words (on, off, above, below. . .) in pairs.

*Materials:* Drawing of a turkey (see Figure 9), five construction paper cutouts of corn or candy corn.
   Note: During the activity, each pair of children should have only one turkey and five corn pieces to share. Each child may later be given a turkey to color if desired.

*Procedure:* Tell the children that they will be working in pairs to feed the turkey to fatten it for Thanksgiving dinner. The teacher will tell the children how many pieces of corn to give the turkey each time they feed it. They will take turns feeding the turkey by putting corn pieces on the drawing. Their partners will check to see that they have the correct number of corn pieces.

1. one piece of corn
2. three pieces of corn
3. two pieces of corn
4. no pieces (The turkey is not feeling well.)
5. five pieces of corn
6. four pieces of corn

To practice vocabulary words:

1. one piece on the turkey
2. two pieces off the turkey
3. one piece on, one piece off
4. two pieces on, two pieces off

5. three pieces on, one piece off
6. two pieces on, three pieces off
(Change the order of the words.)
7. three pieces off the turkey, one piece on the turkey
8. four pieces off, one piece on
9. one piece off, no pieces on
10. no pieces off, two pieces on

"Above" and "below" may be substituted for "on" and "off." Example: one piece of corn above the turkey, one below (meaning one at the top of the turkey picture and one at the bottom of the turkey picture, but not within the outline of the turkey).

*Group Reward:* Candy corn or cornbread can serve as a reward to be eaten following the activity.

Figure 9

# DIRECTION FOLLOWING

One form of communication that teachers continuously use is that of direction giving and direction following. Children need to learn very early that following directions is extremely important. Whether the children follow those directions precisely is another problem altogether.

The lesson "Parts of a Flower" can be used during the spring season and indicates the importance of communication and direction following within the cooperative setting.

---

Parts of a Flower
(Spring)
*Lori Skolnick*

*Goal:* The children will follow directions, individually and as a group.

*Objective:* The children will work cooperatively and collaboratively, making a group spring mural by following specific teacher directions.

*Process Skills:* Cooperating, communicating, explaining, identifying, listening, and counting.

*Grouping:* Groups of four. The teacher makes cards prior to the lesson. On one side of the card is a number from 1 to 4, and on the other side of the card is a flower type. The numbers determine which team member performs each task.

*Procedure:* This lesson uses the leap frog Cooperative Learning approach.

Child 1 will go up to the teacher and obtain the first set of directions. The teacher states, "Give each person in your group a piece of paper and tell each one to cut out a stem for a flower."

The child gets materials and takes them to the group. The child then relays the teacher's directions to the group, and the group members follow the child's directions.

The teacher monitors all groups and checks on their progress. When the majority of the children have completed the task, the teacher calls up child 2 and states the following, "Go and get two leaves for each person in your group and have them cut them out." Child 2 gets the materials and relays the directions to the group.

Child 3 is called by the teacher. The teacher states, "Get enough flowers for each member of your group. Ask your friends what color each one would like." The teacher pauses to allow child 3 to complete this set of directions before giving the next set of directions to child 3. The teacher tells child 3, "Tell your team members that they are to glue their flowers onto their stems." Child 3 relays the directions to the group.

Child 4 is called by the teacher. The teacher states, "Have your group glue their flowers on the paper—first, the flower with the stem and, second, the leaves." Child 4 gets the background paper and relays the directions to the group.

Child 1 is called by the teacher. The teacher states, "Ask your group whether or not they would like to add anything else to their beautiful picture." Child 1 carries the directions to the group. If the group decides to add something, then child 2 can be in charge of getting any additional materials that are needed.

Cleaning up of the materials and returning them to the correct location are the tasks of children 3 and 4. Once the area is cleaned up, each group shares its mural with the class. With a prekindergarten class or a kindergarten class with a high percentage of non-English-speaking children, each child from the group should say something about the mural.

---

A Halloween project can be a context for direction following on the part of young children. In the lesson "Peanut Butter and Jelly Sandwiches," the children not only hear a teacher read a story, but also make a Halloween peanut butter and jelly sandwich by following the teacher's interesting directions.

# Peanut Butter and Jelly Sandwiches
## (Halloween)
### *Jan Morehead*

*Objective:* The children will become aware of the importance of following directions while thinking logically and sequentially in order to make a peanut butter and jelly sandwich.

*Grouping:* Groups of four. The teacher assigns four different jobs to each group. Each group will be responsible for making a sandwich. Some groups will be responsible for distributing the finished product, plus other related snack items.

*Anticipatory Set:* The teacher reads the book *The Giant Jam Sandwich* to the class. The teacher leads a discussion about what would be needed to make a sandwich, especially a peanut butter and jelly sandwich.

*Sandwich-Making Roles:*

- Baker: Brings the supply tub to the group; opens and removes the bread from a package of bread.
- Spreader: Spreads the peanut butter on the bread.
- Jammer: Spreads the jelly.
- Slicer: Puts the bread slices together in sandwich form and cuts it into four pieces.

*Table Helper Roles:*

- Mouth Cleaner: Passes out napkins.
- Milk Person: Passes out milk.
- Sipper: Passes out straws.
- Munchy Muncher: Passes out sandwiches.

*Input:* As a whole group, the teacher has the children give verbal directions for making a peanut butter and jelly sandwich. The teacher writes the directions on the chalkboard or chart paper. When the list is completed, the teacher makes the sandwich according to the children's directions. (If the children say to put the peanut butter on the bread, then the teacher puts the jar of peanut butter on the unopened package of bread, and so on.) The teacher talks about the importance of thinking logically, doing things in sequential order, following directions, and making decisions. The teacher passes out job necklaces to four children (see Figure 10), assigning one of the sandwich roles to each child. The class is then asked to restate the directions for the sandwich in a logical and sequential order.

*Guided Practice:* Four children come to the front of the classroom to act as role models. The teacher has assigned jobs according to the corresponding necklaces. The teacher talks to the entire class about the importance of thinking logically, doing things in sequential order, following directions, and making decisions. Safety rules are talked about in regard to opening jars of food and using a knife. The class is asked to restate the directions. The teacher writes each new direction on the board as one child demonstrates that direction as a role model. The teacher can compare the original directions with the new directions.

*Independent Practice:* Cooperative Learning groups of four are formed. Each group is given four necklaces with differing pictures on them. The job pictures include a peanut butter jar, a jelly jar, a slice of bread, and a knife (see Figure 11). Each group member has previously been assigned a number (1–4). The teacher assigns a number to each picture. The children can then determine what each job will be and begin making the sandwich. (The teacher has previously placed all the supplies in a tub. The supplies include small containers of peanut butter and jelly, two slices of bread, a plastic knife, and a sheet of waxed paper.)

*Closure:* Table helpers can be assigned the job of distributing the snacks. These jobs can be randomly assigned by the teacher. Job necklaces assign the various roles. (Another variation would be to pass out four different jobs to each group of four.) Stick puppets might be made for each picture. Each puppet can be held up in the air, one at a time, and everyone with that job can pick up the appropriate items from the tub and pass them out to the table group members. (Separate items may be kept in separate tubs—i.e., bread in the bread tub, etc.)

*Group Evaluation:*

1. Elicit verbal responses from the children.
2. Make a word web using the vocabulary words: peanut butter,

jelly, knife, bread, spread, and so on (see Figure 12).

3. Review the directions, comparing the first set to the second set.
4. Discuss how important it is to follow directions, not only during this lesson, but always.
5. Ask how the children liked their sandwiches.

*Note:* This activity was done originally during the week of Halloween. The food products and equipment were renamed, using Halloween vocabulary words (see Figure 13). In addition, the directions were sent home for the parents to enjoy. The children can come up with their own names for each item used and each role carried out.

---

Figure 10

Figure 11

Figure 12

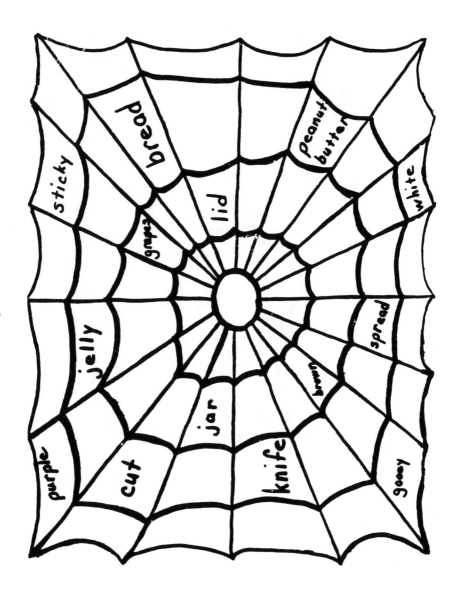

Figure 13

## SHARING TEAMS

Most teachers have had Show & Tell and have had it turn into Drag & Brag. The children drag something into the room and go on about how great their favorite "whatever" is and how they love it so much. This may draw limited attention from other children who want to talk about their favorite item. Cooperative Learning can change this large-group setting, which can cause hurt feelings, into one of mutual concern and listening.

Sharing teams, developed by Lyman, Foyle, and Thies, is a simple Cooperative Learning structure that allows children to share ideas while practicing roles and developing listening skills. Teams can have three or four members who rotate the following roles:

- Sharer: Tells the group her response to an idea or question.
- Stretcher: Asks one or more questions to get more information from the sharer.
- Applauder: Tells one or more things he liked about what the sharer or the stretcher said. (Groups of four have two applauders.)

A time limit for the sharer should be given. Short time limits of two to four minutes are appropriate when beginning. Later, longer sharing times can be given, if desired.

After each team member has shared, the team members can write about their sharing. The topic sentence can be "Today, our group talked about. . . ." The roles of writer (writes the ideas of the group), teller (tells what should be written), and checker (checks for completeness, grammar, and punctuation) can be used for the writing activity.

For prewriting four- and five-year-olds, sharing pairs of children could replace groups. The pairs could generate a sentence to dictate for a Sharing Chart. The chart might be labeled "SHARE PAIRS CHART" and have the words "Today

We Shared . . ." on the first line. Then the children's names could be listed in the following way:

- Mike shared his (in the space Mike draws what he shared).
- Susie told me about her (in the space Susie draws what she told).

## SHARING TEAMS STARTERS

Listening in the sharing teams can be enhanced by using one or more of the following sharing teams starters. The children start their statements with "What I like to do best is. . . ." This provides the children with some structure in their sharing time. Active involvement of all children is encouraged. Following are some possible sharing teams starters:

1. What I like to do best is. . . .
2. What I like about school is. . . .
3. School could be better if. . . .
4. Something really fun I did was. . . .
5. Things I like to see [hear, taste, feel, smell] are. . . .
6. Something that makes me happy is. . . .
7. My favorite food is. . . .
8. A good friend is. . . .
9. Hot weather [cold, snow, rain] makes me feel like. . . .

(Negatives may be introduced after trust has been built in the classroom. Some negative statements might include the following.)

10. Something that bugs me is. . . .
11. Something that scares me is. . . .
12. Something that makes me angry is. . . .

# THINKING OUT LOUD TOGETHER, SHARING (TOTS)

Children are self-centered and do not share "why" they choose to do or say something. This can be alleviated by fostering communication between children in a spoken manner. One way to do this is by following the thinking out loud together, sharing (TOTS) approach developed by Foyle, Lyman, and Thies.

TOTS combines the cognitive and affective domains. In the cognitive domain, the process includes five steps (thinking out loud together):

1. *Wondering:* The child thinks about what the teacher presented.

   "I want to know. . . ."

2. *Telling:* The child verbalizes or orally rehearses that wondering/thinking to others.

   "I want to tell others about what I know."
   "I want to tell others about what I think."

3. *Listening:* The child attends to or listens to the ideas of others. This listening is a form of showing respect for others.

   "I want to know what others think."

4. *Building:* The child restates the other child's telling and attempts to add to it by improving on it.

   "We have a good idea."

5. *Evaluating:*

   "This is a good idea because. . . ."
   "We did a good job because. . . ."

In the affective domain, the process includes the following five steps (sharing):

1. *Motivating:*

   "I need to know. . . ."

2. *Sharing:* Learning by teaching each other; oral rehearsal; peer practice.

   "I have a good idea. . . ."

3. *Accepting:* Individual attention; listening.

   "My friends have a good idea. . . ."

4. *Liking (self-esteem):*

   "I like myself and others. . . ."

5. *Celebrating (evaluating):*

   "We work well together because. . . ."

Young children not only need to achieve success in the cognitive domain, but especially need to achieve success in the affective domain. Young children need to verbalize (thinking out loud together) and to actually use social skills (sharing). An additional reason for young children to verbalize is that oral language is a concept-building tool. The task of preschoolers, kindergartners, and even primary students is to shift from concrete and action-stimulus-bound thought to an internalized action—a mental construct that can be referred to without repeating the action or events externally over and over again. The next lesson, "The Block Tower," uses manipulatives to illustrate the TOTS approach.

## The Block Tower
### (A Thinking Out Loud Together, Sharing or TOTS Approach)

*Objective:* Communication will be enhanced as each child expresses what she is thinking while making a block tower.

*Grouping:* Teams of two.

*Process:* As children work together, they verbalize why they are doing something. The teacher helps the children go through this process. Any activity can be substituted for building a tower.

1. Child 1: "I want to know how high we can pile these blocks." (Wondering)
2. Child 1: "I think we should put the first block here." (Telling)
3. Child 2: He pays attention to child 1, who is talking. (Listening)
4. Child 2: "That's a good idea. Let's put the next block here because it will. . . ." (Building)
5. Child 1: "I think the next block should go here because. . . ."
6. And so on. Each child helps build the blocks up while stating what she is thinking or doing.

# MANIPULATIVES

The lesson "The Block Tower" uses manipulatives. Early childhood teachers recognize the importance of using objects that provide hands-on experiences for young children. These objects are called *manipulatives*. Manipulatives provide many opportunities for children to be actively involved in cooperative interaction with others. Some cooperative strategies that utilize manipulatives are

- Cooperative counting: Children practice counting skills, using a variety of objects, in teams of two or more.
- Cooperative sorting: Children sort objects by color, shape, size, texture, or other attributes in teams of two or more.

- Cooperative constructing: Children build a structure or put a puzzle together in teams of two or more. One set of materials should be used that leads to one finished product.
- Cooperative listening: Children arrange one set of objects by following auditory directions given by the teacher in teams of two or more.
- Cooperative shaping: Children arrange one set of objects in the shape of given shapes, letters, or numbers in teams of two or more.

A variety of objects lend themselves to use as manipulatives for these cooperative strategies (see Figure 14). Having only one set of materials to be shared (by a team or pair) is very important in order to promote positive interdependence.

## Figure 14
### Selected Manipulative Objects

| Item | Description and Use | Manufacturer |
|---|---|---|
| Barrel of Monkeys | 14 plastic monkey shapes with tails used to connect them | Milton Bradley Company |
| Blockhead | 24 wooden blocks in a variety of shapes and colors | Pressman Toy Corporation |
| Jumbo Pick-Up Stix | 24 sticks in 4 colors | Rose Art Industries |
| Magnetic Shapes | 10 shapes in 6 colors | Tootsietoy Corporation |
| Parquetry Blocks | 32 blocks in 3 shapes and 6 colors | Learning Resources |
| Super Shapes Monsters | Pasta monster shapes, which can be colored to make them easier to tell apart | Mueller (Best Foods) |

## CONCLUSION

Communication goes beyond speaking to one another. It is the sharing of ideas and the understanding of others. Cooperative Learning uses communication skills, and the growth of these skills is at the heart of the interactive process. When understanding is communicated well, true cooperation can occur. Young children can learn this process through oral language development, sharing teams, and the use of manipulatives within Cooperative Learning groups.

# Chapter 6

# COOPERATION AND PLAY

*Play is a particularly powerful form of activity that fosters the social life and constructive activity of the child.*

—*Jean Piaget*

Play is a major vehicle for enabling children to learn about their world. It is a channel for exploring, for testing the limits of their environment, for engaging their minds in new patterns of thought, and for devising alternative actions. During play, children can master basic concepts and skills. They can express ideas or feelings, construct new knowledge, and develop oral language as they interact with objects and people.

The *process* of play activity—not the product—is significant. Play is characterized by its self-directedness, active involvement, and intrinsic motivation *to satisfy self* rather than to meet basic survival needs or adult demands.

Children's play has been the subject of much study. Some principles that emerge as common denominators in the findings are that (1) play is child-directed, child-initiated, and child-involved; (2) play is autonomous of external goals; (3) play occurs when basic needs are met and the child feels secure; (4) play is fun; and (5) play supports and enhances all areas of development.

There are several theories about the stages and types of play. Researchers usually differentiate between "free" play and "teacher-guided" play. These two forms of play differ in the level of adult control. Stage theories vary, but most indicate an initial, motor-oriented play stage from infancy to about two years of age. During this time, children practice and refine motor skills and are egocentric in their behavior. These experiences form the basis

95

for other forms of play, social interactions, and oral language development. This isolated play enables children to distinguish themselves as separate from their surroundings and their actions as affecting events in their world.

A second stage, toddler to about three years old, generally depicts play that is parallel (side by side) without purposeful interaction between players. This is the forerunner of cooperative play. Teacher encouragement to interact and share play materials with peers and adult dialogue with toddlers about others' needs and feelings lay the foundation for cooperative behaviors.

Associative or cooperative play begins when children can decenter enough to interact in collaborative ways while playing. This can occur in socially skilled three-year-olds or perhaps not until well into the primary grades for a child with few social experiences. The task of educators of young children is to know when to intervene in play, to know how to structure the play environment for maximum autonomy, and to know the children well enough to do all this with their appropriate developmental needs in mind.

## THE TEACHER'S ROLE IN COOPERATIVE PLAY

By encouraging autonomy and intervening only when necessary to stimulate conversation or to model appropriate social behavior, the teacher can promote cooperative play and enrich social interactions. The purpose is to support the children and minimize adult control as much as possible so that the play process is child-initiated and child-satisfying. Children learn to be interdependent with peers much more quickly with minimal adult involvement (Spodek, Saracho & Davis 1991).

Planning for flexible spaces, materials, and time frames within a secure, predictable environment will provide an appropriate framework for play. Children's play ideas can be stimulated by a diversity of literature experiences, field trips, pets, centers, and access to interesting people in the classroom.

The teacher's role changes slightly if the children are playing organized games, but the need to support independence is still important. This may mandate "walking" through the problem-solving process and spending lots of time discussing what to do about peer conflicts—even if this limits the actual play time. Reduced adult intervention encourages cooperation among the children and allows them to build competence as negotiators and cooperative problem solvers. Games may need to be modified to be compatible with young children's thinking. They can become frustrated and have negative experiences when rules are imposed on them by an adult or older children.

Adults need to keep in mind that autonomy and independent thinking are the goals of play activities. It is the young children's play—*their* games and *their* competence—that needs the time to grow. Early childhood teachers can become overly concerned with the adult interpretation of "success" in these play activities.

An example of the difference in young children's thinking during games is cited by Kamii and DeVries (1980): "When four-year-olds run a race, everybody can win. When they play Hide and Seek, a hider often yells, 'Here I am, come and find me!' In a guessing game, a player often gives the answer away and others do not object to this" (p. 202). As in other activities, play and games must be compatible with the child's developmental needs and abilities. Early childhood teachers will reap tremendous, continuing benefits if preschoolers and kindergartners experience productive cooperative play.

## BENEFITS OF COOPERATIVE PLAY

As in Chapter 1, in the discussion of an appropriate curriculum, the central consideration must always be appropriately meeting children's needs, whatever the activity may be. Play promotes development in all areas: physical, social, emotional, and cognitive. This is especially true when the play is cooperative and other children's actions and thoughts impact the players.

*Physical* activity and the development of fine and gross motor skills are an obvious part of play, especially in outdoor activities. Whether the play is inside or outside, children are *actively involved*, which is a basic learning prerequisite for young children. The *self-concept* is enhanced as young children gain confidence (self-efficacy) in what they can accomplish independently of adults. Pride in their accomplishments, individual or cooperative, is a positive experience. As children are encouraged to choose activities and invent their own play processes, they have control over the environment and sense a responsibility for their activity. Creativity and flexibility of action and thought are direct cognitive growth benefits. Situations, problems, and solutions are ingeniously arranged, developed, and solved during play.

The decentering process allows children to entertain others' viewpoints. This movement away from egocentrism is a major factor in the ability to *construct knowledge* and modify it as new experiences occur. Piaget calls this "confrontation of points of view" and emphasizes its importance to the assimilation/ accommodation cycle of cognitive development: "It is clear that the confrontation of points of view is already indispensable in childhood for the elaboration of logical thought . . . [He commends study] . . . on such an important terrain as play, where the confrontation of points of view is constantly at work" (quoted in Kamii & DeVries 1980, vii).

The child constructs knowledge of her environment and continually modifies that knowledge based on play experiences— exploration and experimentation with objects and people. External actions are internalized through the channel of language. Eventually, the objects and actions are not necessary for the child to think about the concepts; they have been internally "filed" for retrieval as needed.

Wehman & Umansky (1985) reported four values of play for handicapped children. Play helps achieve educational goals; develops gross and fine motor, language, and social skills; reduces socially unacceptable behavior; and provides enjoyment.

Educators of young children have long known the value of cooperative play in the acquisition of *appropriate social behaviors*. When children learn to decenter and see other viewpoints, they are able to adapt their behavior to be compatible with social situations. Learning to share, to negotiate, and to problem solve helps the child compromise, when necessary, in the best interest of the peer group. These adaptive behaviors are positively influenced in special needs as well as regular needs children.

The direct effect of cooperative play on the social behaviors of special needs children is evident. It teaches them acceptable modes of socialization, such as sharing, taking turns, and being responsible. Also, during play there is a reduction or elimination of aggressive behavior and bizarre vocal sounds (Wehman & Umansky 1985).

The benefits of play are multiple, and the relationship of skills acquired to later learning success is evident. A closer look at the actual implementation of cooperative learning built on cooperative play experiences is the final piece of this puzzle.

## COOPERATIVE LEARNING AND COOPERATIVE PLAY

A primary goal in Cooperative Learning is the development of positive interdependence among group members as they interact to succeed at a task and evaluate their own performance. The essential communication and social skills necessary for success in Cooperative Learning are practiced and refined during cooperative play. The benefits of cooperative play, previously cited, combine to produce increased social and intellectual competence, which enables children to learn effectively in a cooperative group.

During play, children invent guessing games with a hidden object, and playmates guess its location or description.

Hints are given (generously) until someone is successful at finding the object. Building on this play format, a first grade teacher can use a low-level "trivia" game format and put children into heterogeneous groups of three. Each group sits closely around one desk so that they can confer before giving their group answer to the trivia question. Each team has a Scorekeeper, an Encourager, and a Speaker. (The Encourager makes sure that each member has input and that all agree on the answer given by the Speaker.) After all the groups attempt a particular question without giving the right answer, the teacher answers it and puts it back in the stack to be asked again. After the game, the children work together to evaluate their individual effectiveness and their group teamwork. Questions they used included "Do we all help answer questions?" "What makes us a really good team?" and "What could we do to work together better next time?"

## DRAMATIC PLAY

Dramatic play is a natural occurrence for young children in the playhouse area. Sociodramatic play (pretending to be persons from your social circle and "trying on" different roles) is not scripted in advance and is usually quite impromptu. Teacher-directed role-play is defined by specific characters/events. Scripted lines may even be used. For example, The Three Billy Goats Gruff may be re-enacted with a table as the bridge, children as the goats and the troll, and the audience as the sound effects makers (slapping their hands on their thighs and saying "trip-trap" with the appropriate volume for each size goat). The Little Red Hen can be role-played with groups of children saying the lines for the cat, duck, mouse, and other characters.

Children might also select parts of stories to pantomime or role-play. The following lesson was contributed by a teacher whose goal was to use dramatic play to enhance reading comprehension.

# Girls Can Be Anything
## *Mary McDonnell Harris*

The story used in this lesson is *Girls Can Be Anything* by Norma Klein (E. P. Dutton, 1975). The story develops in parts or episodes. An episode is action that takes place at one time and place. The episodes are as follows:

Episode 1: Adam and Marina play hospital. Adam is doctor.
Episode 2: Marina and her father discuss her Aunt Rosa, a surgeon.
Episode 3: Marina plays doctor and confronts Adam.
Episode 4: Adam and Marina play airplanes. Adam is pilot; Marina is stewardess.
Episode 5: Marina and her mother discuss a female pilot.
Episode 6: Adam and Marina play airplanes; both are pilots.

In interpreting a story dramatically, it seems best to develop only one episode, unless all the episodes are the same, as in The Gingerbread Boy. In the case of *Girls Can Be Anything,* parallel episodes 4 and 6 were chosen for dramatic interpretation. Episode 4 was much better developed in the story and provided more dramatic possibilities; the dramatization of episode 6 was essential to the theme of the story.

Preparation for reading a story that will be interpreted dramatically often includes a dramatic warm-up. This is very useful in helping children begin to identify with the story situation and to predict character actions and reactions. In preparation for reading *Girls Can Be Anything,* each child pantomimed a job he or she might like to do as a grown-up. The teacher led a discussion about whether certain jobs were only for men or only for women in the context of their selections.

The lesson sequence was as follows:

1. Preparation for reading
   a. Dramatic warm-up
   b. Discussion of sex-linked careers
   c. Introduction of story characters/vocabulary
2. Silent reading/discussion
   a. Episodes 1, 2, and 3

3. Silent reading/dramatic interpretation of episode 4
   a. Chairs moved into an airplane to establish setting
   b. Silent reading/discussion
   c. Character selection
   d. Dramatic interpretation
4. Silent reading/discussion
   a. Episodes 5 and 6
5. Dramatic interpretation of episode 6

Lesson time: about 45 minutes.

## SONGS AND FINGERPLAYS

Songs and fingerplays are often done cooperatively. Partners can do collaborative motions, and groups can sing the parts of simple rounds like "Row, Row, Row Your Boat." By tightening the structure a bit, roles can be devised for some of these activities. A cooperative strategy for using music with young children is to break the song down into phrases and have as many people in the group as there are phrases in the song. For very young children, even a section of a song is almost always too much for an individual to carry alone vocally. An example of this would be the song "This Old Man." The following music lesson is an example of cooperative roles and positive interdependence built into a singing activity.

---

### This Old Man
### (Music)
### *Susan B. Lyman*

In "This Old Man," the first phrase of the song is "This old man, he played one." The second phrase is "He played nick-nack on my thumb." The third phrase is "With a nick-nack, paddy-whack give the dog a bone!" The fourth phrase is "This old man came rolling home."

Because there are four phrases in this song, there could be four people in each group. Each person would sing just one phrase of

102

the song and do only the actions for the phrase that is sung. If all ten verses of "This Old Man" are used, the teacher may stop between verses and assign new parts so everyone learns all the parts.

By singing cooperatively, children quickly realize that without each person's participation, the song will not sound right or be complete. Cooperation will also make singing like a game as the children put the parts together to form a complete whole.

---

It takes a good deal of planning and careful orchestration for teachers to provide stimulating play environments with minimal adult control. But the dividends from acquiring the basic skills needed to succeed in Cooperative Learning interactions with peers are tremendously valuable. Major benefits can be realized when teaching styles are changed to include Cooperative Learning approaches. The investment of time, energy, and effort to add Cooperative Learning to the early childhood teacher's repertoire is worth the benefits immediately gained in the classroom as well as the benefit of providing a foundation for future successes.

Cooperative experiences in free play, game playing, drama, music, and verse are "rehearsals" for the processes and skills encountered later in cooperative classroom groups. Cooperative play promotes positive interdependence, which is the drive shaft of Cooperative Learning.

## COOPERATIVE PLAY ACTIVITIES

Cooperative play activities often take the form of physical education activities. These physical education activities give teachers an excellent opportunity to foster challenging and cooperative behavioral attitudes among children. Specially designed activities require a cooperative spirit to achieve group prowess *and* individual attainments. Most importantly, cooperative activities can build positive self-concepts. No matter how well-planned activities may be, teachers' attitudes and encouragements are what motivate cooperative play among young children.

Some general guidelines for developing cooperative play include the following: (1) keep everyone active, (2) keep frustration at a minimum, (3) downplay the competitive nature of the activity, and (4) have evident outcomes from successful cooperation.

Some examples of cooperative activities are described in the lesson entitled "Cooperative Play Activities." It is apparent that some of these are traditional activities adapted to enhance the cooperative values of play.

---

## Cooperative Play Activities
### *Bill Stinson*

### *Help Your Neighbor*

Each child moves around the room with a beanbag on her head. If the beanbag should fall off, the child must "freeze." She cannot move until someone can pick up the beanbag and place it back on her head. Keep encouraging the children to "help their neighbor" and praise them when they do.

### *Busy Bee*

Each child has a partner. A body part is called out and each child must touch that body part to the same body part of his partner. Whenever the words "Busy Bee" are called out, they change partners.

### *Trio Beanbag Catch*

One child tosses a beanbag to a pair of children joined arms to arms. They catch the beanbag together without letting go and transport it to a basket.

### *Peanut Butter*

The children pair up and decide on a code word. It should be a two-syllable word or two words (e.g., football, peanut butter). The partners go to opposite sides of the room or playground, close their eyes (or are blindfolded), and begin to call out their part of the code word until they find the person calling out the other part of the code word. Younger children may move one pair at a time to find their partners.

### Move the Fence

Blindfolded, the children hold a rope and try to form various shapes asked for (square, circle, triangle) as a group. The group members may talk to and coach each other, but never let go of the rope or take their blindfolds off until they think they have the desired shape. Younger children may do this with their eyes open.

### Seeing-Eye Dog

One child leads another child (blindfolded or with her eyes closed) through a series of obstacles (chairs, tires, benches, etc.).

### Three-Legged Walk or Run

Partners tie or strap their near legs together and move.

### Chain Race

The children form a chain by joining hands. On a signal, the chain sees how quickly it can run down to a goal line, reverse itself, and return to the starting line without letting go of the joined hands.

### Caterpillar

The children lie on their stomachs, side by side and closely packed. The person on one end of the line rolls onto his neighbor and keeps rolling down the line of bodies. At the end of the line, he lies on his stomach again. The next person at the other end starts rolling.

### Beach Blanketball

The children gather in groups of eight to ten around a blanket or large sheet and grasp its edges. A beach ball or cage ball is placed on the blanket. The children practice throwing the ball up and catching it with their blanket. Then the teams pass their balls back

105

and forth in unison toward the receiving teams. A team can toss the ball straight up and move out of the way to let the other team move in and try to catch it. A net may be used for a form of volleyball.

## Giant Get-Up

The children form a circle, turn their backs to the center of the circle, and lock arms. Then as a group they try to sit and stand up again without letting go of their arms.

## Growing Centipedes

Each child "hooks" up with another child. As partners, they move across the floor in one direction, then another. On the command "hook-up," they join up with another pair without changing their original hook-up pattern and move as a group of four. The centipedes eventually grow into one large centipede.

## Together

This game has an infinite number of variations. The common thread running through the different activities is that the children must achieve the objective by performing the task or acting out the motion together with one or more friends.

1. Can you walk through a field of sticky glue with your partner?
2. Can you swim through gelatin with your partner?
3. Can you be real tall with your partner?
4. Can you be real small with your partner?
5. Can you be one frog with your partner?
6. Can you do a round thing with your friend while holding his hand?
7. Can you and your partner hold hands and saw wood together like lumberjacks?
8. Can you make a human chair for your partner to sit on? A two-people chair? A four-people chair?
9. Can you skip around with three friends?
10. Can you get behind your partner, wrap your arms around her front, and walk at the same time as she does? Can four people do it?
11. Can you make a fort with your friends and all get inside it?
12. Can you go through an obstacle course (e.g., under a

bench, through a hoop, across a beam) without letting go of your partner's hand?

13. Can you make a people tunnel that someone can go through?
14. Can you take turns going through the tunnel, while keeping the tunnel as long as possible?
15. Can you find your partner's heartbeat? After a quiet game? After an active game?
16. Can you each get a stick (or broom) and together with a partner try to bounce and catch a beach ball using both your sticks?
17. Can you get in groups of three or four and see if you can carry a beach ball across the gym holding it way over your heads with floor-hockey sticks or brooms?
18. With your back stuck to your partner's back, can you move around the gym? Jump forward toward this wall? Jump backward toward this wall?
19. Can you both get inside a hoop and move around while still stuck back to back?
20. Can you roll a big hula hoop on its edge so your partner can run through it?
21. Can you make a people sandwich with four or five friends (i.e., with ham, lettuce, mustard, and two slices of bread)?
22. Can you sit down across from your friend, feet to feet, and row a boat?
23. Can you roll your partner(s) like a log? Can you jump over your log(s)?
24. Can you drag your log(s) across the floor? Can you (and a friend) stand your log up like a telephone pole?
25. Can you think of some other neat things to do together?

---

# SELECTED TEACHER RESOURCES
# FOR COOPERATIVE PLAY ACTIVITIES

Cratty, B. *Learning About Human Behavior Through Active Games.* Englewood Cliffs, N.J.: Prentice-Hall, 1975.

Fluegelman, A. *The New Games Book.* New York: Headlands Press, 1976.

Harrison, M. *For The Fun of It.* Philadelphia: Friends Peace Committee, 1975.

Hoper, C., and others. *Awareness Games.* New York: St. Martins Press, 1975.

Jenkins, P. *The Joyful Child.* Tucson, Ariz.: Harbinger House, 1989.

Morris, G. *How to Change the Games Children Play.* 2d ed. Minneapolis: Burgess, 1980.

Orlick, T. *The Cooperative Sports and Games Book.* New York: Pantheon Books, 1978.

_____. *Winning Through Cooperation.* Washington, D.C.: Hawkins & Associates, 1978.

Rohnke, K. *Cowtails and Cobras.* Hamilton, Mass: Project Adventure, 1977.

Simpson, B. *Initiative Games.* Denver: Colorado Outward Bound School, n.d.

Sobel, J. *Everybody Wins: Non-competitive Games for Young Children.* New York: Walker & Co, 1983.

Stinson, B. *To Move, To Learn, To Grow.* 2d ed. Emporia, Kans.: Emporia State University, 1989.

Wayman, J., and L. Plum. *Secrets and Surprises.* Carthage, Ill.: Good Apple, 1981.

# Chapter 7

# MAKING DECISIONS

*Every student must take responsibility for his or her own individual learning. At the same time, students must also be encouraged to take responsibility for the success of other students in the classroom.*

—*Lawrence Lyman and Harvey Foyle*

As young children enter social situations with peers, the ensuing interactions trigger the need for decision-making skills. Through guided interactions, teachers can facilitate positive decision making, and children can gain confidence in their abilities as they become successful decision makers. Real, everyday choices (e.g., interactions during play, mealtimes, learning centers) must serve as the concrete base for developing these skills.

Teachers serve as decision-making models for young children. Since children are usually self-centered, their individual decisions tend to support and enhance personal gratification. Cooperative Learning attempts to decenter children, moving them from self-interested decision making to decision making for the good of the whole group. Teachers can use Cooperative Learning activities to provide structured situations that allow interactions and provide opportunities for decision making on the part of children.

According to Glasser (1986), power is one of the basic psychological needs that must be met in education. Cooperative Learning lessons for young children can be structured so that decision making is encouraged. When appropriate decisions are made, students have gained power over their own lives and over their relationships with others. According to Johnson and Johnson (1990), positive interdependence is one element of Cooperative Learning. This positive interdependence can come about only when children freely make appropriate decisions that empower them to be successful in their relationships with others.

Everyday classroom activities can provide opportunities for cooperative decision making. As the students get ready for recess, for example, the teacher can say, "Will we need our coats this afternoon? Turn to your partner and give a reason why or why not." The students may respond by noting the trees are blowing or by recalling their experiences at lunch. The teacher then helps the group process these data and arrive at a shared, appropriate decision. Decision making can also take place during more structured learning activities, such as role-playing, lessons on holidays and heroes, and special projects.

In the lesson "Wonders of the World," children are encouraged to make decisions related to science content.

---

### Wonders of the World
*Mildred Hackler*

*Objective:* In groups, students will investigate and make predictions about science.

*Procedure:* Students are grouped in twos, threes, or fours, as appropriate for the needs and skills of the class. Groups are assigned various problems dealing with science.

1. *Can you tell what I am?* At a center or designated area, various substances are available for students to smell, taste, or touch, as appropriate. The teacher specifies which sense the students will use. Groups work with substances and try to agree on what they are. Examples:

| *Taste/Touch* | *Smell* |
|---|---|
| baking soda | chocolate syrup |
| salt | water |

110

| cornstarch | lemon/lime soda |
| powdered sugar | vinegar |
| sugar | soda water |

*Group Evaluation:* Students discuss what made each substance different.

2. *How many?* The teacher gives students a problem. In their groups, students predict quantities.
   - How many marbles in a jar?
   - How many beans in a bag?
   - How many toothpicks needed to fill in the outline of a house?

*Group Evaluation:* Students discuss how they estimated each quantity.

3. *What animal am I?* The teacher provides information about an animal (food it eats, tracks it makes, habitat). In groups, students decide which animal the teacher is describing.

*Group Evaluation:* One group thinks of an animal and shares information so that other groups can guess the animal the first group's members are thinking of.

4. *How far?* Groups estimate the number of footsteps needed to reach a specified destination. Students can then pace off the distances to see how close the estimates were.

   - How far is it to the nearest outside door?
   - How far is it to the cafeteria?
   - How far is it to the office?

*Group Evaluation:* Students think of other distances that could be estimated using the footstep measure.

---

## THE EASTER EGG MOBILE

Teachers of young children have the initial opportunity to prepare and structure Cooperative Learning activities. These activities can be the same ones that teachers are currently using, but redesigned in order to encourage cooperation and interaction. Decision making now becomes the focus of each lesson.

The lesson "Easter Egg Mobile" is a seasonal project that allows children to make several decisions about the project.

---

### Easter Egg Mobile

*Objective:* The children will practice cutting and using fine motor skills while making decisions about the cooperative design of an Easter egg.

*Grouping:* Groups of three. Each group is given a copy of the Easter egg (see Figure 15). The teacher assigns each child a number (1, 2, or 3).

*Cutting Task:* Child 1 begins cutting out the egg. After a short interval of time, child 2 should have a turn cutting out some of the lines inside the egg. Child 3 should cut the remaining lines inside the egg. All children should have approximately the same amount of time to cut.

*Coloring Task:* Using the children's numbers, the teacher assigns each child a part of the egg to color. Child 1 will do the top (one end), child 2 will do the middle, and child 3 will do the bottom of the egg (the other end).

*The Easter Egg Mobile:* After the children are finished, the teacher has them put the parts of the egg together in order to observe the results. The children decide how the egg should be arranged from top to bottom. The children may decide to trade parts of their Easter egg with other groups. The children should decide on how their egg would look the best. When the parts of the egg have been decided on, the children tie the parts together in order to make a mobile. The completed group eggs can be displayed on a bulletin board or hung from the ceiling. This is accomplished by pasting one group's egg on the back of another group's egg and then hanging the result from the ceiling as a mobile.

---

Figure 15

# THE UNUSUAL PUMPKIN

Decision making can be structured so that students' interests are stimulated. A real decision needs to be put before the children so that they can see the results of their decisions. In "The Unusual Pumpkin," cooperative groups emerged from individual students' tasting of foods.

The teacher provides novelty, interest, or motivation by sharing unique rather than common items for decorating a pumpkin. The cooperative groups are then faced with a problem that only they can solve by making a cooperative decision. How can the class use such strange pumpkin-decorating items and still have a nicely decorated pumpkin? The individual decisions are then reviewed by the class, and more decisions must be made by the whole group. The cooperative decision making worked! Ms. Williams' class won first place from the first grade entries in the schoolwide contest.

---

### The Unusual Pumpkin
*Sandra Williams*

*Objective:* Students will be given novel and interesting items and decide how to design and make a pumpkin.

*Grouping:* Groups of three.

*Background Information:* Each class was asked to decorate a pumpkin for a schoolwide contest. This was a follow-up activity to emphasizing problem-solving skills in the classroom.

*Procedure:*

1. The teacher brought to class a grocery bag with food items: a banana, a zucchini, a yellow squash, red potatoes, walnuts, broccoli, and a package of spaghetti.
2. The teacher told the class that she must have picked this grocery bag up by mistake instead of the bag with items to decorate the pumpkin. (The children wanted the teacher to go home and get the correct bag!) At this point, the teacher told the

children that they should make do with the bag's contents. The children should decide what to do with the bag's contents and try to solve the problem of decorating the pumpkin with unlikely items.

3. During the lesson, the children taste the raw foods and graph who liked which raw foods. From the graph, cooperative groups are formed according to what the children liked, thus grouping children according to their tastes for foods. The actual pumpkin-decorating problem still remains. The food items are displayed so that each child can see them. The children are asked to think about the food items and how those items can be used to decorate the pumpkin.

4. Each group discusses the group's ideas about the problem. Groups are given a piece of paper to sketch how they would use the food items to decorate the pumpkin. After each cooperative group finishes a drawing, the drawings are posted for all the groups to see. The whole class discusses each drawing. In fact, the class may decide to use a combination of the drawings in order to decorate the pumpkin.

5. The teacher should carve the actual pumpkin for safety's sake, so that the selected food items can fit onto or into the proper places on the pumpkin. Then the children decorate the pumpkin.

---

# LIVING OR NONLIVING?

In a science lesson, groups of children can classify living and nonliving things. In classifying objects, children must make decisions based on their own backgrounds and experiences. The lesson "Living or Nonliving?" consists of four activities.

---

Living or Nonliving?
*Verlene Kling*

*Objective:* Children will be able to identify the differences between living and nonliving things and determine what makes living things different from nonliving things.

*Grouping:* Groups of four.

*Activity 1*

*Materials: The teacher provides a variety of items or a collection of living and nonliving objects.*

*Procedure:* Each group collects some items for use during the activity. Pictures of living things can be used in place of the actual living things. The teacher instructs the children to classify the objects into two categories: living things and nonliving things.

The children are given time to classify their materials. The teacher asks the children how they judged such things as water and plants.

The teacher asks each group to share its classifications with the other groups and to explain the group members' criteria for categorizing living things and nonliving things. The children are encouraged to ask questions of each group's members and to discuss the classifications among themselves.

*Activity 2*

*Materials:* The teacher provides a large supply of magazines, scissors, glue, and paper.

*Procedure:* The children cut out pictures of objects that are *either* living or nonliving. When the students have cut out some appropriate pictures, they glue the pictures onto the paper. A bulletin board is made with the headings of Living and Nonliving. The poster projects are placed under the appropriate headings.

*Activity 3*

*Materials:* Crayons and worksheets.

*Procedure:* The teacher makes an appropriate worksheet showing living and nonliving things. The children discuss the objects found on the worksheet to be sure that they recognize what the objects are. The children are then asked to circle the living things in each row and to color the objects.

*Activity 4: Summary Activity*

*Materials:* A single piece of white paper.

*Procedure:* Children fold the paper in half so that a 11" x 8¹/₂" sheet of paper now is 5¹/₂" x 8¹/₂". On the first page, the children print at the top a title for the "book," which states: "This Is a Picture of Me—I Am Alive." On this page the children do a self-portrait in color. On each of the three following pages, the children print "I can _____." The children are to draw three different things they can do that show they are alive and to fill in the blank space of "I can _____." Examples: I can breathe air. I can jump over logs. I can eat.

---

The following primary level lesson, "Native American Dwellings of the Past," is based on a social studies theme. This approach could be adapted to the historical culture of the community and/or the ethnic heritage of the children. This particular lesson indicates that Cooperative Learning can be more extensive than one daily lesson in that it involves children in a two-week group investigation. The Group Investigation approach (Sharan & Sharan in press) to Cooperative Learning requires that students make a wide variety of decisions (e.g., content, presentation format) during the investigation.

---

### Native American Dwellings of the Past
*Jody Drake*

*Objective:* The children study and investigate Native American dwellings, construct models, and make oral reports.

*Group Size:* Heterogeneous groups of three.

*Procedure:*

1. Each group of children selects a different historical Native American dwelling type (tepee, wigwam, longhouse, hogan, pueblo) to study.
2. The various groups study the appropriate portion of the social studies textbook together.
3. Roles are chosen by the children: Reader, Note Taker, and Checker. (The Checker makes sure that everyone understands

what is read; that is, he asks for explanations in each person's own words.)
4. The groups research in the library, with the members switching roles. In addition, audiovisuals can be viewed.
5. Each group contributes a chapter with illustrations to the class book *Native American Dwellings of the Past*, which is printed using a computer.
6. The groups construct models of the dwellings with an emphasis on the equal contributions of group members. These projects can be displayed in the library along with the class book. A variety of materials can be used to build the models:
   - wigwam (papier-mâché)
   - tepee (cloth and sticks)
   - longhouse (milk carton and toothpicks)
   - hogan (dough that hardens)
   - pueblo (construction paper and sand with toothpick ladders)
7. Each group can report to the class about the group's findings.
8. The major components of any body of knowledge (in this case, Native American dwellings) can be cooperatively investigated and reported using this approach. Content could be selected from any subject area (e.g., science, social studies, literature).

## CONCLUSION

Cooperative Learning is an ideal vehicle for group decision making. Decision making is an important life skill, which can be enhanced by teachers of young children. In addition, Cooperative Learning lessons designed for group decision making promote the affective and cognitive goals of early childhood education.

# AFTERWORD

The authors hope that as you, the reader, reach the end of this book, the benefits of Cooperative Learning for the early childhood learner are clear. We hope that you have found ideas and lesson opportunities in this book that you are eager to try with your own students. Cooperative Learning is one strategy that has the potential to make positive, lasting changes in our schools.

Opportunities for Cooperative Learning are present in your classroom every day. It has been pointed out that Cooperative Learning is more than a particular set of materials or a certain curriculum. As you look around your classroom, you will find many activities that you have previously done individually that will lend themselves to cooperation. Do not be afraid to try your own ideas—you know the children you work with best.

It has been the authors' experience that teachers are more successful with Cooperative Learning when they themselves are involved in cooperative interaction—with colleagues, with parents, with family, and with friends. For this reason, it is important that you become involved in sharing your ideas, your successes, and your failures with your colleagues. Opportunities to network with others who are trying Cooperative Learning are available. Ask around—find colleagues in your school, in your district, or in your area who are using Cooperative Learning, and share with one another.

Above all, the authors hope that you will be gentle with yourself as you try Cooperative Learning. Any innovation or change takes time. In many communities, children are coming to school having experienced fewer chances for cooperation than ever before. While these social changes make Cooperative Learning harder to implement, we believe your efforts to implement Cooperative Learning will be rewarded—now, and throughout the years—as you see the children you teach learn more efficiently, get along with others better, and develop the skills necessary for successful participation in society.

# SELECTED REFERENCES

Adcock, D., and M. Segal. *Play Together Grow Together*. Mt. Rainier, Md.: Gryphon House, 1983.

Aronson, E., and others. *The Effects of Cooperative Classroom Structure on Prosocial Behavior*, 1977. (ERIC Document Reproduction Service, no. ED 150 520)

_____. *The Jigsaw Classroom*. Beverly Hills, Calif.: Sage, 1978.

Bereiter, C., and S. Engleman. *Teaching Disadvantaged Children in the Preschool*. Englewood Cliffs, N.J.: Prentice-Hall, 1966.

Boyer, E. "Early Schooling and the Nation's Future." *Educational Leadership* 44, no. 6 (March 1987): 4–6.

Brandt, R. S., ed. "Cooperative Learning." *Educational Leadership* 47, no. 4 (December 1989–January 1990): 1–96.

Bredekamp, S. *Developmentally Appropriate Practice in Early Childhood Programs Serving Children from Birth Through Age 8*. Washington, D.C.: National Association for the Education of Young Children, 1987.

Bredekamp, S., and L. Shepard. "How Best to Protect Children from Inappropriate School Expectations, Practices and Policies." *Young Children* 44, no.3 (March 1989): 14–24.

Brubacher, M., R. Payne, and K. Rickett, eds. *Perspectives on Small Group Learning: Theory and Practice*. Oakville, Ontario, Canada: Rubicon Publishing, 1990.

Bruzelli, C., and N. File. "Building Trust in Friends." *Young Children* 44, no.3 (March 1989): 70–75.

Cartwright, D., and A. Zander, eds. *Group Dynamics*. New York: Harper & Row, 1968.

Cihak, M. K., and B. J. Heron. *Games Children Should Play: Sequential Lessons for Teaching Communication Skills in Grades K–6*. Glenview, Ill.: Scott, Foresman & Co., 1980.

Clark, M. L. *Gender, Race, and Friendship Research*, 1985. (ERIC Document Reproduction Service, no. ED 259 053)

Clarke, J., R. Wideman, and S. Eadie. *Together We Learn.* Scarborough, Ontario, Canada: Prentice-Hall of Canada, 1990.

Cohen, E. *Designing Groupwork: Strategies for the Heterogeneous Classroom.* New York: Teachers College Press, 1986.

Cooper, C. R., and others. *Children's Discourse in Cooperative and Didactic Interaction: Developmental Patterns in Effective Learning,* 1980. (ERIC Document Reproduction Service, no. ED 206 378)

Curran, L. *Cooperative Learning Lessons for Little Ones: Literature-Based Language Arts and Social Skills.* San Juan Capistrano, Calif.: Resources for Teachers, 1990.

Dalton, J., and D. Smith. *Extending Children's Special Abilities: Strategies for Primary Classrooms.* North Melbourne, Australia: Victorian Government Bookshop, 1986.

Davidson, N., ed. *Cooperative Learning in Mathematics: A Handbook for Teachers.* Reading, Mass.: Addison-Wesley, 1989.

Day, B. *Early Childhood Education: Creative Learning Activities.* 3d ed. New York: Macmillan, 1988.

_____. "What's Happening in Early Childhood Programs Across the United States?" *A Resource Guide to Public School Early Childhood Programs,* edited by C. Warger. Alexandria, Va.: ASCD Publications, 1988.

Day, B. D., and K. N. Drake. *Early Childhood Education: Curriculum Organization and Classroom Management.* Alexandria, Va.: Association for Supervision and Curriculum Development, 1983.

Deutsch, M. "A Theory of Cooperation and Competition." *Human Relations* 2 (1949): 129–52.

_____. "The Effects of Cooperation and Competition upon Group Process." In *Group Dynamics: Research and Theory,* edited by D. Cartwright and A. Zander. 2d ed. New York: Harper & Row, 1960.

_____. *The Resolution of Conflict.* New Haven, Conn.: Yale University Press, 1973.

Dewey, J. "Speech to Parents of Dewey School." In *The Dewey School: The Laboratory School of the University of Chicago, 1896–1903,* edited by K. Mayhew and A. C. Edwards. New York: Atherton Press, 1966.

Elkind, D. "The Resistance to Developmentally Appropriate Practice with Young Children: The Real Issue." In *A Resource Guide to Public School Early Childhood Programs*, edited by C. Warger. Alexandria, Va.: ASCD Publications, 1988.

Foyle, H. C., and L. R. Lyman. *The Interactive Classroom: Cooperative Learning*. Emporia, Kans.: Teachers College, Emporia State University, 1989. Two 16-minute videotapes on cooperative learning: "Part 1—Overview"; "Part 2—The Step-by-Step Process."

Foyle, H. C.; L. Lyman; S. Lyman; J. Foyle; and J. Morehead. "Using Cooperative Learning in the Early Childhood Classroom." Paper presented at the Forty-Fifth annual conference of the Association for Supervision and Curriculum Development, San Antonio, March 3, 1990.

Foyle, H. C., L. R. Lyman, and M. A. Morehead. "Cooperative Learning: Possible Solutions to Student and Teacher Problems." *Forward* (Wisconsin Journal for Supervision and Curriculum Development) 14, no. 1 (Spring 1989): 33–36.

Ginot, H. *Between Teacher and Child*. New York: Macmillan, 1972.

Glasser, W. *Control Theory in the Classroom*. New York: Harper & Row, 1986.

————. *The Quality School*. New York: Harper & Row, 1990.

Hatcher, B., ed. *Learning Opportunities Beyond the School*, 1987. (ERIC Document Reproduction Service, no. ED 288 630)

Hohmann, M., B. Banet, and D. Weikart. *Young Children in Action*. Ypsilanti, Mich.: High/Scope Press, 1978.

Hollifield, J., and others. *Children Learning in Groups, and Other Trends in Elementary and Early Childhood Education*, 1989. (ERIC Document Reproduction Service, no. ED 308 993)

Jenkins, P. *The Joyful Child*. Tucson, Ariz.: Harbinger House, 1989.

Johnson, D. W., and R. T. Johnson. *Circles of Learning: Cooperation in the Classroom*. 3d ed. Edina, Minn.: Interaction Book Co., 1990.

Joyce, B., and M. Weil. *Models of Teaching*. 2d ed. Englewood Cliffs, N.J.: Prentice-Hall, 1980.

Kagan, S. *Cooperative Learning Resources for Teachers*. San Juan

Capistrano, Calif.: Resources for Teachers, 1990.

Kamii, C., and R. DeVries. *Group Games in Early Education: Implications of Piaget's Theory*. Washington, D.C.: National Association for the Education of Young Children, 1980.

Katz, L. G. "Engaging Children's Minds: The Implications of Research for Early Childhood Education." In *A Resource Guide to Public School Early Childhood Programs*, edited by C. Warger. Alexandria, Va.: Association for Supervision and Curriculum Development, 1988.

Katz, L. G., and others. *The Case for Mixed-Age Grouping in Early Childhood Education Programs*, 1989. (ERIC Document Reproduction Service, no. ED 308 991)

Kickona, T. "Creating the Just Community with Children." *Theory into Practice* 16, no. 2 (1977): 97–104.

Kohlberg, L. *Essays on Moral Development*. Vol. 2, *The Psychology of Moral Development*. San Francisco: Harper & Row, 1984.

Kohn, A. *No Contest: The Case Against Competition*. Boston, Mass.: Houghton Mifflin, 1986.

Kreidler, W. J. *Creative Conflict Resolution*. Glenview, Ill.: Scott, Foresman & Co., 1984.

Lorber, N. "Inadequate Social Acceptance and Disruptive Classroom Behavior." *Journal of Educational Research*, 59, no. 8 (April 1966): 360–62.

Lyman, F. "The Responsive Classroom Discussion." In *Mainstreaming Digest*, edited by A. S. Anderson. College Park: College of Education, University of Maryland, 1981.

____. "Think-Pair-Share: An Expanding Teaching Technique." *MAACIE Cooperative News* 1 no. 1 (1987): 1–2.

Lyman, L. R., and H. C. Foyle. *Cooperative Learning: Does It Work for Teachers of Young Children?* 1988. (ERIC Document Reproduction Service, no. ED 299 047)

____.*Cooperative Learning Strategies and Children*. (*ERIC Digest* No. EDO-PS-88-5,1988. (ERIC Document Reproduction Service, no. ED 306 003)

_____. *Cooperative Grouping for Interactive Learning: Students, Teachers, Administrators.* Washington, D.C.: National Education Association, 1990.

Madden, N. A., and R. E. Slavin. *Effects of Cooperative Learning on the Social Acceptance of Mainstreamed Academically Handicapped Students,* 1981. (ERIC Document Reproduction Service, no. ED 209 882)

Miller, C. H. "Ready, Set, Write!" *Equity and Choice* 3, no. 2 (Winter 1987): 3–8.

Miller, K. A. "Enhancing Early Childhood Mainstreaming Through Cooperative Learning: A Brief Literature Review." *Child Study Journal* 19, no. 4 (1989): 285–92.

Montagu, A. *The Human Revolution.* New York: World, 1965.

Moorman, C., and D. Dishon. *Our Classroom: We Can Learn Together.* Englewood Cliffs, N.J.: Prentice-Hall, 1983.

Orlick, T. *The Second Cooperative Sports and Games Book.* New York: Pantheon Books, 1981.

Piaget, J. *The Psychology of Intelligence.* London: Routledge & Kegan Paul, 1950.

_____. *The Origins of Intelligence in Children.* New York: International Universities Press, 1952.

Putnam, J. W., and J. Farnsworth-Lunt. *Cooperative Learning and the Integration of Students with Disabilities: An Annotated Bibliography.* Missoula: Montana University Affiliated Program Satellite, 1989.

Ramsey, P. G. *Teaching and Learning in a Diverse World: Multicultural Education for Young Children.* New York: Teachers College Press, 1987.

Rhoades, J., and M. McCabe. *Simple Cooperation in the Classroom.* Willits, Calif.: ITA Publications, 1985.

Sapon-Shevin, M. "Teaching Cooperation." In *Teaching Social Skills to Young Children,* edited by G. Cartledge and J. F. Milburn. New York: Pergamon Press, 1986.

Saracho, O., and B. Spodek, eds. *Understanding the Multicultural Experience in Early Childhood Education.* Washington, D.C.: National Association of the Education of Young Children, 1983.

Schmuck, R. A., and P. A. Schmuck. *Group Processes in the Classroom.* Dubuque, Iowa: William C. Brown, 1988.

Sharan, S., and Y. Sharan. *Small-Group Teaching.* Englewood Cliffs, N.J.: Educational Technology Publications, 1976.

_____. *Group Investigation: Expanding Cooperative Learning.* In press.

Shure, M. B., and G. Spivak. *Problem Solving Techniques in Childrearing.* San Francisco: Jossey-Bass, 1978.

Slavin, R. E. *Cooperative Learning: Student Teams.* 2d ed. What Research Says to the Teacher Series. Washington, D.C.: National Education Association, 1987.

_____. *Cooperative Learning: Theory, Research, and Practice.* Englewood Cliffs, N.J.: Prentice-Hall, 1990.

Slavin, R. E. and N. Madden. "What Works for Students at Risk: A Research Synthesis." *Educational Leadership* 46, no. 5 (February 1989): 4–30.

Slavin, R. E.; S. Sharan; S. Kagan; R. Lazarowitz; C. Webb; and R. Schmuck, eds. *Learning to Cooperate, Cooperating to Learn.* New York: Plenum, 1985.

Sobel, J. *Everybody Wins: Non-competitive Games for Young Children.* New York: Walker & Co., 1983.

Souweine, J., S. Crimmins, and C. Mazel. *Mainstreaming: Ideas for Teaching Young Children.* Washington, D.C.: National Association for the Education of Young Children, 1981.

Spodek, B.; O. Saracho; and M. Davis. *Foundations of Early Childhood Education.* 2d ed. Englewood Cliffs, N.J.: Prentice-Hall, 1991.

Spodek, B.; O. N. Saracho; and R. C. Lee. "Creating a Supportive Social Environment." In *Mainstreaming Young Children.* Belmont, Calif.: Wadsworth, 1984.

Stanely, W. B. *Social Studies Research: Theory into Practice. ERIC Digest* No. 27, 1985. (ERIC Document Reproduction Service, no. ED 268 064)

Stanford, G. *Developing Effective Classroom Groups.* New York: Hart, 1977.

Tudge, J., and D. Caruso. "Cooperative Problem Solving in the Classroom: Enhancing Children's Cognitive Development." *Young Children* 44, no. 1 (November 1988): 46–120.

Van Kleeck, A. E., and C. R. Cooper. *Children's Communication Strategies in a Cooperative Learning Task with Developmentally Delayed and Normal Partners*, 1980. (ERIC Document Reproduction Service, no. ED 184 189)

van Oudenhoven, J. P., and others. "Effect of Cooperation and Shared Feedback on Spelling Achievement." *Journal of Educational Psychology* 79, no. 1 (March 1987): 92–94.

VanSickle, R. L. "A Social Perspective on Student Learning." *Theory and Research in Social Education* 10, no. 2 (Summer 1982): 21–31.

Walsh, H. M. *Introducing the Young Child to the Social World.* New York: Macmillan, 1980.

Warger, C., ed. *A Resource Guide to Public School Early Childhood Programs.* Alexandria, Va.: Association for Supervision and Curriculum Development, 1988.

Watson, M. S., and others. "Cooperative Learning as a Means of Promoting Prosocial Development Among Kindergarten and Early Primary-Grade Children." *International Journal of Social Education* 3, no. 2 (Fall 1988): 34–47.

Wehman, P., and W. Umansky. "Play Skill Development." In *Young Children with Special Needs,* edited by N. H. Fallen. Columbus, Ohio: Merrill, 1985.

Weikert, D. P. "Hard Choices in Early Childhood Care and Education: A View into the Future." *Young Children* 44, no. 3 (March 1989): 25–30.

Wheeler, R., and R. Ryan. "Effects of Cooperative and Competitive Classroom Environments on the Attitudes and Achievement of Elementary School Students Engaged in Social Studies Inquiry Activities." *Journal of Educational Psychology* 65, no. 3 (December 1973): 402–407.

Wilcox, J., and others. "Cooperative Learning Groups Aid Integration." *Teaching Exceptional Children* 20, no.1 (Fall 1987): 61–63.

Yager, S, and others. "Oral Discussion, Group-to-Individual Transfer, and Achievement in Cooperative Learning Groups." *Journal of Educational Psychology* 77, no. 1 (February 1985): 60–66.

_____."The Impact of Group Processing on Achievement in Cooperative Learning Groups." *Journal of Social Psychology* 126, no. 3 (June 1986): 389–97.

# clinical
# geropsychiatry

# clinical
# geropsychiatry

**ADRIAN VERWOERDT, M.D.**

Professor of Psychiatry;
Director, Geropsychiatry Training
  Program
Duke University Medical Center
Durham, North Carolina

 *The Williams & Wilkins Co.*

*Made in the United States of America*

Library of Congress Cataloging in Publication Data

Verwoerdt, Adrian.
  Clinical geropsychiatry.

  Includes index.
  1. Geriatric psychiatry. I. Title. [DNLM: 1. Geriatric psychiatry.
WT150 V572c]
RC451.4.A5V47      618.9'76'89      75-26878
ISBN 0-683-08591-3


Composed and printed at the
WAVERLY PRESS, INC.
Mt. Royal and Guilford Aves.
Baltimore, Md. 21202, U.S.A.

*to my parents*

# *PREFACE*

This book is intended for professionals involved in organizing or providing mental health services for the elderly. While the text is primarily aimed at psychiatrists and psychiatric nurse practitioners, an attempt has been made to reflect the multidisciplinary aspects of aging, and to make the book useful for gerontologic practitioners from other disciplines as well. Its purpose is to be of use to mental health professionals who practice in a variety of clinical settings, including private practice, community mental health centers, general hospitals, geriatric units of mental hospitals, and nursing homes.

Geropsychiatry is the psychiatry of late life. It encompasses the behavioral sciences, psychodynamic concepts, and psychiatric practice with reference to the aging personality and to the mental disorders of late life. This book is written within a medical-psychological frame of reference, in keeping with the concepts of modern ego psychology, and is based on consideration of three levels of human activity: biological, psychological, and social. Since the primary focus of the book is clinical, the presentation of theoretical concepts serves to facilitate a better understanding of the psychopathology of senescence and of an etiologically based treatment approach. Any theoretical construct stands or falls depending on its power to broaden the scope of scientific understanding and to facilitate effective clinical intervention.

Anyone who has done clinical work in the field of aging is confronted with arduous tasks, including the necessity to relinquish one's rescue fantasies, to be faced with death or despair, to struggle for value and meaning, and to keep the humanitarian and the scientist within himself in dynamic equilibrium. If some measure of personal and professional maturation results from this, a proper sense of humility will be part of it. Surprisingly many can be our rewards: the challenge of work in what still is very much a terra incognita, the excitement of the team effort, and the therapeutic response of our patients.

# ACKNOWLEDGMENTS

It has been my good fortune to have been associated with the Duke Center for the Study of Aging and Human Development for many years. Founded by Dr. Ewald W. Busse, who was director from its inception in 1957 until 1970, the Center was subsequently headed by Dr. Carl Eisdorfer (1970 until 1972) and Dr. George Maddox (1972 until the present). I am indebted to them in two ways: first, because of their remarkable success in bringing together a superb team of investigators, educators and clinicians in the field of aging, and providing unique opportunities for multidisciplinary work; and also, because my personal associations with them were a source of rich learning experiences.

The Center for the Study of Aging and Human Development and the Department of Psychiatry at Duke made it possible to develop a formal Geropsychiatry Training Program in 1966. The latter, funded in part by grants of the National Institute of Mental Health, has provided training in geriatric psychiatry, primarily for psychiatrists, but also for professionals of other disciplines. Throughout the years, my function as program director has provided numerous contacts with the training faculty, including Dr. Daniel T. Gianturco, Dr. Daniel T. Peak, Dr. Eric Pfeiffer, Dr. H. S. Wang, and Dr. Alan D. Whanger. I have profited from our collaboration; to each of them I am indebted in a special way. The work we did was an exciting mix of research, teaching, clinical practice, and program planning. Their enthusiastic participation and individual creativity insured the success of the Duke Geropsychiatry Training Program, and provided the impetus for other innovative programs, in the university itself, in the community, and statewide.

Some of the case material presented in this book became accessible to me by way of my participation in the Duke Older Americans Resources and Services (OARS) program, directed by Dr. Eric Pfeiffer, and the Duke Geriatric Psychiatry Inpatient Service, directed by Dr. Alan D. Whanger. Other clinical case material became available through contacts with the Geropsychiatry Units of John Umstead Hospital (Butner), Cherry Hospital (Goldsboro), and Dorothea Dix Hospital (Raleigh). I wish to express my appreciation to the directors and the clinical staff of these programs for the many case conferences I had the privilege to attend.

I wish to thank Mrs. Ruth Wortman for her excellent work in typing the manuscript, proofreading and correcting, as well as keeping track of administrative, technical details too numerous to mention.

# CONTENTS

# 18 environmental planning . . . . . . . . . 223

# 19 protective intervention . . . . . . . . . . . .

## PROTECTIVE SERVICES: LEGAL AND PSYCHIATRIC ASPECTS

## CONDITIONS REQUIRING MODIFICATION IN METHOD

## DIFFERENCES IN APPROACH AND METHODS

## INDICATIONS FOR SPECIFIC TECHNIQUES

# 20 work and retirement . . . . . . . . . . .

## ENGAGEMENT AND DISENGAGEMENT

# 1

# aging and human development

## BIOLOGICAL AGING

### The Concept of Aging

Theories of aging must take into account the fundamental nature of the aging process, the mechanisms by which it comes about, as well as its manifestations and effects on the organism's functions. No generally accepted definition exists regarding the basic nature of aging.[1] What aging essentially is and why it occurs, no one knows. These issues are just as complex as those pertaining to the concept of life. Since we are unable to define "life," we are likewise incapable of drawing a sharp line between such concepts as development, becoming, and aging. Their common denominator, however, is the factor of time-dependent change.

**1.** Definitions of biological aging share the common denominator of the *factor of time*. Thus, a distinction between primary and secondary aging has been made.[2] Primary aging refers to time-dependent biological processes, rooted in heredity, that are independent of stress, trauma, and disease. Secondary aging pertains to the disabilities resulting from trauma and loss. Primary aging, a time-related process, results in a decline in the efficiency of the various functions of the organism, and this deterioration progressively increases the probability of death.

The factor of time is also essential in the Gompertz equation,[3] a mathematical formula expressing the probability of death at any given age. The Gompertz formula expresses not only the fact that the prevalence of aging phenomena increases exponentially with advancing age, but also the age-related rate of loss of functional cells. Thus it represents the rate of aging on a cellular level and the rate of human mortality in relation to age.

**2.** With regard to *longevity*, variations exist between members of a species, but there is a maximum beyond which no system has been known to survive. The life span of members of a species, by and large, shows a fairly narrow distribution. There seems to be an intrinsic time clock for each species, or a genetically determined program that regulates the phases of the life cycle. In this framework, the moment of death is determined by the same genetic programming that determines the onset

1

of the organism. The functional decline intrinsic in the senescent process is related to a logarithmic function of time.

3. Several subsystems of the system as a whole have been considered as possible *time clocks*. One example is the brain. In contrast to certain epithelial cells (*e.g.*, skin or white blood cells) which are capable of mitotic cell division, the neurons are postmitotic all through life. Because these postmitotic neurons have the vital role of regulating the entire organism, the central nervous system may be viewed as a time clock. The brain is the only organ whose size is correlated with potential lifespan in several species. The *cephalization index* is the ratio between the weight of the brain and the body, and seems to be correlated with longevity in the case of mammals and birds.[4]

Another example of a proposed biological clock is the mitochondria.[5] This is based on the premise that longevity in mammalian species is largely an expression of genetic control over the rate of oxygen utilization. The rate of oxygen use determines the rate of accumulation of mitochondrial damage produced by free radical reactions, the rate increasing with the rate of oxygen consumption, which ultimately causes death.

Finally, it has been proposed that no single part or process of the living system contains a time clock but that the time clock is represented by the sum total of the system parameters themselves. The fact that species have fixed longevities which are probably genetically determined implies that the factors present at the beginning of the biological system are the same that result in senescence. In a mathematical sense, the origin of senescence is at the beginning of the system's existence.[6]

4. The phenomenon of aging can also be conceptualized in the framework of *system theory*. A system can be defined as a dynamic order of parts and processes standing in mutual relationship. Living organisms, whether unicellular or metazoa, are open systems that function through the transfer of energy.[7] The phenomena of senescence are encountered only in systems. Only energy systems, not things, grow old. In biological energy transfers, the efficiency of the system reflects its ability to exist in its environment. In any system undergoing senescence, there is a steady decrease in the energy yields and a negative change in the rate at which usable energy is produced. Power is defined as work per unit of time. Hence, a decline in the functional capacity of a system is a negative acceleration in power. Senescence may be conceptualized as a decline in free energy production with time, a decline in power arising from intrinsic changes in the system.[8]

## Mechanisms of Senescence

There are several biological theories of aging which represent attempts to understand and explain the manner, method, or mechanism by which aging comes about. A few of these theories will be mentioned briefly, because any detailed discussion would extend beyond our scope, at this point.

(a). Progressive *loss of reserve capacities* may be attributable to cell death and depletion of functioning units, caused by increasing impairment of processes of energy use, tissue repair, and elimination. Since no physiological process functions with 100 percent efficiency, there would be a progressive accumulation of failure in the course of time. This view is related to the concept of "mean time to failure,"[9] which would view living systems as a sort of biological machine with built-in obsolescence.

(b). Age-related *cell death* has been ascribed to random hits by environmental factors (*e.g.*, cosmic radiation); to depletion of vital substances with an accumulation of insoluble substances (*e.g.*, lipofuscin); to changes in molecules, especially those involved in energy transfer (*e.g.*, cross-linkages between molecules); and to mutations. Somatic cell mutation produces DNA changes which in turn results in changed RNA and altered protein transcription (nonsense protein).[10, 11]

(c). *Stochastic* theories focus on cell depletion through cell death or somatic mutations caused by radiation or other "hits." In time defects develop in all cells, but in organs that can replace cells, the process of mitosis can eliminate aberrant cells. However, organs consisting of postmitotic cells (*e.g.*, neurons) cannot rejuvenate, and hence would seem to have major responsibility for the aging process. From this point of view, aging is fundamentally the progressive increase of nonfunctional cells in organs whose cells are postmitotic.[2]

(d). The *error* theory is linked to the *mutation* theory. The development of chromosomal abnormalities apparently is an intrinsic aspect of cellular aging and suggests the occurrence of mutation.[12] Chromosomal abnormalities occur progressively with increasing age. Radiation further facilitates this phenomenon.

(e). The *cross-linkage* (eversion) theory applies mostly to noncellular material, especially collagen. A cross-linkage between polypeptide strands changes the structure of the collagen molecule and results in functional deterioration.

(f). Immunological factors play a role in the *autoimmune* theory. With time the individual develops mutant (nonsense) protein caused by transcription errors. The development of immune reactions to this "not self" protein may play a role both in the aging process *per se*, and in the causation of certain age-related diseases (*e.g.*, arteriosclerosis, cancer, maturity-onset diabetes).[13, 14]

The various theories of aging are by no means mutually exclusive, but rather tend to complement each other. Some theories focus more on cellular phenomena, others on interstitial tissue (*e.g.*, collagen), and again others on intracellular structures (*e.g.*, mitochondria). The number of possible interactions between intracellular and intercellular activities is so great that it is not possible to determine which action, reaction, or interaction represents the mechanism of aging. The intrinsic processes which bring the cell inevitably to its death are probably the same as those with which the cell begins.[6]

## The Manifestations of Aging

(a). As a rule, biological characteristics show earlier maturation and decline than psychosocial capacities and functions. The *pattern of age decrement* is individual for each person, and the rate of decline varies from one function to another, and from one individual to another.

There is no direct or simple cause and effect relationship between the degree of structural impairment on the one hand, and the presence of impaired function or manifest disease on the other hand. At an autopsy, for example, it is not unusual to find rather extensive changes in the brain vessels although there was little clinical evidence of mental impairment before death.

**(b). The Concept of Health and Illness.** The hallmark of health is the ability to maintain a steady state within, and a dynamic equilibrium between oneself and the environment. A healthy individual can maintain himself and remain inwardly stable in spite of changing external circumstances. This ability is called homeostasis or constancy principle. However, there are definite limits to this capacity. This is true for living organisms at any age, but with advancing age the capacity for homeostasis gradually declines. The range of adjustment and adaptation becomes smaller and narrower.

**(c). Aging versus Illness.**

**1.** Aging is the progressive loss of physiological capacities and functions in the organism. Muscle, fibrous tissue, cartilage, and bone deteriorate with age. Elastic and muscular tissue is replaced by fibrous elements. Changes in the elastic properties of collagen (because of increased cross-linkages between polypeptide chains) cause it to be tougher. Calcification of the arterial system is a linear function of age.[1] Hardening of the arteries begins at an early age and continues to progress slowly. In the skeletal system, resorption of bone and osteoporosis occur, the latter more frequently in women because of the postmenopausal reduction of estrogen secretion. Other examples of age-related deterioration are the decline in myocardial, pulmonary, hepatic, renal, endocrine, and behavioral capacities. These deteriorations have been attributed to increasing loss in functional (parenchymal) cells with replacement by nonfunctional connective tissue.

**2.** The distinction between age-related biological decline and specific diseases prevalent in late life is not always clear. One characteristic of biological deterioration is that the resting level of a function may show no significant change with age, except that during stress, return to the base level is prolonged (for example, displacements in acid-base balance and in blood glucose levels).

Diabetes is an example illustrating the difficulty of distinguishing clearly between *normal* and *pathological aging*. If values indicative of diabetes in young adults are indiscriminately applied to the aged, many of them would be diagnosed as diabetic. Older persons taking a glucose tolerance test often show a diabetic type of curve, but do not necessarily show clinical evidence of diabetes. It is only under the stress of glucose overload that the aged person manifests a decline in the capacity to keep the blood glucose level within certain narrow limits.

**3.** Health status of the aged, therefore, should not be evaluated in terms of the standards for young adults. If one takes the standards for the young as criteria for health, then indeed most of the aged would have to be considered ill. The term "well" in the case of a 30-year-old person and in that of an 80-year-old person has entirely different meanings. Some capacities decline early in life but the decline becomes manifest only in their late twenties (for their specific situation). On the other hand, creative individuals, *e.g.*, musicians, may still be productive and "young" in their sixties.

## HUMAN DEVELOPMENT

The human being is a biological, psychological, and social system developing and moving forward in time. Over the life span, there exists a continuous change of goals and interests, and the awareness of these changes results in a sense of becoming. During each of the phases of the lifespan there are specific opportunities and challenges. The notion of development includes phenomena that are both progressive and retrogressive in nature. The thymus gland, for example, shows retrogressive changes (involution) early in life. On the other hand, in late life, there may be considerable social growth and expansion in spite of age-related biological decline.

### Phases of Human Development

**(a).** Human development has been described in terms of a *cycle of life phases*, each phase being characterized by its own typical opportunities, sources of satisfaction, and specific developmental goals (Table 1).[15] Successful completion of one life phase is a prerequisite to meet the demands and obtain the gratifications of a subsequent phase. Failure in one phase leads to psychological problems related to that phase, and serves as a predisposition for subsequent failures in later phases. Because there are increasingly more chances to fail as time goes on, the last phase of life ("integrity") is necessarily the most difficult one to attain. Erikson's life phases[15] may be summarized as follows:

**1.** *Basic trust* is the period covering the first year of life and is more or less the equivalent of the oral phase in psychoanalytic terminology. Essentially, the infant learns through the experiences of the mother-child relationship that the world is a good place, and that others are trustworthy; included is a sense of trustworthiness as far as the self is concerned. In adults, the impairment of basic trust is expressed in a basic mistrust: a tendency towards withdrawal, alienation, and lack of affiliation.

**2.** *Autonomy* (age 1–3) is the equivalent of the anal phase. During this period the child learns to make use of his basic motor capacities such as walking, talking, and sphincter control. The child begins to stand out as an individual. From a sense of self-control, not associated with loss of self-esteem, comes a lasting sense of autonomy and pride. Failure to reach such autonomy results in a sense of doubt and shame, and in a tenuous capacity for self-control. The sense of shame interferes with standing out as a separate individual, and is related to loss of face and loss of dignity.

TABLE 1.*

| Psychosocial crises | Radius of Significant Relations | Related Elements of Social Order | Psychosocial Modalities | Psychosexual Stages |
|---|---|---|---|---|
| Trust vs. mistrust | Maternal person | Cosmic order | To get<br>To give in return | Oral-respiratory, sensory-kinesthetic (incorporative modes) |
| Autonomy vs. shame, doubt | Parental persons | Law and order | To hold (on)<br>To let (go) | Anal-urethral, muscular (retentive-eliminative) |
| Initiative vs. guilt | Basic family | Ideal prototypes | To make (=going after)<br>To make like (=playing) | Infantile-genital, locomotor (intrusive, inclusive) |
| Industry vs. inferiority | Neighborhood, school | Technological elements | To make things (=completing)<br>To make things together | Latency |
| Identity and repudiation vs. identity diffusion | Peer groups and outgroups; models of leadership | Ideological perspectives | To be oneself (or not to be)<br>To share being oneself | Puberty |
| Intimacy and solidarity vs. isolation | Partners in friendship, sex, competition, cooperation | Patterns of cooperation and competition | To lose and find oneself in another | Genitality |
| Generativity vs. self-absorption | Divided labor and shared household | Currents of education and tradition | To make be<br>To take care of | |
| Integrity vs. Despair | Mankind, my kind | Wisdom | To be, through having been<br>To face not being | |

* Reprinted from Psychological Issues, Vol. 1, No. 1, by permission of W. W. Norton & Company, Inc., and the author. Copyright 1959 by International Universities Press, Inc.

3. *Initiative* (age 4–6) is a period of venturing out, exploring (curiosity), thrusting forward, and discovering what it means to be a boy or a girl. Failure in this developmental stage leads to an undue sense of doing wrong and guilt. Feelings of guilt are now possible because of the maturation of the child's conscience (superego). The phase of initiative is comparable to the infantile-genital stage in psychoanalytic terminology.

4. *Industry* (age 6–12), equivalent to the latency period, is the period of learning specific skills and acquiring knowledge. Failure in this phase leads to a sense of inferiority.

5. *Identity* (age 12–20) is the phase of adolescence (puberty). The task of this difficult period of life is to discover "who one is" —what kind of man or woman one is going to be, what career to pursue, and what one's individual outlook on society and the world is. Identity diffusion leads to uncertainty in one or all of these aspects.

6. *Intimacy* refers to the closeness and affiliation in adult relation-

ships, particularly between man and woman. This phase corresponds with that of mature genitality. To find sexual, emotional and spiritual satisfactions in a socially approved setting is a major developmental task of intimacy. Failure leads to a sense of isolation and self-absorption.

7. *Generativity* pertains primarily to the establishing and guiding of the next generation, although there are people who, for various reasons, do not apply this drive to offspring but to other forms of altruistic activity, or to creativity, which may absorb their kind of parental responsibility. Generativity literally refers to productivity. An individual can generate a great variety of works, such as offspring, money, business, teaching, and good deeds. Self-absorption and a sense of stagnation are typical of failure in the area of generativity.

8. *Integrity* refers to the final identity of a person. Erikson[15] describes it as the acceptance of one's life cycle and the significant people in it as something that had to be and that, by necessity, permitted no substitutions; also, there is the need for accepting one's life and what happened in it, as one's own responsibility. (Note the apparent paradox between the inevitability of one's life and one's responsibility for it). The ideal characteristic of the last phase of life is integrity which, at the same time, is also the specific task of this life phase. Failure in accomplishing this aim is indicated by the term despair.

(b). Integrity, the sense of identity in senescence, presupposes the more or less successful passing through of previous life phases. The successful completion of developmental challenges is not simply an isolated affair on the part of the individual. He needs, besides his own resources, the cooperation of the social environment. Thus, an infant will not develop trust if the mother does not provide the infant with the sense that life is worth living; and the adolescent develops his sense of identity by way of consensual validation in contact with his peers.

It is no exaggeration to say that the social environment up until now has been less than conducive toward successful completion of the ultimate task in life: the final integration of one's self and of all past selves in the present self. Biological and social environmental hazards contribute to a great number of crises and failures.

Inasmuch as intimacy, generativity, and integrity are developmental phases of the adult and late years, they have special significance for understanding the psychological issues of old age. The counterparts of these three phases, *i.e.*, isolation, stagnation and self-absorption, and despair, play a major role in the psychopathological formations of late life.

Comparatively speaking, the senium has remained *terra incognita*. An understanding of this phase of life is a necessary step toward a comprehensive theory of human behavior. A fuller understanding of the later phases of life can provide additional insights into earlier periods of growth and development and their impact on the total personality.

## Senescence as a Developmental Phase

(a). When speaking of psychological experiences of the last phase of life, the emphasis here is on the word "last." Although we usually think of aging in terms of decline, this decline is a movement toward a final end. It is this that distinguishes senescence from previous life phases. The latter have a beginning, and an end which, at the same time, is a new commencement. Besides being a temporal determinant, the term "the end" also connotes an element of purpose, goal, or task. In previous developmental stages, the end of a phase coincides with the goal toward which development is aimed. Toward what end is the stage of senescence aimed? Can we speak of a goal or task in senescence, as we do in previous life phases?

Although death is a fact of life, one's position *vis-à-vis* death is an intensely personal matter. It is here that we may speak of a *developmental task*, in the sense that a person comes to view his own death as the appropriate outcome of his life. Stern[16] offers the thesis that "adaptation to death is necessary for full personality maturation and that deficiency in this adaptation is an integral factor in neurosis. The neurotic uses regressive fixation to symbiotic dependency (which in infancy protected him against trauma) to ward off fears concerning the inevitable final trauma." Since there is no previous experience of death (only the death of others) to serve as a model for death anxiety, this anxiety is a creative act. It involves the synthesis of earlier anxieties (those along one or more specific dimensions of human experience) into a new form of anxiety which overarches all of these.

(b). The statistical definition, that "aging is a process that increases the probability of death," introduces the phenomena of death. The impersonal quality and intellectual detachment inherent in statistics and mathematics, however, are alien to the immediacy of human experience. Inasmuch as aging represents a progressive shortening of the distance to death, there are several corresponding milestones in human development: (1) a cognitive, intellectual comprehension; (2) a subjective, emotional experience; and, (3) a final existential perspective.

1. What distinguishes human aging from biological aging in general is the fact that the human being knows he will grow old and eventually die. This knowledge is not always present, and during the first few years of life, it is completely absent. An intellectual comprehension of the fact of death develops at about the same time that the young individual learns the facts of life, *i.e.*, during early adolescence. A cognitive grasp of the concept of a personal death depends on the attainment of specific psychological capacities, including the completion of the body-image, a mature time perspective, and the capacity for abstract thinking. Through the capacity for abstraction, it becomes possible to imagine one's own death, *i.e.*, to apply the fact of the death of the other to oneself. The mature time perspective enables one to place this end of the self at the horizon of one's existence. And finally, the concept of death of the self is meaningful only to the extent that there is a self concept and body image to begin with.

2. That point in life when the sum total of an individual's biological, psychological, and social capacities are in an optimal configuration, constitutes the peak of prime of life (climacter: Greek term meaning rung of the ladder). Most people perceive the period of life before the climacter

as one of evolution, growth, or ascendance, and the time after the prime of life as a period of involution, decline, or descendance. (Again, these are not simple distinctions or absolute contrasts, because growth and expansion remain possible during the second half of life. What matters, however, is the net effect of the total of all changes at a given time). After the peak there is a change in tempo and direction: a deceleration and a descent which are dimensions of the "change of life." The perception of the onset of age-related phenomena and the subjective experience associated with the awareness of aging (*i.e.*, shorter distance to death) are dimensions of the *midlife crisis*.[17] The crisis presumably is depressive and is often lucidly apparent in the lives of persons with creative genius. As an example, the opening stanzas of Dante's *Divine Comedy* written at the age of 35, may be quoted.[18]

> Midway life's journey I was made aware
> That I had strayed into a dark forest,
> And the right path appeared not anywhere.
> Ah, tongue cannot describe how it oppressed,
> This wood, so harsh, dismal and wild, that fear
> At thought of it strikes now into my breast.
> So bitter it is, death is scarce bitterer.

According to Jacques,[17] who investigated the midlife crisis with regard to its effect on creativity, it occurs around the age of 35. In a random sample of 310 artists, the death rate showed a sudden jump between the ages of 35 and 39. Between the ages of 40 and 44, there is a big drop below the normal death rate, while in the late 40's the death rate returns to normal. The content and mode of creative work before and after the midlife crisis are different. The content of the creativity changes from the lyrical, in early adulthood, to the more tragic and philosophical, after the crisis, and, eventually on to the serene, in the sixties.

3. As the biological phenomena of life, aging, and death are inextricably intertwined, so are, on the existential level, the meaning of life and death inseparable. Hence, the final perspective *vis-à-vis* death comes about by way of a retrospective evaluation of one's life. The task of the *life review*[19, 20] is to integrate one's life as it has been lived in relation to how it might have been lived. The life review is not a passive process, but a constructive effort to achieve a purposeful form of *reminiscence*. These reminiscences serve primarily not to recall facts, but to weave them into a harmonious perspective and to achieve a sense of closure. The old person may want to write a revised autobiography, as it were, to be left with those who survive him.

The forms of life review may range from a nostalgic recall to severe depression with anxiety, guilt and suicidal tendencies. In general, the life review should not be viewed as a psychopathological phenomenon, but as a common, normal experience. The lifelong personality of each individual influences the way in which he handles the life review, and whether he feels he has much time or only a few days to get his psychological house in order. The person's characteristic patterns of coping with conflict may be used to resolve his terminal conflicts.[20]

Reminiscing and the life review may be carried out in the privacy of one's mind, or it may involve an audience. A certain degree of audience participation is desirable, because the issue "Who am I and what have I been?" is intimately related to the notion of what one is and has been for others. In the life review, there is concern with the image that an individual wishes to leave behind. This may lead to forgiveness and reconciliation, and sharing one's own interpretation of the meaning of life with others.

## REFERENCES

1. HENDERSON, E.: The aging process. *J. Am. Geriatr. Soc. 20:* 565–571, 1972.
2. BUSSE, E. W.: Theories of Aging. *In:* Behavior and Adaptation in Late Life, Chap. 2, E. W. Busse and E. Pfeiffer, eds. Little, Brown and Company, Boston, 1969. pp. 11–32.
3. GOMPERTZ, B.: On the nature of the function expressive of the law of human mortality. *Philos. Trans. R. Soc. Lond. 115:* 513, 1825.
4. SACHER, G. A.: Relation of lifespan to brain weight and body weight in mammals. *In:* The Lifespan of Animals, Ciba Foundation Colloquia on Ageing, Vol. 5, G. E. W. Wolstenholme and M. O'Connor, eds. Little, Brown and Company, Boston, 1959. pp. 115–141.
5. HARMAN, D.: The biological clock: the mitochondria? *J. Am. Geriatr. Soc. 20:* 145–147, 1972.
6. CALLOWAY, N. O.: A general theory of senescence. *J. Am. Geriatr. Soc. 12:* 856, 1964.
7. VON BERTALANFFY, L.: General system theory and psychiatry. *In:* American Handbook of Psychiatry, Vol. 3, Chap. 43, S. Arieti, ed. Basic Books, New York, 1966. pp. 705–721.
8. CALLOWAY, N. O.: The role of entropy in biologic senescence. *J. Am. Geriatr. Soc. 14:* 342, 1966.
9. HAYFLICK, L.: Human cells and aging. *Sci. Am. 218:* 32–37, 1968.
10. SZILARD, L.: On the nature of the aging process. *Proc. Natl. Acad. Sci. U. S. A. 45:* 32, 1959.
11. COMFORT, A.: Models of aging, mammals. *In:* Perspectives in Experimental Gerontology. N. W. Shock, ed. C. C Thomas, Springfield. Ill., 1966. pp. 245–256.
12. JACOBS, P. A., COURT BROWN, W. M., AND DOLL, R.: Distribution of human chromosome counts in relation to age. *Nature 191:* 1178, 1961.
13. BLUMENTHAL, H. T. AND PROBSTEIN, J. G.: The pathogenesis of diseases of senescence. *In:* Surgery of the Aged and Debilitated Patient, J. D. Powers, ed. W. B. Saunders Company, Philadelphia, 1968. pp. 44–81.
14. WOLFORD, R. L.: The immunologic theory of aging. *Gerontologist 4:* 195–197, 1964.
15. ERIKSON, E. H.: Identity and the life cycle. *In:* Psychological Issues, Vol. 1, No. 1, G. S. Klein, ed. International Universities Press, New York, 1959.
16. STERN, M. M.: Fear of Death and Neuroses. *J. Am. Psychoanal. Assoc. 16:* 3–31, 1968.
17. JACQUES, E.: Death and the mid-life crisis. *Int. J. Psychoanal. 46:* 502–514, 1965.
18. ALIGHIERI, D.: The Divine Comedy: Inferno, Canto I. *In:* The Portable Dante, L. Binyon, trans. The Viking Press, New York, 1947. p 3.
19. BUTLER, R. N.: The life review: an interpretation of reminiscence in the aged. *Psychiatry 26:* 109–114, 1963.
20. BIRREN, J. E.: Life review, reconciliation and termination. *In:* The Psychology of Aging, Chap. 12. Prentice Hall, Inc., Englewood Cliffs, N. J., 1964.

# 2

# psychodynamic aspects

## CHANGES IN THE MENTAL APPARATUS

Considerations of mental phenomena include several dimensions: the time factor; aspects of energy; the concept of structure; and, the factor of dynamic interaction. The time factor is reflected in the developmental aspects of human behavior, in processes of becoming, and in the time-related changes in aging. Aspects of energy (the so-called economic point of view in psychoanalytic theory) refer to such phenomena as drives and needs; neutralized energy for productivity, creativity, or recreation; energy required for adaptational or defensive purposes; and so on. Structural considerations pertain to concepts, such as ego and superego, which in contrast to the id, represent organization, order, or information. Finally, the term *psychodynamic* refers to the interactional aspects, to an interplay of intrapsychic forces.

Simple as these descriptive notations may sound, they pertain to mental phenomena that are complex in nature. With regard to their existence and characteristics, we can only make inferences, not direct observations. In addition, since there are no separate compartments in the mind, they are closely related and cannot be viewed as being independent. The sum total of the attributes of the mental apparatus makes up the individual's *character* (from the Greek verb which means to groove, *e.g.*, in stone, as a hieroglyph; hence, our use of the term character for a printed or engraved symbol). Thus, one's character is the indelible imprint of life's experiences on one's self. Implied here is the notion that personalities can change over a lifetime. These changes can be described in terms of intrapsychic changes in the id, ego, and superego, as well as in their dynamic interrelationships. Such considerations about the effects of aging on the mental apparatus will be metapsychological on the one hand, and must be in conformance with clinical observations on the other hand.[1]

### Energy, Drives, and Needs

The organism is an intrinsically active system. A stimulus does not cause a reaction in an otherwise inert system, but rather modifies

11

processes in an autonomously active system. Since the organism is able to maintain a disequilibrium (*i.e.*, the steady state of an open system), it can dispense with tension in spontaneous activity or through responses to stimuli.[2]

**(a).** Characteristic of drives is the compelling tendency to seek gratification through activities of consummation. Drives represent bits of energy; this energy can be estimated in terms of the amount of work performed in the process of satisfying the drive. The term *id* (Latin for the English "it") connotes something impersonal. What is impersonal about the drives of the id is that all humans (and animals) possess similar sets of biological drives. Therefore, what makes a human being distinctive, *i.e.*, a personality, is not his id, but how he handles himself in a complex world in which he has to maintain relationships with others.

With regard to the drives, it must be kept in mind that these can be categorized in several ways. Traditionally, a distinction is made between libidinal and aggressive drives. It is clear, however, that the distinction between drives involving the discharge of surplus energy and those involving the need for replenishment is equally important. The former type includes active impulses, which are catabolic in nature and aimed at discharge of tension. The latter can be thought of as (more or less) passive needs, *e.g.*, hunger, sleep, and thirst, which involve anabolic processes and which are aimed at building up of tension.

Typical of the senescence of living systems is the progressive decline in ability to produce energy. A young organism can produce more energy per unit of time than an old one. From the standpoint of energy, an old organism has less power. Applying this concept of biological drives, it seems plausible that with aging the strength of the drives declines. According to this view, the drives would become less powerful, less urgent. This will be particularly true of the active drives (*e.g.*, genital sexuality, generativity in the areas of work and parenthood, mastery of novel situations, etc.).

**(b).** Another general characteristic of biological aging is that the resting level of a function may show no significant change with age, but that during or after stress, return to the baseline level is prolonged (*e.g.*, displacements in electrolytes, blood glucose levels, heart rate). Thus, there is an increase in the amount of time needed to restore and replenish the organism, with advancing age. On the psychological level, this can be expressed in terms of an increase in needs. With advancing age, it takes increasingly more time for anabolic processes or restoration and replenishment to take place, even though the absolute quantity (intensity) of the passive, anabolic needs may decrease with age. For example, an older person may need fewer calories, but the metabolic processes of intake and assimilation of food, as well as production of usable energy, may require more time. Such a constellation amounts to an increase in passive needs. The intensity of such needs, then, becomes progressively stronger because more time is required to fulfill them. With increasing age, the needs for stability, shelter, rest, etc. will become relatively more important. These biological needs, whose intensity increases with age, have a quality of being relatively more "narcissistic," self-oriented, passive, or pregenital, and are aimed at self-preservation. Important in this context is the fact that, because of declining strength and resources, the aged person does not have the same power he used to have, to bring about the fulfillment of his particular needs and wishes.

## Structural Aspects

### (a). The Ego.

1. Whereas the energy of drives lacks structure, in the case of ego energy is used in an organized manner. This corresponds, respectively, to the difference between primary and secondary process. Thus, *ego* is, in a sense, equivalent to order and information. The ego is a set of regulatory principles whose main task is to maintain balance between the pressures from different directions: inner needs and drives, the opportunities and constraints of the external world, and the guidelines of one's conscience. The achievement of adaptation is a creative process involving continuous problem solving, and facilitated by the *synthetic* and the *autonomous* ego functions. The latter, which include the capacities for thought, memory, communication, perception, and neuromuscular control, are largely determined by hereditary factors.

The human organism, as an open system, is capable of maintaining a *steady state*. This is not a simple condition of harmony or of equilibrium but involves the maintenance of constant ratio between input (sensory afferent stimuli, etc.) and output (motor-efferent responses, etc.). This steady state is further characterized by *equifinality*. Whereas the equilibria in closed systems depend on initial conditions, an open system can attain a time-independent state, which depends on the parameters of the system rather than on its initial condition.[2] On the psychological level, this principle corresponds with the phenomenon of personal identity. Thus, the functions of the ego include but also go beyond the traditional concept of homeostasis.

The basic model of cybernetics is the feedback scheme which, in the case of living organisms, is called *homeostasis*. The homeostatic feedback mechanism involves an ensemble of regulations that maintain variables constant and direct the organism toward a goal, with the result of the reaction being monitored back to the receptor side so that the system is held stable or led toward a target. However, the homeostatic scheme does not explain several types of specifically human behavior, such as exploring and curiosity; activities aimed at building up, rather than reducing, tension; creativity; etc.[2] In psychopathology, on the other hand, the homeostatic model is more suitable because nonhomeostatic functions usually decline in mental illness. Thus, mental disease may be described as a series of defense mechanisms, settling down at ever lower homeostatic levels until mere preservation of physiological life is left (*e.g.*, in senile regression).[3] The concept of progressive teleological regression in schizophrenia is similar.[4]

The accurate perception and interpretation of reality is an ego function, called the *reality principle*. It is based on an integration of several part functions: perception, apperception, thought, and memory.

Characteristic of all living systems is the property of boundary. The boundary of the personality (the self) is not simply concrete and spatial such as the skin. Rather, the *ego boundary* is a dynamic structure that functions like a membrane. It is the subjective line of demarcation between self and not-self, me and not-me, inside and outside. The concept of ego boundary is related to other ego functions, such as the reality principle, the self-image and, the body image. In states of depersonalization, there is both a blurring of the ego boundary and impaired reality testing.

The body occupies a unique position with regard to inner and outer reality. In one sense, the body is part of myself so that what occurs to it, occurs inside of me. But, one can also take some distance from one's body, look at it, touch it, perceive sensations coming from within, and so on. In this sense, the body is external to the perceiving self and comparable to other external objects. We may even feel that we own our body—a possession to be proud or ashamed of, to be concerned about or to be taken for granted. The term *body-image* refers to an individual's subjective image of his own body. In addition to this inner mental picture, the body image includes a set of personal values assigned to parts of the body and to the body as a whole (pride in physical prowess, shame about physical shortcomings, etc.). The role of the body and the body image is particularly relevant with regard to somatic expressions of psychiatric illness (*e.g.*, conversion, hypochondriasis).

The ego matures in a gradual way and this involves a great deal of learning, first in the family, and later in school and work, through friendships, marriage, parenthood, and so on. In fact, the ego has the opportunity for a lifetime of continuing education. By the same token, life, through its corrective emotional experiences, may act as a therapist. The autodidact may learn from life's experiences without the formalized instructions of school or interventions typical of therapy.

2. *Age-related changes* may affect the autonomous ego functions or the ego's defense mechanisms, both of which require the expenditure of energy.

—The autonomous ego functions (perception, thought, etc.) may be affected when insufficient energy is available to them, or when there is a withdrawal (decathexis) of the energy normally invested in the operation of these capacities. This can be seen in various psychopathological conditions: decathexis of perception may lead to hysterical conversion symptoms, *e.g.*, hysterical blindness; and, decathexis of memory may cause amnesia. It is possible that in schizophrenia and in certain cases of senile regression, the loss of abstract intelligence is based on a withdrawal of energy from the autonomous ego function of thought.

—One of the earliest functions of the ego is to interpose a time lag between stimulus and response. Thus, motor responses are no longer necessarily automatic. During this *delay of gratification*, there is opportunity for selecting those behavioral responses which are likely to be maximally effective and for creative problem solving. Thus, the mature ego (secondary process) stands in opposition to the pleasure principle (the urge toward immediate gratification, typical of primary process). Regression of this ego function may result in "the geriatric delinquent," dominated by the pleasure principle, and oriented toward immediate gratification, often at the expense of long-range plans.[5]

—The decline in the ability to delay gratification in some old individuals is probably related to an *altered time perspective:* the sense that time is running out and there is no point in continuing to delay gratification. Such a trend is not necessarily pathological; it may be healthy, depending on many factors. In some old persons, however, this ego change may result in acting out of socially undesirable behavior.

—As is true for ego functions in general, *defense mechanisms* require energy to function effectively. Repression, the ego's (unconscious) attempt to prevent certain thoughts or feelings from entering conscious awareness, requires a continuous expenditure of energy (counterca-thexis). With less energy being available to the ego, it may become difficult to maintain repression. In such a case, there are two possible developments. Some of that which was repressed may begin to emerge into conscious awareness; and, if this repressed mental content is threatening or unacceptable to the individual, anxiety will be the result. Or, with repression itself being unable to do the job, auxiliary defenses are called into action, *e.g.*, denial or projection.

—Some individuals, throughout life, habitually use defenses that may require large amounts of energy. As a result, they have little energy left over for work, social contacts, leisure activities, and so on. *High-energy* defense patterns (the "fight" patterns of response) include: reaction formation, counterphobic defenses, overcompensation, obsessive-compulsive defenses, the manic cluster (denial, hyperactivity, and suppression through diversion), and the paranoid cluster (projection, hostile aggression against the externalized problem, or repeatedly fleeing away from the externalized threat).

—On the other hand, defenses that are basically *regressive* (*e.g.*, withdrawal and increased dependency) require less energy. The high-energy defensive patterns become more vulnerable as the years go by, because of physical illness or age-related decline in energy production.

### (b). The Superego.

The *superego* is more or less equivalent to conscience. Like the ego, it develops over a period of years, through assimilation of standards and guidelines from significant people, especially the parents. The mental processes that play an important role in superego development are introjection and identification. The superego may be involved in intrapsychic changes that are favorable or unfavorable.

1. Favorable, adaptive changes are probably related to the phenomenon of "mellowing with age." There may be two ways in which *mellowing* can come about. First, when the instinctual drives are less strong and urgent, the superego may no longer have to be as alert or on guard. As a result, less energy is taken up by the censorship function of the superego. A relaxed superego may be inwardly perceived as a sense of freedom. Whatever energy has been freed, may now become available for other,

possibly creative, purposes. Secondly, an individual who has been "on good behavior" for most of his life, may come to feel that it is now time for a reward. He may allow himself to reap the benefits of a lifetime of work through the experience of leisure during retirement.

2. Unfavorable developments occur when, in the course of aging, needs or impulses emerge which are unacceptable to the superego. For example, an individual who is physically disabled and faced with the need to accept help from others, may consider such dependency gratifications unacceptable, or inconsistent with his self-concept, so that feelings of shame and guilt develop, or an attitude of rebellious protest.

(c). Part of the superego is the idealized self concept, the *ego ideal*, which refers to one's aspirations and life goals. At some point in life, frequently in the middle years, an individual begins to wonder if he will reach the goals he has set for himself. Some people will feel that they have arrived; others, that they have fallen short of their aspirations. The phrases "having arrived" and "having it made" are commonly used to refer to a sense of status in life, or the attainment of a plateau on which success comes in one's grasp. A sense of satisfaction arises from perceiving the merger of the actual self with the idealized self. The success is the sense of succeeding into the ego ideal. Once attained, this succession into the ego ideal will serve as insurance against the risks of loss of self-esteem that would result from being "over the hill."

In contrast to despair, the coming into one's own, the succeeding into the ego ideal, is a moment of integration—of integrity.

## PSYCHODYNAMICS OF ADAPTATION

### The Role of Loss

(a). For any loss or stress to become meaningful, it has to be perceived, registered in the mind, and evaluated through the process of *apperception*. Apperception refers to a mental scanning process of comparing incoming stimuli and images with those already stored in memory. The fact of a loss cannot be undone by the ego, but it is possible for the ego, through its defense mechanisms, to try to prevent the loss from reaching conscious awareness. The situation may become rather complex when the ego itself is changing as well, *e.g.*, in organic brain syndrome (*cf.* case on page 98). In these instances, the ego's ability to perceive reality is impaired and the impact of losses may be blunted. Reality perception may also be diminished through a process of withdrawal which prevents the individual from feeling the pain that would have come with clear awareness of having suffered a loss, a factor that may play a role in the development of senile regression.

(b). **The Quality of Stress and Loss.** Specific clusters of social events requiring change in ongoing life adjustment are significantly associated with the onset of an illness.[6] The relationship between life stress and object loss, on the one hand, and illness onset, on the other hand, has been demonstrated by several investigators.[7] The etiologic significance of stresses and losses is that they represent a necessary, but not a sufficient cause of illness, and that they account in part for the time of onset of illness.[8] In addition to determining the number and type of stressful factors, it is also necessary to be able to assess them in terms of their qualitative aspects, e.g., the subjective meaning of an event or its personal value. As a result of their research in this area, Holmes and Rahe[8] developed a rating scale listing a series of life events, with the qualitative significance of these events being numerically expressed (Table 1). It must be remembered that such a rating scale is based on data obtained from a cross-sectional study of a large number of subjects. Therefore, the rating scale cannot simply be applied to one particular person. In addition, it is very likely that, in a given individual, the qualitative stress aspects of some of the life events would change in the course of time.

According to Levin,[9] loss represents a deficiency of external supplies needed to satisfy drives and needs. Loss of an object into which much narcissistic libido was invested is a precipitating factor for depression. In addition, there are other precipitating factors: attack, restraint, threat, and loss equivalents. Attack refers to any external force producing pain or injury. Restraint is any external force which restricts those actions needed for satisfaction of drives. Freedom from restraint therefore represents freedom to find satisfactory outlets for one's drives. Older people are restrained by physical infirmities, fears of overdoing it, and cautionary attitudes on the part of family and society (e.g., in the area of sex). Threat is a warning of possible future loss, attack, or restraint. Threats may contribute to depression and conversely depression may increase one's feeling of being threatened. Loss equivalents occur when somebody else's gain is experienced as a loss for oneself (as in envy). Or, there may be exposure to a seductive situation which leads to increased desire which cannot be satisfied.

(c). For further understanding of the effects of loss, it is necessary to keep in mind the distinction between losses pertaining to the nonself (e.g., material possessions, love objects) as compared to the self (e.g., the body). Again, a few definitions may be in order. An *object* refers to the instrument that brings about satisfaction of a need or drive (food, sexual partner, etc.). The *aim* of a drive is the specific activity required for satisfying the drive (in case of hunger: biting, chewing, swallowing, etc.; in case of the sex drive: sexual intercourse, masturbation, etc.). The *source* of a drive refers to the body area where the excitation arises, e.g., the upper gastro-intestinal tract or the genital organs.

1. The object, the instrument bringing about drive satisfaction or need fulfillment, may be lost through death, or may be less accessible because of illness. Thus, because of a specific object loss the quality of the sexual drive, for example, may change from a heterosexual to an autoerotic orientation. The loss of an external object may be resolved by a process of *substitution:* directing the drive or interest toward a new object. The economy of the mind is then only temporarily upset.

2. The situation, however, is different in the case of an internal loss. When an important part of the body is lost (or declines in effectiveness), psychic economy may be considerably disturbed. For example, because of the loss of teeth or a gastrectomy, the aim of the hunger drive can be

TABLE 1. *The Social Readjustment Rating Scale**

| Life Event | Mean Value |
|---|---|
| 1. Death of spouse | 100 |
| 2. Divorce | 73 |
| 3. Marital separation | 65 |
| 4. Jail term | 63 |
| 5. Death of close family member | 63 |
| 6. Personal injury or illness | 53 |
| 7. Marriage | 50 |
| 8. Fired at work | 47 |
| 9. Marital reconciliation | 45 |
| 10. Retirement | 45 |
| 11. Change in health of family member | 44 |
| 12. Pregnancy | 40 |
| 13. Sex difficulties | 39 |
| 14. Gain of new family member | 39 |
| 15. Business readjustment | 39 |
| 16. Change in financial state | 38 |
| 17. Death of close friend | 37 |
| 18. Change to different line of work | 36 |
| 19. Change in number of arguments with spouse | 35 |
| 20. Mortgage over $10,000 | 31 |
| 21. Foreclosure of mortgage or loan | 30 |
| 22. Change in responsibilities at work | 29 |
| 23. Son or daughter leaving home | 29 |
| 24. Trouble with in-laws | 29 |
| 25. Outstanding personal achievement | 28 |
| 26. Wife begins or stops work | 26 |
| 27. Begin or end school | 26 |
| 28. Change in living conditions | 25 |
| 29. Revision of personal habits | 24 |
| 30. Trouble with boss | 23 |
| 31. Change in work hours or conditions | 20 |
| 32. Change in residence | 20 |
| 33. Change in schools | 20 |
| 34. Change in recreation | 19 |
| 35. Change in church activities | 19 |
| 36. Change in social activities | 18 |
| 37. Mortgage or loan less than $10,000 | 17 |
| 38. Change in sleeping habits | 16 |
| 39. Change in number of family get-togethers | 15 |
| 40. Change in eating habits | 15 |
| 41. Vacation | 13 |
| 42. Christmas | 12 |
| 43. Minor violations of the law | 11 |

* See T. H. Holmes and R. H. Rahe for complete wording of items. [8] Reprinted by permission of Pergamon Press, Ltd.

significantly altered; the activity normally required for satisfying the drive can no longer be performed. Likewise, an arthritic or cardiac patient may be incapable of performing activities required for certain sexual gratifications.

It is also possible that the decline in the overall amount of available energy may affect the aim of the drive or need. This may involve a shift from being active to being passive. A physically infirm man, for example, may change from active sexual performance to more or less passive participation.

3. Again another consideration pertains to possible changes in the source of the drives. Anatomical and physiological alterations in specific organs may diminish the intensity of excitations, a shift which may involve a simultaneous increase in the urgency of another need. The source (erogenous zone) where the genital-sexual drive is considered to originate, for example, is the genital apparatus. If there should be a major anatomical loss involving these organs, or a physiological change affecting the endocrine glands providing sex hormones, the sex drive itself may be altered. And, the psychological effect will be different, compared with the loss of an external object. Likewise, the source of the hunger drive is altered in conditions such as diabetes or hyperthyroidism.

4. Under certain circumstances, special problems may develop. For example, any acute, sudden change in the drive—its objects, aim, or source—usually represents a major stress resulting in profound psychological reactions. Also, any discrepancy between the rates of change in the aim and the source of the drive sets the stage for conflict. Thus, a young man with a disabling skeleto-muscular condition may be unable to consummate the sexual act while his sex drive is relatively normal. Optimally, losses in the realm of the object, aim, and source would be in keeping with each other so that no discrepancy between wish, capability, and opportunity takes place.

Some of the above is illustrated by the case of a 68-year-old man hospitalized because of chronic depression. The psychodynamics involved a dependent premorbid personality; regression and hypochondriacal concerns were quite prominent in the clinical picture. What actually had brought the patient to the hospital, was his sexual behavior toward his wife: he insisted on being held at her bosom and her nursing him, two hours every day. The wife had become increasingly indignant about this, especially in view of the fact that "he cannot raise a hard one." Thus, in the context of his depression (and some age-related infirmities), the following changes in drive and drive satisfaction had occurred. The source of the sexual drive had changed from being genital to pregenital (oral and skin eroticism); the aim of the drive changed from active consummation to being passive and receptive (being held). The object of the drive shifted from vagina to breasts. The area of sexuality, however, in which these regressive changes occurred, represented a displacement of other, nonsexual concerns (need for security, self-esteem, etc.). The fact that the patient tried to solve a nonsexual problem by way of sexual means, was responsible for his insatiable demands—no amount of breast feeding would have been sufficient. This point was vividly demonstrated after admission to the hospital. As the result of various therapeutic measures, his spirits improved, the regressive and hypochondriacal features disappeared, along with the insatiable oral tension.

## The Role of Sublimation

Although a psychologically healthy person is flexible enough to revise his mental economy, such a readjustment is difficult or impossible for a person with long-standing psychological problems. One reason for this is the often rigid and limited repertoire of defenses; also, the very magnitude of the underlying conflict may be sufficiently frightening that the individual feels he has to be constantly on guard and that he can't afford a period of relative defenselessness during which he could experiment with new coping techniques. In such a situation, then, marked anxiety or depression may develop. The failure to establish new patterns to deal with conflict or stress tends to be resolved finally by resorting to the way of least resistance, *i.e.*, regression or withdrawal. These defensive maneuvers, in fact, may take the person away from the conflict area, but because he has never adequately developed the habit of optimal regression (*e.g.*, regression in the service of the ego), the newly adopted defense tends to overshoot. Examples of this can be seen, when an individual, who used to be compulsively active or excessively self-reliant, experiences an illness or a stressful change, after which he remains unduly passive and dependent.

All important for mental health is the capacity to sublimate. *Sublimation* is the optimal way of handling drives that, in their original form, are not permitted free expression by society. Many such impulses belong to the domain of infantile sexuality; they are drives which, later in adult life, ordinarily find their appropriate niche in the realm of genital sexuality. They are called component drives because they are to become subsidiary to adult genital drives. Normally these infantile drives come under the hegemony of adult sexuality, and being more temperate under the auspices of love and intimacy they become useful and permissible. Another possibility, however, is for one or more of the pregenital drives to be sublimated which involves the following. The drive changes in quality so that it now becomes socially acceptable. The energy involved in the original infantile drive is fully expressed; this is different from repression, where the drive energy is wasted because of its confinement in the unconscious. In contrast to repression, there is no need for a continuous countercathexis in the case of sublimation. The id and the ego join forces, as it were, and are not at cross-purposes; hence, energy is freely available for constructive purposes. Finally, sublimation involves a process of neutralization: the sexual or aggressive-destructive aspects of a particular drive is removed and neutralized.

What is the significance of this for the psychodynamics of senescence? The notion of changing a need, interest, or drive into socially acceptable channels implies an orientation on the part of the individual toward society, its members and values. An *outward orientation* toward others and toward external resources can be an extremely useful coping device when the aging person's inner resources are dwindling and provide less intense gratification.[10] Thus, an aging individual may shift his interests and values, away from himself, toward external objects: his children, business, church, community, and so on. Individuals with a high degree of abstraction may shift their interest to society, the world, science, or art. Further, we might theorize that, because sublimation involves a change of pregenital drives, an age-related decline in genital interest and activity, would not affect the capacity or opportunity for sublimation.

In the previous chapter, we had raised the question, whether it is possible to speak of development in old age. In view of the continued possibility for intrapsychic changes, including the opportunities for sublimation, it is certainly appropriate to speak of continued psychological development in late life.

## REFERENCES

1. ZETZEL, E. R.: Dynamics of the metapsychology of the aging process. *In:* Geriatric Psychiatry, M. A. Berezin and S. H. Cath, eds. International University Press, New York, 1965. pp. 109–119.
2. VON BERTALANFFY, L.: General system theory and psychiatry. *In:* American Handbook of Psychiatry, Vol. 3, Chap. 43, S. Arieti, ed. Basic Books, Inc., New York, 1966. pp. 705–721.
3. MENNINGER, K., MAYMAN, M., AND PRUYSER, P.: The Vital Balance. The Viking Press, New York, 1963.
4. ARIETI, S.: Schizophrenia. *In:* American Handbook of Psychiatry, Vol. 1, Chap. 23, S. Arieti, ed. Basic Books, Inc., New York, 1959.
5. WOLK, R. L., RUSTIN, S. L., AND SCOTTI, J.: The geriatric delinquent. *J. Am. Geriatr. Soc. 11:* 653–659, 1963.
6. RAHE, R. H., MEYER, M., KJAER, G., AND HOLMES, T. H.: Social stress and illness onset. *J. Psychosom. Res. 8:* 35, 1964.
7. GRAHAM, D. T. AND STEVENSON, I.: Disease as response to life stress. *In:* The Psychological Basis of Medical Practice, H. I. Lief and N. R. Lief, eds. Harper and Rowe, New York, 1963.
8. HOLMES, T. H. AND RAHE, R. H.: The social readjustment rating scale. *J. Psychosom. Res. 11:* 213–218, 1967.
9. LEVIN, S.: Depression in the aged. *In:* Geriatric Psychiatry, M. A. Berezin and S. H. Cath, eds. International Universities Press, New York, 1965. pp. 203–225.
10. CATH, S. H.: Some dynamics of middle and later years: a study in depletion and restitution. *In:* Geriatric Psychiatry, M. A. Berezin and S. H. Cath, eds. International Universities Press, New York, 1965. pp. 21–72.

# 3

# dynamic psychopathology

## STRESS AND COPING IN LATE LIFE

The aged person's environment is characterized by changes which are stressful in varying degrees. Stresses in the external environment include loss of occupation, income, and prestige. In the internal milieu, decline in all biological systems is obvious.

In living organisms, the response to a stressful event is a reaction aimed at removing or neutralizing the stress and repairing the damage. On the cellular level, for example, there is the formation of antibodies and other immune mechanisms. Specific cells or organs play a major role in physiological defenses: white blood cells, spleen, adrenal glands, etc. The same principles apply to phenomena on the psychological level. A mental stress or psychotrauma leads to a psychological defense or a behavioral coping pattern.

In dynamic psychopathology, we need to differentiate between the following: the stress itself and the immediate emotional distress caused by it (*e.g.*, loss of a spouse resulting in immediate distress of grief); the defense mechanisms employed to deal with the stress and its associated distress (*e.g.*, denial); and the psychological and behavioral phenomena associated with or resulting from the defense mechanisms (*e.g.*, denial leading to neurotic depression or patterns of hyperactivity). These processes tend to unfold in temporal sequence, but in such a way that each phase is superimposed on the preceding one. There is, of course, some overlap throughout.

## Emotional Distress

Emotional distress includes various negative feelings such as fear and anxiety, grief and depression, shame and guilt, anger and hostility, and so forth. It is important to keep in mind that there is no such thing as an abnormal feeling *per se*. What makes feelings abnormal is not so much their quality, but the extent of their duration, their intensity, and the appropriateness in the context. Thus, sadness and grief are an essential aspect of the experience of living; it would be abnormal to never feel sadness and grief. These same feelings, however, if more prolonged and severe become pathological, *i.e.*, a depression.

Fear is the normal emotional reaction to impending injury or loss. Primary anxiety (or traumatic anxiety) concerns the response of the organism to maximal internal and external stimulation. Signal anxiety is the warning signal in response to impulses and fantasies that might result in disaster. This type of anxiety is the signal of an internal danger situation relevant to ego-alien impulses. In old age signal anxiety becomes less important. Also, traumatic anxiety as a response to overwhelming stress is relatively unusual, although it does occur. Thus, the nature of anxiety in the aged does not correspond to primary (traumatic) anxiety, nor to signal anxiety. According to Zetzel, anxiety in the aged resembles the type of anxiety stimulated by fear of loss and separation.[1]

A danger anticipated may be actual (real) or imagined (existing in fantasy only). The more a person reacts to imagined dangers and losses, the more the psychological capacity of reality evaluation is impaired. In a neurosis there is only a mild to moderate impairment of reality testing, whereas in a psychosis the impairment of contact with reality is severe or total. Thus, a psychotic patient may live entirely in a fantasy world. Some aged individuals, for example, withdraw from reality and retreat into their inner self in order to live off their memories.

The normal emotional response to a loss which actually took place is a *grief reaction*.[2] This should be distinguished from depression which, although difficult to define in exact terms, is generally considered as a pathological emotional reaction. A grief reaction involves a clear and conscious recognition, on the individual's part, of an actual loss. After the initial emotional shock on the part of the bereaved person, there is an increasing realization of the significance of the loss and all its ramifications in every day life. During this period there are recurring episodes of specific physiologic distress, such as waves of sadness. The feelings of bereavement and sadness are expressed verbally and nonverbally, *e.g.*, crying. Toward the end of the grief reaction, which may last for several months, there is a resolution which involves a redirecting of energies and interests toward new people, goals, or activities.[3]

When a close person is lost, the psychic energy invested in that person first has no place to go, but eventually the resolution of the grief reaction results in a reinvestment of this psychic energy in new objects, in the direction of other people. However, when part of the self is lost (*e.g.*, amputation), resolution of the grief reaction is more complex and involves a form of inner realignment and reappraisal of the self and one's relations with others. Adjustment of the latter type is characterized by continuation of self-esteem, rooted in a religious or philosophical framework that views personal worth on the basis of one's intrinsic value as a unique person; by accepting and integrating the limitation into a new self concept; and by finding new ways of maintaining closeness to others and realizing remaining potentials.

## Psychodynamic Aspects of Coping Behavior

The aged individual has to cope with a multitude of losses that often interact and accumulate in the manner of a vicious circle, at a time when the physical and mental energy needed for effective coping is decreasing. This has two implications First, the usual ways of coping, especially the high energy defenses, may have to be replaced by new techniques of adaptation. Active or aggressive mastery, for example, may be replaced by acceptance and the capacity to resign oneself to the inevitable without self-reproach, bitterness, or cynicism.[1]

(a). The *capacity for coping* with stress (the range of capacity, and the types of defenses chosen) is a function of the ego. Ego strength determines, to a large extent, the degree of success in coping. When a person overextends himself in his attempts toward mastery, we can speak of a crisis. Whether or not a crisis will be resolved depends, by and large, on the ego's potential for growth; crisis resolution, in turn, results in further ego growth. We can try to assess ego strength by exploring the individual's manner of coping with stress in the past, his mastery of novel situations, as well as the objective signs of achievement and subjective sense of satisfaction with regard to previous life phases (marriage, parenthood, work, etc.).

(b). The *range* of coping mechanisms is based on a repertoire determined largely by past experiences and relationships to significant people in childhood and young adult life. A person whose earlier life was relatively wholesome and free from major intrapsychic conflicts possesses more flexibility and a greater range of effective behavioral responses to stress, because less effort is expended in dealing with internal (neurotic) pressures. On the other hand, an individual who has always had limited psychological resources and resilience, and who has managed only a precarious adjustment, is more likely to respond maladaptively to stress. The overly independent person, for example who has always resisted any appearance of weakness may perceive a disabling disease as catastrophic, responding to it in a disorganized fashion, whereas another individual with fewer conflicts may be able to adjust to the same disability more gracefully.

The individual's capacity to adapt successfully is also influenced by *organic problems* such as mental retardation, congenital or acquired deformities, organic brain damage, and so on. The person who cannot fully comprehend a problem or who lacks the physical capacity to respond efficiently is clearly limited in his attempts at adaptation.

The aged person's *external environment* is a very influential factor in the ability to adapt successfully. The ability of a spouse or other family member to move in supportively, when greater physical dependence is unavoidable, will enable the aged person to remain in his environment for a longer time.

(c). Whether coping or defense mechanisms are adaptive or maladaptive depends upon the type and intensity of the defense as well as upon its appropriateness to the situation. *Adaptive* coping techniques imply a reestablishment of an equilibrium that was disturbed by a loss. In the case of coping with physical illness, for example, adaptive devices presuppose some amount of cognitive awareness regarding the illness, a willingness to seek medical help, and a realistic adjustment to the sick role. *Maladaptive* defenses aggravate the patient's suffering, deplete his resources, and weaken his resistance. Maladaptive coping behavior typically leads to a vicious circle which aggravates the very problem against which it is directed. In the language of cybernetics: adaptive coping represents a negative feedback leading to corrective intervention, whereas maladaptive coping involves a positive feedback leading to a vicious circle. In the latter case, unpleasant emotions and painful tension do not abate, but accumulate in the individual.

(d). The *selection* of a particular defense frequently results in certain characteristic behaviors. This has definite implications, not only for the individual's adjustment or lack thereof, but also for clinical management.[4] The various defense techniques and the behavioral patterns commonly associated with them can be grouped into three main categories, i.e., those aimed at:

—Retreat and conservation of energy.
—Exclusion of the threat or loss from awareness.
—Mastery and control.

## TYPES OF DEFENSES AND COPING

### Retreat from the Threat; Conservation of Energy

Defenses aimed at retreat from the threat and at conservation of energy include regression, giving up, and withdrawal.

(a). *Regression* is the retreat into earlier, more primitive modes of adaptation and relating to others. Its chief features are restriction of interest in the external world, self-centeredness, bodily overconcern, and increased dependency on others. Regression commensurate with the severity of a disability or illness is useful because it enables the patient to accept appropriate help in a dependent relationship. Excessive regression tends to backfire because others (relatives, medical personnel) will view the patient as "bad and uncooperative."

In some cases, the patient is apprehensive about letting go, and fights against the regressive pull tugging inside of him. Although this may seem convenient for the environment (the patient is not demanding), it presents a problem for the person who clings to an independence which may have been appropriate but now has lost its usefulness. Moreover, once the facade of independence crumbles, the regressive manifestations of the underlying dependency now coming to the fore may be exceptionally severe and all the more difficult to manage.

The egocentricity and bodily overconcern of the regressed patient are closely related. Being engrossed in his own self, little interest is left over for others and the world around. Because of the reduced scope of the patient's world, his reality testing is hampered and he is less able to form reliable judgements about what happens around him. Consequently, he feels insecure and the need for continuous reality testing arises. Some of the resulting disturbing behavior represents attempts to find out where he stands with other people.

The patient is often uncomfortably aware of his dependent state; the guilt feelings generated by it make him easily suspicious of the goodwill of those attending him. He may imagine that they do not come to his aid quickly enough because they resent waiting on him or get exhausted by his demands. The patient also feels ambivalence toward those who care for him. Although he may be grateful for the support, he is resentful because of what seems to him his inferior position. Some patients express this ambivalence by becoming more demanding.

The individual who accepts dependency eagerly causes other problems. He may develop excessive dependency on one person, so that he feels no one else can satisfy his needs. Such patients need to have their relationships with the medical personnel carefully structured to prevent overdependence on any one individual.

> A 69-year-old man of national prominence, hospitalized for a myocardial infarct, irritated and alienated nurses with his demanding, hostile behavior. In contrast to his responsible preillness behavior, characterized by precision in his work and conscientiousness in his relations with other people, the patient's illness behavior was marked by extreme dependence upon his wife, and obnoxiousness toward everyone else. He frequently passed flatus in the presence of nurses and other medical personnel without any appearance of embarrassment.

As regression deepens, dependence upon the familiar and upon the established order extends to routines and to inanimate objects. Patients find small disruptions of daily routine upsetting; they need to have their activities fall into a stable, predictable pattern. One feature of regression, relevant in this context, is the alteration of the time sense and time perspective. Whereas normal, healthy adults look ahead months or years, the regressed patient, like the child, views life in a time scale composed of smaller units such as days or weeks. One of the consequences of this is the patient's inability to wait, and a frustrating sense of impatience.

> The existence of organic problems, *e.g.*, organic brain syndrome (OBS), predisposes to regressive phenomena of psychotic nature. An 85-year-old woman with senile dementia would fill her shoes with bath powder and shredded paper; then she would tear up her clothes. She expressed the delusion that she had just given birth to a baby, even mentioning the baby's father by name. But the baby had died, and now she did not know what to do with the clothing.

> The themes of conception, birth, and death are represented through archaic, primary process symbols. Her own impending death was no longer in sight since she had regressed to a point where she still could give birth (a psychotic restitution fantasy). At the same time, her own death was represented by the young baby who already had died. The baby's death was concretely dramatized by tearing up her clothes.

The delusional and hallucinatory phenomena in patients who are psychotic or profoundly regressed (*e.g.*, schizophrenia, senile regression) are comparable to the manifest contents of a dream. The mental mechanisms causing the distortion of the underlying latent

thoughts and feelings are frequently rather naive and unsophisti-
cated. Hence, it may be relatively easy to arrive at an understanding
of the psychotic manifestations.

(b). The orderly retreat inherent in adaptive regression is a sort of
flexible "giving in." If the retreat is carried to its extreme, however, it
may end in surrender and capitulation to the threat. In this *giving up*,
there is a sense of complete loss of control and intactness of the self. In
such a state of hopelessness and helplessness, the entire homeostatic
machinery may collapse. The organism may lose its capacity for
maintaining order in the internal (psychophysiological) environment.
Giving up the will to live may well have psychophysiological repercussions which lower the individual's resistance, aggravate existing symptoms, and perhaps even hasten the moment of death.[5]

A 59-year-old divorced woman expressed the desire to go to sleep
and never wake up. Her present condition of giving up was the
outcome of a long process of decompensation. Early in her marriage
her husband committed adultery but she stayed with him, and even
supported him, "because he was close to being an alcoholic." She
worked as a personnel director, an illustration of her strong sense of
duty. Because they were unable to have children of their own, she
wanted to adopt a child but he refused. The patient continued to
function responsibly in her work until she had a depression after her
father's death, eight years ago. This depression lasted six months.
Since then, however, she began to drink, and this increased to the
point of her being hospitalized several times because of alcohol
abuse. Meanwhile, her husband left her, which resulted in a divorce
two years ago. After this, he began to do remarkably well as a
salesman, and even stopped drinking. Having lost her husband, the
patient next lost her job, and then her home. Being on welfare, she
had to move into a rooming house. Thus, at the age of 58, she felt
that nothing was left: no parents, no child, no husband, no job, no
home, no meaning, no future. Living alone, she let herself deteriorate, drinking by herself and keeping others away by locking herself
in her room which became more and more filthy. Eventually, she
started to wander about aimlessly at night, was told to pack up and
leave, and lost this last shelter.

(c). Whereas regression is a moving away from adult role responsibilities, *withdrawal* is a moving away from people. As such, it is a more
serious development than regression. The response of withdrawal is often
based on feelings of inadequacy or shame. For example, disfigurements
resulting from illness or surgery may cause a person to expect disgust
from others. To protect himself from this mortification, he withdraws
from the contact with others. The loss of youthful attractiveness also can
prompt a protective withdrawal. The ravages of time may be experienced
as a narcissistic injury that is particularly painful. As a result, there may
be attempts to cover oneself from the exposure to the eyes of others. In
intimate relations, withdrawal sets up a vicious circle. The attitude of
lowered esteem for oneself is contagious: others are likely to end up

feeling embarrassed, too. Thus, withdrawal as a means to maintain self-esteem and avoid shame becomes a self-fulfilling prophecy; and, the price of maintaining dignity through withdrawal is isolation and loneliness.

A woman in her early 60's had been in psychotherapy because of multiple somatic complaints, most of which had a psychogenic origin. As her physical symptoms began to abate, she became more depressed. With embarrassment, she began to relate concerns about her marriage. She accused her husband of not being interested in her, and ruminated that many years ago he might have had a fleeting interest in another woman. Now, she and her husband were estranged and no longer intimate. At this point she confided, with visible shame, that her body was like a battlefield. In the course of many years, multiple surgical procedures had been performed on her abdomen and breasts, leaving scars all over. She hated the sight of it and kept herself under cover. Her embarrassment however, was communicated to her husband. He too began to feel a sense of shame. By participating in the cover up, he confirmed her doubts about herself and consolidated a pattern of mutual withdrawal.

### Excluding the Threat or Its Significance from Awareness

Defenses aimed at excluding the threat or its significance from awareness include suppression, denial, rationalization, depersonalization, externalization (projection), and internalization (introjection).

(a). *Suppression* is a conscious attempt to dismiss certain ideas or feelings from awareness. Typically, the individual tries to push unpleasant thoughts to the back of his mind by getting busy with something else. Such diversionary activities become more difficult when a person becomes weaker as a result of progressive disability or illness. Also, suppression may be put out of commission by the increased idleness inherent in being sick, disabled, or isolated. Nighttime may be especially difficult because of the additional lack of sensory input. Unable to sleep, the patient may find himself increasingly preoccupied with anxiety-provoking concerns.

A 63-year-old man was hospitalized because of addiction to glutethimide. He had taken this for several years, gradually requiring more and more. The patient had been a prominent and successful person in his small community. He viewed his personal identity almost exclusively in terms of his work (director of a community agency) which involved much strain and irregular hours. The thought of retirement in the nearby future was a threat because this loss of social role was equated by him with a loss of identity. During daytime or working hours, he could suppress awareness of this threat by keeping busy, but at nighttime the "ghosts came out of the closet." Hence, the insomnia which in turn led to the addiction pattern.

(b). *Denial* is a mental mechanism by which an observation, fact, or its significance, is denied or not recognized. Denial is frequently manifested by a person's spontaneous negation ("Now, don't get me wrong, what we have talked about doesn't worry me one bit."). Denial may be aimed at the factual existence of a loss, at the implications of the loss, or at one's emotional reactions resulting from the loss. Complete denial of the fact of an illness or loss suggests serious psychopathology of psychotic proportions. Denial of feelings or problems associated with an illness or loss is much more common. Mild forms of denial are often conductive to good adjustment, but extreme denial, frequently coupled with rebellious protest, is self-destructive, since the person tends to neglect appropriate counsel and assistance.

A 66-year-old man was hospitalized repeatedly because of recurrent cardiac decompensation. A psychiatric consultation was requested. During the interview, the patient was in a jovial, expansive mood (denial of feelings of concern about his illness). He acknowledged the fact that he had a heart disease, but denied its importance. At one point, he leaned over and whispered with a mischievious look on his face "Every so often, I get away from here, go downtown, and treat myself to a hearty, salty steak." He opened the drawer of his nightstand and pointed with a chuckle, at a hidden salt shaker.

Closely related to denial is *rationalization*, a type of reasoning whereby true causal relationships are not recognized, minor aspects of a situation are emphasized out of proportion, or major aspects are minimized. Facts, conditions, or symptoms are ascribed to causes that are less threatening than the real ones.

A male patient, in his early 60's, had undergone a prostatectomy and bilateral orchiectomy because of cancer. When asked about his condition, he stated that "my testicles are not gone, they just pull up in here, or maybe they pool (sic) in here" (pointing to his groin).

The ineffectiveness of denial mechanisms may become apparent in several ways: worsening of physical illness, inability to rationalize away traumatic changes in the body, and so on. One interesting example showing the ineffectiveness of denial is the emergence of the denied phenomenon in dreams.

A woman, widowed for more than a year, said "I never look at my husband's pictures, or I would think of him all the time." She had been quite ambivalent about her husband. Since his death, she had a repetitive dream: "I see his casket in the ground. There is no soil on it, no dirt on it yet. The top of the casket is lifted up." The tenuous intrapsychic equilibrium also showed up in nightmares: "I am falling off the top of a building." Rather than heeding these warnings from within, she resorted to sleeping pills to bolster the denial attempts. When this failed, an agitated depression developed, which required hospitalization.

(c). *Depersonalization* is a mechanism that involves a protective blurring of ego boundaries. The usual distinction between self and notself becomes less clear and the result is a sense of estrangement from reality. The protective quality of depersonalization lies in the individual's feeling that "this experience is not really happening to me—it is just like a dream." If the emphasis is on external reality being different, the term derealization can be used.

A 64-year-old woman with several physical illnesses of a serious nature developed an acute trance-like confusion. After the confusion had cleared up, she described her experience as follows: "I felt like I was plumb gone, as if I was facing the end. I looked at my watch and saw that the face of my watch was black." This episode of unreality represented a dying experience: she was facing the end of herself (being plumb gone) and the end of time (the black face of the watch).

**(d).** *Externalization* and *internalization* involve a displacement and a blurring of boundary between the self and the not-self. The former is the mechanism by which one ascribes one's own undesirable condition, thoughts, or feelings to other people. The latter is the reverse process. By means of internalization a person may attribute to himself something that actually came from without.

A patient with lung cancer, told by his physician about the existence of metastases, said later "I am not sure what I was told; I think the idea of malignant spread was, after all, my own idea."

In externalization (or projection), the fact of a loss or illness cannot be ascribed to others unless mental disorganization is of psychotic proportion. Its occurrence suggests massive ego breakdown due to terminal processes.

A woman with terminal uremia thought that it was not she herself, but the nurse and her husband who were going to die.

A patient, terminally ill with leukemia, had the delusion that she was spreading a bad odor throughout the entire hospital.

Much more common is the projection of the cause of one's condition onto somebody or something external. It is as though the person says "it is nothing about me that makes me weak or less valuable, but you outsiders are responsible." Projection of feelings (*e.g.*, anger, envy) is very common. It causes a person to think that the people around him do not like him, not recognizing that the source of this hostility is inside of himself.

An 86-year-old man, living with his 84-year-old wife in a rest home, had been preoccupied with his loss of manhood. Contributing to his general sense of loss were his children's lack of interest, the sale of his home, and the loss of other belongings in a fire. He resented his financial dependency and required his wife to pin their spending money to her underwear. All expenditures needed his authorization. All the losses, however, appeared to converge into the overriding concern of losing his manhood and sexual potency. He then used projection to deal with this specific concern: he accused his wife of having an affair with the rest home operator.

Externalization may also be accomplished by displacement onto objects and situations which can serve as an external symbol of inner concerns, feelings, or drives. Thus, a *phobia* originates. Once the internal problem has become an external threat, *i.e.*, a phobia, the patient may feel in a position to cope, either by flight from the external threat, or, as in the case of counterphobic defenses, by fighting the external enemy.

## Defenses Aimed at Mastery and Control

Defenses aimed at mastery and control include intellectualization, isolation of feelings from thoughts, certain obsessive-compulsive mechanisms, overcompensation, and counterphobic defenses.

(a). *Intellectualization* and the separation of ideas from painful feelings associated with them (*i.e.*, *isolation*) represent attempts at mastery by reliance on a cognitive, intellectual approach. While obsessions usually refer to ideational phenomena, compulsions pertain to behavioral-motor manifestations.

(b). *Obsessive-compulsive* phenomena involve the mental mechanisms of reaction formation, undoing, and isolation. The following case illustrates some of these mechanisms.

A 62-year-old widow had been living with her married daughter for several years. The 9-year-old granddaughter, who had problems in school, was being seen by a counsellor who allegedly recommended that the grandmother would do well to leave the home. Shortly after this, the elderly woman became progressively withdrawn. She stopped taking baths, so that the adult daughter had to bathe her mother. The latter, however, refused to take her clothes off or be touched. She also refused to sit down for a meal, but would eat standing in a corner. She was picky about the food. She began holding her purse in her hand at all times. Finally, she started compulsive handwashing.

In trying to understand this behavior, it appeared that the idea of being-in-the-way was a core theme. The patient saw herself as somebody who did not belong, an untouchable. Hence, she tried to be inconspicuous, taking up minimal space by withdrawing, ready to go at a moment's notice (standing up to eat, not taking her clothes off, having her purse with her). By staying out of touch with others, she intended to stay out of their way and be allowed to stay. But her standing up during mealtime served as an ominous symbol of nemesis; and her complaints about the food also expressed her resentment about being mistreated. The compulsive handwashing represented her self image as being untouchable; it was a subtle but vindictive demonstration that she was given a dirty deal; and, it symbolized that she was taking her hands off them, and washing them in innocence.

Not infrequently, obsessive-compulsive phenomena occur in the context of depression, *e.g.*, involutional melancholia. Their psychodynamic significance depends on the individual case, but not uncommonly this involves attempts to maintain control over unacceptable aggressive or sexual impulses.

A 55-year-old woman complained of depression, a compelling urge to walk, a handwashing compulsion, and a "crazy feeling of wanting to rip off my clothes and go naked on the street." Her husband had gradually become disabled because of cardiac illness. He was now staying at home, doing housekeeping chores, and was no longer sexually interested in her. She was not aware of conscious anger at her husband. Instead, she was preoccupied with "these crazy ideas intruding in my mind like a foreign body—this is not like me—this urge to walk, rip off my clothes, getting irritated when my husband rhythmically pets—I mean taps—his foot."

*Obsessive doubting and indecision*, as well as *compulsive rituals* and ceremonies, may serve the ulterior motive of avoiding decisive action, stalling, and temporizing.

A 74-year-old woman had spent most of her life in a mental hospital. She was released when her schizophrenic symptomatology had become minimal, and was placed in a boarding home. The patient was still remarkably capable of grasping the intellectual, emotional, and social nuances inherent in her new existence. She verbalized regret that so much of her life had passed her by—"would it not be wonderful if [she] could do some catching up?" Soon after this, she began to spend hours in the toilet, refusing to come out even though others were waiting in line. She would also go shopping, spending all her time and energy trying to decide what to buy, but would come home empty-handed.

In this patient, both the toilet and the shopping behavior reflected her wish to temporize; if she could only make time stand still, her wish to make up for lost time in the past would come true.

Obsessive-compulsive mechanisms also may occur in aged persons caught in a regressive drift. With the ebbing away of their energy or resources, their life span and personal hygiene may progressively deteriorate. Compulsive rituals may emerge in a last effort to prevent the life space from decaying into a microslum. In such cases we see the evidence of breakdown scattered all over the place, with the individual concentrating on keeping one tiny detail straightened out.

(c). *Overcompensation* refers to behavioral patterns aimed at repairing deficiencies or overcoming shortcomings, real or imagined. The notion of overcompensation implies a surplus effort. This reminds us of *reaction formation*. In reaction formation, however, the aim is not repair of a deficiency, but sealing off repressed feelings or thoughts. Overcompensation and reaction formation both require the expenditure of considerable psychic energy; and for this reason they become increasingly inappropriate and maladaptive in the course of aging.

A 73-year-old woman had been married for 32 years to a man, ten years her junior. She had two years of college, while her husband never went beyond the fourth grade. At the age of eight, he had lost his left leg in an accident. Throughout their married life, she had supported him, and kept their age difference and his alcoholism a secret. At the age of 65, she refused to apply for financial assistance because of the lien law and wanting to keep her age a secret. Her pattern of excessive self-reliance was based on overcompensating for a self-image of being a weakling. (This negative identity had developed in early adolescence. During a routine physical examination, a heart murmur was discovered and she had been advised to get as much rest as possible, and to avoid dating, dances, etc. Her class mates had made fun of her handicap. After six years of a regimen of getting as much rest as possible, it turned out that the heart murmur was a functional one.) The patient was able to maintain an illusion of strength and dignity by means of this high energy defense until a series of traumatic events pulled the rug from under her. At the age of 68, because of cancer, she got a permanent colostomy. This also forced her to request financial aid for herself. One year later she had a mastectomy. Her sense of having lost strength was reflected by an ever increasing fear that her husband would leave her. Feelings of shame were revealed by her daily dress, a bedsheet. She refused to wear anything that might be insufficient for a complete coverup of her deformities. This idiosyncratic coverup turned her into a caricature (a reactivation of the negative identity during adolescence), and the patient, aware of failure all around, fell back on the next line of defense: projection. She accused her husband of stealing her money.

**(d).** Whereas in overcompensation, the source of the deficiency and the challenge posed by it is perceived to be inside, in the case of *counterphobic* mechanisms, the behavioral pattern is in response to a challenge outside. Thus, counterphobic behavior tends to be aimed at the mastery of a situational, external challenge. When the individual's resources are equal to the challenge, the stage is set for the possible accomplishment of unusual, impressive feats. But, when his resources decline as a result of the aging process, the counterphobic mechanisms become highly maladaptive, or self-destructive. These mechanisms also may play a role in the psychodynamics of certain paranoid states (see page 67).

### REFERENCES

1. ZETZEL, E. R.: Metapsychology of aging. *In:* Geriatric Psychiatry, M. A. Berezin and S. H. Cath, eds. International Universities Press, New York, 1965. pp. 109–119.
2. Lindemann, E.: Symptomatology and management of acute grief. *Am. J. Psychiatry* *101:* 141, 1944.
3. Cath, S.: Depletion and restitution. *In:* Geriatric Psychiatry, M. A. Berezin and S. H. Cath, eds. International Universities Press, New York, 1965. pp. 21–72.
4. Verwoerdt, A.: Psychopathological responses to the stress of physical illness. *Adv. Psychosom. Med. 8:* 92–114, 1972.
5. Verwoerdt, A.: Communication with the fatally ill. Charles C Thomas, Springfield, Illinois, 1966. pp. 59–60.

# 4

# organic brain syndromes

An organic brain syndrome consists of a characteristic symptomatology including impairments of orientation, memory, intellect, and judgement, as well as emotional lability or shallowness. It may be accompanied by disorders of affect and behavior, and the severity of these may be psychotic or nonpsychotic. The syndrome may be *acute* (reversible) or *chronic* (irreversible brain damage). When secondary to somatic illness, it tends to be reversible; a physical illness may also cause an acute exacerbation of an already existing chronic brain syndrome. Serial episodes of acute brain syndrome often represent a step-like progression to the chronic form.

The rate of organic brain syndrome, of moderate to severe degree, among the elderly population, is estimated at about 2.3 percent. Among aged individuals admitted to a psychiatric hospital or extended care facilities, the incidence is much higher. One survey showed that among old patients first admitted to a psychiatric institution, almost 80 percent received a diagnosis of organic brain syndrome, and less than 10 percent received the diagnosis of a functional psychosis. According to a 1964 survey, almost 90 percent of the resident population in nursing and boarding homes was 65 years or older; of these elderly residents, about two-thirds were considered to have organic brain syndrome (36 percent attributable to vascular pathology, and 30 percent attributable to senile dementia).[1]

There seems to be no consistent relationship between intellectual deterioration and organic brain changes. In one study, 20 percent of the patients with a diagnosis of senile psychosis had little or no senile plaque formation on autopsy examination, whereas moderate or severe senile plaque formation occurred in 9 percent of patients with a functional psychosis.[2]. In another investigation, no evidence of dementia was found in almost one-fourth of individuals who turned out to have severe brain atrophy. Although all patients with severe intellectual impairment had demonstrable cerebral atrophy, in some cases the extent of atrophy was less than what had been anticipated on the basis of neuropsychological test data.[3]

Obrist *et al.*[4] found that in a group of patients with presenile or senile dementia cerebral blood flow was normal in about one third of the cases.

Furthermore, demented patients may have a normal EEG, whereas aged individuals in apparently good psychological condition can have gross abnormalities in their EEG.[5] These discrepancies can be taken as evidence that multiple factors play an etiologic role in dementia and other organic brain syndromes.

## ETIOLOGY

Structural damage to the brain tends to be irreversible because neurons have limited recuperative capacity and do not reproduce. Structural alterations include a loss of neurons, and increase in senile plaques and the amount of neurofibrillary degeneration. Physiologically, there is a reduction in the metabolic activity of brain.

Although brain impairment is usually accompanied by deficits of those cognitive functions which depend on the intactness of the tissue involved, the pathogenic role of organic factors should not be overemphasized. Usually, multiple factors are operating, either simultaneously or as successive links in a cause-and-effect chain. These factors may be physical, psychological, or social and environmental, and may have various effects on each other. The outcome of such interactions is the formation of one or more vicious circles: one pathogenic process exerting a positive feedback effect on another. Hence, it is useful to consider organic brain syndrome as being sociopsychosomatic in origin and nature.[6].

In several types of organic brain syndrome, especially senile and presenile dementia, the etiology remains enigmatic. In other instances, *e.g.*, cerebral arteriosclerosis, the etiological factors are less obscure but this does not necessarily enhance the prospects for effective therapy. For example, certain drugs can increase cerebral blood flow under normal conditions but have little or no impact when cerebral atherosclerosis is present.[6]

### Physical Factors

Physical factors which may cause organic brain damage can be grouped in two major categories: (a) organic-cerebral and (b) extracerebral-somatic factors.

**(a). Organic-Cerebral Factors** include:

1. Trauma (*e.g.*, concussion, contusion, subarachnoid hemorrhage).
2. Infection (*e.g.*, tertiary syphilis, postencephalitic syndromes).
3. Neoplasm.
4. Metabolic deficiencies (*e.g.*, hypoglycemia, hypothyroidism, vitamin $B_{12}$ deficiency, etc.).
5. Chemical (toxins such as CO, lead, alcohol).
6. Drug-related (*e.g.*, CNS side effects of psychotropic drugs, the central anticholinergic syndrome).
7. Vascular (*e.g.*, atherosclerosis of cerebral arteries, cerebral thrombosis).
8. Atrophy and neuronal loss (*e.g.*, senile dementia, and presenile dementia [Alzheimer's and Pick's disease]).
9. Other: multiple sclerosis, amyotrophic lateral sclerosis.

**(b). Extracerebral-Somatic Factors.** Many diseases frequently occurring in old age can have an adverse effect on the brain, thereby causing a secondary organic brain syndrome. Physical illnesses which may interfere with brain function include cardiovascular and pulmonary disease. For example, elderly persons with cardiovascular disease have a high incidence of EEG abnormality,[7] and a greater decline in intellectual function.[8] Other somatic disorders may be metabolic, *e.g.*, diabetes, uremia, and other electrolyte disturbances.

Physical factors that may interfere with brain metabolism can be classified as follows:

**1. Decreased Supply of Oxygen.**
—*Hypoxic hypoxia:* low ambient oxygen, respiratory depression, pulmonary diseases.
—*Anemic hypoxia:* various anemias.
—*Ischemic hypoxia:* hypotension, insufficient pulse pressure, arteriosclerosis of vessels supplying blood to the brain, (especially carotid arteries).

**2. Decreased Supply of Glucose.**
—*Essential hypoglycemia.*
—*Insulin*-related decrease.

**3. Decreased Utilization of Essential Brain Nutrients.**
—*Drug-related decrease:* barbituates interfere with the cerebral metabolism of oxygen and glucose.
—*Vitamin* deficiencies: *e.g.*, vitamin B$_{12}$.
—*Metabolic* disorders: *e.g.*, hypothyroidism, diabetes, alcoholism.
—*Electrolyte* disturbances: dehydration; acidosis and alkalosis; uremia.

The metabolic disturbances in the brain may, in turn, lead to anatomic-structural brain damage. It is because of the latter that it is so important to diagnose as quickly as possible, any physical factors which could interfere with brain function. By treating such physical diseases one may prevent the development of permanent brain damage.

### Psychological Factors

**(a). Premorbid Personality.** The possible existence of a link between certain premorbid personality traits (compulsiveness, aggressiveness, rigidity) and an increased vulnerability to dementia is mentioned by several authors. Patients whose premorbid personality is characterized by versatility in adaptation tend to have relatively less intellectual impairment in association with a certain amount of cerebral neuronal loss.[9, 10] It is indeed reasonable to expect that any premorbid behavioral style involving aggressive and high energy defenses is especially vulnerable to the psychotrauma of loss of mastery (resulting from organic brain changes); and that compulsive, rigid individuals are prone to react with profound anxiety when faced with the necessity of changing their habitual style and accommodating themselves to ego-alien constraints.

**(b). Psychodynamic Aspects.** The stress of intellectual decline produces the immediate response of anxiety and mobilizes specific defenses. The latter are often precisely those defenses whose continued operation is being threatened. Thus, the aggressive, ambitious person may try to defend against the threat of loss of control by becoming even more aggressive and controlling; likewise, the compulsive person may become more rigid and set in his usual ways. Inasmuch as the patient tries to meet the threat head on, there will be more opportunities to experience failure. The emotional distress is compounded by more anxiety and frustrating helplessness, as well as feelings of shame and anger. A second vicious circle is set in motion when auxiliary defenses, such as projection, are called into action. When this entails accusatory behavior, the patient may alienate the very persons whose support is vital. If, on the other hand, he tries to cope by withdrawal, the net effect will be similar: again the loss of external support, this time by being out of reach. Still other vicious circles may be set in motion, linking up with those already there and adding to their momentum. The combination of persisting high energy defenses, intensifying negative emotions, and weakening environmental support, sets the stage for another systems breakdown, e.g., a new physical illness.

In other individuals, the course of events is less stormy, because they use defenses that are less harmful, such as mild or moderate degrees of regression or denial. Some patients are almost naive in their attempts to deny. For example, they may respond to a question from the interviewer by saying, "I never learned that in school" (offering an alibi). Others are somewhat more sophisticated; e.g., "Let's see now, what was it you asked me? Oh, yes, well, I often ask myself the same thing.—What do you think yourself, doctor?" (turning the tables). A third type tries to cover up the deficit by beating around the bush: by circumlocution, he is stalling and temporizing. Or, a patient may smile and wave with his hand—a waiver of the question—and say "This is not important. I already answered that yesterday." Thus, the ways and means of denial are legion, and they often strike the audience as funny, prompting giggles or laughter. The patient may then join in and feel off the hook: he is learning that being funny is one way to escape disaster.

The disaster dreaded is that particular situation of failure referred to as the catastrophic condition. The catastrophic reaction tends to occur especially in patients with impairment of abstract capacity. According to Goldstein, the catastrophic condition is not a conscious awareness of, and reaction to the failure, but rather belongs intrinsically to the overall situation of the organism-in-failure.[11] This represents a total systems failure and the collapse of all homeostatic mechanisms. In this disintegration of the personality as an intact organism, the anxiety experienced is in the nature of nameless terror (the primary anxiety, or traumatic anxiety in psychoanalytic terminology). Because of the risk of this devastating experience, the patient's defenses should be handled gingerly. (For an illustrative clinical example, see page 203.)

## Social and Economic Factors

Dementia relates to many social factors including family organization housing conditions, type of household, social outlets, and so on.[5] The common denominators for most of these are economic status and level of education. Elderly persons of low socioeconomic status tend to have more physical illness, which is associated with inadequate housing, nutrition, and medical care, as well as lack of social contacts. Social isolation, commonly associated with chronic illness, facilitates regression and withdrawal which, in turn, contribute to the development of intellectual deterioration. These elderly persons, especially when their health is poor and they live alone, have a low level of morale. Consequently, the low socioeconomic status frequently predisposes to an early onset and a rapid rate of intellectual decline.[1]

## Environmental and Situational Factors

Because of difficulties in perception, comprehension, and memory, as well as slowness in psychomotor skills, aged persons become more sensitive to environmental changes. Relatively minor alterations, such as a shift in household arrangements or family relationships, can cause severe psychological upsets. The brain is the organ of adaptation, and whether it is in a state of compensation or decompensation depends on the demands made on it. Cardiac status, by way of analogy, may decompensate when the input presented or the output demanded exceeds the heart's potential for work. Likewise, the brittle brain status of an old person may decompensate because of changes in the input or the output.

(a). *Abnormal Sensory Input* may be quantitative or qualitative in nature.

1. *Quantitative* input changes include:

—sensory overload, i.e., an increase in the amount of stimuli reaching the aged brain, e.g., chronic overcrowding of a three-generational family in a small dwelling. Another example is the acute sensory overload experienced by an old person who is hospitalized for the first time in his life, undergoes a battery of examinations and tests by many specialists, then is operated on, all within a few days.

—sensory underload, i.e., an undue decrease in the number of stimuli (exteroceptive, proprioceptive, kinesthetic, etc.) reaching the central nervous system via afferent pathways.

These quantitative changes can be chronic or acute, abrupt or insidious, or of minor or major proportions. Sensory deprivation or social isolation may be imposed on the individual (*e.g.*, being alone in the hospital room; having the eyes covered following cataract surgery); the changes may be the outcome of life-long ego-syntonic character traits (*e.g.*, the isolation which the schizoid prefers); or, they may be the consequence of major psychopathology (*e.g.*, self-absorption in severe depression).

2. *Qualitative changes* in the input pertain to exposure to unfamiliar stimuli, *e.g.*, sudden transfer of elderly persons from their homes to an institution.

(b). In addition, it is possible for the brain to decompensate because of *changes in the output*. The latter include quantitative or qualitative changes pertaining to the individual's behavior activities or motor patterns, changes in the demands of performance and work, and modifications in coping techniques (*e.g.*, exhaustion from manic hyperactivity).

**(c).** Inasmuch as the brain, in our cybernetic schema, is interposed between the sensory input and the motor output, the term *throughput* can be used to refer to the "black box" function of the CNS. Disturbances in the throughput (apart from organic brain changes) may develop on the basis of progressive accumulation of disturbing emotions. Accumulating anxiety and tension may produce a neuronal turmoil, which reduces the homeostatic and information processing capacity of the brain. When the status of the brain is already borderline, any further decrease of its efficiency is enough to tip the balance toward decompensation.

The clinical manifestations of such cerebral decompensation are similar to those of an acute OBS. When such acute confusion states have been precipitated by environmental changes or transient internal pressures, however, it would be appropriate to speak of a functional brain syndrome, rather than an organic brain syndrome.

## EVALUATION

### Physical Methods

#### (a). Organic-Cerebral Factors.

1. A brain biopsy is the only procedure which permits direct examination of brain tissue *in vivo*. Yet, even such *histopathological* techniques do not always provide conclusive information.[12]

2. A definitive diagnosis of cerebral atrophy depends on *pneumoencephalographic evidence*, which is usually present in senile and presenile dementia.[13] The injection of air into the subarachnoid space permits clear outline of the ventricular system, thus providing information about the extent of cortical atrophy.

*Echoencephalography* employs high-frequency, ultrasonic waves and is less traumatic than pneumoencephalography. It is useful to demonstrate a midline shift (caused by a space-occupying lesion, or unilateral cerebral edema), and to measure the size of the ventricles. The width of the third ventricle is greater in persons aged 70 or older, than in young adults (a mean of 7.0 *versus* 5.0 mm).[14]

3. *Nuclear diagnostic techniques*, *e.g.*, the radioactive iodinated serum albumen (RISA) scan, make it possible to measure the rate of supracortical absorption of radioactive substances injected into the cerebrospinal fluid of the lumbar subarachnoid space. This is of special value in detecting so-called normal pressure hydrocephalus. In the case of a true hydrocephalus, a ventriculo-peritoneal shunt may be helpful. However, poor absorption is not a clear indication for such operations, especially when brain syndrome is of long duration.

*Static brain scanning* involving the use of radioactive materials (*e.g.*, technetium 99) has some value as a screening test. It is indicated when a localized lesion, such as a metastatic tumor or subdural hematoma, is suspected. The *dynamic brain scan* involves the intravenous injection of a radioactive substance. Uptake and flow of patterns of radioactive dye are recorded on tape and played back through programmed computers. Dynamic brain scanning makes it possible to pick up gross deficiencies in blood flow of major arteries.

**4. Cerebral Metabolism and Blood Flow.** Since the brain obtains its energy mostly from aerobic oxidation of glucose, cerebral metabolism is reflected by the rates of oxygen and glucose utilization. In old persons with good physical and mental health, the values of cerebral oxygen consumption and blood flow are similar to those in healthy younger persons.[15]

—*The cerebral uptake of oxygen* (represented by the difference between the amount of oxygen in arterial blood and that in the internal jugular vein) is a reliable indicator of oxygen utilzation only when the cerebral blood flow is constant.

—Methods for measureing *cerebral blood flow* depend on a diffusible indicator, usually an inert gas administered by inhalation. Its uptake by, or clearance from the brain is determined by monitoring intracranially in the case of a radioactive indicator. The inhalation method using [133]xenon is not traumatic but less reliable than other techniques.[16]

—*Regional cerebral blood flow* can be measured by inhalation of a radioactive inert gas, and provides specific information about different areas of the brain. Metabolism and blood flow in specific regions of the brain may differ greatly under normal circumstances, and likewise, in pathological conditions.

—By means of *cerebral angiograms*, it is possible to determine the location of space-occupying lesions. Cerebral angiography, by way of injecting radio-opaque compounds in the brachial or carotid artery, permits the visualization of the entire cerebro-vascular network, the measurement of ventricular size, and the estimation of cortical atrophy.

**5. Electroencephalography.**

—The incidence of abnormal EEG's is higher in elderly persons with brain disorders than those with psychogenic disorders. Among hospitalized elderly patients, EEG abnormalities are very common. Patients with diffuse slowing in the EEG are more likely to remain hospitalized and have a shorter life expectancy than those with a normal EEG. These abnormalities consist of *diffuse slow activity* in the theta or delta range and are probably attributable to reduced metabolic activity. Usually, the EEG abnormalities correlate well with the severity of intellectual and clinical deterioration. However, the EEG may be normal in patients with definite organic brain syndrome, and old persons apparently in good psychological health may show abnormalities in their EEG.[5, 17]

—Other common EEG abnormalities are *focal disturbances* which seem to appear first during middle age. With advancing age, their incidence increases. They usually consist of slow wave activity, mostly over the left anterior temporal region. Although such focal disturbances are not uncommon in organic brain syndromes (*e.g.*, because of arteriosclerosis or neoplasm), they may persist for several years without manifest symptomatology. But there is some evidence that aged persons with such foci undergo a faster rate of decline in verbal intelligence than those without such foci. Decline in performance abilities tends to be associated with diffuse slowing in the occipital rhythm or decreased blood flow in the left parietal cortex. Decline in verbal abilities tends to be related to focal EEG disturbances in the left anterior temporal region.[5, 17]

Because the EEG changes are not pathognomonic and because of the wide variations among old persons of comparable age and health, a single EEG tracing has limited value. On the other hand, serial EEG's are quite useful, especially to follow up patients suspected of having a brain syndrome. Healthy old persons with consistently normal EEG do not show an intellectual decline over a period of several years. Finally, in order to demonstrate any relationships between neurophysiological factors (EEG, CBF, etc.) and intellectual variables, it is necessary to control for sociocultural differences, to assess the verbal and performance aspects of intelligence separately, and to use specific procedures for the evaluation of particular regions of the brain.[18]

**(b).** *Somatic-extracerebral aspects* include all the physical factors and somatic illnesses which secondarily affect brain function, and in the course of time may produce brain damage. They include disorders which may be endocrine, metabolic, or nutritional, systemic infection, intoxication with drugs or alcohol, and so on. The prompt diagnosis and treatment of these somatic conditions is important, as was already emphasized, and often requires consultation with the internist, neurologist, or other specialists.

### Neuropsychological Aspects

Psychological testing may be more sensitive than clinical examination in demonstrating intellectual or perceptual impairment. Although these impairments usually indicate the presence of brain damage, they cannot be directly related to the location or extent of the pathological process. An impaired intellectual function may be the result from any one of a number of anatomical or physiological abnormalities in the brain.[19] The efficacy of neuropsychological test procedures is limited by the level of the patient's motivation, the consistency and scope of his attention span, the degree of his anxiety, and various defensive responses *vis-à-vis* the test situation. The psychological test data must be viewed in the light of such factors and must be interpreted in a framework that takes into consideration the clinical history, psychiatric examination, laboratory data, and so on.

Among the aged, intellectual decline is so common that intelligence tests must be evaluated with a corrective factor for age. An old person is expected to have a verbal ability of 7 to 27 percent below that of a young adult and a performance ability of 26 to 50 percent below that of a young adult. Most intellectual abilities seem to reach a peak in early adulthood and then gradually decline.[20] Verbal abilities and stored information show relatively little deficit, in contrast to psychomotor skills, especially those involving speed and perceptual-integrative abilities.[21] This increasing discrepancy between verbal and performance abilities can be used to indicate the degree of intellectual deterioration. Generalizations about age-related decline of intellect, however, are usually based on cross-sectional studies. Longitudinal studies, on the other hand, indicate that intellectual changes within a given age group show considerable individual variation.[22]

## Behavioral Manifestations

On the basis of psychiatric history and mental status examination, it may be feasible to differentiate types of organic brain syndrome (*e.g.*, senile dementia, cerebral arteriosclerosis), especially in cases of rather severe brain damage. But in patients with brain impairment of mild to moderate degree, the anamnesis and the mental status may not be sufficient to make a certain diagnosis, and auxiliary diagnostic techniques will be required.

Specific refinements of, and additions for the psychiatric examination of elderly patients have been developed.[23] The issue of reliable behavioral rating scales has particular relevance for clinical research projects aimed at evaluating responses to psychotropic drugs.[24]

(a). *Sensorium* refers to the extent that a person is capable of utilizing data from his sense organs. If the sensorium is intact, the individual is attentive and alert to his environment. If the sensorium is not intact, consciousness may be clouded and the person may be confused. In severe cases, there is stupor and coma.

(b). *Orientation* is the process by which a person uses sense data (from internal and external origins) to gain information about the spatio-temporal characteristics of his whereabouts, the position he occupies in his milieu, and how and why he came to be there. For orientation to be intact, the sense organs must provide a minimum of sensory input, to be integrated centrally in an intact brain (apperception). Thus, disorientation can be caused by peripheral or central factors, or by a combination of both.

(c). *Attention is* the ability to focus in an alert way on a particular phenomenon. This ability depends, among other things, on the state of consciousness. A disturbed sensorium leads to a disturbance in attention, *e.g.*, inability to concentrate, distractibility. Attention may also be affected by intense emotional states. In severe depression, for example, there may be intense preoccupation with depressive thought content.

A professional woman in her mid-50's was admitted to the mental hospital with the diagnosis of presenile dementia. Before this admission, she had spent several weeks in a university-affiliated hospital, where she had undergone numerous tests and examinations. The primary symptomatology which had prompted hospitalization consisted of a profound inability to concentrate and shortened attention span. As a result, she began to make more and more mistakes in her work which involved a great deal of abstract thought and delicate judgement. Since the patient was clearly not depressed, organicity was suspected right from the beginning. Having undergone a thorough checkup in the university-affiliated hospital, the patient was finally told that her condition was "irreversible, and was a case of premature aging." She was then transferred to a nearby state mental hospital, with the diagnosis of presenile dementia. It so happened that the alert internist of the state hospital began to pursue some leads along a pathway that eventually established the diagnosis of myxedema. Immediately after the patient began to receive thyroid replacement therapy, her "senility" cleared up. Commenting in retrospect on her initial symptoms of impaired concentration and attention, the patient stated: "It was not like me to be that way. That problem in concentrating came over me, as something foreign, that was not part of me. I was too weak to resist it." Such a discrepancy between an intact observing ego on the one hand, and a specific severe mental impairment on the other hand, would indicate an organic brain syndrome other than (presenile or senile) dementia.

(d). *Perceptual abnormalities* include illusions and hallucinations. An illusion is a misinterpretation of an actual stimulus. Such perceptual distortions frequently occur in acute confusional states and other psychiatric disorders, but are also occasionally experienced by normal individuals. Hallucinations are perceptual experiences in the apparent absence of external stimuli, and indicate the existence of a psychosis. When examining the patient in this respect, it would not be wise to simply conclude that a patient is hallucinating when he reports that he sees or hears things. One should also ascertain to what extent imagination or perceptual imagery play a role. This can be done by inquiring whether the visions or voices are inside the patient's head—inside of him—or whether he perceives them as coming from outside of himself. In the case of visual and auditory imagery, the perceptual experiences are felt to be inside; they can be evoked and dismissed at will. Hallucinations, on the other hand, are not evoked and dismissed voluntarily.

In some cases, one can observe the following pathogenesis of a hallucinatory experience. The patient may have certain age-related changes in perception and alterations in sensory modality, such as paresthesias. For example, a dry skin may cause itching—"as if ants are crawling over my skin." When the patient undergoes regression, the abstract capacity may be replaced by concrete thinking. As a result, the metaphor becomes the real thing. What was figurative becomes literal. Thus, the sensory experience is expressed in a literal, concrete form: "ants are crawling over my skin."

(e). The capacity of *memory* includes the ability to register, store, and retrieve information. Learning, the storing of new information, is related to the intactness of memory capability. Memory disturbances may result from impaired registration, retention, or retrieval of stored information. *Confabulations*, a form of paramnesia, are products of fantasy being substituted for memory gaps. These accounts of past experiences may be rather fantastic, like a fable; hence the name confabulations. Confabulations, frequently colored by wishful thinking, occur in Korsakov's syndrome (an organic brain syndrome caused by vitamine B deficiency usually associated with chronic alcoholism) and in presbyophrenia (a form of senile dementia).

A 74-year-old man had suffered a stroke when he was 55 years. Since then he had been moderately disabled because of hemiplegia. He had been able to walk with a cane until recently, when he had become so infirm that he was confined to bed or wheelchair. All these years, he wife had taken care of him, accepting their fate with courage and matter-of-factness. But her matter-of-factness, which had served both of them so well and so long, became a focal point for periodic friction. Whenever the patient would boast that he had gone for a walk around the block (a reassuring confabulation), she would correct him by pointing out the facts of the matter. Thereupon the patient, usually a mild-mannered man, would angrily repeat his boastful assertion.

1. *Recent recall* is tested by asking the patient to remember something (a word, number, or name). After a while, *e.g.*, one to five minutes, the patient is asked to reproduce the item. Recent memory can be further tested by asking questions, such as: Where do you live? How long have you lived there? How long have you been here? Where were you one week ago? How many meals did you have today? What did you have for breakfast? What is my name? When did you see me for the first time? Have you been in this room before?

2. *Remote memory* can be tested by asking the following type of questions: Where were you born? Where did you go to school? What was the highest grade you completed? How old were you when you finished school? How old were you when you began working? What was the name of your first employer? Who was U. S. President when you began your first job?

Kahn and Goldfarb[23] introduced a Mental Status Questionnaire consisting of ten questions that pertain to orientation for time, place, and person; recent and remote memory; and general information. The patient's performance is scored in terms of the number of wrong answers. The error scores seem to be a reliable indicator of the degree of organicity (Table 1).

(f). Another approach is the *Face-Hand Test* (FHT), a series of double simultaneous stimulations of the face and hand.[25] Failure to correctly report touch on the back of the hand is presumptive of cortical neuronal loss. The patient, his hands resting on his knees, sits facing the examiner. He is touched simultaneously on one cheek and the dorsum of one hand, in a specific order. The Face-Hand Test is done first with the patient's eyes closed, then repeated with eyes open. Anxious persons may make more errors with eyes open than with eyes closed. In 80 percent of persons who make errors with the eyes closed there is no improvement with eyes open. In the four initial trials the patient gets used to the procedure. In the teaching trials, 5 and 6, the examiner informs the patient where he is touched, or reinforces a correct response by saying "that's right." A person who learns to report correctly where he is touched after trials 5 and 6 is presumed free of brain damage. Only errors on steps 7 through 10 (which are a repeat of 1 to 4) are considered presumptive of brain

TABLE 1. *Mental Status Questionnaire (MSQ)**

| 1. Where are we now? | Orientation for place |
|---|---|
| 2. Where is this place located? | Orientation for place |
| 3. What is the day of month? | Orientation for time |
| 4. What month is it? | Orientation for time |
| 5. What year is it? | Orientation for time |
| 6. How old are you? | Memory—recent or remote |
| 7. When is your birthday? | Memory—recent or remote |
| 8. What year were you born? | Memory—recent or remote |
| 9. Who is president of the U. S.? | General information—memory |
| 10. Who was president before him? | General information—memory |

Rating of MSQ

| Number of errors | Chronic brain syndrome |
|---|---|
| 0–2 | absent–mild |
| 3–5 | mild–moderate |
| 6–8 | moderate–severe |
| 9–10 | severe |

* Modified from Kahn *et al.*[23] Reprinted by permission of the American Psychiatric Association and the authors.

damage. Major changes in score upon repeat testing are rare when chronic brain syndrome is present. However, in acute brain syndrome the score may vary over a short period of time.

Errors include not reporting the touch to the hand (extinction); localizing the hand touch to the cheek, the knee, or elsewhere (displacement); pointing to the examiner's hand (projection); or pointing outside in space (exsomesthesia). The test results correlate with the degree of brain syndrome as measured by the MSQ or psychiatric evaluation. Extinction of the touch to the face is rare and suggests a functional disorder (Table 2).

## DIFFERENTIAL DIAGNOSIS

### Psychogenic *versus* Organic Disorders

A categorical dichotomy between organic and psychogenic conditions is theoretically not justified, and clinically not useful. There has been a tendency to regard some patients as "organic," and others as "psychogenic," and to reserve one's therapeutic zeal for the latter. In reality, organic and psychogenic factors are operating in each individual patient, and both sets of factors can be treated with varying degrees of success. The therapeutic management of one aspect should not be held up until completing the treatment of other aspects. Rather, all pathogenic factors need to be treated simultaneously.

(a). **Psychological Reactions with Organic Brain Syndrome.** Impairment of brain tissue may or may not be associated with psychological disorders. For example, organic brain syndrome, attributable to cerebral

TABLE 2. *Sequence of Stimulation in Face-Hand Test*\*

| | |
|---|---|
| 1. Right cheek—left hand | Initial trials. Response evaluated in context |
| 2. Left cheek—right hand | of further trials. |
| 3. Right cheek—right hand | |
| 4. Left cheek—left hand | |
| | |
| 5. Right cheek—left cheek | Teaching trials. Usually reported correctly. Examiner |
| 6. Right hand—left hand | informs, or reinforces response that there were two touches. |
| | |
| 7. Right cheek—left hand | Brain damage suggested by: |
| 8. Left cheek—right hand | —Incorrect response and stimulation not |
| 9. Right cheek—right hand | reported; |
| 10. Left cheek—left hand | —felt but displaced; |
| | —projected or located in space. |

\* From Goldfarb.[25] Reprinted by permission of Grune & Stratton, Inc. and the author.

arteriosclerosis, could be associated with neurotic depressive reaction, or with psychotic depression, or with behavioral disorder, as the case may be. The patient with cerebral arteriosclerosis is usually aware of his loss of mental powers and reacts with feelings of depression. Attempts to defend onseself against the threat of disintegration are sometimes facilitated by anosognosia. This is a rare case of brain damage in which the patient "does not know, and knows not that he knows not," and even major physical defects, such as hemiparesis, may not come to conscious awareness.

Psychotic reactions commonly seen with chronic brain syndrome are paranoid states and depressions, with or without agitation. The involutional types of depressions with guilt feelings, rumination over previous failures, suicidal tendencies, and so on, rarely occur in conjunction with CBS. It is almost as if a brain-damaged person does not possess the resources for the elaboration of complex psychological modes of reaction. Nevertheless, under the pressures of illness and pain, suicidal tendencies may occur, and this risk is especially great in elderly male patients.

**(b). Psychogenic Depression.** Depression in senescence is frequently overlooked because it does not always follow the same clinical picture as depression in younger ages. The affective manifestations such as sad feelings, self-depreciatory thoughts, crying spells, and so on, are frequently inconspicuous whereas psychomotor retardation, impairment of attention and memory, somatic symptoms, and loss of energy and initiative are more prominent. Such manifestations can easily be mistaken as being of organic origin. At times, only a therapeutic trial with antidepressant or electroconvulsive treatment may help to clarify it. All too often, an elderly patient who is essentially depressed receives the diagnosis of organic brain syndrome, after admission to the hospital, and is then treated accordingly. The result is that the patient begins to conform to the attitudes of his environment; *i.e.*, he will start behaving more and more like a senile patient.

TABLE 3.

Differential Diagnosis of Organic Brain Syndromes

| Factors | Depressive psychosis | Cerebral arteriosclerosis | Senile dementia | Alzheimer's disease | Pick's disease |
|---|---|---|---|---|---|
| Usual age of onset | any age | 55–70 average: 65 | 70+ average: 75 | 50–60 average: 56 | 45–55 average: 50 |
| Sex distribution | early life: more women late life: more men | men–women = 3:1 | men–women = 2:3 | men–women = 2:3 | men–women = 2:3 |
| Duration | varies from weeks to years | varies from days to many years average: 4 yr | varies from months to years average: 5 yr | average: 4 yr | average: 4 yr |
| Mode of onset | gradual or sudden; precipitating stress often apparent | gradual or acute | insidious | more sudden and less gradual than S.D. | slow and insidious |
| Course | self-limited, but with tendency to recur | intermittent, fluctuating | slowly or rapidly progressive | rapidly progressive | progressive and fatal |
| Prognosis | responsive to drugs or ECT | varies depending on multiple factors | poor (in moderate or severe cases) | very poor | very poor |
| Outcome | usually recovery; sometimes suicide or regression to paranoid level | death from CVA, heart disease, or infection | death from general organismic failure, or infection | | |
| Hereditary and precipitating factors | involution; previous history of depression | some familial tendency | multiple genetically determined factors | multifactorial inheritance, genetic factors causing premature aging | heredo-degenerative process |

TABLE 4.

Differential Diagnosis of Organic Brain Syndromes

| Factors | Depressive psychosis | Cerebral arteriosclerosis | Senile dementia | Alzheimer's disease | Pick's disease |
|---|---|---|---|---|---|
| Signs of brain damage | none | diffuse or focal | diffuse, generalized | diffuse, generalized more severe than in S. D. | circumscribed atrophy; frontal, temporal, or parietal lobes |
| Impairment of higher cortical functions | no structural impairment | some isolated impairments, e.g., aphasia, apraxia, agnosia | progressive dementia | involvement of cerebral associative areas; transcortical aphasia, agnosia, apraxia, etc. | focal cortical impairments, e.g., motor or sensory aphasia |
| Neuromuscular | psychomotor retardation or agitation | paralyses; minor extrapyramidal signs | tremors, uncertain gait, variable muscular rigidity; incontinence | transient or progressive paresis; unsteady gait; increased muscle tone; occasional tremors; incontinence | primitive reflexes; extrapyramidal signs; attacks of muscular hypotonia; incontinence |
| Seizures | none | epileptiform attacks | rare | occasional | rare |
| Medical | physiological concomitants of depression (sleep, appetite, weight, energy) | common history of CVA; headaches, dizziness & syncope (in 50%); "little strokes"; arteriosclerosis in heart, kidney, legs, etc. | infections, contractures, fractures, decubitus | infections, contractures, fractures, decubitus | infections, contractures, fractures, decubitus |

TABLE 5.

Differential Diagnosis of Organic Brain Syndromes

| Neuropathology | Depressive psychosis | Cerebral arteriosclerosis | Senile dementia | Alzheimer's disease | Pick's disease |
|---|---|---|---|---|---|
| Macroscopic | none characteristic | large or small areas of softening and hemorrhage | diffuse generalized shrinkage of brain, especially gray matter; dilated ventricles; internal hydrocephalus | general cerebral atrophy; dilated ventricles; internal hydrocephalus | circumscribed lobar atrophy, mostly orbito-frontal and temporal |
| Microscopic | none characteristic | granular atrophy of cortex diffusely with hypertensive cardiovascular disease; destruction of neurons, nerve fibers and glia; focal neuronal & selective cortical degeneration; | neuronal degeneration and shrinking; most damage in upper layers of cortex; deposition of lipofuscin & intracellular fibrils; | diffuse loss of neurons, especially in cortex layers 3 & 5; disturbed cortical layers; neuron degeneration: pyknosis, granulovacuolar, Alzheimer's neurofibrillary change; | progressive atrophy of neurons; no predilection for cortical layers; neuron degeneration, increased pigment, pyknosis; swollen cells; argyrophilic cytoplasmic inclusions; |
| | | secondary gliosis; | moderate gliosis, especially in outer layer of cortex; | gliosis more severe than in S.D.; | gliosis prominent; |
| | | senile plaques not typical | senile plaques | senile plaques throughout cortex | senile plaques rare |
| Vascular | none characteristic | Vascular: large arteries: atherosclerosis small vessels: endothelial proliferation; medial hypertrophy; intima hyalinization | endothelial degeneration; media fibrosis; adventitial proliferation; vascular loops | degenerative changes of endothelial and adventitial cells | endothelial proliferation; hyaline degeneration |

TABLE 6.

Differential Diagnosis of Organic Brain Syndromes

| Psychiatric symptomatology (I) | Depressive psychosis | Cerebral arteriosclerosis | Senile dementia | Alzheimer's disease | Pick's disease |
|---|---|---|---|---|---|
| Orientation | intact, except in depressive stupor | episodes of acute confusion; lucid intervals | progressive disorientation in all spheres; loss of time perspective | | |
| Perception | occasional auditory hallucinations | auditory and visual hallucinations during acute exacerbations | various types of hallucinations in advanced stages | occasional hallucinations | |
| Intellect and thought | no mental impairment; delusions consistent with affect; insight varies | lacunar types of intellectual deficit; delusions rare; insight present in early stages | progressive, generalized dementia; delusions depend on degree of regression and premorbid personality; no insight | progressive dementia & loss of abstraction; aphasia, alexia, agnosia, asymbolia, agraphia, apraxia; no insight | *Frontal lobe* syndrome: progressive loss of abstraction; *Aphasic* syndrome: aphasia, alexia, etc. *Alogic* syndrome: agnosia, apraxia, etc.; no insight |
| Memory | transient memory problems due to C.N.S. slowing | varying deficits of recent & remote memory, of retention & recall; confabulations rare | progressive impairment of all memory functions; confabulations in presbyophrenic type | progressive impairment of all memory functions; confabulations rare | progressive impairment of all memory functions; confabulations common |

TABLE 7.

Differential Diagnosis of Organic Brain Syndromes

| Psychiatric Symptomatology (II) | Depressive psychosis | Cerebral arteriosclerosis | Senile dementia | Alzheimer's disease | Pick's disease |
|---|---|---|---|---|---|
| Affect | depression; guilt; low self-esteem | emotional lability; anxiety and depression; later, blunting of affect | depends on subtype—simple: apathy depressed: agitation delirious: anxiety paranoid: hostility presbyophrenic: shallow euphoria | variable at first; later, apathy | apathy and indifference |
| Psychomotor | retardation; sometimes, agitation | hypoactive or hyperactive or restless agitation | hyperactive or hypoactive, or restless agitation | hyperactive; repetitive, primitive motor behavior; extrapyramidal signs | hypo- or hyperkinetic; primitive reflexes; stereotyped activ. perseveration; echolalia; logoklony |
| Personality changes | transient regressive changes | regressive changes are intermittent or slowly progressive | progressive deterioration of social behavior and personal habits | | |

**(c). Schizophrenia.** The symptomatology of chronic schizophrenia may be almost indistinguishable from senile dementia. In both conditions, regressive changes may produce apparently similar disorders in thought, affect, perception, and psychomotor abilities. But similar symptomatology does not imply an identical pathogenesis. The schizophrenic patient has his neuronal equipment still intact but he makes no use of it. The patient with organic brain syndrome has suffered damage of his equipment, and much as he would want to use it, it would be of no use. In the case of the schizophrenic, proper therapy may reverse the patient's regression to the point where he again begins to make use of his mental faculties.

**(d). Dissociative States (Hysterical Psychoses).** These are included in the category of hysterical disorders. In a dissociative state, psychological conflicts may result in apparent personality disorganization. Repressed, unacceptable impulses, wishes, or fantasies may find expression or are acted out, during a state of altered consciousness. Clinical manifestations of the dissociative state include depersonalization, stupor, trance states, and hysterical fugues. Typically, there is amnesia for the dissociative episode. Often it is difficult to draw the line between neurosis and psychosis. The differential diagnosis of hysterical dissociation includes temporal lobe epilepsy and other types of organic brain syndrome which involve an alteration of consciousness.

A man in his 60's was hospitalized in a state of stupor. He would not respond to questions, and was, in fact, mute. Although there was extreme restriction in psychomotor activity, the few movements which he did perform were not remarkably slowed. The behavioral response to any question was stereotypical: he would lie down on his bed, cross his hands over his chest, and close his eyes. It was obvious, from occasional eye contact, that the patient was aware of what went on around him. But his consciousness and attention seemed to be focused exclusively on one point. The nature of these ideas could be inferred from his ritual behavior—acting out a fantasy of being dead. The patient's trance-like behavior, the narrowing of his consciousness onto one exclusive thought, and the enactment of the fantasy of being dead suggested the diagnosis of dissociative reaction (hysterical psychosis). It would not have been incorrect to make the diagnosis of a psychotic depression, but the point is that the depression presented itself in the form of an hysterical psychosis (*i.e.*, profound personality disorganization, an altered state of consciousness, and the acting out of a dominant fantasy). Electric shock treatment in this case resulted in immediate improvement.

## Primary *versus* Secondary Organic Brain Syndrome

This is an important differential diagnosis because secondary organic brain syndrome, *i.e.*, caused by extracerebral-somatic factors, can usually be ameliorated by active treatment of the primary physical illness. In addition, timely treatment of acute organic brain syndrome will prevent the development of permanent brain damage.

## Types of Primary Organic Brain Syndrome

(a). *Cerebral arteriosclerosis* is a chronic brain syndrome associated with episodes of focal brain damage, frequently cerebral thrombosis or carotid artery occlusion. Vasopastic episodes, cerebral anoxemia, hypotensive crises in hypertensive patients, or cardiac failure may also be responsible. Massive cerebral hemorrhage rarely causes chronic brain syndrome because only a few patients survive the acute episode. Diffuse brain damage is necessary in order for the signs of chronic brain syndrome to develop. A single cerebro-vascular attack usually causes signs of focal rather than diffuse damage unless systemic disease contributes to diffuse brain damage through its effect on blood supply or metabolism. Several strokes may occur before chronic brain syndrome is evident, in spite of neurological signs indicating focal brain damage.

(b). Senile brain changes are etiological factors in *senile dementia* in the absence of focal neurological signs or a history of stroke. In contrast to cerebral arteriosclerosis, senile dementia usually occurs after the age of seventy. Its onset is usually insidious; its progression may be characterized by ill-defined emotional disorders.

Clinical subtypes of senile dementia may be catagorized as follows:

1. **Simple Deterioration.** This type refers to uncomplicated cases of brain syndrome with memory loss, diminished emotional responsiveness, disorientation, wandering and nocturnal restlessness.

2. **Delirious.** This term describes an acute confusional state in patients with chronic brain syndrome. Most of these patients are physically ill (metabolic disturbances, dehydration, malnutrition, trauma, exhaustion).

3. **Depressed.** Depressed patients often display agitation and disorientation. Hallucinations and delusions (especially somatic delusions) may occur.

4. **Paranoid.** Patients with senile dementia who are suspicious, hostile, and who blame others. There are poorly organized delusions which may be persecutory or self-aggrandizing. While consciousness and orientation are usually intact, there are frequent perceptual distortions and hallucinations.

5. **Presbyophrenia.** This term (literally, old mind) refers to patients with confabulations who in spite of gross memory defects, retain superficially good social habits.

(c). *Other types of primary organic brain syndrome* include those caused by infection; neoplasm; trauma; alcohol (*e.g.*, Korsakov's syndrome); and drugs (*e.g.*, CNS depressants, or the central anticholinergic syndrome [see Chap. 10]).

For further details of differential diagnosis, see Tables 3 through 7.

### REFERENCES

1. WANG, H. S. AND BUSSE, E. W.: Dementia in old age. *In:* Contemporary Neurology, Chap. 9, C. E. Wells, ed. F. A. Davis Co., Philadelphia, 1971. p. 155.
2. CORSELLIS,, J. A. N.: Mental Illness and the Ageing Brain. Oxford University Press, London, 1962.

3. WILLANGER, R., THYGESEN, P., NIELSEN, R. AND PETERSEN, O.: Intellectual impairment and cerebral atrophy—a psychological, neurological, and radiological investigation. *Dan. Med. Bull. 15:* 65-93, 1968.

4. OBRIST, W. D., CHIVIAN, E., CRONQVIST, S., AND INGVAR, D. H.: Regional cerebral blood flow in senile and presenile dementia. *Neurology 20:* 315-322, 1970.

5. BUSSE, E. W. AND WANG, H. S.: The value of electroencephalography in geriatrics. *Geriatrics 20:* 906-924, 1965.

6. WANG, H. S.: Organic Brain Syndrome. *In:* Behavior and Adaptation in Late Life, Chap. 13, E. W. Busse and E. Pfeiffer, eds. Little, Brown and Company, Inc., Boston, 1969.

7. OBRIST, W. D. AND BISSELL, L. F.: The electroencephalogram of aged patients with cardiac and cerebral vascular disease. *J. Gerontol. 10:* 315-330, 1955.

8. EISDORFER, C.: Psychologic reaction to cardiovascular change in the aged. *Mayo Clin. Proc. 42:* 620-636, 1967.

9. GIANTURCO, D. T., BRESLIN, M. S., HEYMAN, A., GENTRY, W. D., JENKINS, C. D., AND KAPLAN, B.: Personality patterns and life stress in ischemic cerebrovascular disease: I. Psychiatric findings. *Stroke 5:* 453-460, 1974.

10. KIEV, A., CHAPMAN, L. F., GUTHRIE, T. C., AND WOLFF, G.: The highest integrative functions and diffuse cerebral atrophy. *Neurology 12:* 363-385, 1962.

11. GOLDSTEIN, K.: Functional disturbances in brain damage. *In* American Handbook of Psychiatry, Vol. 1, Chap. 39, S. Arieti, ed. Basic Books, New York, 1959. pp. 770-793.

12. SMITH, W. T., TURNER, E., AND SIM, M.: Cerebral biopsy in the investigation of presenile dementia. II. *Br. J. Psychiatry 112:* 127-133, 1966.

13. HAUG, J. O.: Pneumoencephalographic studies in mental disease. *Acta Psychiatr. Scand.* (Suppl. 38) *165:* 1-104, 1962.

14. GARG, A. G. AND TAYLOR, A. R.: A-Scan Echoencephalography in Measurement of the Cerebral Ventricles. *J. Neurol. Neurosurg. Psychiatry 31:* 245-249, 1968.

15. DASTUR, D. K., LANE, M. H., HANSEN, D. B., KETY, S. S., PERLIN, S., BUTLER, R., AND SOKOLOFF, L.: Effects of aging on cerebral circulation and metabolism in man. *In:* Human Aging: A Biological and Behavioral Study. J. E. Birren, R. N. Butler, S. W. Greenhouse, L. Sokoloff, and M. R. Yarrow, eds. U. S. Government Printing Office, Washington, D.C., 1963.

16. OBRIST, W. D., THOMPSON, H. K., JR., KING, C. H., AND WANG, H. S.: Determination of regional cerebral blood flow by inhalation of 133-xenon. *Circ. Res. 20:* 124-135, 1967.

17. OBRIST, W. D., SOKOLOFF, L., LASSEN, N. A., LANE, M. H., BUTLER, R. N., AND FEINBERG, I.: Relation of EEG to cerebral blood flow and metabolism in old age. *Electroencephalogr. Clin. Neurophysiol. 15:* 610-619, 1963.

18. WANG, H. S., OBRIST, W. D., AND BUSSE, E. W.: Neurophysiological correlates of the intellectual function of elderly persons living in the community. *Am. J. Psychiatry 126:* 1205-1212, 1970.

19. BENTON, A.: Psychological Tests for Brain Damage. *In:* Comprehensive Textbook of Psychiatry, A. M. Freedman and H. I. Kaplan, eds. Williams & Wilkins, Baltimore, 1967. pp. 530-538.

20. WECHSLER, D.: The Measurement and Appraisal of Adult Intelligence, 4th Ed. Williams & Wilkins, Baltimore, 1958.

21. BOTWINICK, J.: Cognitive processes in maturity and old age. Springer Publishing Co., Inc., New York, 1967.

22. BIRREN, J. E.: Increments and decrements in the intellectual status of the aged. *In:* Aging in Modern Society: Psychiatric Research Report 23. A. Simon and L. J. Epstein, eds. American Psychiatric Association, Washington, D.C., 1968.

23. KAHN, R. L., GOLDFARB, A. I., POLLACK, M., AND PECK, A.: Brief objective measures for the determination of mental status in the aged. *Am. J. Psychiatry 117:* 326-328, 1960.

24. SALZMAN, C., SHADER, R. I., KOCHANSKY, G. E., AND CRONIN, D. M.: Rating scales for psychotropic drug research with geriatric patients. *J. Am. Geriatr. Soc. 20:* 209-221, 1972.

25. GOLDFARB, A. I.: The evaluation of geriatric patients following treatment. *In:* Evaluation of Psychiatric Treatment, P. H. Hoch and J. Zubin, eds. Grune & Stratton, New York, 1964. p. 291.

# 5

# thought disorders and paranoid phenomena

The thought disorders and paranoid phenomena of late life in the absence of organic brain damage include chronic schizophrenia (carried over from earlier years into old age), late paraphrenia, and paranoid states. Thought disorders and paranoid reactions also can occur in the context of organic brain syndrome.

## THE NATURE OF THOUGHT DISORDERS AND PARANOID PHENOMENA

The term dementia praecox was coined in 1857 by Morel, to designate psychoses which would end in deterioration. The word praecox (i.e., precocious) implied that this process started in early life, in contrast to the mental deterioration in old age. In 1896 Kraepelin delineated dementia praecox as a group of mental disorders, and in 1911 Bleuler introduced the term schizophrenia, because in his view the illness did not necessarily lead to dementia. The term dementia nowadays is reserved for thought disorders that have an organic basis. Schizophrenia, however, is considered to be based on a primary disorder in thinking which is not secondary to brain damage but is associated with autism. Paranoid states are distinguished from schizophrenia by the narrowness of the reality distortions and by the absence of other psychotic manifestations.[1]

### Evaluation of Thought Processes

The only satisfactory method to examine a person's thoughts is through the medium of words, spoken or written. The communicative framework in which thoughts are transmitted to the receiver includes verbal messages and the metacommunicative signals accompanying them.

(a). *Quantitative* changes in thought may be reflected by changes in the tempo of speech, e.g., pressure of speech in mania, or slowing of speech in depression. But there is not always a close correlation between thought and speech. For example, a hostile, fearful, or withdrawn patient

55

may be tight-lipped while his thoughts are racing at high speed. Quantitative abnormalities are not essential features of a primary thought disorder. In fact, these are more typical of affective disorders.

**(b).** The types of words selected, the configuration of speech patterns, and other formal aspects of speech may be an indicator of *qualitative* disturbances in thought. In true thought disorders, there is a qualitative abnormality affecting the *formal* aspects of thought.

A 63-year-old chronic schizophrenic woman, when asked if she was the head of the household, answered, "My is a residential president." When asked about her health, she responded, "The united crusaders of the medical sciences have some gifts to give each individual as to prosperity." The inappropriateness and incoherence of this speech pattern reflects the patient's thought disorder. To other questions, she would respond by whispering telephone numbers. The patient had with her many scraps of paper on which she had written numerous telephone numbers. A few words were scattered throughout these numbers, adding up to a cryptic message of reassurance from God. Each phone number represented a person considered helpful and friendly (illustrating the typical features of autism, magical thinking, telecommunication with supernatural powers, etc.).

**1.** *The Concept of Association.* The relatively unencumbered flow of thought that occurs in the stream of consciousness is called free association. When examining a series of thoughts, we may discover that each thought in the sequence expresses the same underlying theme. The associative links between the thoughts represent a "red thread" tying them together into a cohesive statement. A single thought is not an association; an association can only exist between two or more thoughts. A pattern of thought processes is evaluated by examining the associative links between thoughts. The nature of these links can be predominantly logical and orderly (secondary process), or illogical and irrational (primary process).

Primary process corresponds with the pleasure principle and is characterized by a tendency to immediate discharge of drive energy and by extreme mobility of cathexes, so that substitute ways of discharge are easily achieved. Primary process thinking is characterized by the absence of negatives and conditionals; by absence of time sense; and by the use of allusions, analogies, displacements, condensation, and symbolic representation. The secondary process refers to the reality principle and involves the delay of immediate discharge or gratification, the use of logic, the presence of the time sense, the awareness of alternative modes of action, and the ability of decision-making.

The primary process quality of psychotic thought processes is illustrated by the following delusion of an 82-year-old schizophrenic woman. This patient who had been preoccupied for years with sex and pregnancy, stated that "When I put my hand on the red knob of the railing, my thumb becomes swollen." Such a delusion can be viewed in the same way as the manifest content of a dream. The latent dream content (the underlying wish) undergoes elaborate distortions involving primary process mechanisms. Thus, the underlying wish is probably the wish to be pregnant which, in turn, represents a denial of death's approach. The pregnancy is to come about through contact with a phallic object: the hard railing with the red knob (glans). (This is an example of the use of displacement and symbolic representation.) Touching the phallic symbol causes part of her body to swell. The swelling represents the idea of pregnancy, but it is displaced to her thumb, another phallic symbol. Thus, through symbolic representation, displacements, and so on, an underlying fantasy is highly distorted and condensed into a brief somatic delusion. (This is the same patient as on page 112.)

**2.** Essential features of a thought disorder include the presence of paleologic thought, concretization of the concept, and the loss of abstract capacity. In *paleologic* thought, a common predicate leads to the establishment of an identity of two nouns. *Concretization of the concept* involves loss of the abstract capacity and transforming the abstract into the concrete.[2] The *abstract capacity* comprises the ability to assume a specific mental set; to imagine the merely possible; to shift reflectively from one aspect of a situation to another, and to keep in mind several aspects of a task simultaneously; to find common denominators; and, to use concepts and symbols properly.[3] The following case illustrates a thought disorder in a patient with senile dementia.

An 80-year-old woman (without a past history of schizophrenia) complained "I have stones inside of me and it is hard for them to come out." This patient had occasional fecal impaction, and her stools were hard, like stones. Because her abstract capacity was impaired, she could not conceptualize the "as if," and make proper use of a metaphor. Whereas normal thought accepts identity only on the basis of identical subjects, paleological thinking accepts identity based on identical predicates.[4] Thus, an associative link becomes an identifying link: the attribute, hard, common to both feces and stones, leads to the identity, feces = stones.

In this patient, the somatic delusion (feces are stones) was over-determined. She had a feeling that she had been given stones for bread. This phrase of a biblical parable expressed her feeling of having been abandoned by caretaking parental figures. But again, the figurative aspects were lost and the parable had become a concrete event. The sequence of her thoughts could be represented as follows:

| Content of Thought | Formal Aspects |
| --- | --- |
| (1) I am stopped up, because of constipation. | Statement of fact. |
| (2) My stools are stones, and can't come out. | Concretization of the metaphor results in somatic delusion. |
| (3) I have been given stones to eat. | Rationalization to explain (1) and (2). |

| | |
|---|---|
| (4) Somebody gave me stones for bread. | Projection of cause of the problem; the parable is concretized, and used for further explanation of (1) and (2). |
| (5) I feel helpless and confused. | Loneliness and helplessness activate memory of the parable. |

A 91-year-old woman, who was admitted to the mental hospital because she constantly talked about death, was suspicious that her family was too interested in her will, and was calling various relatives "Peter" or "Judas". After hospitalization, she expressed fear that death would come about by way of electric shock treatments (EST). During the interview, she declared suddenly that "Jesus comes as a thief in the night" (reference to biblical metaphor—Jesus comes unexpectedly).

The explanation of her concerns and accusations was considered to be as follows. The thought of her own death is concretely personified and externalized as a thief in the night. The externalized threat is not only disarmed, but changed into its opposite, Jesus, the Savior. The notion of thief now finds its way toward some of her relatives: Judas was a thief who betrayed Jesus for some money. Even Peter disowned, betrayed Jesus—and that, just before His death. Likewise, her own offspring might abandon, disown, or betray her for money.

This patient was found to have diabetes and a duodenal ulcer. Significantly, she actively resisted diagnostic tests as well as recommended treatment. Thus, she appeared ready to die, and yet was very much frightened by that thought—Judas, Peter, and Jesus Himself had died painful, cruel deaths.

The logical association between one thought and the next may be disturbed in thought disorders resulting in *loose associations*. A simple way of testing abstract capacity is to ask the patient "What is the same about an orange, an apple, and a grapefruit? " One correct answer is that all three are fruits (the common denominator is that they belong to the general category of fruits). A person with an impaired abstract capacity might respond that his mother used to buy all these fruits; he can only think of a concrete event and cannot generalize from the particular toward the general. At times, the manifestations of a thought disorder may be quite subtle. Under routine circumstances, schizophrenia or brain-damaged patients may not reveal their impairment, in contrast to situations which require an initiative, making a choice, or shifting from one mental set to another.

A woman in her late 50's had a 15-year history of vague psychiatric symptoms: a phobia about eating in public places; often changing jobs because she did not feel appreciated; and occasional crying spells "out of a clear blue sky." Her diagnosis had been involutional depression, but in spite of antidepressant therapy, her complaints persisted. The diagnostic riddle was eventually solved through a careful analysis of verbatim transcripts of some clinical interviews: repeated, subtle nonsequiturs suggested a thought disorder. For example, she reported that her neighbor had said to her "I haven't seen you for some time. Where have you been? I thought maybe you were shopping for Christmas." The patient had answered, "No, I have done my Christmas shopping already." Thus, she could not conceive of shopping as the merely possible, *i.e.*, some general type of situation that could account for her absence from home at any time. Instead, "shopping" referred to one particular, concrete event.

   **(c).** In addition to the formal aspects, the *contents of thought* must be explored. The contents may be highly abnormal and indicative of a psychosis; yet this phenomenon is not restricted to the domain of thought disorders. In affective psychoses, for example, all sorts of psychotic thought contents may occur, but these delusions are considered to be secondary to, and in keeping with, the primary disorder in affect.

   **1.** Characteristic of *ideas of reference* is that the meaning of events or people's actions is interpreted as being especially related to oneself. The terms reference and relationship have a common etymological derivation: the past participle of the Latin *referre* is *relatus*. Thus a reference implies a type of relatedness. Ideas of reference signify thoughts that establish a special relationship between the thinking subject and one or more external objects, between "me here" and "them over there". The second feature of ideas of reference pertains to the nature of this special relationship. The subject (patient) may see himself as being active (influencing the other) or passive (being at the receiving end); the type of interaction may be good and pleasant, or evil and painful.

   **2.** Mild, fleeting ideas of reference occur at some time in almost all individuals. In contrast, when their duration becomes extended and the sense of conviction more intense, they indicate a pathological relationship between oneself and the world around. This type of disordered relationship is referred to as *paranoid* (etymology: para = besides; noia = knowledge; hence, paranoia denotes knowledge that is besides the point).

   A 65-year-old woman, with a diagnosis of schizophrenia since age 51, had the idea that "whenever somebody passes my window, the food in the refrigerator sours." Illustrative of a paranoid idea of reference, the patient considered herself the passive victim of evil forces. This patient also had covered every mirror in the house with towels, presumably part of a delusional schema to protect herself against the evil eye.

   **3.** *Delusions* represent a serious thought disorder indicating illness of psychotic proportions. A delusion is a false idea that is out of keeping with the beliefs generally held by society and that cannot be corrected. Delusions may be grandiose (as in manic and schizophrenic states), persecutory (paranoid schizophrenia and organic brain syndrome), hypochondriacal (depression, schizophrenia and organic brain syndrome), and so on. Delusions may be systematized or logically built up on a basic premise but because the premise is incorrect, the deductions constituting the delusional system are equally incorrect. In senile dementia, paranoid delusions tend to be poorly systematized because of impairment of intellect. The delusions of affective disorders are consistent with the prevailing mood, but in thought disorders, there often is a discrepancy between the delusional thought content and the patient's feelings.

## Differential Diagnosis of Thought Disorders

The true thought disorders need to be differentiated from pseudo-thought disturbances, which may occur in depression, manic conditions, and obsessive-compulsive states.

(a). **Depression.** In depression thoughts emerge at a slow tempo, but the nature of the associative links is not affected. What may happen in profound depression, however, is that the patient may replace the verbalization of certain thoughts by a period of silence. In such a case, the first thought in a sequence of thoughts may be verbalized, whereas the next several thought components are not verbally expressed, *e.g.*, because of self-absorption or depressive apathy. After the silence, the patient may verbalize the last thought in the series—one that probably shows little logical connection with the first thought. The absence of a logical connection, in this case, does not signify true incoherence, but pseudo-incoherence, because the intermediate associative links between the first and the last statement were not verbalized.

(b). **Manic States.** Hypertalkative patients at times seem to show incoherence or irrelevant thoughts. The manic patient, however, may think so fast that there is not enough time to verbalize all his thoughts. Thus he may leave some of them out, resulting in an apparent loosening of the association. Although his speech may seem rambling or incomprehensible, this does not reflect a true disturbance in logical thinking, but rather the inability of the speech apparatus to keep up with the increased tempo of thought production.

(c). **Circumstantiality.** The obsessional, perfectionistic individual may depart tangentially at each station of the train of thought—going into details, producing rococo verbal structures—but he will always return to the main trend ("as I was saying a while ago"). In spite of the baroque style, the circumstantial patient eventually makes his point.

(d). **Rambling.** In the case of rambling, the point is never made. The patient with organic brain syndrome may set out with thought no. 1, and proceed towards thoughts nos. 2, 3, and so on. While doing this, he loses sight of the point to be made, goes astray, and gets lost. The mental impairment may not permit him to carry out the dual task of remembering the point to be made and elaborating the successive steps needed to get to the point. Inasmuch as the brain-damaged patient forgets where his train of thought is heading, the essential deficit is in the area of memory, rather than in formal thought processes.

## AGING AND SCHIZOPHRENIA

With regard to the relationship between aging and schizophrenia, we are interested in exploring four aspects: the usual age of onset of the clinical subtypes; the pathogenetic effects of aging; the pathoplastic effects of aging in modifying the symptomatology; and, the possible effects of schizophrenia on the aging process itself.

## Age of Onset

Compared with other forms of schizophrenia, the paranoid type becomes clinically manifest at a later age, usually after age 30. One plausible factor is that, compared with other forms of schizophrenia, the paranoid type is relatively less severe. A disorder that, intrinsically or for whatever reasons, is less severe, would proportionately need more time to become manifest. And, if the premorbid personality in paranoid schizophrenia has relatively more strength, not only would it take longer for overt symptoms to develop, but also, once the disorder became manifest, it would leave the overall personality more intact.

## Pathogenetic Effects of Aging

The role which the aging process may play, in terms of contributing to the etiology of thought disorders and paranoid phenomena, includes the following possibilities:

**(a).** In the course of time, as a result of progressive accumulation of stresses, schizoid or paranoid personalities may develop an intensification of their pathological character traits. This process may take only a few years or almost a lifetime. The psychodynamics and the duration of this process depend on biological, psychological, social, and environmental factors, and their interaction. In some cases the character disorder may decompensate, transiently or permanently in early adulthood; in other cases the regression toward autism and thought disorder may not come about until the prospective patient has arrived in old age.

An 82-year-old widow had recently developed extensive paranoid delusions. At first, the diagnosis late paraphrenia was considered because the schizophrenic disorder seemed to have started in old age. A careful anamnesis, however, revealed, that during her early 20's, the patient had had a brief episode of hearing voices (telling her "to jump in the well"), excessive religious preoccupation, and marked ambivalence of affect. She apparently had a remission of this, and it was some sixty years later that the schizophrenic disorder again became overt.

**(b).** Some cases of progressive decompensation take as their point of departure the midlife crisis. Normally, the awareness of entering the second half of life and the realization of its significance involve an involutional grief reaction. Failure to resolve this grief reaction may lead to an involutional depression (second step). Such a depression may be mild or severe, short or long lasting, a one time thing or recurrent problem. Individuals differ greatly in their ability to overcome the depression and to develop mechanisms of psychological immunity against subsequent involutional losses. Some involutional depressions do not fully recover, and in fact, do not even hold their own in terms of remaining on a level of chronic depression. Rather (and this would be the third phase), they settle down at a lower level of adjustment, *i.e.,* hypochondriasis. This involves a disengagement from external objects and a withdrawal of interest onto the self. The distancing from others and the somatic self-absorption produce further object losses and impoverishment, because the patient alienates others with his complaints. Because of the prolonged disengagement from the basic human dimensions of love and work, the patient's social and vocational skills suffer from decathexis and disuse atrophy. Some patients may succeed in finding a new support base on the hypochondriacal level, depending on multiple factors. However, when the unstable, brittle adjustment does not hold up, the final phase sets in: a further withdrawal (from the realm of the body to the sphere of the inner self); regression to autism, with concomitant loss of contact with reality; and the onset of a thought disorder and paranoid ideation.

A 65-year-old divorced woman had become an overwhelming problem to all agencies in the community, because she was perennially dissatisfied with any place, person, or program arranged to meet her demands. At the age of 40, she had been admitted to a mental hospital because she had been accusing her husband of being "immoral and unfaithful", and she expressed suicidal threats (i.e., an involutional depression, with paranoid features). During her stay in the hospital, the depressive symptoms cleared up, and were replaced by hypochondriasis. She was discharged after a few months with the diagnosis "neurasthenia". At the age of 43, she divorced her husband, who later remarried. She has not had any contact with him, nor with her two sons, since that time. Reportedly, the sons will have nothing to do with her, and the patient blames this on her husband ("He taught them to hate and despise me").

Over the last fifteen years, the patient (still an attractive, well-dressed lady) has sent out 41 formal change-of-address notes. In one two-year time span, she moved 15 times. Over the past 10 years, she has lived in 30 different boarding homes. No one would allow her to return, once she left. The depressive symptoms never returned and were permanently replaced by hypochondriasis. At all times, her conversation revolved around herself, her ailments, doctors, medicine, and diet. After a few years of moving ceaselessly and alienating people, she also became more hostile and suspicious. She began to write letters to heads of agencies and directors of departments, explaining her plight, asking for help, and making assorted accusations. Some of her gossip was so vicious that she acquired a reputation of being like a snake in the grass, ready to strike any time. By the time she was in her late 50's, the accusations began to acquire decidedly paranoid aspects (e.g., "I heard the cleaning woman beating up some old people in the room next to mine."). She was constantly planning to litigate against various boarding homes, or to bring suit against some social service department. In her early 60's, grandiose thoughts and behavior were superimposed on the symptomatology (e.g., calling the police department to deliver her medicine to her from the drug store). By age 65, her litigious correspondence had reached for higher and higher echelons, eventually including letters to the U. S. President.

## The Pathoplastic Effects of Aging

The passage of time may influence existing psychopathology in numerous ways. There seems to be evidence suggesting certain general types of age-related effects on schizophrenic and paranoid conditions.

(a). *Hallucinations* become less frequent and less exciting in chronic paranoid schizophrenia,[5] although in late paraphrenia, threatening or exciting hallucinations occur often.

(b). *Psychotic motor activity* tends to decrease with aging. Patients who were initially hyperactive have a better chance for trial visits or discharge after 20 years of hospitalization.[6]

(c). *Delusions* may remain unaffected by aging, or may show various changes. In one study, about half of the aged schizophrenics showed no change in their delusions; in the other half, the delusions had disappeared, expanded, or consolidated. Five possible mechanisms by which the delusions in old schizophrenics could be modified were observed: liquidation through suppression and retrenchment; shift of delusional content by restructuring of the milieu; conversion of a productive delusion into a nihilistic, depressive configuration; disappearance of the delusion, coincident with a psychoorganically-induced regression; and expansion and fantastic generalization of the delusional themes.[7]

The extent of adherence to the same delusional thought content is roughly parallel to the degree of withdrawal.[6] Delusions may become less prominent or even disappear in the course of aging, due to the development of physical illness which facilitates recathexis of the body. The switch from a persecutory delusion to a grandiose one is, psychodynamically, probably comparable to the shift from depression to mania (involving a mechanism of psychotic restitution fantasies).

(d). There are chronic schizophrenics, who have been on phenothiazines for 10 to 15 years, and finally are able to leave the hospital. In these cases, it is not logical to assume that the phenothiazines became fully effective after all these years, nor that improved community facilities can better handle such patients now. When these aged schizophrenics leave the hospital after some decades, they usually are placed in simple boarding home settings, of the same kind that has existed throughout the years. This is further evidence that the aging process has a pathoplastic effect in certain schizophrenics.

## Effect on the Aging Process

There is no way of answering in a generalizing way whether or not schizophrenia can have an effect on the aging process. Bleuler was of the opinion that organic cerebral changes occurred less often in schizophrenics than in the average population.[5] Riemer[8] and Bychowsky[9] found no clinical evidence of organic brain syndrome in the aged schizophrenics studied by them. The notion whether or not schizophrenia would provide some type of immunity or protection against the effects of senile brain changes certainly requires a lot more systematic investigation. Apart from this, a few points can be made on a common sense basis.

First, schizophrenics, as a group, if not protected and treated by society would show a drastically reduced life span. They would succumb to illness, accident, and deprivation. Second, persons with a schizoid character structure may have a built-in protection against the stresses of old age. The withdrawn schizoid does not engage himself with others, may not acquire objects of value—in short, he travels lightly. Hence he has little to lose later in life. Third, the fact that many schizophrenic patients find permanent shelter in the refuge of a hospital, or protection in the custody of a family, implies that they are not being exposed to the stress and strain of the daily rat race. Fourth, the idea that schizophrenics may have a special resistance to dementia is probably a deceptive mirage. Rather, it is more logical to consider the fact that a schizophrenic suffers from a functional disorder of thought. When, in old age, structural cerebral impairment sets in, the dementia is no longer functional but organic. But the clinical difference between not using intact brain equipment, and not using nonintact equipment, may be hardly noticeable.

## CLINICAL TYPES AND DIFFERENTIAL DIAGNOSIS

### Paranoid Schizophrenia

Paranoid schizophrenia may appear as late as the middle adult years and leave the personality relatively intact, in contrast to other types of schizophrenia. The symptomatology includes delusions of persecution or grandeur, ideas of reference, auditory hallucinations, and frequent preoccupation with religion or supernatural topics. A distinction is made between a hostile and a grandiose subtype. The *hostile* subtype is characterized by delusions of persecution and injustice, extensive use of projection, a tendency to develop a systematized network of interrelated delusions, and auditory hallucinations of a threatening or violent nature. The *grandiose* subtype has delusions of grandeur and occasional persecutory delusions, autistic restitution fantasies (regression to infantile omnipotence), inclusion of protective supernatural powers in the delusional system, and auditory hallucinations involving communication with the supernatural powers.

The difference between these clinical subtypes probably has little significance. Whenever an individual feels singled out for persecution, it is easy for him to rationalize that he must be special, and from here it is only a small step to get on the road toward grandiosity. Conversely, any one who feels grandiose, extra special, or chosen by God, may well conclude that lesser mortals envy him. Thus he will start imagining that evil elements are ganging up on him to get even with him, or rob him of his treasure. Because of the ideas of reference and paranoid delusions, such patients are often constantly on the move.

A 66-year-old man had started to have progressively severe ideas of reference in his mid-40's. Before that, most of his life had been taken up by a see-saw battle with tuberculosis. When the disease was finally brought under control, at age 55, the patient had a full-fledged mental breakdown which necessitated commitment to a psychiatric hospital. Two years later he was discharged with a diagnosis of paranoid schizophrenia. He continued to have persecutory delusions, including the idea that other people gave him their colds, and that he would catch these any time he was in a draft. Thus, he would try to maintain a no-man's-land around him. However, these efforts always failed: the draft would still come across, and so he felt compelled to move elsewhere. Over a period of eight years, he moved in and out of 14 boarding homes.

## Late Life Paraphrenia

The term paraphrenia dates back to the early nineteenth century, and has been used by authorities (Kraepelin, Freud, etc.) in different ways. In 1911, Freud formulated his views on the relationship between paranoia and homosexuality in his analysis of the Schreber case. He suggested the term paraphrenia because he felt that Schreber was suffering from paranoia as well as schizophrenia. Nowadays, the term refers to a mental illness characterized by a thought disorder with paranoid, systematized delusions, but without dementia or progressive personality deterioration. Contact with reality is maintained except in the specific area of the delusional system.[10] The onset of late paraphrenia is usually after age 60.

Kay and Roth conclude that late paraphrenia must be regarded as the mode of manifestation of old age schizophrenia.[11] Its clinical symptomatology is characterized by many schizophrenia-like disorders of thought, mood, and volition; by relatively good preservation of formal intellect, personality, and memory; and by conspicuous hallucinations. These patients may survive for a long period of time; recovery is the exception and prolonged hospitalization is the rule. The paraphrenic is most often a female, single or widowed, who has few close relatives. Most have been living alone for many years before hospitalization. Few of the paraphrenics have children, and those with children have only limited contact with them. Good physical health is common, except for frequent problems with hearing and vision. The presence of these sensory losses and long-standing social isolation, along with the premorbid personality traits (usually schizoid or paranoid), seem to be the main etiological factors.

Herbert and Jacobson provided further support for the concept of late paraphrenia as a distinct psychiatric disorder.[13] Their sample included 45 female and 2 male patients, all of whom were 65 years old or older. Their diagnostic criteria for paraphrenia include: systematized delusions, with or without hallucinations, in a setting of clear consciousness; onset of illness in late middle age; and absence of organic dementia. Elderly patients with a "carry over" schizophrenia (chronic schizophrenia persisting into the senium) were not considered paraphrenic. Patients with late paraphrenia may have had premorbid personality disorders, but these disorders apparently had not prevented them from coping with their environment before the onset of paraphrenia.

A 71-year-old widow, with no children and no close relatives, had been living alone for several years. Reportedly, she had an episode of acting peculiarly seven years ago, but since then she had succeeded in maintaining an independent adjustment. Recently, however, her neighbors reported that she acted strangely. A psychiatric referral revealed that she had the delusion that men from a nearby amusement park were "making marks on her window, and sleeping on her front porch" and that "some people were burying dead children in her back yard." On one occasion the patient, apparently under the influence of her delusions, had torn out the flowers from her neighbors' planters. It must be emphasized that, even during the acute psychosis, she maintained a social facade. She visited all over town, and was well known and liked by many people. Of particular interest in the delusional thoughts are the themes of birth and death (the men are sleeping on her front porch—but she is a marked woman—the child is dead—and her revenge is to destroy what grows in her neighbor's planter).

Persecutory delusions include ideas of being drugged, thoughts being read, being influenced by rays, machines, or electricity, and so on. Auditory hallucinations occur in most cases, particularly at night (threatening, jeering commentaries, obscenities, loud bangs, etc.). The delusions and hallucinations frequently have a sexual slant or erotic coloring. The responsible parties are often jealous, hostile neighbors. These experiences are intermittent; behavior and thought content during intervening episodes can be relatively undisturbed. Once hospitalized, these patients do well, but as the years go by, their adjustment becomes more brittle.[12]

A 74-year-old widow, living alone and still taking care of herself and her home, had the delusion that a night watchman, hiding in her attic, was spying on her. To protect herself, she undressed and bathed in the dark (projecting her reluctance to see her own deteriorating body, onto an evil eye). The night watchman "kept [her] awake for almost three months, trying to make [her] think he was a bird by tapping on the ceiling; one night he even threw a bucket of water on [her]." She changed locks on her house, but discovered he would enter by lifting a part of the roof. A few months later, however, she reported that the night watchman was acting very nicely. She talked to him all the time. At first, he had been an old man with only one thing on his mind—her money. But now, he is a young boy interested in helping her; "and he knows I have a gun that will shoot twenty-five times."

The delusion of the watchman is overdetermined: it represents the evil eye that sees ugly things; it is the projection of the concretized concept of loss (he is after her money); and, it is the externalization of her wish to have somebody watch over her. The figurative watch "over" becomes a literal, spatial "above, in the attic." The delusion of the man upstairs fails to reassure her: neither the old spy-thief nor the young boy would be much of a protection, and so she has her magic gun ready.

A few comments are in order regarding the external enemy, intruder or foreign body in this type of delusions. In the early stages of the illness, the enemy is perceived as being well outside the patient's house, beyond the perimeter of personal space. Typically, they are hoodlum types on the street, in front of the house, acting obnoxiously or speaking vulgar language. During the next phase, the undesirable elements make their way across the property line, into the garden, or onto the front porch. The third stage is that of penetration into the house. This intrusion usually involves damage, *e.g.*, to the plumbing or wiring in the basement. During the last stage, the protective symbolic equation (body = house) breaks down and now the enemy is felt to intrude into the patient's body space itself (tactile hallucinations). This last phase may also be described by the patient as "something coming through the wall toward me."

A 72-year-old woman, with a long history of schizoid behavior and recent evidence of organic brain syndrome, was placed in a home for the aged. There she developed a confusional state, with agitation and depression. She had the delusion that a machine in the room next door was pushing pictures through the wall, which would then appear on her T.V. screen. Clinical management in this case included dispensing haloperidol 0.5 mg t.i.d., encouraging her to stay in the home and to get to know the other residents, and arranging for regular visits by relatives. When the patient returned for the first follow-up, she reported that the pictures were no longer on the T.V. screen, but just on the wall itself, and she was undecided how they got there. Two weeks later, she reported the pictures were gone altogether and she disowned any memories about the recent delusional-hallucinatory experiences. Meanwhile, she was gaining weight, looked calmer, and spoke favorably about the home. In this case, the mental decompensation producing paranoid manifestations was precipitated by a "transplantation shock." What is further illustrated is that the degree of closeness of the intruding element and its proximity to the self, tend to correspond with the degree of psychopathological regression.

## Paranoid States

Paranoid states are psychotic disorders in which a delusion, usually persecutory or grandiose, is the essential abnormality. Disturbances in mood and behavior are dependent on, and determined by, this delusion. This distinguishes paranoid states from the affective psychoses and schizophrenia, in which mood and thought disorders, respectively, are the central abnormalities.[1] A precipitating factor, which may be any of the common age-related losses, is often apparent. The question arises why some individuals respond to such ubiquitous losses by developing a paranoid state. The following factors may play a role.

(a). The *premorbid personality* may have counterphobic features and an inclination to use defenses of the "high energy" variety (mastery through attack; projection), with subsequent attempts to move aggressively against the externalized threat. Another type of premorbid personality, also inclined to use projection, may be less aggressive, and thus may prefer to move away from the external danger (a phobic pattern).

**(b).** Whether the patient will aggressively move against the external enemy, or flee in apprehension, depends on his *relative strength, i.e.,* whether he unconsciously views himself as being potentially stronger or weaker than the persecutor, and on whether or not he feels backed into a corner and thus becomes a desperado who has nothing to lose by attacking.

**(c).** The *nature* of the loss is important, in the sense that the tendency to respond with projection and intense hostility or fear, is greater, the more the loss pertains to an exquisitely sensitive area (in the case of men, masculine attributes, such as power, "manhood", or sexual potency; and in women, notions of feeling love-less or life-less). Also, the *acuteness* and *rate of speed* with which the loss takes place play a role. The more sudden and acute, the more likely it is that ego strength will fail, and maladaptive defenses are employed.

A 78-year-old widow had long been a chronic complainer, accusing the operators of the boarding homes where she had been of being mean and mistreating her. Although she was married twice, she had no children. In both marriages she was dominant and decidedly in charge. Her first husband died when the patient was in her mid-40's. She met her second husband through a lonely hearts club and married him at age 51. Over the next 15 years, the couple moved 25 times. During this period of uprootedness, the patient became a determined hypochondriac. She would see various physicians for indigestion and arthritis, but would never use their prescriptions, and instead would buy patent medications according to her own judgment. In the course of time, her tendency to be dominating and demanding became more aggressive. After her second husband's death, 12 years earlier, she moved into a boarding home, but the earlier pattern of frequent moves persisted. Finally, having run out of places to stay, and having seemingly lost everyone's good will, she developed an acute delusion that the water in the home was poisoned and that her roommate was trying to kill her.

Delusions pertaining to water and food are common in paranoid states. Another patient, an 81-year-old widow, developed a fairly extensive delusional system to the effect that somebody was putting lime in her water. Her original concern had been about the (realistic) issue of fluoridation of the water. From here on, she developed the lime delusion. As a result, she sold her house and moved into a new one, only to discover that "this time they were sprinkling lime on the snow." To protect herself, she started to buy water and stored it in jars. But even this provided no escape from the enemy. Somebody began to put deliberately too much sugar in her food—and that, while she is a diabetic.

## Paranoid Reactions in Organic Brain Syndrome

**(a).** Paranoid phenomena frequently occur in the setting of *organic brain syndrome.* In most cases, they represent nonspecific manifestations of a severe mental disorder, in the context of which the emergence of primitive defense mechanisms is no surprise. Typical for the paranoid phenomena, secondary to cerebral decompensation, is their lack of sophistication and systematization, as well as their variability. It is as if the patient improvises on the spot, changing his story without regard for consistency. The paranoid delusions or hallucinations tend to clear up, as the patient's overall condition improves.

A male patient in his 70's had the delusion that he was being poisoned because uranium in his blood was sinking down into the veins of his legs. In actuality, his legs were swollen because of thrombophlebitis and cardiac decompensation. He had been in renal failure and attempts had been made to treat his uremia. The patient had been aware that the element of urea was poisoning him. The idea of something toxic became the focal point of a delusional elaboration. Urea was transformed into uranium, an element that is both heavy and toxic; this served to explain his state of being poisoned and the heaviness in the legs. A few days later, the patient casually changed this delusion into another one: that his heart was to be cut out.

(b). *Senile Dementia, Paranoid Type.* These patients may show paranoid delusions (usually persecutory) and quarrelsome, demanding behavior; chronic complaints about being mistreated are characteristic.

A 74-year-old widow phoned various community agencies, complaining that neighborhood boys kept her awake at night and damaged her property. She feared the boys would burn her house if she made any complaints (concretization and projection of her own sense of feeling "burned up" about being victimized). A few weeks later, the delusions changed: she accused the pharmacy of giving her pills with the wrong color. Again a few weeks later, she became acutely apprehensive during the night and called the police for help. After this, she complained it had taken the police many hours to come, and they had searched her house for illegal liquor. The progressive deterioration is suggested by increasingly prominent oral concerns (being poisoned, illegal liquor) and feelings of utter helplessness. Even the parental symbols (pharmacy and police) are corrupt. It is significant that once this patient was placed in a boarding home the paranoid symptoms subsided.

(c). *Alcoholic paranoid state* develops in chronic alcoholics, usually male, and is manifested by extreme jealousy and frequent delusions of unfaithfulness on the part of the spouse.

A 60-year-old man, a chronic alcoholic, was committed to the mental hospital because of his violent threats to his wife. He accused her of having had many lovers throughout their married life, and stated that of the five children born of this marriage, only the oldest had been fathered by him. In reality, the patient himself had had numerous extramarital affairs. His wife had stayed with him, in spite of his abusive behavior "to keep the family together." In fact, when the children had grown up and left, she began to help her husband in running their small business. Thus, the patient's paranoid accusations flew directly in the face of the evidence; the delusions of jealousy came about by projecting his own impulses and fantasies onto his wife.

In alcoholic paranoid reactions (as in many paranoid states), there is a serious risk of violent, destructive behavior, even to the point of homicide. Because of this, immediate intervention, usually involving hospitalization, is indicated.

## REFERENCES

1. A. P. A. Diagnostic and Statistical Manual of Mental Disorders, 2nd Ed. American Psychiatric Association, Washington, D.C., 1968, p. 37.
2. ARIETI, S.: Schizophrenia: symptomatology and mechanisms. In: American Handbook of Psychiatry, Vol. 1, Chap. 23, S. Arieti, ed. Basic Books, Inc., New York, 1959. pp. 475–484.
3. GOLDSTEIN, K.: Functional disturbances in brain damage. In: American Handbook of Psychiatry, Vol. 1, Chap. 39, S. Arieti, ed. Basic Books, Inc., New York, 1959. pp. 770–793.
4. VON DOMARUS, E.: The specific laws of logic in schizophrenia. In: Language and Thought in Schizophrenia, J. S. Kasanin, ed. University of California Press, Berkeley, 1944. pp. 104–113.
5. BLEULER, E.: Dementia Praecox, or the Group of Schizophrenias. International Universities Press, New York, 1952.
6. EHRENTHEIL, O. F.: Behavioral changes of aging chronic psychotics. In: New Thoughts on Old Age, Chap. 7, R. Kastenbaum, ed. Springer Publishing Company, Inc., New York, 1964. pp. 99–115.
7. MULLER, C.: The influence of age on schizophrenia. In: Processes of Aging, Chap. 23, R. H. Williams, C. Tibbits, and W. Donahue, eds. Atherton Press, New York, 1962. p. 511.
8. RIEMER, M. D.: A study of the mental status of schizophrenics hospitalized for over 25 years into their senium. Psychiatr. Q. 24: 209–313, 1950.
9. BYCHOWSKY, G.: Schizophrenia in the period of involution. Dis. Ner. Syst. 13: 150–153, 1952.
10. HINSIE, L. E. AND CAMPBELL, R. J.: Psychiatric Dictionary, 4th Ed. Oxford Universities Press, New York, 1970.
11. KAY, D. W. K. AND ROTH, M.: Schizophrenias of old age. In: Processes of Aging, Chap. 20, R. H. Williams, C. Tibbits, and W. Donahue, eds. Atherton Press, 1963. pp. 402–448.
12. ROTH, M.: The natural history of mental disorders in old age. J. Ment. Sci. 101: 281–301, 1955.
13. HERBERT, M. E. AND JACOBSON, S.: Late Paraphrenia. Am. J. Psychiatry 113: 461–469, 1967.

# 6

# affective disorders

## DIMENSIONS OF AFFECT

With regard to emotion there are three specific dimensions: subjective feelings which can be communicated through speech; physiological concomitants in the autonomous nervous system; and motor behavior involving the musculoskeletal apparatus. In affect states or disorders, all of these dimensions may be equally manifest, or one of them may be relatively dominant. The physiological concomitants, for example, are more prominent in patients with a depressive equivalent[1] (a depression masked by physical symptoms). Emotional expression, primarily by way of motor behavior, can be seen in the action language (acting out) of certain behavior disorders.

### The Subjective Experience

The subjective experience of an affect can be assessed by the examiner only if the feelings are formulated and verbalized by the patient. Not infrequently, active inquiry into these feelings is indicated, because some individuals are not used to putting their feelings into words. One can then help the patient by presenting him with various mood statements (*e.g.*, sad, blue, edgy, annoyed, let down, aggravated, etc.). When the patient recognizes and acknowledges the appropriate affect, this may be accompanied by noticeable physiological concomitants or motor expressive behavior.

A 62-year-old minister's wife, hospitalized because of depression, had always been concerned about making a good impression. In her many contacts with church members she had to set a good example, turning the other cheek when she was hurt or frustrated. This pattern of suppressing anger had become second nature, until she got caught in a tug of war between two factions in the congregation, and was being slapped on both cheeks. During the interview, she could describe her feelings only as "being upset"; but at the same time she made a fist with both hands, pressing them against each other. After her attention had been drawn to this, she could verbalize the sensation of pressure and counterpressure in her fists, and recognized in this gesture her feelings of deadlock and the state of impasse in her life.

71

## Physiological Concomitants

Some physiological concomitants of specific affects can be directly observed during the interview (*e.g.*, tearfulness, sighing, holding one's breath); others are obtained from the anamnesis (*e.g.*, loss of appetite, fatigue, insomnia). Certain patients communicate primarily by way of organ language. By carefully tuning in to such an organ recital, one can be alerted to clues about the patient's affect; *e.g.*, a heavy sensation in the chest (depression); butterflies in the stomach (anxiety); a pain in the neck (suppressed anger); feeling choked up (acute grief). Somatization refers to the relative prominence of the physiological concomitants *vis-à-vis* the subjective-experiential aspects of specific affects.

Depression involves a slowing down, and any of all organ systems and personality functions may be affected by it. There are frequent exceptions to this rule, however, because an individual may try to defend against a depression by way of increased activity of particular physiological functions. Thus, changes in metabolism and energy production can vary considerably. Although appetite is usually decreased, in some cases there may be an increase, even to the point of bulimia. Most depressed patients complain of insomnia but some tend to become more sleepy, somnolent, or even lethargic. And whereas psychomotor activity is usually slowed down, the reverse is true in agitated depressions. These apparent exceptions are not paradoxical phenomena, but probably serve the purpose of warding off the depression or facilitating its remission. Repetitive movements, for example, as in agitated depression, may not only reflect and express anxiety (co-existing with the depression), but also may involve self-stimulation and tension accumulation which is preferable to the lifeless, empty quality of the inner world of the depressed patient.

Total sleep time is decreased in depression; the patient awakens more frequently, and there is a reduction of Stage 4 sleep.[2] By and large, the extent of the sleep disturbance is in keeping with the severity of the depression.[3]

## Motor and Behavioral Dimensions

In some instances, the affect is manifested primarily through its motor aspects and behavioral dimensions. Specific action language (e.g., gestures, psychomotor patterns) will suggest the presence of depression or anxiety. The general posture may convey lack of vitality, as if the patient is burdened down by a heavy weight. In contrast, the manic patient seems to pit himself actively against the force of gravity. For the depressed patient, personal time drags, so that the world around is perceived as going too fast.

A 64-year-old woman with a psychotic depression was bothered by the idea that all the clocks on the hospital ward were running fast.

In manic states, personal time flies (everthing around going proportionately slower), and spatially there is an exhilarating sense of soaring. Whereas the depressed patient is oriented backwards toward the past, the manic patient is going forward in a "flight into health." The former is a captive of the past, the latter escapes into the future.

The various dimensions of depressive affect states have been investigated by Zung and incorporated in a rating scale (Self-rating Depression Scale).[4] The specific items in the depression scale refer to subjective experience, physiological concomitants, and psychomotor behavior (Table 1).

## AGING AND AFFECTIVE DISORDERS

Since there is no clear definition as to what constitutes an affective disorder, statements regarding their incidence in old age must be viewed with reservation. The same caution is necessary with regard to generalizations about the effects of aging on the symptomatology of depressive and manic disorders.

Some authors state that depressions are mitigated by the aging process.[5, 6, 7] This would be particularly true for *neurotic depressions* that developed in early life. Some questions that concern us here pertain to

TABLE 1. *Criteria for the Diagnosis of Depressive Disorders and the Self-rating Scale Items using them*

| Diagnosis of Depressive Disorders | Self-rating Depression Scale Items* |
|---|---|
| Pervasive affect | |
| A. Depressed, sad and blue | 1. I feel down-hearted and blue. |
| B. Crying spells | 2. I have crying spells, or feel like it. |
| Physiological disturbances | |
| A. Rhythmic disturbances | |
| 1. Diurnal variation | 3. Morning is when I feel the best. |
| 2. Decreased sleep with early or frequent waking | 4. I have trouble sleeping at night. |
| 3. Decreased appetite | 5. I eat as much as I used to. |
| 4. Weight loss | 6. I notice that I am losing weight. |
| 5. Decreased libido | 7. I still enjoy sex. |
| B. Other disturbances | |
| 1. G. I.: constipation | 8. I have trouble with constipation. |
| 2. C. V.: tachycardia | 9. My heart beats faster than usual. |
| 3. M. S.: fatigue | 10. I get tired for no reason. |
| Psychological disturbances | |
| A. Psychomotor activities | |
| 1. Agitation | 11. I find myself restless and can't keep still. |
| 2. Retardation | 12. I find it easy to do the things I used to. |
| B. Ideational | |
| 1. Confusion | 13. My mind is as clear as it used to be. |
| 2. Emptiness | 14. My life is pretty full. |
| 3. Hopelessness | 15. I feel hopeful about the future. |
| 4. Indecisiveness | 16. I find it easy to make decisions. |
| 5. Irritability | 17. I am more irritable than usual. |
| 6. Dissatisfaction | 18. I still enjoy the things I used to. |
| 7. Personal devaluation | 19. I feel that I am useful and needed. |
| 8. Suicidal rumination | 20. I feel that others would be better off if I were dead. |

*Item numbers 3, 5, 7, 12, 13, 14, 15, 16, 18, and 19 are worded symptomatically negative. From Zung.[4] Reproduced by permission of the author.

lack of an unambiguous, clear operational definition of depression, and to whether the data were obtained through longitudinal follow-up of certain neurotics over a period of decades or through cross-sectional studies of various age groups. Psychoneuroses may seem to improve in late life because the severe neuroses have dropped out because of death or decompensation into more severe psychopathology. The dropping out of severe neuroses in the course of time would leave available the milder types, thus creating the false impression that the neurotic process *per se* is favorably affected by the passage of time. This is not to say that such favorable changes cannot occur. But the only satisfactory way to study the effect of aging on neuroses is by way of longitudinal follow-up of individuals with specific neuroses.

Other authors emphasize the high incidence of late life depressions.[8, 9] There seems to be a consensus that *reactive depressions* become more frequent in old age. Loss of physical health is probably a major factor in the development of such depressive feeling states.[4, 10, 11] A reactive depression, however, is more like a grief reaction than a neurotic depression. Because aged persons often have multiple illnesses and other types of losses, it is reasonable to expect an increasing incidence of reactive depressions with advancing age.

The onset of *manic-depressive illness* usually occurs in middle age, although occasionally a first episode occurs after age sixty-five.[12] As will be discussed later, the question is whether such late life manic disorders are an expression of manic-depressive illness or a separate entity. Apparently, manic disorders in general become less frequent with advancing age.[9]

Hereditary factors apparently play a role in depression and mania, and may well be the same for both disorders.[13] Although the genotype is fixed, the phenotype may change in the course of aging. Because mania is an illness involving the use of high-energy defenses (hyperactivity, extroversion), it may become increasingly difficult to choose mania as a mode of expressing affective disorder in late life.[14, 15]

Relevant in this context is the finding that monoamine oxidase levels steadily increase and that norepinephrine levels decrease with aging. This *relation of age to enzyme activity* might reflect a predisposing factor to depression.[16, 17] According to some epidemiologic studies, the incidence of affective disorders increases with age,[18] and this has been related to the fact that MAO-levels also increase with age.[19] It seems that with advancing age bipolar depressive illness occurs with increasing frequency, severity, and duration of episodes, and with increasing resistance to treatment. Reportedly, the prognosis for recovery of recurrent depressions becomes worse in old age.[20, 21]

The difference between unipolar and bipolar affective disorders is reflected by differences on the neurophysiological level. Thus, the administration of L-Dopa can differentiate between patients with unipolar *versus* bipolar depressions.[22] (Bipolar refers to patients with a past history of manic-depressive illness; unipolar, to those without such history).[23] The administration of L-Dopa causes the formation of more dopamine in the brain, and this is associated with an increase in anger in patients with unipolar depression, without improving the depressive affect. In patients with a history of manic-depressive illness, however, L-Dopa can precipitate manic or hypomanic behavior.[22] According to Coppen, the administration of lithium to bipolar patients causes improvement in the affective disorder, in contrast to its effect on unipolar patients.[24] On the other hand, unipolar patients respond well to tricyclic antidepressants, although bipolar patients do not. Some bipolar patients tend to become hypomanic when taking tricyclics. Finally, bipolar patients in contrast to unipolar patients, show a significantly decreased level of MAO in blood platelets.[25] Such a deficiency could produce an increased amount of biogenic amines, which in turn serves as a predisposition for mania.[22]

At the present state of our knowledge, it would be premature to make final generalizations concerning the effects of age on affective disorders. It does seem that, in the course of time, affective disorders can change by following a plurality of pathways, and that the symptomatology may be expressed through a diversity of clinical manifestations.

## PSYCHODYNAMIC ASPECTS AND CLINICAL MANIFESTATIONS

### Involutional Grief Reaction

An involutional grief reaction may occur in early middle age as part of the mid-life crisis. Among the factors responsible for it are failure to attain ideals, realization of one's transience, relinquishing illusions of perennial progress, and other disillusionments, as well as biological or social stresses emerging around this time. More than likely, this grief reaction is the first in a series, although this is not to say that the second half of life consists only of successive losses and grief.

The depressive feelings do not amount to a depression unless the grief reaction derails, e.g., into a neurotic or psychotic depression. If losses occur in rapid succession, multiple grief reactions can be superimposed. When, during a period of grief, a second loss occurs, then a third, and so on, a situation develops in which the person has persistent depressive feelings. Yet, this persistence is not to be interpreted as chronicity, but it reflects a succession of superimposed losses and episodes of grief. A grief reaction may derail in several ways, and as a result, various types of affective disorder may develop.

### Neurotic Depression

(a). *The Role of Ambivalence.* If the individual used to have ambivalent feelings about the lost object, the grief reaction comes to an impasse. If a person had mixed feelings about having something, he will also have mixed feelings about not having it. Thus, the working through of the loss tends to get into a deadlock.

If a person had mixed feelings about his father, for example, there will be a sense of unfinished business after the father has died. Because of the positive feelings (love, admiration), the negative emotions (hostility, envy, fear) are repressed. But in their repressed state, they maintain an influence, leading to unconscious wishes that are vindictive in nature. If the father should die after a long and painful illness, the following developments may occur. Inasmuch as the patient loved his father, he experiences a major loss resulting in a grief reaction. But to the extent that he hated or resented him, he may have a sense of satisfaction that the negative wishes were fulfilled. The affection and respect for his deceased father cause him to feel guilty that the hostile fantasies came true. By way of primitive magical thought processes, he now holds himself responsible for his father's death. (What is magic here, is the notion that one's wishes or thoughts can cause something to happen. Because the hostile feelings are unconscious, they are out of reach for the corrective influences of rational thought).

The next sequel in the chain is the need for a punishment that fits the crime. At this point, two currents of feelings converge. Because of his affectionate feelings, the patient tries to hold onto the lost object by introjection or identification. By becoming like his father, he is better able to retain an image of him and maintain a sense of closeness to him. But because of the other feelings (hostility and guilt), the identification is highly selective; the patient identifies with those features that are painful, i.e., his father's illness. By including these painful elements in his identification, he suffers the way his father did and atones for his hostility.

(b). Such a *hostile identification*, however, is not a stable, satisfactory state of affairs. The grief reaction is not being resolved and the patient develops a neurotic depression or is suffering from physical symptoms.

A middle aged woman was hospitalized for disabling attacks of "asthma," which were, in fact, caused by hyperventilation episodes. She had been married to an alcoholic who "had been running around with other women," while she had been a "good wife." One reason she suppressed her feelings of outrage and resentment was the fact that he had heart disease, with a lot of shortness of breath. One day he asked her to go fishing with him, but she refused; a few hours later she was informed that he had drowned. Presumably, he had an acute heart attack, fell in the water, and drowned. Soon after this, she began to have "asthma." The symptom choice was determined by the husband's cardiac dyspnea and his death by drowning. Through the mental mechanism of hostile identification with her dead husband, she developed an illness of her own, which represented a punishment for her resentment toward him and alleged negligence of him ("If I had gone fishing with him, I could have saved him.").

## Psychotic Depression

(a). *The Role of Overreaction and Generalization.* A person who has experienced a loss may overreact. Having experienced one loss, the individual feels more easily threatened and may develop a mental set involving the anticipation of multiple losses. The nature of these anticipated losses is that they are not factually real, but have psychic reality. And it is this psychic reality that counts with regard to the development of emotional responses. In addition, there may be a process of generalization from one particular loss to losses in the realm of general categories and ideals. For example, the loss of a spouse may be the first step on a pathway leading to the conclusion that marriage in general is no good; loss of a child, to the conclusion that parenthood in general is not worth it; loss of a job, to the feeling that it does not pay to be a good worker. In this manner, disappointments and disillusionments may wreak havoc with personal ideals and cherished sets of values.

(b). The *predisposition* to overreacting is related to certain premorbid character features. First, there may be a tendency to function according to the all-or-none principle, and to think in terms of black or white instead of shades of gray. Such a rigid framework leaves no place for flexibility, relativity, and nuances. The second feature refers to over-valuation of meaningful objects and personal ideals. Because the object is overvalued, its loss becomes a disaster. The patient is not responding to the actual value, but to something inflated by fantasy. These two tendencies combined (*i.e.*, the idea of a disaster, plus the all-or-none principle) lead the patient to believe that everything must be bad all over. This is the intrapsychic counterpart of the domino theory: once the first domino stone falls, the rest will automatically follow.

There is also evidence that the premorbid character has compulsive features. Compulsive individuals tend to be rigid and reserved. They may be emotionally inhibited and sexually incapable of attaining true intimacy. The ambivalent feelings about one's feminine or masculine role come into sharper focus during the involutional years.

In this type of premorbid character, a loss produces a depression which feeds on itself, and which may progressively decompensate into a depressive psychosis. The more pervasive the sense of disillusionment, the more the future becomes constricted, with doubts about life being worth living. The more the lost ideals and objects were a source of pride, the more the self-esteem will be lowered.

(c). With regard to the *role of hostility* in the psychodynamics of a psychotic depression, there are two considerations. The first one pertains to the well-known mechanism of introjection, and turning the hostility against the self. Second, the more the lost object had been inflated in fantasy, the more there will be an angry protest. Knowing that his anger is not reasonable is of little comfort to the patient, and makes matters even more frustrating—the thought that he only has himself to blame. The destructive elements of his anger, having little in the way of a realistic outlet, now may flow through the channels opened up by the process of generalization. As a result, the hostility is not aimed at real objects but at their abstractions: ideals and values. This may have a lethal effect on the symbols of life and love. The scene of Armageddon overwhelms the patient with remorse and guilt; he feels doomed having committed the unpardonable sin. In this context, the delusion of unpardonable sin reflects not only the patient's guilt about his destructiveness, but also the irrevocability of the damage.

(d). The *nosological* distinction between involutional melancholia and psychotic depressive reaction does not appear to be logical or practical. *Involutional melancholia* is defined as a "disorder occurring in the involutional period and characterized by worry, anxiety, agitation, and severe insomnia; frequent feelings of guilt and somatic preoccupation, which may be delusional." A *psychotic depressive reaction* is distinguished by a "depressive mood attributable to some experience."[26] This seems to imply that, in order to make the latter diagnosis in an elderly patient, one would need to prove that the experience to which that patient is reacting is unrelated to involution, even though it occurs during involution. What the two diagnostic entities have in common is the spectrum of clinical symptomatology, and the absence of recurrent affective disorders in the past history.

(e) In the *symptomatology*, the disturbance of affect is the outstanding manifestation with disturbances of thought and behavior being secondary. The sensorium is clear, but depressive stupor may occur because of extreme introspective preoccupation. The affect is one of profound depression, guilt, worthlessness, or hopelessness, often accompanied by agitation and anxiety. When illusions or auditory hallucinations occur, their content is in keeping with the depressive affect. The voices may tell the patient, for example, that he will be punished for an unpardonable sin. Delusions are frequent and are also consistent with the depressive affect. Psychomotor activity may show retardation or agitation in varying degrees. The physiological concomitants may be quite prominent. Some cases are characterized chiefly by depression, and others, by paranoid ideas. The difference between the depressed and paranoid subtypes can be quite subtle indeed.

One middle-aged man with a psychotic depression had the delusion of having given syphilis to the entire world. Certainly, this was a delusion that might qualify as unpardonable sin. But the element of paranoid grandiosity is just beneath the surface: only a sexual superman could give syphilis to the whole world.

## Manic Disorders

(a). **Psychodynamic Aspects.** A person may respond to a loss by denying its significance (*i.e.*, rationalization), by denying the emotions associated with the loss (suppression), or by denying the actual fact of the loss (*e.g.*, psychotic restitution fantasies). Psychotic restitution fantasies may occur not only in manic disorders, but also in schizophrenia and dementia.

Denial and suppression are often facilitated by hyperactive behavior, the pursuit of external diversions, and a general stimulus hunger. These patterns of behavior facilitate the pushing of painful thoughts to the back of one's mind. With advancing age, it will become progressively more difficult for the individual to select the manic cluster of defenses, and it becomes increasingly likely that the affective disorder will be manifested in terms of an agitated depression or a depressive psychosis.

The actual onset of manic-depressive illness is precipitated by a combination of endogenous (hereditary, constitutional) factors and external, situational stresses. The following case example (dating back to the pre-lithium era) illustrates the interaction of multiple factors: family history, premorbid personality, ambivalence toward the lost object, cyclic mood swings with clockwork regularity for thirteen years after acute onset in middle age.

A 62-year-old woman had recurrent moodswings, since the age of 49, when her husband died. Her first depression began a few days after his death and she was already receiving ECT within a week after the funeral. During the next 13 years, she had her annual fall depression and spring elation. During the first nine years, the manic episodes were treated with ECT, although ECT was given during depressive episodes only if they were severe.

The family history revealed that both parents and one brother had suffered from recurrent moodswings, while a sister was chronically depressed. The patient described her father as being "supermanic."

The patient's premorbid personality was characterized by passive-aggressive traits, and by an inability to assert herself or to express anger ("I never ask for anything."). Her marriage had been unhappy because her husband allegedly ran around with other women. The patient stayed with him "only to raise my children—I kept everything to myself." During her husband's prolonged terminal illness, she had taken care of him because she used to be a nurse. When interviewed during a followup visit in early fall, she stated "I am getting ready for my depression."

**(b). Clinical Manifestations.**

1. In *manic-depressive* illness, the essential features are alternating, marked mood swings, remission, and recurrence of episodes. The manic type demonstrates increased verbal and psychomotor behavior, and rapid flow of ideas. The patient may engage in unwise business activities or inappropriate extramarital romances. The depressed type manifests depression of mood. Psychomotor retardation usually is prominent, but agitation may occur. The depressed phase of manic-depressive illness is differentiated from other depressions on the basis of the cyclic pattern of the depressive episodes. In some cases the periodicity has a seasonal character. The patient may report, for example, that "spring is my time to feel up, and autumn is my time to feel down." When the recurrent episodes of affective disturbance tend to be similar, the patient (and family members) often learn how to recognize the onset of the disorder at an early stage.

In the case of a 58-year-old woman with a clear history of manic-depressive illness, the earliest sign of a manic phase was an increased preoccupation with household chores. The patient would get up at 5 AM and start cleaning, washing, and cooking; this activity would go on until midnight. During the first manic episodes, the patient thought "this was just great," and she would glow with joy about her excessive work. Only later did she learn to recognize the keyed-up behavior as being part of an illness. She also had to learn to recognize the onset of depressive episodes. During the initial stages of her manic-depressive illness, she would ignore a depression until she was suicidal.

According to Stotsky[27] manic-depressive disorders continue into old age. Most of these disorders are of the depressed type with psychomotor retardation, and have a tendency toward paranoid ideation, seclusiveness, and apathy. In some cases, pseudosenility tends to be prominent.

The *differential diagnosis* between a manic disorder and *agitated depression* can be rather difficult. Patients with agitated depression may report that they feel unable to resist the surge of energy that compels them to be active, and also that "going so fast" lifts their spirits and makes them feel good. Typically, there is a pattern of decreased sleep; the appetite may be up or down, but since the patient usually "does not have time to sit down and eat," weight loss is common.

Manic episodes may be attributable to *drug reactions* (steroids) or idosyncratic drug responses (*e.g.*, tranquilizers and sedatives). Also, it may be the first sign of an O.B.S.

2. When a manic disorder appears for the first time in late life (and a careful scrutiny of the past history does not reveal previous episodes of affective disorder), the diagnosis of manic-depressive illness would not be appropriate. In many of these patients there is a constellation of social, environmental, and psychodynamic factors which we would expect to cause a psychotic depressive reaction. Instead, we are confronted with mania. In such patients, the protective aspect of the manic defense cluster (denial, flight into health, shallow euphoria) is usually rather transparent. The manic element is represented by grandiosity on the ideational level rather than elation on the emotional level. In these cases of isolated mania, there is not a joyous grandiosity, but a solemn, austere grandeur. Furthermore, because these manic conditions seem to be reactive in nature, it would be proper to designate them as a *psychotic manic reaction*, as a counterpart of the psychotic depressive reaction.

A 75-year-old man was hospitalized because he expected the end of the world. He also had the delusion that his house was surrounded by enemies. During the alleged siege, however, the patient had suddenly felt that the "Lord was on my side so I went outside and stood in front of my house facing my enemies. I raised my cane and the crowd opened up, so I could walk through."

This man was found to have a carcinoma of the lung, which had not been expected by anyone before or right after hospitalization. The manic delusion replaced a depressive-paranoid one (expecting the end of the world). The latter delusion may have been precipitated by the enemy within (cancer) which would end his world. The projection allowed the intrapsychic gain of externalizing and making concrete the internal (physical) threat. The next defensive procedure involved the creation of enough help to defeat the external enemy: the Lord, Himself, came to the patient's rescue. The resulting sense of invincibility and grandiosity was expressed by his identification with Moses, who also had been beleaguered, raised his cane, and opened a path through the sea, toward the promised land.

### Depressive Withdrawal

A person who has experienced a painful loss may decide that he is not willing to expose himself again to such a risk. The full resolution of the grief reaction does not take place because the bereaved person is unwilling to invest his interests into a new object. The world around contains potential substitute objects, but the feeling is "I won't get hurt twice—once is enough." Such a person may resolve his grief up to a point, but what remains is an emotionally sensitive scar. The absence of a new object or activity brings about an impoverishment. As with most maladaptive patterns, the process does not stop here; it may further decompensate in the direction of hypochondriasis or a narcissistic self-absorption. The patient's remaining object relationships are endangered because he may alienate people by being self-centered and neglecting his interpersonal contacts. Withdrawal, self-absorption, and hypochondriasis, having a positive feedback on each other, become a vicious circle, and lead to progressive impoverishment of the self.

## Paranoid Decompensation

(a). At almost any point during the decompensation of a grief reaction, paranoid elements may enter. This is usually attributable to a further weakening of the patient's position, or to increasing regression. Paranoid features must be distinguished from the expression of anger, which can be a sign of clinical improvement in depressive states. Such outwardly directed anger is not the same as the hostility frequently associated with paranoid phenomena; the latter are chiefly characterized by the use of projection and the presence of ideas of references (see page 59). Thus, the development of "anger-out" phenomena is a favorable sign, whereas paranoid changes indicate further decompensation. The depressive position essentially conveys, "I am bad, you are good." The paranoid position reverses this to "I am good, you are bad," whereas the schizoid view is "I am bad, you are bad." Developmentally, the paranoid position precedes the depressive position, which emerges at a developmental level of four to six months. There is a tendency to regress, in varying degrees, to the paranoid position when the working through of depressive anxieties is interfered with.

(b). Not only may affective disorders undergo a paranoid decompensation, but so can *hypochondriasis*. Initially, the hypochondriac still has faith in the system. The withdrawal from others was not primarily on the basis of depreciating them. Rather, they are perceived as valuable; otherwise the patient would not keep on making contacts in his search for aid. After some time, however, the hypochondriac usually becomes more and more disillusioned. He begins to feel mistreated, angry, and bitter. Ideas of reference exist when the patient feels especially singled out for abuse or neglect. Further decompensation produces vindictiveness and active depreciation of others, with a proportionate elevation of himself.

(c). In *depressive bitterness*, the individual feels embittered by the failure of providence to allot him the good life. There is a sense that life in general can be good but that fortune has smiled on others, not on him. While others found their place in the sun, he feels an outsider, left out in the cold. Considering his misfortune, it is impossible to remain resigned and not to feel envy toward the lucky ones who are counting their blessings. A paranoid shift may occur when the "have not" accuses "those who have."

(d). In *cynical depressions*, the concept of providence disappears and is replaced by that of fate, a power which rules blindly according to the laws of necessity. In such a fatalistic ideology, there is no place for the good life or gifts of fortune, but only submission to the inevitable, without understanding. The cynic may sustain a misanthropic consolation, that all those happy people are merely deceiving themselves—they don't know that life is a cruel joke. He may live his life in quiet desperation, comforted only by his secret that, in his nihilism, he knows more than his fellow humans. The secret is kept intact through arrogance and distantiation. The arrogance discourages trespassers who might question him on his ideology. The patient may also resort to other behaviors to keep others away, becoming dirty, living in filth, or developing his private system of thinking (delusions).

The misanthropic depressions and their paranoid features can be regarded as manifestations of a perspective of hopelessness, or specific dimensions of despair.

## REFERENCES

1. GOLDFARB, A. I.: Masked depression in the elderly. *In:* Masked Depression, Chap. 14, S. Lessee, ed. Jason Aronson. New York. 1974. pp. 236–249.
2. ZUNG, W. W. K., WILSON, W. P., and DODSON, W. E.: Effect of depressive disorders on sleep EEG responses. *Arch. Gen. Psychiatry 10:* 439, 1964.
3. SNYDER, F.: Sleep disturbance in relation to acute psychosis. *In:* Sleep Physiology and Pathology, Chap. 13, A. Kales, ed. J. B. Lippincott Company, Philadelphia, 1969. pp. 170–182.
4. ZUNG, W. W. K.: Depression in the normal aged. Psychosomatics *8:* 287–292, 1967.
5. SILVERMAN, C.: The Epidemiology of Depression. Johns Hopkins University Press, Baltimore, 1968.
6. ERNEST, K.: Die Prognose der Neurosen, Springer-Verlag, Berlin, 1959.
7. MEYER, J. E.: Psychoneuroses and neurotic reactions in old age. *J. Am. Geriatr. Soc.* 22: 254–257, 1974.
8. BATCHELOR, I. R. C.: Suicide in Old Age. *In:* Clues to Suicide, Chap. 14, E. S. Shneidman and M. L. Farberow, eds. McGraw-Hill, New York, 1957. pp. 143–151.
9. ROTH, M.: The natural history of mental disorders in old age. *J. Ment. Sci. 101:* 281–301, 1955.
10. NOWLIN, J. B.: Depression and health. *In:* Normal Aging, Chap. 5, Vol. 2, E. Palmore, ed. Duke University Press, Durham, 1974. pp. 168–172.
11. VERWOERDT, A. and DOVENHUEHLE, R. H.: Heart disease and depression. *Geriatrics 19:* 856–864, 1964.
12. DAVIS, J. M., FANN, W. E., EL-YOUSEF, M. K., and JANOWSKY, D. S.: Clinical problems in treating the aged with psychotropic drugs. *In:* Advances in Behavioral Biology, Vol. 6. Psychopharmacology and Aging. C. Eisdorfer and W. E. Fann, eds. Plenum Press, New York, 1973. pp. 111–125.
13. WINOKUR, G., CADORET, R., DORZAB, J., BAKER, M.: Depressive disease: a genetic study. *Arch. Gen. Psychiatry 24:* 135–144, 1971.
14. PRANGE, A. J.: The use of antidepressant drugs in the elderly patient. *In:* Advances in Behavioral Biology, vol. 6. Psychopharmacology and Aging. C. Eisdorfer and W. E. Fann, eds. Plenum Press, New York, 1973. pp. 225–237.
15. COURT, J. H.: Manic-depressive psychosis: an alternate conceptual model. *Br. J. Psychiatry 114:* 1523–1530, 1968.
16. COPPEN, A.: The biochemistry of affective disorders. *Br. J. Psychiatry 113:* 1237–1264, 1967.
17. ROBINSON, D. S., NIES, A., DAVIS, J. N., BUNNEY, W. E., DAVIS, J. M., COLBURN, R. W.,

BOURNE, H. R., SHAW, D. M., AND COPPEN, A. J.: Aging, monamines, and monoamine-oxidase levels. *Lancet 1:* 290–291, 1972.

18. ROWNSLEY, K.: "Epidemiology of affective disorders. Recent developments in affective disorders. *Br. J. Psychiatry*, (Special Publication No. 2) pp. 27–36, 1968.

19. NIES, A., ROBINSON, D. S., DAVIS, J. M., and RAVARIS, C. L.: Changes in monoamine oxidase with aging. *In:* Advances in Behavioral Biology, Vol. 6. Psychopharmacology and Aging. C. Eisdorfer and W. E. Fann, eds. Plenum Press, New York, 1973. pp. 41–54.

20. PERRIS, C.: "A study of bipolar (manic depressive) and unipolar recurrent depressive psychoses". *Acta Psychiatr. Scand. 42* (Suppl 194): 7–189, 1966.

21. VAN DER VELDE, C. D.: "Effectiveness of lithium carbonate in the treatment of manic-depressive illness". *Am. J. Psychiatry 127:* 345–351, 1970.

22. BRODIE, H. K.: Affective changes associated with L-dopa therapy. *In:* Advances in Behavioral Biology, Vol. 6. Psychopharmacology and Aging. C. Eisdorfer and W. E. Fann, eds. Plenum Press, New York, 1973. pp. 97–104.

23. LEONHARD, K.: Aufteilung der Endogenen Psychosen, 2nd Ed. Akademie Verlag, Berlin, 1959.

24. COPPEN, A., NOGUERA, R., BAILEY, J., BURNS, B. H., SWANI, M. S., HARE, E. H., GARDNER, R., and MAGGS, R.: "Prophylactic Lithium in affective disorders. *Lancet 2:* 275, 1971.

25. MURPHY, D. L., and WEISS, R.: Reduced monamine oxidase activity in blood platelets from bipolar depressed patients. *Am. J. Psychiatry 128:* 1351, 1972.

26. Diagnostic and Statistical Manual of Mental Disorders, 2nd Ed. American Psychiatric Association, Washington, D.C., 1968. pp. 36; 38.

27. STOTSKY, B. A.: Psychoses in the elderly. *In:* Advances in Behavioral Biology, Vol. 6. Psychopharmacology and Aging. C. Eisdorfer and W. E. Fann, eds. Plenum Press, New York, 1973. pp. 193–202.

# 7

# personality disorders

This group of disorders is characterized by deeply ingrained patterns of behavior that are different in quality from neurotic and psychotic manifestations. By and large, they are lifelong patterns recognizable by the time of adolescence, or even earlier.[1] In contrast to the neuroses, internal discomfort and a sense of anxiety from within are lacking, and maladaptive interaction with the environment is prominent. While a neurotic conflict remains contained within the boundaries of the self, in personality disorders conflicts are often acted out or externalized. As a result, the individual himself is relieved of the tension while the environment now has to put up with it. The pathology is no longer in the person, but in the society—hence the term sociopath.

The problems that society has to put up with, in terms of its relationship with personality disorders, are of the following kind: the consequences of acting out of specific impulses or fantasies, intrapsychically invested with much drive energy; the consequences of poor impulse control, in general; and, the consequences of social and vocational inadequacies, resulting in the need for all types of assistance, especially money.

The broad category of personality disorders comprises numerous types: paranoid, cyclothymic, schizoid, explosive, obsessive-compulsive, hysterical, antisocial, passive-aggressive, inadequate, immature, and passive-dependent personality. Sexual deviations, alcoholism, and drug abuse are included as well. From a psychodynamic point of view, the common denominator in these types is considered to be a deficiency in the ego. This ego deficiency may pertain to the ego's basic tasks of adequate impulse control (delay of immediate gratification) and defense against anxiety, or to one or more of the autonomous ego functions.

In addition to reviewing the clinical manifestations of various personality disorders in late life, the issue of the relationship between aging and personality disorders (and their mutual interaction) is of particular interest and relevance.

## AGING AND PERSONALITY DISORDERS

With regard to the relationship between aging and personality disorders, the following questions can be raised:

How does the aging process influence the various lifelong patterns of personality disorder (pathoplastic effects)?

What are the adaptational assets and liabilities of specific character disorders *vis-à-vis* the stress of the aging process?

Which types of behavioral disorder can arise, for the first time, in the context of senescence (pathogenetic effects)?

## Effects of Aging on Personality Disorders

No systematic longitudinal studies exist which would provide information about the effects of the aging process on various personality disorders. Such a study might not be feasible anyway, in view of the lack of adequate operational definitions of what constitutes a personality disorder, and because of the innumerable variables impinging on the individual in addition to the factor of aging.

Statistical data pertaining to first admissions to U.S. public mental hospitals show that the diagnosis of personality disorder occurs most frequently in the 25 to 44 age range (about one out of every three admissions), whereas the incidence of personality disorders in the two adjacent age groups (18–24 and 45–64) is only slightly less.[2] In contrast, the frequency in the 65+ age group drops below five percent, whereas the incidence of organic brain syndromes soars to 84 percent. A similar type of distribution is obtained for neurotic disorders. Statistical data on the incidence of neuroses and personality disorders obtained from community mental health clinics are along the same lines.[3] Thus, cross-sectional studies seem to indicate that the incidence of neuroses, as well as personality disorders, gradually increases in early life, reaching a peak during the 25 to 44 age range, and then tapering off during senescence and old age. But such cross-sectional studies do not tell us what happens to particular individuals over a period of many years.

The data suggest that, inasmuch as personality disorders are thought to originate early in life, a pattern of repeated failure and maladjustment increasingly takes its toll as the individual is confronted with the tasks of adulthood. But the statistical finding that the incidence of personality disorders decreases after middle age does not justify the conclusion that such disorders therefore ameliorate with advancing age. Although such a favorable development is certainly possible, it is just as possible that the behavior patterns undergo unfavorable changes. For example, what had been diagnosed as a personality disorder early in life may decompensate in various ways: an alcoholic may develop organic brain syndrome; an obsessive-compulsive person may develop involutional melancholia (perhaps with recurrent depressive episodes from then on); inadequate personalities, who often also have a poor educational background, may be more vulnerable to early onset of dementia; or, a schizoid type may become paranoid or schizophrenic.

An 85-year-old man, never married, had lived alone in a remote area ever since age 20. During his early teens, his father was killed by a sheriff, who was himself killed in the fight. The patient's mother then became mentally ill and was unable to care for the seven children. The patient, being the oldest child, reportedly took care of his mentally ill mother and his six siblings for a few years. Then he moved away to live by himself. During all these years (from age 20 until 85), he lived in a one-room shack, keeping other people away, and refusing all offers of medical or financial assistance. Eventually, his physical condition necessitated placement in an extended care facility. After this, he became acutely belligerent and paranoid. Once he discovered, however, that in the rest home he could have his own private room, his behavior calmed down. His life-long schizoid patterns were restored and remained intact, when he locked himself in his room and refused contacts with others.

Finally, it is possible that a certain number of personality disorders simply do not survive until old age. They become the victim of their deficiency in adaptation, and succumb due to accidents, lack of proper self-protection, and so on.

Personality types which the clinician may diagnose as a disorder are not necessarily considered abnormal from the patient's viewpoint. First, because the personality defect is built into the character structure, it is ego-syntonic, and is therefore not perceived by the individual, himself, as a handicap. Second, the existence of certain personality assets may be used to minimize or compensate for the character deficiency, or even to turn the handicap into an advantage. A "manipulator", who is lacking in intimacy, trust, and affiliation, may succeed in building an empire for himself, and his character deficiency may never catch up with him. A dependent personality may be lucky enough to find the protective niche essential to his happiness. The inadequate personality may find out that society will take care of him by putting him on welfare, by giving him refuge in the sickrole, or even by securing him as a career prisoner.

A 73-year-old man, whose father had been a sheriff, succeeded going through life always being taken care of by one person or another. He lived off and on with various relatives; spent time in a few sanatoriums for alleged tuberculosis; married and lived off his wife's earnings; and after her death, made a suicidal gesture which assured him the protection of a mental hospital; and finally, moved into a boarding home living off a small disability check.

Certain types of impulse disorders (including alcoholics or habitual trouble-makers) tend to settle down after the mid-point in life, at some time between 35 and 45 years of age. The explanation for such phenomena is probably in terms of an interaction between intrapsychic shifts and social changes. These would include changes in the drives (their aim, source, object, and intensity), changes in the ego (belated mastery of skills, increased ability to deal with drives of lesser intensity) and superego changes (mellowing, or the discovery that society's standards are not so confining that personal satisfaction can be obtained only by way of rebellion). Social-interpersonal developments can contribute to the amelioration of behavioral disorders. An alcoholic may come to the point where the satisfactions of the group experiences of Alcoholics Anonymous, or of religious conversion, are felt to be more rewarding than the euphoric oblivion of alcohol. And, an individual with a long history of breaking the law, may find himself at a point where he can use his inside familiarity with delinquency as the very basis for efforts aimed at rehabilitating law breakers. In such instances, intrapsychic shifts and social opportunities interact and complement each other to bring about the behavioral improvements and turn a loser into a winner.

The past life of a 75-year-old man consisted primarily of a series of defeats and rejections. He never had a steady job and spent his money as fast as he could earn it. His only son was killed in the military service. His wife left him for another man, and he did not know the whereabouts of his two daughters. By the age of 70, he had no home, no family, no belongings. Arrangements were made by the social service department for placement in a boarding home. In the first home, he courted a woman employee, but after a while he lost out to another resident who was also in the competition. After this defeat, the boarding home operator gave him added responsibilities in the home to boost his morale, but the patient felt he was being used as a janitor. Next, he focused his attention on another woman, this time a resident in the home; and again he lost out to a competitor. Thus, he went from one boarding home to another, for a period of years. The pattern of defeats and rejections stopped when he was placed in a small rest home managed by a widow. She gave him special responsibilities, and made him feel worthwhile. Because there was no other man in the house, and no competition, he felt progressively more secure. For the first time in as long as he could remember, he felt at home and had a sense of belonging.

In studying the life histories of character disorders, we frequently see a lifelong pattern of deficient personality functioning, of which the patient himself was not aware. As a result, the individual has been losing out all along, but without clearly realizing this. The losses are not the kind we usually have in mind (loss of something of value), but they represent missed opportunities. The individual is missing out on any number and type of basic elements in the spectrum of human experience. Because what is being missed are opportunities, he tends not to know about such a loss and may not feel like a loser. But when such a person arrives in old age, he has little to show for his earlier years. At his station in life there is a paucity of external objects, a poverty of external support systems. At this point, awareness begins to grow that something is amiss. In keeping with the lifelong pattern of not seeing the deficiency as related to the self, the patient now is aware only of the deficiencies around him: somebody else must be responsible, somebody else is not giving him enough. Thus, a variety of personality disorders may end up in late life as losers, have-nots, putting the blame for this on the environment.

The clinical symptomatology of such patients is characterized by hapless complaining and a persistent bitterness. The accusations are directed at whatever people happen to be around or at various community agencies. These individuals are usually in their 60's or 70's, and show no evidence of organic disorders, schizophrenia, or recurrent depressions. Their histories reveal lack of significant achievement in areas such as education, marriage, parenthood, work, and social relationships. They are characterized by failure to learn from experience, increasing impoverishment of self and milieu, and the absence of recognizable depression.

### Adaptational Assets and Liabilities

Regarding the adaptational assets and liabilities of personality disorders *vis-à-vis* the stress of aging, the following points may be considered:

**(a).** Character disorders relying largely on *coping patterns requiring little energy* may be relatively better equipped to deal with the stresses of aging. These low energy patterns (see Chap. 3, under "Retreat from the Threat; Conservation of Energy") would apply to passive-dependent, schizoid, asthenic, and inadequate personalities. Such individuals may feel quite comfortable with the regressive modes of adaptation frequently encountered in old age.

**(b).** Persons using primarily *high-energy defense patterns* are likely to be more vulnerable. The paranoid personality tends to react with anger and aggression. The cyclothymic personality relies on hyperactivity and diversions. The obsessive-compulsive personality requires much time and energy for pursuing perfectionism or for repeating rituals. In the case of many passive-agressive personalities, an aggressive or overly independent facade covers underlying passivity and dependency.

**(c).** Personalities in which the central deficiency is *inadequate impulse control* include the explosive personality and the hysterical personality, as well as the alcoholic and the sexual deviates. In these personality disorders, life may act as a therapist, inasmuch as the strength of the drives declines with age. However, this is still a far from simple proposition. Active and aggressive impulses may well decrease in intensity, while passive needs are becoming more prominent. Thus, whether personality disorders involving poor impulse control will improve or deteriorate with age depends on the nature of the impulses.

### Age-specific Behavior Disorders

Age-specific behavior disorders are those that arise for the first time in old age, and may reflect the pathogenetic effect of aging. This category includes three types of psychopathological constellations: (a) changes in the personal time perspective; (b) regressive ego changes leading to (re-)activation of latent conflict and acting out; and (c) behavior disturbances secondary to other age-related mental illness.

**(a).** As was mentioned in Chapter 2, specific alterations in the *time perspective* occur with advancing age. Some individuals feel that time is running out and want to make the most of whatever time remains. Those who discover that they have missed out on this or that subjectively important experience may want to catch up. Depending on many factors (ego strength, appropriateness of belatedly attaining overdue goals, situational opportunities and constraints, etc.), such endeavors will succeed or fail. For example, an old person may always have had the wish to see the world. Sir Francis Chichester, in his 60's, succeeded going around the world alone in a sailboat, but the goal was reached after a lifetime of preparation. Likewise, a person, well-to-do in his retirement, may appropriately decide to go around the world. On the other hand, there are situations in which old men and women who, having missed out on true romance, now become libidinal desperadoes, willing to exchange their fortune for a mirage of romatic love.

Persons who have been on good behavior all of their lives may feel that now the time has come for a reward. This may reflect a process of genuine mellowing, but it can also be a caricature of it. The latter situation occurs when the individual used to resent being on good behavior. His resentment may have betrayed itself through his getting irritated at people who indulged without qualms in those pleasures which our patient had renounced. In such cases, the old person will reach for his reward with a vengeance, as though in finally doing what he wants, he is getting back at the authority that had kept him so long in line.

A 71-year-old woman, married to a man 24 years her senior, had acquired notoriety of being "a conniver, demanding and bitter." The patient, the oldest of seven siblings, had wanted to become a nurse but her father had not permitted it, "since this was not considered proper for young ladies during those days". The patient was bitterly disappointed and really never forgave her father for this. When she married a man who was old enough to be her father, there was no doubt as to who was in charge this time. Having taken revenge in this manner, life dealt her a cruel blow when her only two children died at an early age. ("They are buried in the cemetary across from my home, and I can see them from my window.") During the last ten years or so, her behavior has become more dominating. She calls her doctor, caseworker or family members for the slightest reasons, no matter what time of the night. She also periodically puts the money allocated for attendant care for her husband in her own pocket.

(b). *Ego changes* in old age may affect psychological conflicts which throughout life had remained relatively dormant or latent. Because of age-related stresses, the ego may function ineffectively and ego strength may decompensate. Because of weakening of repression or reaction formation, impulses that used to be kept in check are now coming to the fore and finding expression in specific behavior patterns. These behavior patterns tend to be the opposite of what used to be the life-long dominant ego-style.

In the case of acting out, we deal with a specific wish or a cluster of wishful fantasies, which used to be repressed. When the ego's capacity to maintain repression is diminished, these wishes can gain access to the motor apparatus, and may be acted upon. Related to this, and often an essential part, is the reactivation of a childhood neurosis.

A 67-year-old man was hospitalized because of combative behavior, especially toward his oldest son whom he accused of plotting to take away his 500-acre farm. The patient had taken his son into several business endeavors, the last of which was (ironically) a funeral parlor. In addition, the patient had grandiose delusions and a euphoric affect. He stated that he "did not feel like 67, but like 17 years old; and when I was young, I had sex four times per night." (The patient's wife had expressed her irritation at his agressively romantic demands.) He also was preoccupied with fantasies about meeting a queen, and reported that, in fact, he had met a queen on several occasions. In the absence of a history of affective or schizophrenic disorder, the diagnosis "psychotic manic reaction" was made. Of special relevance in this context is the role played by the reactivation and acting out of a neurotic conflict dating back to childhood. At the age of five, he wanted to be a millionaire and had been preoccupied with fairy tales in which a poor boy marries a princess; as a millionaire he would be able to marry the queen herself. This oedipal fantasy (marrying the mother if only he could be as powerful as the father) remained with the patient throughout his life. It became a near-reality inasmuch as he became a near-millionaire. Then, during senescence, came the painful realization that he was no longer powerful. Now, it was his son who possessed power. The patient then developed envy and jealousy toward his son much like the mixture of envy, awe, and hostility he once had felt toward his father. This psychodynamic constellation we may call a reversed oedipal complex. The patient's manic and paranoid behavior represented a defense against depression and a sense of helplessness; regressive forces resulted in a reactivation of an early childhood oedipal conflict. As soon as the patient began to improve, the regressive forces lost their power and the childhood conflict was once more repressed. Concomitantly, he disowned any accusations toward his son. The idea of the son rising up against his father disappeared along with other derivatives of the childhood neurosis: he disclaimed any acquaintance with queens. Significantly, as clinical improvement occurred, the more severe psychopathology (paranoid) disappeared first, while it took longer for the less serious psychopathological elements (mania) to clear up.

**(c). Behavioral Disturbances Secondary to Senescent Psychopathology.** In these cases, the behavioral disorder emerges, not as a carry over from the past, but as the result of specific psychopathology that develops in late life (organic brain syndrome, affective disorders, paranoid states, late paraphrenia). Of course, in many cases, late life psychopathology will only bring into sharper profile, behavioral traits that had existed throughout life without being unduly troublesome.

An 87-year-old woman, who was known to have always had a "mean and ugly" disposition, gradually developed increasingly severe temper tantrums. During these outbursts, she would hit and flail at people, and spit on them.

**1.** In *organic brain syndrome*, behavioral disturbances are the consequence of profound regression, unlearning of previously acquired skills, loss of impulse control, impaired judgment, and so on. Examples include regressive sexual behavior (*e.g.*, pedophilia), combativeness, loss of social decorum, incontinence, tendency to hoarding, deterioration of personal hygiene and personal milieu, and excessive wandering.

The main problem in the case of a 78-year-old woman with early presbyophrenia was her constant moving around. Over the last several years, she had moved more than thirty times, in four southern states. The patient had been born on a plantation in the Deep South. "I lived in a big house with many servants, and had everything I wanted." In contrast to her fairy-tale childhood, her adult years were marred by tragedy. Her two marriages ended in failure.

Her only child, a boy, died at age 11. When asked about this, the patient responded: "I don't know. I can't think about that, it is too sad. I tried to forget. I have forgotten" (illustrating the role of "forgetting" and "loss of memory" in depressive reminiscing). In old age, she ended up lonely and penniless. Her constant moving around represented a search for the utopia she once had known in childhood.

2. In contrast to *mania* in younger age groups, hyperactivity is not as prominent in older patients. What may be striking, however, are behavior patterns reflecting an underlying sense of grandiosity or invulnerability (*e.g.*, expansive business transactions, inappropriate romantic pursuits).

3. *Depressive conditions* may cause behavioral disturbances, such as self-destructive activities. In cases of extreme depression where the element of hopelessness enters, the ultimate act of despair is to take one's loved ones along in death (homicide-suicide).

4. *Paranoid states* are frequently associated with outward aggression, tendencies toward malice, ill will, vicious gossip, and litigation. There is a risk of combative, and occasionally even homicidal, behavior.

## CLINICAL TYPES

The *schizoid* personality avoids close involvement with others and has difficulty in being normally assertive. He is seclusive and sometimes eccentric. The *paranoid* individual has certain schizoid traits and a tendency to use projection, which results in suspiciousness. Emotional stress, including age-related losses, may increase the tendencies toward withdrawal and projection, resulting in overt symptomatology.

A 63-year-old unmarried woman was hospitalized because of hallucinations, delusions, and arguments with her family about a piece of land. The patient had always been a shy, reticent person who preferred staying close to home. Her father had died when she was two years old. The mother remarried and when the patient was 16 years old, she and her stepfather began to have sexual relations. This continued, until, at age 30, she became pregnant by her stepfather and gave birth to a daughter. The family knew all about it and forgave her. In fact, the patient lived without interruption with her mother until the latter died. Her mother died a few years before the patient's hospital admission. The death forced the patient to live on her own and support herself for the first time in her life. Meanwhile, disagreement was building up about a sizeable piece of land which the stepfather had left to the patient, who in turn had given it to her illegitimate daughter. The combined stresses of lifelong social isolation, constant bickering about her status and estate, and being forced into independence exceeded her coping ability.

The dynamics and symptomatology of her mental illness included: 1) *Regression and withdrawal.* She stayed in her home, refusing to go out. Increasing preoccupation with her self and a regressive drift into the past led to reactivation of feelings about her stepfather, especially guilt. 2) *Projection.* The guilt about her stepfather and the suspicion that her family would take her land were projected in the form of a single delusion ("people are following me") which lacked any elaboration or systematization. 3) *Concretization of the percept.* There had been visual and auditory hallucinations in keeping with the delusion of being followed. She "saw" and "heard" the people following her around. 4) The psychological test data showed a surprisingly *low intelligence* (70 on the WAIS). It was obvious that her intellectual potential was not that low. The lowered I.Q. and the feature of concreteness in the test findings were interpreted as a consequence of the regressive drift and autistic withdrawal. When proper environmental support was given to this patient, her symptoms quickly disappeared.

In the loneliness of old age, an individual with mild schizoid tendencies may well feel relatively comfortable. Such persons have traveled through life with a minimum of belongings. They had little to begin with, and have little to lose in the end.

On the other hand, a severely schizoid person may become a recluse living in marginal circumstances. Some old persons, often female, are hospitalized because of paranoid delusions. Typically, such a woman is unmarried, childless, has long been living alone, and has few social contacts. Age-related physical problems add the element of helplessness to the isolation. The resulting anxiety is dealt with by way of projection: the internal threat is externalized and becomes an enemy "out there." This enemy is given attributes which the patient always considered particularly threatening or alien. In unmarried, isolated women, these often pertain to sexual-erotic notions. Thus, the troublemakers have sexual schemes. But this autistic fantasy is usually not expressed in a direct fashion. By way of (primary process) symbolization, another distortion is added: the patient's body is symbolically represented as a house, and the evil designs of the troublemakers, as a foreign body coming inside. The sexual aspect is illustrated by the frequent delusion that the foreign man intrudes in the basement and messes up the plumbing or the electric wires. When such paranoid delusions are chronically persistent in the absence of organic brain damage, the diagnosis of *late paraphrenia* would be appropriate.

In some cases, the patient's isolation is seemingly not as absolute or severe if there is another person around who shares the patient's house, or life, and sometimes the delusions as well. This is the condition of *Folie à Deux*, a paranoid illness involving two individuals. Because their relationship is typically a primitive symbiosis, however, the two persons function as one unit; and, as a unit, they are just as isolated (perhaps more so even) as the above described cases (see Chap. 17 for description of Folie à Deux).

The *hysterical personality* is emotionally unpredictable, dramatic, or even histrionic. The self-dramatization has the aim of seeking attention, and may involve seductive behavior. These personalities are immature, vain, egocentric, and have a tendency to erotize interpersonal relationships, but their emotions are shallow. Underlying this changeable surface behavior, there are often strong dependency needs.[1] In the language of psychoanalysis: oral dependency needs are being gratified by genital sexual means; the sexuality of the hysterical personality is in the service of pregenital oral needs.

The aging process, especially the involution of the genital apparatus, may have a profound effect on the adjustment of such persons. It becomes more difficult or inappropriate to employ the instrument of genital sex for pregenital aims (*i.e.*, dependency wishes). Hence, such persons are predisposed to involutional depressions, hypochondriasis, and hysterical exaggeration of physical illness. Before the onset of a depression, there may be a period of heightened sexual inclinations and romantic activities, or attempts to deny the existence or significance of involutional processes. Ideally, such individuals would learn (through life's experiences, or through psychotherapy) that closeness, intimacy, or dependency can be achieved in many different ways, not just through the experience of genital sexuality.

The *passive-aggressive personality* is characterized by passive, as well as aggressive, behavior. The aggressive feelings, thoughts, or tendencies are expressed by passive means: oppositional behavior (obstructionism, stubbornness), being out of step with the environment (procrastination, intentional *faux pas*, deliberate misunderstandings), and a tendency toward brooding and cherishing old hurts. The element of passivity does not only apply to the method of expressing aggressive impulses, but also pertains to underlying passive-dependent wishes. Thus, the surface behavior may be the opposite of deeper, hidden tendencies.

The repertoire of dependency wishes not only centers on the functions of the upper G. I. tract (lips, mouth, stomach), but also includes submissive wishes (to be held and to follow), passive wishes (*e.g.*, stimulation by touch and warmth), and narcissistic wishes (to be in the center of attention).

Conflicts may develop because the aggressiveness and independence are not genuine, and are therefore difficult to maintain. In addition, the underlying dependency needs are not being met. An individual who covers his dependency needs with a facade of self-reliance is pseudoindependent. But the facade of strength has the effect of attracting others who are passive or dependent. The day of reckoning comes, when there is no longer enough energy to maintain the independent facade. The patient will fight the loss of face, first by way of an increase in aggressiveness or in the appearance of self-reliance; this defense often suddenly gives way to helpless dependency and depression.

An intelligent and attractive woman, in her mid-50's, had tried to commit suicide several times over a period of five years. She was married to a professional man of some prominence, and had two grown daughters. Throughout the years, she had worked in public relations jobs. During the interview she appeared outgoing and quickly took control. She claimed she was "the dominant type," while her husband was "passive." Her first depression (age 20) occurred right after her father's death. He had been a strict, strong man who kept her on the straight, narrow path. After his death, she searched for similar men who were strong and dominant. When she met her husband-to-be, she was "impressed by his silence." After having been married to him for some years, she discovered that the silent type is not always the strong type. The depressions recurred, each episode being more severe. This patient's aggressive, dominating exterior covered a core of intense wishes for dependency, passivity, and submissiveness. The choice of marital partner was made on the basis of a mutual misunderstanding: she mistook his silence for strength; he felt attracted to her aggressive, extroverted facade. In this neurotic mismatch, the patient's real needs were not being met, and feeling hopelessly trapped in the marriage, she became suicidal.

The *passive-dependent* personality, without the cover of an aggressive facade, may not fare too badly in the course of life. If the dependency features are out in the open, the issue is at least unambiguous. Some people may feel attracted to a passive, dependent person, for whatever reasons of their own. A strong marital partner may provide the needed gratifications. And if he or she should die, a variety of substitutes may be available (children, the security of a home or hospital, etc.). The behavior pattern of *inadequate personalities* is characterized by the lack of efficiency. Even though the individual is not physically inadequate, nor mentally retarded, his overall adaptation is deficient, as manifested by lack of physical and emotional stamina, by socio-economic instability, and by a paucity of object-relations. Much of the same applies also to *immature* personalities. When the environment happens to be strongly supportive, such personalities may maintain themselves for long periods of time. They may feel quite contented about retirement (often an early and forced retirement), because they do not have to cope with the demands of work any longer. Many depend for their happiness on the support from social service and other agencies.

The *obsessive-compulsive* personality is characterized by undue concern with conformity and adherence to standards of conscience. Such individuals are rigid, inhibited, and unable to relax.[1] Compulsive personalities who were able to make a virtue out of necessity and use their compulsiveness adaptively and to their advantage, may, in old age, draw the benefits from this orderliness and regularity. On the other hand, if the emphasis used to be on rigidity and inhibition, the losses in old age may precipitate an involutional depressive reaction. Generally, this type of personality disorder is considered to have more than average susceptibility to involutional depressions and a greater tendency to react maladaptively to the stress of intellectual decline in later years.[4]

The *cyclothymic* personality has an extroverted approach to life. Alternating moods of elation and depression, though not of psychotic degree, are characteristic. Periods of euphoria or hypomania are characterized by an optimistic outlook, spirited ambitiousness, emotional warmth and a high degree of energy. Periods of downswing are marked by pessimism, a sense of futility, and low energy. These mood changes are not usually attributable to external factors; hence, the idea that genetic-constitutional factors play a role. The development of manic-depressive illness later on in life usually requires the occurrence of an external precipitating factor, which can be any type of loss or trauma.

## REFERENCES

1. Diagnostic and Statistical Manual of Mental Disorders, 2nd Ed. American Psychiatric Association, Washington, D.C., 1968.
2. U. S. Department of Health, Education, and Welfare, Biometry Branch, Washington, D.C., No. 7, 1971.
3. U. S. Department of Health, Education, and Welfare, Biometry Branch, Washington, D.C., No. 59, 1970.
4. Gianturco, D. T., Breslin, M. S., Heyman, A., Gentry, W. D., Jenkins, C. D., and Kaplan, B.: Personality patterns and life stress in ischemic cerebrovascular disease. I. Psychiatric findings. *Stroke 5:* 453–460, 1974.

# 8

# psychological responses to physical illness*

The psychological responses to physical illness include coping and defense mechanisms, as well as emotional reactions subjectively experienced as feelings. The type and intensity of these somatopsychic reactions, adaptive or maladaptive, depend on the interaction of a great many factors, which can be grouped into three categories: (A) stresses pertinent to the physical illness *per se*; (B) characteristics of the "host"; and (C) situational factors. Processes of interaction among the foregoing factors may be considered as yet another category.

## CHARACTERISTICS OF THE SPECIFIC PHYSICAL ILLNESS

### Severity of the Illness

This factor includes considerations regarding the magnitude of the actual physiological disorder, the severity of subjective symptoms, the degree of anticipated disability, and the extent to which the illness is life-threatening.[1]

### Time Factors

Severity of the illness at a given moment is not a reliable basis for accurate prediction of the psychological response. One must also take into account the *duration* of the illness and its *rate of progression* in the course of time. A study of cardiac patients,[2] for example, showed that the severity of the depressive response varied inversely with the length of the illness. Both in mild and in severe cardiac disease, severe depressive symptoms were apt to occur early in the course of the illness. These symptoms tended to disappear in patients with mild cardiac disease after three years. Severe cardiac illness, on the other hand, was associated with severe depressive symptoms throughout its course. Thus it seems that in its early phases, any cardiac illness is interpreted by the

---

* Portions of this chapter, which originally appeared as "Psychological Responses to the Stress of Physical Illness" in Adv. Psychosom. Med. 8: 119–141, are reprinted by permission of S. Karger AG Basel.

patient as something very serious, and the initial psychological response tends to be in the nature of a shock reaction, based on the patient's feeling that an organ of vital importance has been damaged. Only after some time (in this particular study, three years) does the patient begin to recognize that the illness has different degrees of severity.[3]

Another time factor is the rate of progression of the pathological process. Slowly developing conditions allow time for adaptation, both on the somatic and psychological level. A rapidly progressing illness, on the other hand, may have an overwhelming psychic as well as somatic effect. For example, patients with quickly growing malignancies show more evidence of anxiety than patients with slowly growing maligancies.[4]

One specific measure in which the time factor is used retrospectively is *distance to death*. This is the interval between the point in time at which the investigator observes certain phenomena about the patient and the time at which death occurs. This longitudinal approach was used in an investigation of 30 patients thought to have a fatal illness.[5] They were studied with regard to feelings of hopelessness, changes in time sense, and other variables. A follow-up study one year later revealed that 22 patients had expired, the median distance to death being two months. Patients who had died within two months had manifested more evidence of hopelessness and had been less future-oriented than those who had died two to nine months after the time of testing.

## Organ System Involved

Some organ systems (*e.g.*, cardiopulmonary) are essential to biological functions; others (*e.g.*, musculoskeletal) are vitally less important. Systemic diseases have widespread repercussions throughout the entire organism; in other conditions the effects remain more or less localized. Some illnesses (*e.g.*, skin disease) affect body parts accessible to the patient's sight; others, such as intestinal malignancies, are hidden. Nevertheless, it is reasonable to assume that disease in any organ system produces specific signals which originate at the site of the disturbance and are transmitted along somatic or visceral afferent pathways to the central nervous system, where they are registered as messages about the state of the interior.[5]

A woman who suffered from periodic diarrhea caused by diverticulitis of the colon would dream about "falling in a mudhole," one or two days before the onset of each episode.

In some patients with a disease that has widespread, systemic repercussions, such as carcinoma of the pancreas, a careful history reveals that the very first symptoms consisted of a vague, ill-defined depression. Thus, it would be wise to suspect early systemic disease when one encounters a patient complaining of nonspecific depression, especially if there have been no depressive episodes in the past.

The apperceptive capacity of the central nervous system can be defined as its capacity to evaluate the significance of afferent stimuli by comparing them with past experience. Because apperception is often impaired in organic brain damage, it is important to distinguish between illnesses involving *cerebral* impairment and those involving *extracerebral* pathology. In the former, the organ of adaptation, itself, is affected, so that the final psychological response reflects the specific distortion caused by the mental impairment.

A man in his 50's who had chronic brain disease was constantly preoccupied with that time in his life when he was an airplane pilot. He actually would appear to relive the experiences of that era. This preoccupation and reliving represented a primitive attempt to deny the impact of the present illness. The mental mechanisms of denial and negation require a certain amount of abstract capacity, and having lost this capacity, the patient substituted a reliving of the past.

## CHARACTERISTICS OF THE HOST

Among the personality-related variables contributing to the final psychological response are constitutional endowment, including intelligence and other ego apparatuses, as well as preferred response patterns;[6] experiental factors and interpersonal relationships; educational level; and vocational achievements. All of these interact in the process of personality development and maturation, as well as in the response to illness.

A person free from major intrapsychic conflict will possess flexibility, resilience, and an adequate repertoire of effective coping strategies. Individuals with intrapsychic conflict, on the other hand, must expend valuable energy in dealing with the internal, neurotic pressures. Thus the range and efficacy of their coping mechanisms tend to be reduced. As long as they do not encounter stresses too great for the narrow range of their homeostatic capacity, they may present an appearance of well-being and psychological equilibrium. Even minor stresses, however, can throw this tenuous balance out of kilter. The psychic economy of such individuals does not have the reserve capacity to absorb and buffer the impact of stressful events.

The capacity to adapt is also greatly influenced by congenital defects or acquired disabilities. Patients with mental retardation, for example, may respond to illness-related stresses in a primitive fashion (by projection or primitive motor patterns) or, they may decompensate, becoming agitated and confused.

### Age and Sex

The role of age is illustrated by the observation that, at age seven, the loss of a tooth signifies growth and is a source of pride, whereas at seventy it signifies decline and is a cause of grief. Various mental and physical capacities develop at different rates of speed, reaching peak performance levels at different points in the life cycle. In considering the influence of age upon a particular illness, therefore, it is necessary to go beyond merely chronologic age, and to define age in terms of the *maturational level* of specific biological, psychological, and social capacities.

Because general homeostatic capacity, recuperative ability, resilience, and energy gradually decline with advancing years, stresses in late life may have a greater impact than those occurring earlier. The stress involved in sexual involution serves to illustrate the roles played by both age and sex. Women usually cope with the stress of menopause during their forties. Sexual involution in men tends to occur later, when the overall capacity for coping may not be as great as during the middle years. The advantage to the male of a longer period of reproductive ability may well be offset by the advantage that women have of coping with the stress of involution while they still have many other resources.[7, 8]

## The Body Image

Sociocultural conditions being what they are, disabling illness may present a more specific threat to men whereas disfiguring illness may be more threatening to women. In both instances, the psychological reaction depends not only on the actual impairment but also on its symbolic significance. The latter is determined by many personal and interpersonal factors, one of these being the body image. This is the conceptualization of the body's structure and functions, and includes the ego's perceptions, ideas, and feelings in reference to its own body.[9]

As illness interferes with different physiological functions, different psychological concerns are activated. Patients with emphysema, for example, often present somatopsychic phenomena based on fears of suffocation.

> One patient with long-standing emphysema had repetitive, anxious dreams of being underneath a house, in the narrow space between floor and ground, with just enough space to crawl along on his stomach.

Less intense in the immediate anxiety it produces, but profound in its disruption of body image, are illnesses which affect psychically significant sites. Involvement of the reproductive organs may bring loss of sexual capacities and disturbance in sexual identity. Disease in the lower intestines may result in bowel incontinence and concomitant fears of helplessness and losing control in general. Many fears and fantasies associated with disease which impair organ function are *somatopsychic elaborations* of the physiological disturbances. Such psychological manifestations cannot be separated from their basic physiological causes. Hence, they must be distinguished from body image disturbances which occur on a purely psychodynamic basis, such as cancerophobia, conversion reaction, hypochondriasis, and the somatic delusions encountered in schizophrenia and psychotic depression.

The psychological reaction to the loss of a body part or the loss of a function includes grief and depression, shame and embarrassment, as well as apprehension about the future impact of the body alteration on interpersonal relations, occupational performance, and so on. Patients with a colostomy, for example, experience a serious narcissistic injury; embarrassment can be intense, and the patient is anxious about the effects of the colostomy on sexual intimacy. It may be difficult for him to *reorganize the body image* and to integrate the colostomy as part of it. When the colostomy is not accepted, it continues to be viewed as something alien, a foreign body. Such lack of integration into the body image sets the stage for psychological "rejection" of the foreign element

—often in the form of denial. This response is maladaptive because the patient's negative attitude poorly equips him for the task of adjusting and attuning the physiological processes of elimination to the structural limitations of the colostomy. The result may be chronic discomfort and dysfunction.

Another example of discomfort associated with altered body image is the painful phantom limb. Apparently this phenomenon is frequently related to unresolved emotional conflicts concerning the loss of the limb, the circumstances in which the injury occurred, or the type of premorbid personality.[10]

A 71-year-old man had undergone an amputation of his left arm because of a malignancy, at the age of 44. Soon after the surgery, he developed a painful phantom limb which persisted through the years, and about which he still is complaining. Psychiatric consultation revealed that the patient had always been considered as "the queer one in the family." He never had a regular job, but became a self-styled preacher. He did not go beyond the third grade in school, but he taught himself to read after he had heard the call to preach. Reportedly, his preaching was not bad, but he never was called to a church, and this caused him much bitterness. The patient's mother had walked out on his father, leaving him with 12 children. Shortly after that, the father became embroiled in a lawsuit against a neighbor. At the day of the trial, the father was shot and killed in an ambush. The patient was married and divorced twice. The last few years he has been living alone. He is constantly afraid that someone will burglarize his home, and for protection he has two vicious dogs, one gun, and seven locks on the door. None of his relatives visit him anymore.

Psychodynamically, this patient illustrates a paranoid personality disorder who in the course of his life, gradually decompensated into a chronic schizophrenic. His history shows exposure to violence, and presently he is excessively preoccupied with violence and the threat of being attacked. The occurrence and persistence of the painful phantom limb in this context of violence is plausible.

When a relatively minor physical injury triggers a major psychological response, the explanation may lie in the symbolic significance of the physical trauma. When the premorbid personality includes conflicts regarding fear of physical injury, castration, or aggressive competition, even minor injuries may acquire tremendous significance. The types of injuries (traumatic or surgical) which, in men, are likely to precipitate such neurotic reactions are those involving the hand, the inguinal area (hernia repair, appendectomy), and the nose. In such cases, the accidental or surgical alteration of the body image may have become symbolic of genital injury.

## Characteristics of Premorbid Personality

Knowledge concerning the premorbid personality may enable the clinician to anticipate the psychological responses to stress. In some cases, a premorbid behavior pattern will be intensified under the impact of the illness. A *passive-dependent* individual may welcome illness as a means of permitting him to gratify his dependency needs. Physical illness may not be unwelcome to *guilt-ridden* or *machochistic* personalities. Because the disease satisfies their need for punishment, their emotional state may actually improve during the illness. For *immature* and *inadequate* persons, illness can provide escape from adult responsibilities.

Sometimes physical illness is the lesser of two evils. For example, an *ambitious*, hard-striving, middle-aged man who discovers that he has fallen short of the goals set by his ego-ideal, may find in illness an alibi that covers his shortcomings, be they real or imagined.

Individuals whose premorbid personalities showed prominent reaction formations may react to physical illness in a surprising way. The *emotionally distant* personality, whose coldness is the result of reaction formation against tender feelings, may use the illness for an excuse to express emotional warmth and experience intimacy. Thus, physical illness may come to be the currency that permits the exchange of emotional warmth between persons who otherwise have a distant relationship. Physical illness may be used in a similar way by patients who are *overly self-reliant.* They may publicly protest but secretly enjoy being sick, because the illness forces them temporarily into a position of dependency and receptivity. If, however, the illness becomes prolonged or disabling, so that the reaction formation of excessive self-reliance is jeopardized, the patient may first fight back with an exaggeration of the very traits of self-reliance. Later, when he no longer has enough energy to sustain this behavior, this rigid line of defense may suddenly give way to regressive behavior such as excessive helplessness and dependency.

An elderly male patient had been a most prominent and respected citizen of his community before an accident resulted in quadriplegia. Every time he was cleaned after defecation, he unleashed a torrent of invectives and profanities at the male attendant, but as soon as the procedure had been completed he quieted down. His rage at the attendants was overdetermined and involved projection of the cause of his discomfort onto the attendants; a regressive, primitive attempt to be the big shot he used to be; a desperate, paroxysmal exaggeration of the reaction formation against passive-dependency wishes; and an attempt to ward off homosexual feelings and thoughts stimulated by the enforced passivity and fostered by the regular attention from male attendants.

*Schizoid* personalities, or lonely and isolated persons, may view illness as a secure bridge leading toward another human being. They may wish to hang onto their illness or their sick role, because the contacts with nurses and physicians provide them with closeness which, however, does not necessarily involve true intimacy. Such patients may, in the course of their illness, develop an attachment to the hospital or clinic in general, rather than to specific members of the medical or nursing staff.

*Schizophrenic* patients occasionally display a most interesting reaction to the development of a physical problem.

A skin lesion appeared on the foot of a male patient suffering from chronic undifferentiated schizophrenia. This was treated effectively by his physician. As soon as the skin had closed over the wound, however, the patient became acutely psychotic. When the foot lesion reappeared a short time later, the patient's mental condition improved. Each time the lesion healed, the schizophrenic symptoms flared up; when the lesion reappeared the schizophrenia improved. It finally became clear that the patient himself reopened the wound as soon as the bandages were removed.

This example illustrates the fact that the body represents an "intermediate station" between external reality and the inner realm of the mind. In autistic regression, the ego withdraws from external reality and the body may become the recipient of the withdrawn cathexes—a situation that tends to manifest itself as hypochondriasis. When this last anchorage point in reality—the physical body—is given up, the patient withdraws into his inner realm, where memory and fantasy images are cathected. A physical condition, especially one which is painful or visible to the patient, draws his attention back toward the sphere of the body, a part of actual reality.

In persons who are *action-prone* or tend to act out, illness interferes with the habitual pattern of activity. Anxiety, depression, and regressive behavior may be the result, especially if action had been used to ward off intrapsychic tension. Physical illness may also bring about anxiety and depression in persons who are *obsessive-compulsive* or perfectionistic. It simply becomes impossible for the perfectionist to live up to his high standards. Likewise, the compulsive individual may no longer have sufficient energy to maintain repetitive behavior rituals.

For *narcissistic* personalities, physical illness is a special threat because it represents an attack on the integrity of the body and the body image. Such individuals may have prided themselves on possessing unusual attractiveness, physical strength, or sexual prowess. The loss (either real or imagined) of these attributes leads to lowered self-esteem.

## SITUATIONAL FACTORS

### The Illness Situation

(a). The individual with a physical illness is confronted with the necessity of assuming the *sick role*. The patient must adapt to his restricted pattern of living by withdrawing from many of the usual pursuits engaged in by healthy people. He transfers the right to make decisions concerning his welfare to his physician and family; and society frees him from the discharge of ordinary duties. For many people, this new pattern of dependent behavior is not easy to adopt, because dependency may connote inferiority and create feelings of guilt and hostility. Nevertheless, the physically ill patient generally responds by gradually surrendering to dependency needs. When strong denial and counterphobic mechanisms are active, however, this adaptive device is obscured and the patient tends to resist appropriate regression, ignore limitations imposed by the disease and the treatment program, and reject support and supervision by the physician.

**(b).** The *physician-patient relationship* is an important factor in shaping some of the patient's reactions to illness. Difficulties in the doctor patient relationship may arise from a great variety of sources.[11] For example, the greater the class differences between physician and patient, the more difficult it becomes to communicate. On the patient's side, dissatisfaction results, which in the lower classes often takes the form of evasiveness in deference to the doctor's status, whereas in the middle and upper classes, it may be expressed with more self-assertiveness. Other obstacles to communication result from cultural differences. For example, a patient from a cultural group given to overt expression of feelings may make much of his pain and create the impression that he is a complainer. Some ethnic groups attach little importance to time as a regulator of behavior. When a person from such a background is told to take his medicine twice a day, he may translate this as "any time it occurs to me."

**(c).** *Hospitalization* may be refused by the patient who interprets it as confirmation of the seriousness of his illness. The patient who accepts hospitalization is usually faced with difficult adjustments, with separation from home being the most consistent traumatic factor.[12] The hospital tends to foster an impersonal atmosphere; for many, it represents a strange environment where one loses personal identity for the sake of institutional efficiency. Hospitalization can also produce stress through informational overload or excessive sensory stimulation. Preconceived anxieties are often reinforced by fearful sights, smells, and sounds, by unaccustomed proximity to other patients, lack of privacy, routines that clash with the patient's personal habits, and by the expectations of the medical staff concerning his behavior.[13]

## Family Relationships

The family may not easily accept the patient in the sick role. They may resist decisions made by medical personnel which tend to remove the patient from his usual activities, and may attempt to view his symptoms within the framework of normality. When it becomes necessary to hospitalize the patient, the family may feel that they have in some way rejected him. This feeling of guilt causes some families to make unwarranted financial sacrifices or give the patient an excessive amount of attention.

If the patient is hospitalized for a long time, it is often necessary for the family to reorganize itself, establishing new patterns of relationships to fill the gap left by the patient. These may work out so well that problems arise when the patient returns home.

Problems of an *intergenerational* nature are not uncommon between elderly patients and their adult children. The latter have to recognize that they can no longer look to their parents for the support they used to receive in earlier years. The ability to relate to one's parent as a mature adult involves seeing him as a person separate from his role as head of the family. Thus, the adult child ceases to be dependent and becomes dependable. It is a critical point, when a person realizes that his aging parents are no longer pillars of support but that they themselves now need the support of their children. If the relationship between adult children and their parents has been mature, the transition of roles can be made without difficulty. But when the adult child has remained immature or dependent, a crisis occurs, and he may not permit the aging parent to become dependent. Because he continues unrealistically to regard his parent as capable and competent, the latter is subjected to the stress of having to play a role he does not want, nor would be capable of. In other cases, the problem originates with the parent, who may cling to an obsolete set of roles* or outdated self-concept. In most instances, however, difficulties in the role reversal are attributable to psychological factors in both the aging parent and his adult child.

## PROCESSES OF INTERACTION

Physical illness is associated with disturbed function on three different levels. *Intrasystemic level* refers to processes taking place within the molecule, the cell, or the organ. *Systemic level* refers to the functions of the organism as a whole, and to the personality (ego, character). *Intersystemic level*, includes interpersonal phenomena such as dyadic relationships (marriage), small groups (nuclear family), larger groups (extended family, community).

*Funtional* integrity on a particular level depends on the *structural* intactness of the preceding lower levels. Damage at one level affects the functions of other levels, the effect depending on the properties of these adjacent levels. For example, prostatic hypertrophy requiring a prosta-tectomy represents physical illness on the organ level. The extent to which the patient can continue to function sexually after the operation depends not only on the structural and functional properties of other components of the genital apparatus, but also on systemic characteristics of the patient (*e.g.*, psychosexual maturity) and intersystemic factors (*e.g.*, marital adjustment).

The interactional processes among these various levels must be viewed in a *sociopsychosomatic* framework. Even the manifestations of organic brain syndrome can be more adequately understood when the illness is studied in this framework. The clinical picture of organic brain syndrome depends not only on the nature and extent of the brain damage but also on the patient's educational level and emotional maturity, on the quality of interpersonal relations, and on environmental support.[14]

To varying degrees, chronic illness in general (for example, cardiovas-cular disease, stroke, diabetes) interferes with sexual interest and activity. The majority of men, however, who have had a coronary occlusion or a prostatectomy continue sexual activity.[15][16] When illness interferes with the capacity for sexual initiative or sustained perform-ance (secondary consequence), the patient and his (or her) spouse face the task of seeking new ways of sexual intimacy. This requires a spirit of open-mindedness and cooperativeness which permits experimentation with new sexual techniques. For aggressive men, the change from an active role to a less active one may mean a difficult adjustment. If a mutually satisfactory readjustment cannot be achieved, marital conflicts may develop. These problems are not an immediate (secondary) result of the illness but represent more remote (tertiary) consequences. Now, when these third-order problems (the lack of marital harmony) are not effectively resolved, another set of repercussions is set in motion. These fourth-order reverberations in the interactional network may consist of maladaptive coping behavior (regression, withdrawal) and further problems within or outside the marriage (sexual acting out). This last set of events is likely to have an unfavorable (positive feedback) effect on the primary condition (such as, coronary heart disease).

Similar *cause-and-effect sequences* involving other functional capacities are also set in motion by physical illness. Decreased work capacity, for example, often causes lowered self-esteem and depression, which in turn can affect sexual interest and capacity. Conversely, sexual problems may adversely affect work capacity.

A 60-year-old man with heart disease had become progressively short of breath. Eventually, he had to stop work and was hospitalized because of violent coughing spells caused by pulmonary congestion. During a psychiatric interview he was tearful and depressed. The immediate cause for this was his feeling of loneliness in the hospital; but he had already been feeling dejected for some time before hospitalization. He admitted, with visible embarrassment, that since he had quit work, his wife had gone to work to make a living. The patient stayed at home doing household chores. Somewhere along the line he lost his potency. He related that his family physician had explained the heart condition by comparing the heart valves with the worn out valves of a car. Since then, the patient had come to think of his heart as an engine, and the coughing spells as the ominous sounds of a machine ready to explode. Finally, he mentioned that he probably only had himself to blame for getting in this shape, because he never took care of himself when he had a cold.

This case illustrates the wide range of somatopsychic reactions: a reactive depression (because of loss of physical health, loss of job and social role, and separation from home because of hospitalization); changes in body image (fearful fantasies about the illness); complex phenomena (such as the loss of potency) caused by the interaction effect of physical illness, depression, changed social role and self-concept, and fear of exertion; and finally, feelings of guilt (holding himself responsible for his predicament). Psychiatric treatment in such a case would aim at preventing the patient from settling down permanently in the sick role. This would involve giving the patient adequate information about his symptoms without frightening him; reassuring about the prognosis and his ability to continue to do some type of work; correcting his fearful fantasies about his symptoms; removing guilt feelings; exploring ways in which sexual intimacy can be continued, and so on.

Complexity is a fact of life and in the living system countless forces interact dynamically. One cause may have effects in several directions, or may even have repercussions throughout the entire system. Further, an effect can become a cause for new effects. Eventually, some kind of endstate develops when a balance of forces is reached in the interactional network. Although it is impossible, in view of the infinite complexities of a living system, to trace the nature, intensity, direction, and interaction of all factors operating at a given moment, the big lines and major themes can usually be discerned without too much difficulty. Clinical judgement involves this capacity to see the essential phenomena and grasp their interaction. The experienced clinician uses the comprehensive approach, or sociopsychosomatic framework, to his advantage and that of the patient.

## REFERENCES

1. VERWOERDT, A.: Communication with the Fatally Ill. Charles C. Thomas, Springfield, Ill. 1966. p. 183.
2. DOVENMUEHLE, R. H. AND VERWOERDT, A.: Physical illness and depressive symptomatology. I. Incidence of depressive symptoms in hospitalized cardiac patients. *J. Am. Geriatr. Soc. 10:* 932–947, 1962.
3. DOVENMUEHLE, R. H. AND VERWOERDT, A.: Physical illness and depressive symptomatology. II. Factors of length and severity of illness and frequency of hospitalization. *J. Gerontol. 18:* 260–266, 1963.
4. BEIGLER, J. S.: Anxiety as an aid in the prognostication of impending death. *Arch. Neurol. Psychiatry 77:* 171, 1957.
5. VERWOERDT, A. AND ELMORE, J. L: Psychological reactions in fatal illness. I. The prospect of impending death. *J. Am. Geriatr. Soc. 15:* 9–19, 1967.
6. FRIES, M. E. AND WOOLF, P. J.: Some hypotheses on the role of the congenital activity type in personality development. *Psychoanal. Study Child 8:* 48–62, 1953.
7. SZALITA, A. B.: Psychodynamics of disorders of the involutional age. *In:* American Handbook of Psychiatry, Vol. 3, Chap. 5, S. Arieti, ed. Basic Books, New York, 1966.
8. VERWOERDT, A., PFEIFFER, E., AND WANG, H. S.: Sexual behavior in senescence. II. Patterns of sexual activity and interest. *Geriatrics 24:* 137–154, 1969.
9. HINSIE, L. E. AND CAMPBELL, R. J.: Psychiatric Dictionary, 4th ed. Oxford University Press, New York, 1970.
10. KOLB, L. C.: Disturbances of the body image. *In:* American Handbook of Psychiatry, Vol. 1, Chap. 38, S. Arieti, ed. Basic Books, New York, 1959.
11. BOGDONOFF, M. D., NICHOLS, C. R., KLEIN, R. F., AND EISDORFER, C.: The doctor-patient relationship. *J. Am. Med. Assoc. 192:* 45, 1965.
12. VERWOERDT, A. AND DOVENMUEHLE, R. H.: Heart disease and depression. *Geriatrics 19:* 856–864, 1964.
13. SCHOTTSTAEDT, W. W., PINSKY, R. H., MACKLER, D., AND WOLF, S.: Prestige and social interaction on a metabolic ward. *Psychosom. Med. 21:* 131, 1959.
14. WANG, H. S.: Organic brain syndromes. *In:* Behavior and Adaptation in Late Life, Chap. 13, E. W. Busse and E. Pfeiffer, eds. Little, Brown, Boston, 1969.
15. HELLERSTEIN, H. K. AND FRIEDMAN, E. H.: Sexual Activity and the post-coronary patient. *Med. Aspects Hum. Sexual. 3:* 70–96, 1969.
16. FINKLE, A. L.: Sex after prostatectomy. *Med. Aspects Hum. Sexual. 2:* 40–41, 1968.

# 9
# somatic expression of psychiatric illness

The somatic aspects of psychiatric disorders can be considered under various headings depending on the type of etiology (physical *versus* psychogenic), the site of pathology (cerebral *versus* extracerebral), and the temporal factor in the cause-and-effect sequences (primary *versus* secondary). Following this approach, four major categories can be delineated:

*Organic brain syndrome* caused by organic-cerebral etiologic factors, or secondary to extracerebral-somatic pathology (See Chap. 4).

*Functional psychiatric disorders* in the absence of organic brain syndrome, *e.g.*, schizophrenia, depressive psychosis and neurotic disorders (See Chaps. 5, 6, and 7).

*Somatopsychic reactions* in which psychological responses are secondary to physical illness, with the central nervous system being structurally intact, *e.g.*, a reactive depression in cardiac illness (See Chap. 8).

*Psychophysiological disorders* in which neither the physical nor the psychological factor alone is sufficient to lead to illness, but both are necessary. Again, there is no structural impairment of brain tissue.

Several psychosomatic aspects of psychiatric illness were already mentioned in previous chapters. At this point, it will be useful to review those types of physical symptoms which represent the outward manifestations of an underlying mental disorder. These somatic expressions of psychiatric illness include: (A) hysterical phenomena (conversion neurosis; hysterical exaggeration of physical illness); (B) somatization phenomena (depressive equivalent; anxiety equivalent); (C) somatic delusions in schizophrenia, depression, organic brain syndrome, senile dementia; and (D) hypochondriasis and related states.

## HYSTERICAL CONDITIONS

### Conversion

In a conversion reaction, a psychological conflict is converted into a physical symptom. This mechanism decreases anxiety (primary gain) and often also produces a secondary gain (a gain derived from the sick role). Characteristic of conversion are the following:

The psychological conflict is *converted* into a somatic symptom, which at the same time expresses the conflict.

The somatic symptoms involve components of the *motor* system whose innervations are under voluntary control, or the *sensory* organs of the perceptual system. There is no primary physical impairment, but secondary disuse atrophy may develop in rare cases.

The nature of the symptom is in terms of a *loss* of function (*e.g.*, hysterical paralysis, hysterical blindness) or an *alteration* of function (*e.g.*, hysterical paresthesia).

The hysterical symptom expresses the psychological conflict in a *symbolic* way. Related to this is the fact that the nature, location, and extent of the conversion symptoms do not correspond with objective, anatomic facts. Instead, the somatic manifestations correspond with the *body image.*

The physical discomfort from the hysterical symptom can serve as *atonement for the guilt* from the unacceptable impulses.

Because the unacceptable impulse is indeed expressed (symbolically, through conversion), while the patient at the same time does penance through his suffering, the net total amounts to a balance of forces. The patient may have a peculiar *equanimity vis-à-vis* the physical symptom (la belle indifference).

Conversion reactions must be differentiated from *psychophysiological disorders.* In the latter, there is no symbolic expression of psychic conflict. These disorders are located in organs under control of the autonomous nervous system and have a physiologic origin (mediated through the limbic system, hypothalamus, etc.). Anatomic-structural changes may develop that can even be life-threatening; and, the physical symptoms do not relieve anxiety or guilt as in conversion. The diagnosis of conversion can be established only by meeting two basic requirements: *positive* evidence of a psychological conflict, and its symbolic, somatic expression; and *negative* evidence, in terms of ruling out possible physical pathology which, of course, is particularly relevant in the case of aged patients.

A 62-year-old woman, who had always lived in an isolated rural area, had recently started to have persistent chewing movements. She herself was not bothered by these, and her hospitalization had been prompted by a cardiac problem. The psychiatric interview revealed that she had been feeling neglected by her husband. When asked how she felt about this, she shrugged her shoulders indicating that she was resigned to it. She was then asked if she ever felt as if she "wanted to chew him out." The patient looked up surprised and acknowledged remembering having felt just that, but she had dismissed the idea of chewing her husband out, because of a mixture of fear and love for him. Significantly, her chewing movements stopped the moment she remembered the wish to chew her husband out. To establish the diagnosis of conversion in this particular case, it was also necessary to rule out lingual-facial-buccal dyskinesia, either the spontaneous type or as part of tardive dyskinesia.[1]

Generally, the classical type of conversions seem to occur less frequently nowadays than a few decades ago. Specifically, they are considered to be rare in old age.

## Hysterical Exaggeration of Physical Illness

Much more frequent among elderly patients, is the phenomenon of hysterical exaggeration of physical illness. As mentioned above, the primary gain in a psychodynamic constellation is an intrapersonal gain, *i.e.*, the re-establishment of an intrapsychic equilibrium. Secondary gain is interpersonal and refers to advantages that secondarily accrue from the sick role, or to unexpected fringe benefits from a neurotic illness. A patient may exploit any illness (emotional or physical) for ulterior motives, and usually this involves a hysterical exaggeration of the symptomatology. In the case of physical illness, the primary motive would be to obtain effective treatment. But if an ulterior motive is operating, the patient is interested in receiving not only treatment, but also something more, such as attention, commiseration, or financial assistance.

This type of patient can be recognized fairly readily. In a typical case, the patient has been quietly sitting in the waiting room, until his name is called; it is his turn to see the doctor, and now a dramatic display of distress is suddenly enacted. A cardiac patient may clutch his chest, as if in pain; assorted types of dyspnea may appear (often the dyspnea is slightly histrionic, inasmuch as the type of dyspnea is contrary to what one would expect, *e.g.*, a shallow, superficial blowing out of air, almost like a puffing or whistling). By the same token, a patient with a mental illness may exaggerate his psychiatric symptoms, *e.g.*, by appearing dazed, by answering ordinary questions with "I don't know," or even by cheerfully volunteering on the way from waiting room to office that the "voices keep me awake all night long." The purpose is to convince the physician, nurse (or other parental and authority symbols who have the power to give and to take away) that he, the patient, is sick indeed, and deserves help. This exaggeration of symptoms is not malingering which is conscious and deliberate. Instead, these patients are unaware of their dramatization. Furthermore, we are talking about individuals who have an illness to begin with. In view of the dramatic, naive over-reacting, of which the patient himself is not aware, it is appropriate to designate such exaggeration of illness as hysterical. This phenomenon is related to the "search for aid," described by Goldfarb.[2] This may be a rational search for skilled aid, or an irrational search prompted by dependency striving for parental substitutes. Part of the irrational search for aid is the element of regressive behavior, and the appeal to powerful caretakers by the display of personal suffering.[2] Occasionally, the search for aid is less dramatic, more conniving, and borders on malingering.

A 68-year-old woman had been confined to a wheelchair since an accident at age 38 caused a paralysis of both legs. For some reason, she disliked her present nursing home and made no secret of her wish to be admitted to the local general hospital. Then, because of a urinary infection, her wish came true. In the hospital, an indwelling catheter was inserted in the bladder. A few days later a nurse discovered that the patient periodically cut the catheter with her fingernails, in the apparent belief that this would prolong her hospitalization. On subsequent occasions this patient was observed to pick at her decubitus sores, again in the apparent hope that if these did not improve she would return to her favorite hospital.

The development of secondary gains and ulterior motives may complicate not only a conversion neurosis or a physical illness, but also other conditions, e.g., phobic states, traumatic neuroses, and depression. An individual may have a *phobia* about staying by himself at night. A deeper fear of death is being displaced onto an external symbolic substitute, *viz.*, being alone in the dark. This phobic displacements leads to the primary gain (remaining unaware of death-anxiety); but once the phobia is a *fait accompli*, other people may be moved to stay with the patient (secondary gain).

Some traumatic neuroses (caused by war, accidents, etc.) develop into protracted *compensation-neuroses*, when the patient receives financial compensation because (or, as long as) he is disabled. Such a patient may conclude that he is being rewarded for being sick.

The differential diagnosis between conditions of hysterical exaggeration *versus* true conversion is not always easy, as is illustrated by the following case.

A 66-year-old married woman was hospitalized because of inability to walk for the preceding two months. Before this time, she had been able to walk a mile every day to the local shopping center. A neurological consultation was requested and the conclusion was that the patient had no neurological disease. A consultation from the cardiologist stated that the patient had no exercise intolerance and could take the stress of walking quite well. The only positive finding was X-ray evidence of an old, partially healed fracture of the fifth metatarsal of the left foot. This fracture was incurred in a fall three years before, and she had continued walking until two months before admission. The reasons why this minor, old injury suddenly became a major disability seemed to be as follows. Shortly before her "paralysis," an elderly lady next door had fallen, broken her leg, and died. The idea of falling and becoming disabled and dependent, frightened the patient who saw herself as a strong, independent person. She would resent her husband's inadequacies and accuse him of "putting on" a lot of his problems. Since she repressed her own dependency wishes, she would be all the more irritated by her husband's pattern of dependency gratifications. The combination of her anger and envy toward him, and the sudden frightening reminder (the neighbor's accident) that she would have nobody to depend on, resulted in the hysterical inability to walk. Inasmuch as the symptom was an exaggeration of the disability from the old fracture, we could make the diagnosis of hysterical exaggeration of physical illness. On the other hand, the classical features of conversion were also present; the converting of her psychological conflict (involving anger toward her husband, and repressed dependency wishes) into a physical symptom (the loss of a motor function). The patient expressed the psychological conflict in a symbolic way: "I can't walk, so I am helpless. Sorry, I can't take care of you any more. Why don't you do your best, for a change?"

## SOMATIZATION PHENOMENA

The term somatization apparently was introduced by Stekel who referred to it in terms of organ language.[3] The concept of somatization is based on the assumption that emotion has several dimensions (subjective experience, physiological concomitants, action and motor behavior, and interpersonal-communicative functions), and that individuals may vary considerably with regard to the relative prominence of these aspects. The term somatization here is reserved for those cases when the physiological concomitants of an emotion (or affective disorder) are conspicuous while the other affective dimensions are proportionately less distinct. Thus, the mechanism of somatization may influence an emotional disorder so that the clinical picture shows a paucity of subjective, inner experiences, and a prominence of physiological manifestations. Because the emotional disorder does not express itself openly, but indirectly through physical distress, the term affective equivalent has come to be used. In the differential diagnosis of various illnesses two affect-equivalents must be frequently considered: depressive equivalent, and anxiety equivalent.

### Depressive Equivalent

The somatic equivalent of a depression[4] is a special instance of a masked depression. The masking effect is attributable to the predominance of the physiologic concomitants of the depression and the relative paucity of subjective depressive feelings.

This characteristic discrepancy was strikingly illustrated during an interview with an elderly male patient, hospitalized because of multiple physical complaints. When asked how he felt, the patient responded by talking at length about his headaches. Having finished that, he was again asked how he felt, and now the patient recited the discomforts in his chest and around his heart. The interviewer then inquired about his stomach ("It hurts all over. It is swollen. I feel sick."); about his back ("It always hurts, down in my lower back."); about his arms and legs ("They ache and feel stiff."). Thus, in effect the patient was hurting all over. At the finish of the organ recital, he was asked once more, "Now, with all this going on, how do you really *feel?*" To which the response was, "Feel? Oh, I feel fine."

Usually, however, the physiological symptoms do not represent such a formidable, impenetrable barrier. In many cases, the depressive affective experience is just behind a thin facade of physical symptoms.

A 58-year-old woman, recently widowed, would begin each interview with a quick matter-of-fact rundown of numerous physical problems. After this, she would talk about her two children, both of whom were a source of pride and satisfaction. Only after these prolegomena, the topic of her husband's death would come up. It was necessary for her to approach this topic gingerly and after some preliminary circumlocution, because of her intense ambivalence toward him. By the end of the interview she was usually able to experience the feelings of grief and sadness, and tearfully express these in words.

## Anxiety Equivalents

Somatization may also pertain to anxiety, and the following case illustrates an anxiety equivalent.

After a coronary attack two years before, a 65-year-old man had been suffering from frequent angina. This was poorly relieved by nitroglycerin, which he took in large amounts. Sometimes he would wake up during the night feeling that he could not catch his breath and would try to relieve the pressure on his chest by gasping for breath. He stated that he did not feel frightened at such times; all his attention was focused on the sensations of his chest. His father had died of a heart attack at an age close to the patient's current age. Significantly, he emphasized that this did not bother him. When he had another episode of shortness of breath during his hospitalization, it was clear that he was hyperventilating.

This case illustrates that anxiety can be manifested physiologically without the patient being subjectively aware of the anxiety (caused, in this patient, by the psychological threat of having heart disease and the fact that his father had died of a similar illness). Hyperventilation is a common physiological concomitant of anxiety, and in this patient the disordered breathing aggravated his anginal pains.

Other physiological concomitants of anxiety, which can be dominant manifestations in the clinical picture (and so mask the underlying anxiety state), may be cardiovascular (*e.g.*, palpitations), gastro-intestinal (over-eating; "butterflies" in the stomach; episodic urgency to defecate), urogenital (urinary frequency; sexual dysfunctions), neuromuscular (tension, tremors); and episodes of weakness and insomnia.

## SOMATIC DELUSIONS

Somatic delusions are frequent in schizophrenia, psychotic depression, organic brain syndromes, and senile dementia. Interestingly, there seem to be significantly fewer somatic delusions in manic and paranoid conditions. This is probably related to the fact that the latter two disorders tend to be "centrifugal," i.e., the patient tries to escape from his problem, in an extrovert flight away from the center of his being. In contrast, schizophrenia, depression, and dementia are "centripetal," as it were, with the patient becoming more introverted and absorbed in the self.[5]

Somatic delusions involving sex, pregnancy, and childbirth are not uncommon among aged female patients with a diagnosis of chronic paranoid schizophrenia, late life paraphrenia, or senile dementia.

An 82-year-old woman with a diagnosis of chronic paranoid schizophrenia had the delusion she was 2½ months pregnant. She even identified the alleged father by name. Her delusional system included various schemes that would make her have intercourse with this man, while under a spell, and so make her receptive to him.

Even in the presence of the somatic delusions of psychotic disorders, one has to remain alert to the possibility that actual physical disease may develop, and that the idiosyncratic somatic delusions may obfuscate the signs of physical illness.

An elderly schizophrenic woman had been complaining of "flashes of electricity shooting through [her] body." She had been on phenothiazines for many years. Recently, she began to add complaints of feeling washed out. Because she had had so many bizarre somatic complaints for so long, not much attention was given to this until she returned for a routine follow-up and appeared to be jaundiced. The prime suspect, of course, was the phenothiazine drug; but it turned out that she had metastatic liver cancer. In retrospect, the complaint of feeling washed out was a realistic symptom of the malignancy, not a somatic delusion.

## HYPOCHONDRIASIS AND RELATED STATES

Hypochondriasis refers to excessive preoccupation with the body or a portion of it, whether physical illness exists or not. The crucial element is bodily overconcern and the manner in which the patient relates to his body. The self-absorption and undue attention focused on the body is at the expense of interests in other objects. The hypochondriacal position may be associated with negative feelings, such as anxiety, depression, loneliness, bitterness, shame, guilt, or hostility. Or, the hypochondriac may derive certain private, narcissistic pleasures from cherishing and nurturing (part of) his body. In the context of hypochondriasis, such pleasurable aspects represent secondary developments and fringe benefits.

Normally, individuals with a physical illness continue to be interested in other people. They can maintain their interpersonal relationships in spite of their suffering, and may even feel a greater need to be close to others. Likewise, in cases of regression, the patient withdraws from certain adult role responsibilities, but this does not mean that he is withdrawing from people. To the contrary, because the regressed patient is more dependent, his interpersonal relationships tend to be more, rather than less, intense. In hypochondriasis, however, there is a disengagement, a shift in cathexes, away from external objects in the direction of the self. In this light, the somatic self-absorption does not have a symbolic significance or communicative function (as in hysterical conditions); neither does it reflect the patient's preoccupation with the physiologic concomitants of an affective disorder (as in a depressive equivalent).

Hypochondriasis may occur at any age, but it is more common late in life. There are several reasons for this.

### Chronic Physical Diseases

These diseases can serve as nuclei around which hypochondriacal concerns can be precipitated and crystalized. Physical illnesses do not cause hypochondriasis but may facilitate the redistribution of cathexes. In cases of physical illness, we can speak of hypochondriasis only when the somatic preoccupations are out of keeping with the realities of the physical illness. It is fitting, in this context, to remind ourselves of the risk of *iatrogenic hypochondriasis*. The casual mentioning by a physician of what may happen (a future complication) may become a focal point around which hypochondriacal fantasies are elaborated.

**Disengagement**

The fact that many old persons are socially isolated sets the stage for increased preoccupation with the one object that remains available, *viz.*, one's own body. Isolation *per se* is not sufficient to bring about the disengagement of interest inherent in hypochondriasis. Although the absence of human objects is a potentially serious psychological stress, an isolated person may protect himself in two ways against a drift toward pathological self-absorption. First, one can establish a relationship with the memories of objects once present in one's life. Inasmuch as this stored information represents an ensemble of reasonably accurate historical records, contact with historical reality is maintained. Second, in the absence of human objects, one can nevertheless relate to the world (inanimate or animate) by engaging oneself with it. Through the instrumentalities of his body and mind, a person can create his own world and recreate himself. There are many examples of isolation, involuntary or self-imposed, illustrating that such modes of existence are feasible and that the drift into self-absorption is not inevitable.

In addition to the actual loss of external objects, the self may be isolated by a loosening or a rupture of the ties between onself and those objects. This may come about in several ways. Failure in the area of intimacy may, through *distancing oneself from people*, bring about loneliness and isolation. Failure in the area of generativity, through *disengagement from work*, may result in stagnation of the self. Thus, disengagement either from love or from work leads to self-absorption, of which hypochondriasis is a specific example.

**(a). Flight into the Sick Role.** An individual may feel that a particular relationship is too difficult or demanding. Not being able to keep up one's end of the bargain generates a sense of failure and guilt, of letting the other down. As a result, one may wish to terminate the partnership—not a happy solution, but the lesser of two evils. However, the persistent lack of closure, and the situation of unfinished business, ask urgently for repair. And now a regressive (pseudo) solution presents itself. The combination of various free-floating negative feelings and undue self-attention produces hypochondriasis. The feelings of unpleasure attach themselves to the mental contents of the self-image, specifically the body image. The next step is the rationalization: "I am not feeling well—No wonder that I failed in this or that (marriage, parenthood, work, etc.). It's because I was sick." Thus, hypochondriasis becomes an alibi which removes responsibility for failure, an alias that restores self-esteem. This defense may be successful until others discover the excuse of illness as being physically unjustified and see through the patient's alibi. By this time, additional maneuvers, defenses, or coping are called for, in order to re-establish closure or self-esteem.[6]

**(b).** The self-absorption and disengagement of the hypochondriac has the effect of irritating and alienating others. The patient now experiences further losses of affection and approval. His feelings of being neglected increase in strength, as do his feelings of anger. Thus, any discomfort associated with the hypochondriacal concerns may serve as the *atone-*

*ment for guilt,* not only for his failures, but also for hostile, vengeful feelings. (This is related to the common neurotic pattern in depression and masochism in which the patient himself provokes a certain amount of misery to avoid punishment at the hands of somebody else. It is the lesser of two evils: by punishing oneself, one can choose the type of suffering and control the amount.)

Thus, hypochondriasis may play an important role in attempts to avoid responsibility for shortcomings, real or imagined. And because the question of whether one has been a success or a failure is often a critical issue during the later years, we are prepared to encounter hypochondriasis with greater frequency during this period of the life span.

A 66-year-old woman reportedly "had been enjoying ill health" since a hysterectomy at the age of 54. In spite of her numerous, persistent physical complaints, the family physician could find nothing wrong, and he told the family so. After this, the patient declared that she could hardly take care of herself anymore, let alone her husband. The latter had been moderately disabled by a stroke and the patient had become more and more resentful about helping him (mostly in getting him dressed). She began to seclude herself in her home, allegedly because she lacked money to buy proper clothes. In reality, she had both enough money and clothes. Her withdrawal into the home expressed her sense of having been short-changed by life. She vented the anger which followed in the wake of her disillusionment with her husband, by accusing him of never giving her any money, by being oblivious to his presence, and by covering the floors and furniture with newspapers ("so he won't be able to mess things up").

**(c). Devaluation and Depreciation of Others.** When one's experiences lead to the conclusion that this or that object is "no good," the crucial issue is whether one can find a new object that really is all right. The repudiation of objects that have become truly obsolete is a sound move, provided one can find an adequate substitute. But declaring another person to be no good, may represent an act of self-deception (involving rationalization and projection). The devaluation pertains to the other, not to me myself, as in decreased self-esteem. In fact, I may conclude (*e.g.*, because of unrealistically high expectations) that there is no use in trying to find a substitute object (or new relationship, or interest area) because "people are all alike—no good—and I am tired of getting hurt and disappointed." This form of disengagement is more serious because of the underlying narcissism and premise of arrogance. The hypochondriasis developing in this way may have a selfish, demanding streak—"Don't you see I am suffering? Why don't you do something? Obviously, you are no good either, like all the rest."

A 75-year-old divorced man lived alone in a hotel room, eating all his meals at a nearby cafe. His daily menu was always the same: a cup of coffee for breakfast, a bowl of soup for lunch, a hamburger for supper. At the age of 56 he stopped working, explaining that he was physically ill. He was "examined by twelve different doctors, and was told there was nothing physically wrong." After this, his wife left him and remarried a younger man. The patient still often talks about his wife's leaving him ("There is no one to take care of me, but I am against all women."). Over the years, he moved from one boarding home to another. Not long ago, he bought a gun and threatened some relative if they refused to keep him. It was after this blow-up that he moved into the present hotel. At all times, he carries with him two objects: a large bottle containing different pills (always eager to explain what they are for), and a brown briefcase containing a change of clothes ("I never know when I may have to spend the night away from home.").

A common type of hypochondriac who combines various of the above described features is the chronic complainer, often a woman who has reached middle age. She is the martyr type, sacrificing for her children, yet demanding certain compensations. She has neglected those dimensions of her life which could remain a source of satisfaction when her children have become adults. The undue amount of satisfaction gained from her children was neurotically determined. When her main source of satisfaction is gone, the extra energy has no pathway other than toward herself.[6]

A 58-year-old woman had a long history of multiple physical complaints. In the course of the years, her husband had obtained a divorce and the children had left home. The patient had had physicians and medications too numerous to mention. She would present herself at the clinic with a long-suffering look on her face. In the office she would, without saying a word, place empty medicine bottles on the desk, then sit back. The long-suffering look on her face was now compounded by stubborness and defiance. The therapist, aware of his own sense of irritation, nevertheless would try to convey to her that he was available to help in any possible way, offering her a new prescription, as well as regular time to review her problems. Her curt response was, "Just write the prescription." When the physician showed some hesitation, she unleashed a vicious barrage of rage, leaving no question about her resolve to persevere in the martyr role and to go to any length to provoke rejection.

## Further Decompensation: Autism

For elderly persons who have become disengaged or isolated, the world around has become empty. What remains is the world of the self: the concrete, physical body, and the intangible, invisible mental self. The bodily self is more directly in touch with the outside world. In fact, to the mind or inner self, the body is perceived as a peripheral zone that extends toward the physical world of which it becomes a part. In this framework, the body is a bridge extending from the intimate center of "me," toward what is out there, the "not me." Using the analogy of bridge, we can think of traffic in two opposite directions: toward external objects and toward the self. In a general way, this corresponds to extroversion and introversion, respectively. The withdrawal of cathexes from external objects onto the self is narcissistic in nature. It may be attributable to actual loss of the object *per se*, loss of love of the object (real or imagined), devaluation of the object, and depletion of energy.

If, in the course of a traffic pattern from external objects toward the self, the units of energy remain at the halfway station of the body, they will be invested at this point. This hypercathexis of the body results in hypochondriasis. If, however, this movement pattern is not halted at the halfway point, but proceeds on its inward course, the consequences will be more profound. The last contact point with the real world, the body, is abandoned, and the psychic energy is now mostly used to cathect the inner domain of the self, its thoughts, images, fantasies, and memories. This pathological immersion in the inner self is *autism* and signifies a rupture with the real world. Thus, both hypochondriasis and autism are instances of pathological self-absorption, the former, in the body, and the latter in one's innermost self. What makes autistic immersion especially pathological is the fact that the individual now is out of touch with his environment and his own body, and out of reach for the people around him. In autism, the focus of attention is no longer on the real object world, but on psychic reality. The consequences of such progressive withdrawal include loss of contact with reality, disturbance in time perspective (due to hypercathexis of memories, the past becomes a new present, a new temporal reality), and a progressive unlearning of acquired skills, including loss of abstract capacity. Secondary process functions become less effective, and primitive manifestations of the primary process type of mental functions emerge. Such processes of disengagement and decathexis are typical of schizophrenic disorders, and probably also occur in many cases of progressive senile dementia.

Corresponding to the above two phases of introversion, are two phases of extroversion. The hypochondriac may emerge from the preoccupation with his body and become engaged in the world out there. Or, the autistic, severely withdrawn person may proceed on a pathway leading back to the real world. On this pathway the body is encountered as the first object, external to the innermost self. Thus, we see sometimes that when withdrawn, autistic or schizophrenic patients improve, they first become hypochondriacal.

The psychodynamics of a 55-year-old man with paranoid schizophrenia involved a latent homosexual conflict. The patient made extensive use of projection: he felt followed around by "the element—men in bars who were clean and well dressed and who'd offer him beer and bargains." Finally, a homosexual panic erupted and the patient called the hospital emergency room requesting help in contacting the F.B.I. Fortunately, help could be provided in a more realistic way. Physical examination revealed the presence of a mild heart disease. The decision was made to have the patient come to the clinic at regular times for treatment of his heart condition. The element of physical illness was emphasized in terms of its potential seriousness, to persuade the patient of the need for regular out-patient visits. Almost immediately, the paranoid panic subsided. Thus, a treatment plan based on the notion of trying to con-

vert an autistic person into a hypochondriac seemed to be successful. (See also case example on page 101).

## REFERENCES

1. WEINER, W. J. AND KLAWANS, H. L.: Lingual-facial-buccal movements in the elderly. *J. Am. Geriat. Soc. 21:* 314–320, 1973.
2. GOLDFARB, A. I.: Masked depression in the elderly. *In:* Masked Depression, Chap. 14, pp. 236–249. Stanley Ussee, ed. Jason Aronson, New York, 1974.
3. STEKEL, W.: The Interpretation of Dreams. Liveright, New York, 1943.
4. EWALT, J.: Somatic equivalents of depression. *Tex. J. Med. 60:* 654, 1964.
5. VERWOERDT, A.: Psychopathological responses to the stress of physical illness. *Adv. Psychosom. Med. 8:* 92–114, 1972.
6. BUSSE, E. W. AND PFEIFFER, E.: Functional psychiatric disorders in old age. *In:* Behavior and Adaptation in Late Life, Chap. 10. E. W. Busse and E. Pfeiffer, eds. Little, Brown and Company, Boston, 1969. pp. 183–235.

# 10

## psychopharmacology: some theoretical and practical considerations

**CLASSES OF PSYCHOPHARMACOLOGICAL AGENTS**

The psychopharmacological agents of interest to the geropsychiatrist include a great number of drugs which can influence the CNS directly or indirectly. These psychoactive drugs can be grouped in the following categories:

—*Antipsychotics* (phenothiazine derivatives, the butyrophenones and thioxanthene derivatives).

—*Antidepressants* (the MAO-inhibitors and tricyclic antidepressants)

—*Anticholinergics* (*e.g.*, the antiparkinson drugs)

—*Antianxiety agents* (benzodiazepine derivatives and propanediols).

—*Sedatives* and hypnotics.

—Drugs alleged to improve *cognitive* function, (*e.g.*, the dihydrogenated alkaloids of ergotoxine [Hydergine]).

—A *miscellaneous* group including vitamins (*e.g.*, Vitamin $B_{12}$), folic acid, hormones (estrogens, thyroid, anabolic hormones), vasodilators and anticoagulants.

The clinical significance of some of these drugs is reflected by the fact that they are therapeutically potent, can cause major side-effects as well, and are in widespread use. A survey conducted at 12 V.A. hospitals revealed that 61 percent of the elderly patients studied were receiving psychoactive drugs. Psychoactive drugs were administered to 55 percent of the patients with organic brain syndrome, 70 percent of those with schizophrenia, and 66 percent of those with other mental illness. Antipsychotic drugs were prescribed most frequently (44 percent), followed by antidepressants (11 percent), antianxiety drugs (10 percent), and cerebral vasodilators and dihydroergotoxine (10 percent). Of the patients receiving antipsychotic drugs, 20 percent received antiparkinson drugs. In this particular survey, 16 percent of the patients received multiple drug combinations.[1]

119

Much basic and clinical research is conducted in psychopharmacology. Thus it has been found that the mode of action of psychotropic drugs (antipsychotics and antidepressants) is probably in terms of altering the chemical substrates of synaptic transmission or axonal conduction within the CNS. The synaptic transmission may be mediated by a biogenic amine, such as acetylcholine, norepinephrine, serotonin, or dopamine. Norepinephrine and dopamine are synthesized, in the neuronal cytoplasm from the amino acid tyrosine, whereas serotonin is synthesized from tryptophan. In the CNS, ascending and descending pathways have been identified which are noradrenergic, dopaminergic, or serotonergic in nature.[2]

The antipsychotic agents probably exert their tranquillizing effect by inhibiting certain noradrenergic and dopaminergic receptor sites in the CNS. It has been hypothesized that these drugs make the reticular system in the midbrain less sensitive to impulses from the sensory pathways. The blocking of dopaminergic receptors in the corpus striatum is responsible for the extrapyramidal side effects of antipsychotic drugs. The pharmacodynamic action of MAO-inhibitors occurs by inhibiting the deamination of biogenic amines, resulting in increased amounts of norepinephrine, dopamine, or serotonin at receptor sites in the CNS, and other tissues. The tricyclics are also considered to have an effect on the catecholamines in the CNS. They may exert an influence on the balance between the central cholinergic and adrenergic mechanisms.[3] By blocking the reuptake of catecholamines into presynaptic terminals, and by inhibiting the deamination of biogenic amines, these amines become available at central receptor sites in increased amounts.

Other important research areas include, for example, the recent identification of the "acute anticholinergic syndrome"; the massive problem presented by tardive dyskinesia; the exciting potential of Gerovital H3; the efforts to improve cerebral blood flow and metabolism by hyperbaric oxygenation or other means; and so on. All of this leaves no doubt that psychopharmacology will play an increasingly important role in geropsychiatric practice.

In order to be adequately prepared to make optimal use of these psychoactive drugs in treating elderly patients with mental illness, essentially three requirements must be met. First, it is necessary to have sufficient theoretical knowledge concerning the pharmacodynamic properties of specific drugs. Second, the clinician needs to know the characteristics of the host, that is, in which ways the elderly patient responds differently to drugs, compared with patients in younger age groups. Third, the application of theoretical knowledge in the clinical setting is another, indispensable skill. Such practical know-how is acquired through clinical experience over a period of years. In this chapter, the emphasis will be on the latter two points. Information on the pharmocodynamics of specific drugs will be presented, in the appropriate context, in subsequent chapters.

## DRUG RESPONSES IN THE ELDERLY

Although many aged patients are treated with psychotropic drugs, little evidence is available from well-controlled studies on the effectiveness of these drugs in specific geropsychiatric conditions. The factors which influence drug responses in elderly patients can be categorized according to whether they are specific (age-related) or nonspecific (unrelated to age), and whether they are physical or nonphysical.

## Age-related Factors

(a). **Physical Determinants.** With increasing age, drug reactions in the individual change. This is related to specific factors such as changed absorption and distribution patterns of the drug, alterations in its metabolism, decreased capacity of the liver to detoxify, reduced renal capacity to excrete, decreased cerebral blood flow and cerebral metabolism, organic brain syndrome, and so on. In addition to considering these part functions separately, it is important to keep in mind that the overall capacity for homeostasis, as a general systems characteristic, is reduced in range and resilience. Hence, the margin for error is narrowed and the probability of side-effects is increased. Furthermore, once side-effects develop, they tend to be more incapacitating. Because the homeostatic mechanisms of the component organs and of the system as a whole are diminished, the threshold for toxic side-effects is proportionately lowered.[4] Drug responses in older persons are often comparable to those in the very young. This has been related to renal function which is undeveloped in the young and declining in the aged, and to age-related changes in the capacity to metabolize drugs (microsomal enzyme activity, for example, may decrease in old age).[5] It must be kept in mind, however, that such age-related decrements are not equally applicable to all individuals in a given age group.

1. **Absorption.** The absorption of drugs may be slowed or diminished in aged persons, because of various reasons such as a decrease in gastric acid output with an associated reduction of drug solubility, reduced abdominal blood flow, reduction in size of absorbing surfaces, and impairment of enzyme systems responsible for transport across gastrointestinal membranes.[4]

2. **Drug Distribution.** Once a drug reaches the circulation, its distribution depends on the extent to which the drug is protein-bound in the plasma, the distribution patterns of blood flow, the ability of the drug to pass through various membranes, and the specific properties of tissue affinity. Drugs in circulation may be bound to plasma proteins, especially albumin. Inasmuch as plasma albumin decreases with advancing age, the amount of bound drug may be reduced proportionately.[6] With regard to the factor of peripheral blood flow, a lowered cardiac output in older patients results in a redistribution in favor of cerebral and coronary circulation at the expense of blood flow to the liver and kidneys.[7]

3. **Excretion and Metabolism.** Once a drug is in the circulation, its concentration in the blood reflects the rate at which it is eliminated. The kidney is the primary route for elimination. Increasing age is accompanied by diminished glomerular filtration and tubular secretory capacity. Likewise, the ability of the liver to metabolize drugs decreases with advancing age. The effect of age on the blood level and half-life of the drugs indicates a decrease in the rate at which drugs are metabolized and

eliminated. The longer half-life of drugs may be attributable to a decreased ability of elderly patients to excrete or metabolize them, and the resulting higher blood level may contribute to the higher incidence of adverse drug effects.

4. **Other Age-related Effects.** Altered drug activity in older individuals may occur in the absence of changes in the drug level in blood. This may be caused by changes in the number of receptors, structural changes in the responsive tissue, and less effective homeostatic capacity.[4] Drugs with central nervous system effects, for example, show changed activity with advancing age, which is probably attributable to a reduction in the number of receptors. This is related to the fact that the action of stimulants is reduced with age whereas the action of depressants is enhanced.[8] Barbiturates, for example, tend to have erratic or paradoxical (stimulating) effects. Changes in homeostatic capacity may also influence the overall response to a drug. For example, elderly persons have an impaired capacity to respond effectively to orthostatic stress, and this particular homeostatic loss may be aggravated by phenothiazines and antidepressants.

(b). **Nonphysical Determinants.** The aged individual probably also reacts differently to drugs as a result of age-related psychological and behavioral factors. Research efforts aimed at comparing therapeutic effectiveness of psychotropic drugs in younger and older patients may be hampered by the probability that psychopathological processes (and hence, psychiatric syndromes and target symptoms) in the two age groups are not comparable. For example, there may well be profound differences in the etiology, pathogenesis, psychodynamics, and clinical symptomatology of depression in old people, as compared with younger adults. In previous chapters, the question was raised if and how the aging process can modify the overt manifestations of a psychiatric disorder, and to what extent the age-specific psychiatric disorders (developing for the first time in old age) fit the diagnostic cubbyholes designed several decades ago, when the psychiatric problems of old people and late life were not as much in focus as nowadays.

## Nonspecific Factors

(a). **Physical Determinants.** This category pertains, by and large, to the *interaction between drugs* and drug-drug toxicity. A thorough review of this important topic would go far beyond the scope of this text. Only a few points will be presented to illustrate and emphasize the need to familiarize oneself with information already available and to keep informed about future research findings.

Therapeutic effects can be antagonized by compounds interfering with absorption of the drug, increasing the rate of its metabolism, or blocking the transport mechanism to the drug's site of action. On the other hand, inhibition of the drug's metabolism facilitates transport of the drug to its site of action, enhancing therapeutic as well as adverse effects.

1. **Interference with Transport of Drug to Site of Action.**
—*Interference with absorption.* Antacids interfere with the gastroin-

testinal absorption of antipsychotic agents.[9] Diphenylhydantoin and other anticonvulsants impair the absorption of folic acid.

—*Induction of hepatic microsomal enzymes.* The action of many drugs depends on the rate at which they are metabolized by enzymes in the hepatic endoplasmic reticulum (microsomes). The activities of these enzymes can be increased by several drugs, *e.g.*, phenobarbital. Drugs which induce microsomal enzymes, decrease the action of other drugs. Phenobarbital, for example, can facilitate the metabolizing of chlorpromazine, heparin, coumarin, corticosteroids, and diphenylhydantoin, thus lowering their plasma levels.[10] Other barbiturates and glutethimide also induce hepatic microsomal enzymes. Methylphenidate, on the other hand, inhibits the liver mocrosomal enzyme system,[11] and may reduce the metabolism of diphenylhydantoin, tricyclic antidepressants, phenothiazines, and anticoagulants. As a result, the blood level of these drugs is increased.

—*Blocking drug transport.* Guanethidine, an antihypertensive drug, is concentrated at its site of action in adrenergic neurons by a transport system in the membrane of the neuron. Antidepressant drugs inhibit the uptake of guanethidine into the neuron terminal and thus prevent its action. In hypertensive patients who are taking antidepressants of the imipramine type, this type of drug-drug interaction can be quite serious. Antipsychotic agents, especially chlorpromazine, also antagonize the hypotensive action of guanethidine, probably by the same mechanism as that of the tricyclic antidepressants. Haloperidol and thiothixene have a similar effect, although less prominent. These antipsychotic agents probably prevent the access of guanethidine to the neuron by blockading the amine uptake pump.[12].

**2. Transporting Excessive Amounts of Drug to Site of Action.**

—*Displacement of drugs bound to plasma proteins.* Drugs may be reversibly bound to plasma protein (especially albumen) and not be active pharmacologically. Another drug can have the property of competing for the same binding sites. When one drug is competitively displaced by another drug, the former becomes pharmacologically active, intensifying its effect. For example, tolbutamide (Orinase) is mostly bound to plasma proteins, but can be displaced by sulfaphenazole; the resulting increase in pharmacologically active tolbutamide may cause critical hypoglycemia.

—*Inhibition of the metabolism* of drugs will increase their action. The metabolic inactivation of diphenylhydantoin, for example, is reduced by bishydroxycoumarin and isoniazid; thus, signs of diphenylhydantoin overdosage may occur if the patient is taking these drugs in combination.

**3. Change in Response at Site of Drug Action.** In patients taking MAO inhibitors, hypertensive crises may result from ingesting foods (*e.g.*, cheese) which contain tyramine, or from indirectly-acting sympathomimetics. Excessive release of norepinephrine is the cause of the hypertensive crises in patients receiving MAO inhibitors. The clinical signs of such attacks essentially consist of the manifestations typical of a pheochromocytoma. In view of this, the appropriate treatment consists of administering phentolamine (an alpha-adrenergic blocking agent).

In rare cases, the combination of a MAO inhibitor with a tricyclic antidepressant, or the starting of a tricyclic within a few days after stopping a MAO inhibitor, causes hyperthermia, delirium, and coma. Although this occurs infrequently, the combination of these drugs should be prescribed with great caution.

**4.** That *gender* may play a role in the effect of a drug is suggested by the finding that methylphenidate is a more effective antianxiety agent for females than for males, whereas in the case of diazepam, the reverse is true.[13] Elderly male patients seem to be more responive to the antidepressant effects of alertonic and imipramine.[14]

**(b). Nonphysical Determinants.**

**1.** According to the *law of initial value*, the response of an organism to a stimulus depends, among other things, on the prestimulus (baseline) condition of the organism. Thus, a stimulating drug is likely to be less effective if the organism already is in a state of excitation; and a sedative is less effective in a state of inhibition. In fact, there may be a paradoxical reaction: the excited patient may become less excited following administration of a stimulant, and the inhibited patient may become restless from a sedative. An example of the latter situation is seen in patients who are inactive, take frequent daytime naps and then cannot sleep at night; a sedative at nighttime is likely to have no effect or, paradoxically, may result in restlessness, or confusion. The proper approach here is to promote activities during daytime so that the patient is fatigued in the evening.

**2.** *Personality characteristics* such as extroversion, introversion, aggressiveness, passivity, emotionality, and obsessiveness undoubtedly also contribute to interindividual differences in drug responses.[15] In patients who are intelligent, introspective, and self-observing, certain physical side-effects of antipsychotic drugs may accentuate depersonalization, resulting in further instability of the body image and psychological instability. In other cases, a drug may specifically affect a major defense or interfere with a coping mechanism, such as obsessive-compulsive behavior.

> In the case of an elderly man, preoccupied with his sexual impotence, antidepressant drugs had the effect of energizing his tendency to act out, and precipitate pedophiliac behavior.

Passive types of men are probably less disturbed by side-effects interfering with ejaculation or erection than are aggressive, cocky characters. Narcissistic types of women may be quite upset about the weight gain caused by certain phenothiazines. Hypomanic, extroverted, active, and compulsive individuals of all ages tend to feel guilty when, under the influence of tranquilizers, they slow down, work less, and spend more time in bed.

**3.** Related to the factor of personality characteristics is the variable of *social class*. In a study of comparing the effects of pemoline *versus* methylphenidate, it was found that middle class patients responded better to both drugs than lower class patients did.[16]

**4.** The *placebo effect* refers to any reaction not attributable to specific pharmacodynamic effects but derived from the subjective meaning that the drug has to the patient. The doctor-patient relationship is one of the most important factors in determining which meaning the patient unconsciously assigns to the drug. Therapies and drugs seem to be more effective when the physician himself is convinced of their usefulness. Depending on these factors, the placebo effect will be favorable or unfavorable. In the latter case, the placebo effect may be described as a side-effect. In some instances the placebo effect overshadows the pharmacodynamic effects.

A chronically depressed woman, who was showing a progressive shift toward hypochondriasis, expressed enormous trepidation about taking an antidepressant medication (amitriptyline). She insisted that some years ago she had been given this drug, and it had not helped. Now she was afraid that it would make her "violently sick." She finally agreed to try taking just one tablet daily—as if it were a favor on her part. During subsequent weekly follow-ups, she would relate how "that pill makes me sick. It makes everything back up on me. It is like getting choked." The only indication that she did ingest and assimilate some of the drug was her improved appearance and a gain in weight.

## CLINICAL APPLICATION: SOME GUIDELINES

### Side-effects

Side-effects are all those drug effects that are undesirable, adverse, unwanted, untoward. The precise *definition* of a side-effect is not always possible, because the patient and his physician may disagree as to what constitutes an untoward, unwanted drug effect *versus* a therapeutically desirable one. In certain situations, the sedative effects of psychotropic drugs could be welcomed by the busy personnel of a geropsychiatric ward; but it is clear that any sedative effect that amounts to a chemical straight jacket is antitherapeutic. On the other hand, many outpatients who are maintained on antidepressant drugs, and function well during the day at home and at work, welcome the sedative side-effects of tricyclics (*e.g.*, doxepin and amitriptyline) when the hour of sleep arrives.

Generally, aged patients have a lower tolerance for psychotropic drugs, and require smaller doses than younger patients, to reach a desired therapeutic effect. Likewise, side-effects in the elderly usually develop at lower dosage levels. The *incidence* of side-effects reported in the literature depends on the definition of side-effect, the particular patient population under study, and the accuracy of the assessment techniques. The issue of accuracy of measurement techniques involves the reliability of the various rating scales being used, the problem of achieving inter-rater reliability, and the nearly impossible task of controlling the innumerable variables encountered in a clinical setting. In spite of all these constraints which limit precise determination of the incidence of side-effects, there is general agreement that the incidence of serious adverse drug reactions is simply too high.[17, 18]

The risk of adverse drug reactions increases with age. Seidl *et al.*[19]

observed an increase with age in the incidence of adverse drug reactions, from 11.9 percent in the 41- to 50-year-old age group, to 24.9 percent in the 80+ age group. In Hurwitz's study, 7.5 percent of patients in the 40- to 49-year-old age group had side effects, and 21.3 percent in the 70- to 79-year-old age group.[20] Drugs which tend to produce a higher incidence of adverse reactions in older patients include digitalis, barbiturates, thiazide diuretics (more risk of potassium depletion), and phenothiazines (a higher incidence of extrapyramidal symptoms).[4]

Not only does the incidence of adverse drug reactions increase with age, but also the extent of their *severity*. In addition, some side-effects can cause new complications, *e.g.*, postural hypotension causing a fall with resulting fracture, or causing a cerebrovascular accident.

At times, it may be difficult to distinguish between a true side-effect and a placebo effect. In addition, it is possible to mistake side-effects for a worsening of the primary psychiatric disorder. For example, motor restlessness and akathisia are side-effects of antipsychotic drugs, but may prompt one to increase the dosage on the assumption that the psychosis is worse, thereby setting up a vicious cycle.

A good example of the complexity of *differential diagnosis* is presented by the central anticholinergic syndrome. There are many causes of confusion in the aged, but one type is basically an atropine toxicity caused by the anticholinergic effects of the phenothiazines, tricyclic antidepressants, and antiparkinson agents. Antipsychotic, antidepressants, and antiparkinson drugs all have an anticholinergic effect. Hence, patients using combinations of these drugs are more likely to develop anticholinergic side-effects.[3]

The *central anticholinergic syndrome* is characterized by marked disturbance of short-term memory, impaired attention, disorientation, visual and auditory hallucinations, and increased psychotic thinking. The syndrome can be associated with peripheral anticholinergic signs. It can present a difficult diagnostic problem in psychiatric patients because the anticholinergic toxic signs may resemble the symptomatology of the primary psychosis. This may prompt one to increase the dosis of the psychotropic drugs with a resulting aggravation of the symptomatology. By keeping alert to the possibility of central anticholinergic toxicity and performing careful mental status and physical exams (especially looking for peripheral anticholinergic signs), a correct diagnosis can be established, and appropriate intervention started (lowering the dosis, or stopping the drug). Antiparkinson drugs are perhaps the most frequent cause of the central anticholinergic syndrome. This is especially relevant because many patients do not really need these drugs in conjunction with antipsychotic medications.[3]

Physostigmine reverses the toxic symptomatology but does not modify the symptomatology of the primary, underlying psychosis itself. The central anticholinergic syndrome can be treated by 0.5 to 1.0 mg of physostigmine, intramuscularly, to be repeated every two hours as indicated.[21] In the exceptional case where the diagnosis remains obscure, physostigmine salicylate can be used as a diagnostic tool. Physostigmine may be used only after thorough medical evaluation because of the danger of excessive parasympathetic stimulation. Because atropine sulfate is effective in reversing cholinergic toxicity, it is wise to have this drug ready when the physostigmine test is done. The importance of this test is to obtain proof that the confusional syndrome indeed represents atropine toxicity.[3]

## Some General Guidelines

In view of the multiple factors influencing drug effects in aged patients, it is not surprising that there is such a great variety in drug requirements, therapeutic responses, and side-effects. The correct type and amount of drug is usually determined by a cautious trial and error approach.

The discontinuance of current psychotropic medication to get a *drug-free baseline state* is useful to obtain an accurate assessment of the efficacy of a prospective drug. Once this behavioral baseline is known and a specific drug is administered, the behavioral changes are recorded at regular intervals. The optimal setting for this would be the hospital, but this procedure can also be carried on an out-patient basis, provided the patient returns regularly to the clinic for follow-up evaluations.

Evaluation of the patient's *medical status* and of the drugs used for his medical problems is essential to be alert to potential drug-drug interactions.[12] Multiple physical illnesses being treated with multiple drugs increase the risk of drug-drug toxicity in a geometric fashion. Side-effects in aged patients may be difficult to differentiate from actual age-related physical disorders, including organic brain syndrome, cardiac disease, neurological disorders, glaucoma, prostate hypertrophy, impotence, and so on.

In clinical practice, the selection and dose of a psychotropic drug are usually determined by the presenting psychological symptoms and behavioral signs, rather than the specific underlying psychiatric syndrome. Yet, in planning the treatment it is important to be as specific as is possible. The physician must formulate some explicit notions concerning the etiology, pathogenesis, and psychodynamics of the disturbed behavior. By adhering to these general principles, several risks can be reduced or prevented: overmedication, undermedication, and the "shotgun" approach.

*Polypharmacy* clouds clinical signs. It may become impossible to distinguish among the intended effect of the drug, its side-effects, the placebo effect, and the manifestations of the patient's initial symptoms. Because aged patients frequently have several chronic conditions simultaneously, overmedication is especially likely to occur in their management. A number of elderly patients are actually hospitalized because of multiple drug-related symptoms. In these cases, hospitalization is required to discontinue the questionable drugs, evaluate the patient's physical and psychological baseline on this drug-free (or reduced-drug) status, and determine what medications are really indicated. Learoyd *et al.* emphasize the hazards of polypharmacy.[18] Their study showed that 16 percent of the elderly patients who were on psychotropic drugs before hospitalization and showed abnormal behavior, improved dramatically when the drugs were stopped. About 20 percent of the geropsychiatric admissions were precipitated by adverse effects of psychotropic drugs.

Another risk is *undertreatment*. Many psychotropic drugs begin to exert their maximum therapeutic effect only some weeks after the initial doses. To stop treatment before that time, or to fail to increase the dosage to optimal levels, may be worse than no treatment at all.

The *shot-gun approach* refers to the practice of indiscriminately blanketing the target symptoms with a barrage of drugs, in the hope that at least one of them will be effective. Drug combinations should be used with caution because the side-effects may multiply. If a second drug must be used, it is wise to give the first medication alone long enough to be able to evaluate its therapeutic and side-effects.

In view of the many different types of psychotropic drugs available, it is advisable to develop an *in-depth acquaintance* by working consistently with a few representative drugs, selected from the major drug categories, that seem to have withstood the test of time. Such a systematic approach stands in contrast to browsing around with drugs. What happens often is that the patient is subjected to inconsistent drug patterns because he is periodically transferred from one doctor to another. And, each physician may decide to try out "his own" drug.

The opposite of therapeutic inconsistency is *therapeutic obstinacy*, *i.e.*, the continuation of a particular drug when the clinical evidence does not support its efficacy, or even suggests possible harmfulness. This is a risk in some outpatient clinic settings with a high turnover of physicians and with revolving door type of consultants. Each new physician is likely to start off by continuing the drug (and its dose) prescribed by his predecessor. Changing the drug or the dose would be time consuming and would require a series of visits at regular intervals; the new physician is usually more involved in getting acquainted with his overall case load. By the time he has accomplished that, six to twelve months have passed, which is pretty close to the "half-life" of psychiatric consultants in some out-patient settings. Thus, by the time review and reappraisal of the patient's drug regimen would be possible, a new consultant arrives, who again starts off by continuing the same drug and dose prescribed by his predecessor, and so on.

An elderly woman with a "psychotic depression" turned out to be taking perphenazine (Trilafon) 16 mg 3 times daily. Over a period of several weeks this was reduced to 4 mg t.i.d. By then, the "depression" had begun to lift, but it took about three months before the improvement in her mood and attentiveness had stabilized. Essentially, this patient was schizophrenic, with minimal residual symptoms. Unfortunately, she also began to have, at the lower dosage level, a moderate degree of oro-bucco-lingual dyskinesia. The patient, however, preferred this type of disability to her zombielike status at higher dosage levels.

*Dosage Level:* Because neither the optimal dose nor the maximum dose tolerated are known beforehand, in a given elderly patient, it is useful to follow an individualized approach. Starting with low doses, one gradually increases the amount, while observing the patient's response and remaining alert to the development of side-effects, until therapeutic effects are achieved. Generally it is best to start treatment at a dosage level about one-quarter to one-third of the recommended adult dosage, particularly for the more debilitated patients. The dosage can be increased according to tolerance.

In the acute phase of a psychosis it is wise to start at a low level but move rapidly to effective dosages of the drug; during the chronic phase the dosage should be gradually reduced to the required minimum. Not infrequently, the dosage level may be too low during the acute phase of a psychosis, and too high during the chronic phase. It is particularly easy to leave a hospitalized patient on a high dose of psychotropic drugs even after the acute phase of the psychosis has subsided. In the case of antipsychotics, this will increase the risks of dyskinesias, parkinsonism, and other complications. Therefore, periodic review and readjustment of dosage levels are required.

*Dosage Patterns:* Particular attention must be given to instructing the patient (or family, or responsible others) regarding the amount of drug to be taken, the times of day, and so on. It is frequently useful to write instructions on a prescription form, so as to be clear and to emphasize the importance of the regimen. There is no general agreement about the practice of spreading the dosage of psychotropic drugs throughout the day *versus* taking the entire amount at bedtime. The latter is sometimes recommended for the sake of convenience and to obtain maximum benefit from any sedative effects, *e.g.*, in the case of tricyclics. However, aged patients may be less able to tolerate the sudden absorption of a relatively large drug dose into their blood circulation. In addition, the physician's emphasis on precise regularity of drug schedules enhances the patient's respect for the therapeutic regimen, and results in optimal use of the placebo effect.[22]

When patients are being maintained on psychotropic drugs, in the community after release from the hospital, it is good practice to inform both the patient and the relatives (or boarding home operator, etc.) of the manifestations of possible side-effects, and to caution them regarding certain drug-drug incompatabilities.

Patients maintained on psychotropic drugs should be *regularly reviewed* with regard to indications to adjust dosage (up or down); the risk of insidious, progressive side-effects; the possibility of a developing physical illness that would require other drug treatment, with the subsequent increased risk of drug-drug interactions; and to make sure if the patient is indeed taking the drug as prescribed. Some geropsychiatric patients who are maintained on antipsychotic drugs may undergo a change in their responsiveness to the drug, either in terms of greater or lesser sensitivity. Such variations in responsiveness usually involve time periods of several months, and point out the necessity of regular checkups at least two or three times a year.

Certain drugs (*e.g.*, barbiturates, antihistamines, tranquillizers, lithium) can have a *prolonged action* resulting in confusion, ataxia, or other side-effects. In an out-patient setting, the patient himself may stop (or "forget") taking the drugs without disclosing this to the physician at the time of follow-up. It is useful to ask the patient to describe the drugs he is supposed to be taking, and how often and at what times of the day he takes each one. When the drug regimen has been delegated to a relative (or rest home operator, etc.) the information should be obtained from them.

Finally, although the need for drug maintenance varies from patient to patient, and an empirical, individualized approach is called for, a few general points may be kept in mind:

—Aged schizophrenics seem to tolerate discontinuation of antipsychotic drugs better than younger schizophrenics.

—Patients maintained on antianxiety drugs report rather often that the efficacy of the drug seems to decrease in time. In such cases, one may periodically switch to other related drugs, and after an interval (usually several months), start the patient again on the original drug. The same approach may be useful in the case of sedatives and hypnotics.

—Antiparkinson drugs should not be used routinely to prevent extrapyramidal side-effects, since not all patients will develop these. Although antiparkinson drugs may play a primary role in producing the central anticholinergic syndrome, they also happen to be the type of drug that can be most easily discontinued.[3]

—In maintaining patients on antipsychotic drugs for long periods of time, the benefits of the drug must be weighted against the risk of tardive dyskinesia in the future.

## REFERENCES

1. PRIEN, R. F., HABER, P. A., AND CAFFEY, E. M.: The use of psychoactive drugs in elderly patients with psychiatric disorders: survey conducted in twelve Veterans Administration hospitals. *J. Am. Geriatr. Soc. 23:* 104–112, 1975.
2. FRIEDEL, R. O.: The biochemical basis of psychopharmacology. *In:* Drug Issues in Geropsychiatry, W. E. Fann and G. L. Maddox, eds. Williams & Wilkins, Baltimore, 1974. pp. 9–17.
3. DAVIS, J. M., FANN, W. E., EL-YOUSEF, M. K., AND JANOWSKY, D. S.: Clinical problems in treating the aged with psychotropic drugs. *In:* Advances in Behavioral Biology, Vol. 6: Psychopharmacology and Aging, C. Eisdorfer and W. E. Fann, eds. Plenum Press, New York, 1973. pp. 111–125.
4. BENDER, A. D.: Pharmacodynamic principles of drug therapy in the aged. *J. Am. Geriatr. Soc. 22:* 296–303, 1974.
5. KATO, R., VASSANELLI, P., FRONTINO, G., AND CHIESARA, E.: Variation in the activity of liver microsomal drug-metabolizing enzymes in rats in relation to age. *Biochem. Pharmacol. 13:* 1037, 1964.
6. RAFSKY, H. A., BRILL, A. A., STERN, K. G., AND COREY, H.: Electrophoretic studies on the serum of "normal" aged individuals. *Am. J. Med. Sci. 224:* 522, 1952.
7. GOLDMAN, R.: Speculations on vascular changes with age. *J. Am. Geriatr. Soc. 18:* 765, 1970.
8. VERZAR, F.: The age of the individual as one of the parameters of pharmacological action. *Acta Physiol. Acad. Sci. Hung. 19:* 313, 1961.
9. FANN, W. E., DAVIS, J. M., JANOWSKY, D. S., AND SCHMIDT, D. M.: Chlorpromazine effects of antacids on its gastrointestinal absorption. *J. Clin. Pharmacol. 13:* 388–390, 1973.
10. CONNEY, A. H. AND BURNS, J. J.: Factors influencing drug metabolism. *Adv. Pharmacol. 1:* 31–58, 1962.
11. WHARTON, R. N., PEREL, J. M., DAYTON, P. G., AND MALITZ, S.: A potential clinical use for the interaction of methylphenidate with tricyclic antidepressants. *Am. J. Psychiatry 127:* 1619–1625, 1971.

12. JANOWSKY, D. S., FANN, W. E., AND DAVIS, J. M.: Chlorpromazine reversal of guanethidine hypotension. *Am. J. Psychiatry 130:* 808–812, 1973.
13. SALZMAN, C. AND SHADER, R.: Responses to psychotropic drugs in the normal elderly. *In:* Advances in Behavioral Biology. Vol. 6: Psychopharmacology and Aging, C. Eisdorfer and W. E. Fann, eds. Plenum Press, New York, 1973. pp. 159–168.
14. PRANGE, A. J., WILSON, I. C., KNOW, A. E., McCLANE, T. K., BREESE, G. R., MARTIN, B. R., ALLTOP, L. B., AND LIPTON, M. A.: Thyroid-imipramine interaction: clinical results and basic mechanism. *In:* Brain Chemistry and Mental Disease, B. T. Ho and W. M. McIsaac, eds. Plenum Press, New York, 1971. p. 197.
15. DI MASCIO, A.: Personality and variability of response to psychotropic drugs: relationship to paradoxical effects. *In:* Non-Specific Factors in Drug Therapy, K. Rickels, ed. Charles C. Thomas, Springfield, Ill., 1968. pp. 40–49.
16. RICKELS, K., GORDON, P. E., GAUSMAN, D. H., WEISE, C. C., PERERIA-ORGAN, J. A., AND HESBACHER, P. T.: Pemoline and methylphenidate in mildly depressed outpatients. *Clin. Pharmacol. Ther. 11:* 698–710, 1970.
17. MADDOX, G. L.: Drugs, Physicians, and Patients. *In:* Drug Issues in Geropsychiatry, W. E. Fann and G. L. Maddox, eds. Williams & Wilkins, Baltimore, 1974. pp. 3–6.
18. LEAROYD, B. M.: Psychotropic drugs in the aging patient. *Med. J. Aust. 1:* 1131, 1972.
19. SEIDL, L. G., THORNTON, G. F., SMITH, J. W., AND CLUFF, L. E.: Studies on the epidemiology of adverse drug reactions. III. Reactions in patients on a general medical service. *Bull. Johns Hopkins Hosp. 119:* 299, 1966.
20. HURWITZ, N.: Predisposing factors in adverse reactions to drugs. *Br. Med. J. 1:* 536, 1969.
21. EL-YOUSEF, M. K., JANOWSKY, D. S., DAVIS, J. M., AND SEKERKE, H. J.: Reversal by physostigmine of antiparkinsonian drug toxicity. *Am. J. Psychiatry 130:* 141–145, 1973.
22. PRANGE, A. J.: Use of antidepressant drugs in the elderly patient. *In:* Advances in Behavioral Biology, Vol 6: Psychopharmacology and Aging, C. Eisdorfer and W. E. Fann, eds. Plenum Press, New York, 1973. pp. 225–237.

# 11

# psychotherapy and sociotherapy

## CHARACTERISTICS OF THERAPY WITH THE AGED

Psychiatric therapy with the aged involves more than the average number of emergencies; complex problems of scheduling (time, place, duration); problems related to the fact that the patient, although an adult, is often dependent on other members of his family; the typically multigenerational nature of the problem; and frequent coincidence of organic brain disease and psychogenic trauma. Home visits, in view of the physical difficulties of the patient, are also a necessity to the practice of geropsychiatry.[1]

### Goals of Treatment

The characteristics of the illness, of the patient's environment (family, economic resources, etc.), and of the aging process itself usually determine what are rational treatment goals. Sometimes the primary goal may be to provide relief for the relatives rather than for the patient.

One woman, in her 60's, had visited her demented husband in the hospital, every day for years. The nursing personnel disliked her because she was bossy, and interfered with the institutional routine. But her husband was all this woman had: she had no children, no nearby relatives, and only a few friends. The treatment goal here was in terms of helping her to develop new interests.

In another case, a professional woman in her early fifties consulted the psychiatrist regarding her 80-year-old mother. The latter had been living with her for 15 years, and had become quite senile. The mother's confusion had become so severe that the daughter realized a new arrangement was in order. While talking about the alternatives, it became apparent how much feeling she had invested in her mother. She stated she was happily married, "but all my time is spent on my work and taking care of my mother." When it was pointed out that nursing home placement for her mother was already overdue, she wondered instead how much longer she could keep her mother at home. The question was raised as to what extent she tried to avoid the inevitable loss of her mother, and to what extent the attention focused on her mother for so long had served to avoid grief about not having children. After thinking this over for a while, she agreed that this was both plausible and probable. Finally the point was brought up that not only would she soon face the loss of her mother but also the unsettling prospect of an essentially empty marriage.

Some aged patients, on the other hand, can be helped by insight therapy, when, for example, deterioration is minimal, ego strength is adequate, the patient is motivated, and adequate environmental support is present. Usually, however, treatment goals with elderly patients are more limited in scope. Once this has been realized and accepted by the physician, he is likely to find that geriatric therapy can indeed be quite rewarding in terms of obtaining tangible improvements in the patient and professional satisfaction for himself. Therapeutic failures with the aged do not have to be more frequent than in many categories of younger patients. Many failures are caused by inadequate diagnostic formulation, deficiencies in the comprehensive treatment plan, or prematurely abandoning the therapeutic program.

## Patient Factors

(a). Because of age-related sensory decrements, intellectual impairment, or slowing of central nervous system processes, the patient often has difficulty communicating and cooperating with the physician during the anamnesis and physical examination. It may take him longer to comprehend and respond to questions, he is more likely to forget treatment instructions, and so on. Therefore, one may need to talk more slowly (not necessarily louder), to repeat questions and instructions, and to write down advice and suggestions, or date of return visit.

(b). Because the older patient often "lives in the past," the therapist may be seen more as a person in the patient's past. Thus, the patient may not be able to distinguish the therapist as a real person from the therapist as a *transference* figure. In contrast to therapy with younger adults, the use of transference, which can be subjected to analysis, is less feasible in the aged.

Transference factors play a role in most interpersonal relations, including the doctor-patient relationship. Only in insight-oriented psychotherapy is the transference analyzed. In other types of doctor-patient relationships, the transference is left, by and large, untouched. It is of practical importance that an (unanalyzed) positive transference can play a significant role in the patient's clinical improvement.

## Physician Factors

(a). Younger physicians may have some difficulty in understanding the experiences of their aged patient. The understanding of another person usually involves the mental process of *empathy*, *i.e.*, a transient identification that requires imagining what it would be like to be in the other fellow's shoes. For physicians who have not had the experience of being old, empathic understanding is difficult.

(b). The counterpart of the transference in the patient is the *countertransference* in the physician. Countertransference is common. It may represent a counter-role to the patient's transference roles and expectations. If the roles are fitting and appropriate, the participants in the relationship have something to offer to each other. An elderly woman patient, for example, may unconsciously regard the physician as the son she never had. If the physician's behavior toward this elderly woman contains elements dating back to the relationship with his own mother, then there may be a fit between mutual expectations and roles. A countertransference, like a transference, becomes a problem in the relationship when it contains relatively strong neurotic components or unconscious ambivalence.

**(c).** The possible existence of *gerophobic attitudes*[2] on the part of the physician, or his own unresolved fears of aging and death will make it difficult for him to approach disorders in the aged with enlightened detachment and rational compassion. The obvious constraints in having to set limited therapeutic goals and the lack of opportunity for modifying lifelong patterns of adaptation are added burdens, as is the contemporary cultural emphasis on youth and attractiveness.

**(d).** Finally, early emotional conflicts which existed between the physician and his own parents may be reactivated, causing specific countertransference attitudes. In such cases effective therapeutic intervention is likely to be seriously handicapped. From a practical point of view, the physician then has two options: refer the patient to a colleague or have counsel with himself regarding the nature of his personal countertransference attitude. As a rule of thumb, it is not wise to continue treating patients for whom one has either excessive likes or dislikes.

## Referrals to the Geropsychiatrist

Many aged patients have minor emotional problems. The majority of these patients are seen by the nonpsychiatric practitioner. The frequency of psychiatric referrals depends on a number of factors including availability of psychiatrists in the area, the physician's own knowledge in the field of geropsychiatry, the attitudes of the patient and his family, socioeconomic factors, and so on. When should a psychiatrist be called in? Psychiatric referral and consultations may be needed for two reasons: diagnosis or therapy.

**(a).** Some questions and conditions likely to lead to *diagnostic referral* are the following:

**1.** To what extent do psychological factors contribute to physical symptoms? (These factors include psychophysiologic reactions, conversion reactions, depressive equivalent, hypochondriasis, etc.)

**2.** What are the effects of the patient's physical illness on his psychological functions? (These somatopsychic reactions include reactive depression, regressive behavior, paranoid reactions, acute confusion, etc.)

**3.** Evaluation of aged patients preoperatively, and of postoperative complications.

**4.** Diagnosis and differential diagnosis of organic brain syndrome, senile regression, depressive states, paranoid phenomena, and so on.

**5.** Behavior disturbances, such as vindictiveness, combativeness, self-destructive tendencies, overt sexual acting-out, or "geriatric delinquency".[3]

**6.** Determinations of mental competence.

**(b).** Referrals for *treatment and management* include the following:

**1.** Management of psychotic conditions that require electroconvulsive therapy, lithium therapy, and so on.

**2.** Advice concerning disposition, such as admission to mental hospitals, commitment, release from mental hospitals, placement in specific types of extended care facilities, and counseling the relatives with regard to implementation and implications of such decisions.

**3.** Periodic follow-up and reevaluation of outpatients maintained on psychotropic medications; recommendations for changes in the spectrum of various treatment modalities.

**4.** Individual psychotherapy for selected patients with such problems as reactive depressions, identity crisis of late life, marital difficulties, and family problems involving multigenerational conflicts.

## PSYCHOTHERAPY

### General Considerations

**(a).** Psychotherapy is the planned application, by a professional therapist, of specific psychological techniques to help the patient, by decreasing or removing psychological disability or misery, and facilitating optimal functioning and well-being. The *basic skills* involved in conducting psychotherapy include the ability to make accurate observations of behavior and to draw proper inferences from these; to synthesize the inferences in a tentative psychodynamic formulation, which serves as a theoretical model and has implications for the type of therapy indicated; to apply specific psychotherapeutic techniques in the therapist-patient relationship, and observe the effects of such interventions on the patient; to use this feedback information for the purpose of testing (confirming, refining, rejecting, etc.) the adequacy of the initial psychodynamic formulation; and to recognize one's personality limitations to avoid creating additional conflict in the patient.

**(b).** Basically, psychotherapy is *therapeutic communication*. The goal of the therapist is, first of all, understanding and comprehension, rather than sympathetic agreement or polite disagreement. He must try to discover why the patient is reacting in this way and at this time. Thus, insight is, first and foremost, a requirement for the therapist, regardless of the type of psychotherapy (insight-oriented *versus* supportive). Whether or not the therapist communicates his insights to the patient is a separate issue.

**(c).** All forms of psychotherapy are essentially aimed at *changing and modifying behavior*. They differ with regard to their specific techniques and to the theoretical premises that represent the framework for, and the basis of, these psychotherapeutic techniques. Not infrequently, there seems to be a tendency to overemphasize alleged differences between various schools of thought, and to create artificial dichotomies. In the case of psychoanalytically oriented therapy, for example, the ultimate goal is not insight *per se*. Insight, like an X-ray picture, makes translucent what is inside, but such elucidation is not an end in itself. The reason that insight-oriented therapy takes so long is that so much time is needed to apply the newly acquired insights to practices of everyday living. Thus, the psychoanalytic concept of "working through" involves many procedures which can also be understood in the framework of learning theory, behavior therapy, reality therapy, and so on.

(d). There are many ways in which elderly people with psychological disturbances can be helped. It is both necessary and possible to determine for each patient what factors contribute to producing a psychological disorder. Only then will it be possible to *formulate a plan of action*, which will contain one major therapeutic aim and appropriate subsidiary ones. Usually, psychotherapy with aged patients is supportive in nature. Few patients need or want an extensive personality change. Some are content with solving a minor problem, others are capable of little change.

## Psychotherapeutic Approaches

(a). The distinctive feature of *insight-oriented psychotherapy* is the use of free association and the analysis of the transference. The goal is not primarily to solve of practical problems but to alter the personality structure so that it may function more effectively. Through intrapsychic alterations the ego emerges as a more mature and effective mental agency. This involves conscious recognition of maladaptive defenses and reduction of character rigidities. Regression and transference (brought about by the patient's free associations and the therapist's relative inactivity) are characteristic. Early memories are reactivated. These memories mobilize the feelings associated with them, thus making it possible to explore their role in the present. Insight-oriented therapy is much like an in-depth learning experience. To recognize the problem, its cause and effect, is intellectual insight, whereas true insight includes a reasonable solution. It is this latter point, *i.e.*, attaining a practical solution, which so often represents a problem and constraint in therapy with elderly patients. It may be easy to arrive at insight, but there may not be much opportunity to do anything with it.

A 62-year-old woman was hospitalized because of a progressively severe neurotic depression. She had been the youngest of four children, and as the only girl, she was "her father's darling." At the time of her birth, the father, being 29 years older than the patient's mother, was 62 years old. As a young girl, the patient felt very close to her father, and looked up to him with awe and admiration. Then when she was 5 years old, he died suddenly, leaving the family in financial chaos. During the next few years the patient learned that her father was really not all that admirable, but rather was irresponsible. This discovery had been a painful disillusionment for her.

At the age of 22, she married a prominent, respectable man who was financially well off, and who was 29 years her senior (attempt to repair the disappointment she had as a little girl). When her husband, now 91 years old, reached his 80's, he gradually became senile. The resulting personality changes on his part (becoming less dependable, more irresponsible, etc.) reactivated the patient's original childhood conflict. She became gradually more and more depressed, and received psychotherapy for several years. She did failry well in therapy and depended a great deal on her therapist. Then, a few months ago, he died suddenly. Since then the patient's depression has been significantly worse.

The psychodynamics of her depression are rather transparent. Intellectual insight might be achieved in a short period of time. But the issue is this: what would this woman, at age 62, with her 91-year-old senile husband, actually do with her insight? In fact, it is conceivable that this type of knowledge about herself and the course of her life could exacerbate her depression.

Thus, it is not surprising that insight frequently comes about when the patient intuitively feels that he can, as it were, afford it.

A well-to-do businessman, now in his late 60's, had his first major depressive episode at the age of 48. His premorbid personality was characterized by extreme ambitiousness, aggressiveness, and obsessive-compulsive features. His goal in life (during his 20's and 30's) had been to make a lot of money (which he did), and to become number one in his field (which he did, too). He married a socialite, primarily as a way to facilitate his commercial endeavors. At the apex of his career, his wife left him, and the patient had a major depressive episode (age 48). After recovering from this, he found himself unable to return to his previous work patterns. The next crisis was an acute myocardial infarct at age 55. The pattern of semiretirement now changed into full retirement. About this time, the patient married his second wife, 20 years his junior. He needed her youth, she needed the economic security. The marriage worked out surprisingly well, but the patient continued to have recurrent depressive episodes. The origin of these depressions could be understood in the context of what happened in his second marriage. First, a daughter was born, the patient then being 60 years old. This event made it possible to explore his feelings about his mother who had died when he was still a little boy. Then, at 65 he became the father of a son. Having a son was a source of intense pride for him. And, it was only now that he was prepared to come to grips with the ultimate source of his neurotic problem, *viz.*, his own father. He had never been able to resolve the ambivalence—a mixture of intense admiration and hatred—toward this powerful, capricious man. Being now himself the father of a son, he was able to transcend the ambivalence toward his father, an act involving a retroactive conciliation and forgiveness. Thus, at the age of 65 he accomplished what optimally should have been done 60 years earlier (the resolution of the oedipal conflict). He reported that, for the first time in his life, he was experiencing a sense of serenity and gratitude. He retrieved a picture of his father's, framed it, and placed it side by side with that of his son.

**(b).** In *supportive therapy*, regression and transference are carefully kept within boundaries and are not interpreted. The goal is not insight, but support of existing coping mechanisms in the face of current hardships. Adaptive defenses are strengthened so that they can replace maladaptive ones. In supportive therapy, the goal is to bring the patient back to a satisfactory condition which, for example, could be a prepsychotic neurotic equilibrium. Insight is not achieved deliberately. In order for the patient to be involved in supportive therapy, he should be able to develop positive transference feelings, or feelings of trust and confidence in the physician. Guidance and counseling are forms of supportive therapy which aim at resolving external problems, strengthening ego functioning, and enhancing the self-image.

1. In *counseling*, one assists the client or patient in problem solving by suggesting a course of action and providing support in following that direction. The interviews, usually few in number, are focused on actual interpersonal or situational problems. Likewise, explanations are reality-oriented. Solutions are considered according to the opportunities and constraints of the patient's situation. Although the counselor actively functions as a teacher, the best solution is the one at which the learner arrives through his own efforts. Counseling is based on the assumption that the patient's ego can deal with the problem once a course of action has been outlined and that, in implementing it, there is minimal interference from anxiety or other disturbing emotions.

2. In *guidance*, the emotional factors involved are of such magnitude that the ego cannot function effectively until they are brought to light, and their nature and roles are understood. Because of the disturbing emotions, the individual finds himself unable to carry out solutions which he himself may already have thought out. The support of the therapist, who can exert leverage as an authority or parent substitute, and his permissiveness, act to free resources restricted by intrapsychic or situational impediments. Clarification of the problem often cannot be achieved without elimination of guilt, fear, or anger. Because these are not traced to their unconscious sources, improvement is accomplished by the therapist's support (empathy, acceptance, and permissiveness) which permits the patient to develop a new emotional perspective.

## Sociotherapy

(a). Usually, supportive psychotherapy with aged patients is best carried out in a group context. Group experiences enhance a sense of belonging, an appreciation for the value of external sources of satisfaction, and the effectiveness of reality testing. The group provides an opportunity for ventilation of emotions and discussion of relevant issues (retirement, societal attitudes, religion, the good old days, complaints about the institution, etc.). Patient groups may also be engaged in activities such as occupational therapy, art therapy, and so on. Recreational therapy carried out in a group setting may employ a form of psychodrama in which elderly patients are assigned specific roles to play; these roles may be therapeutic inasmuch as the roles entail the expression of specific emotions and ideas. In the setting of role playing.

the patient may experience catharsis without undue feelings of inhibition or guilt.

   **(b).** The *membership* of a therapeutic group preferably should number between six and twelve, and provide enough variety and stimulation between group members, as well as protection against disruptive factors. The criteria for selecting patients for group therapy include an explicit wish to join, relative alertness, ability to communicate, adequate personal hygiene and locomotion, and some degree of emotional responsiveness.[4] In institutional or out-patient settings, however, ideal criteria are often outweighed by practical considerations. Frequently, groups are started with elderly patients who happen to be available, and this can work out surprisingly well. The group evolves into an organism that eliminates those elements that don't fit and takes in those types who do fit. Once such a group has developed into a relatively cohesive structure, it may go on for a long time.

   One rather loosely structured group in a retirement home has been in continuous existence for many years now. The group survived periodic changes both in its membership and leadership. In this case, the group became, in the sociological sense of the word, an institution all of its own. The secret of its longevity probably was the high caliber of its constituency and the *leitmotiv* of the discussions: counting one's blessings in the present, and a tendency to see the past in an aura of gold.

   **(c).** Group therapy can be carried out in many different settings, such as out-patient facilities, day care centers, psychiatric clinics, geriatric wards, or homes for the aged. It can be conducted by a psychiatrist, nonpsychiatric physicians, clinical psychologists, social workers, nurses, and other health personnel, provided they have had some training in this area. There are several types of group therapy, characterized by differences in goals or methods.

   **1.** *Remotivation groups* are aimed at reaching out toward, and getting in touch with chronic patients who are withdrawn or apathetic. A few such patients meet at regular, frequent times with members of the ward team. The latter are selected on the basis of specific qualities, in particular, emotional warmth and natural friendliness. Through the medium of this warm relationship, the patient is brought in contact with elements of reality, such as pictures and objects closely related to his background (things typical of his work in the past, or his home area). In this manner, he may be drawn out, and his interest in the world around him rekindled.

   **2.** In *resocialization groups* the therapeutic goal is on a level just above the previous one. Given a patient who is still interested in his surroundings, it may be useful to maintain or relearn basic social skills and the instrumentalities required for daily living activities (grooming, eating, cleaning, cooking, etc.).

   **3.** On a next higher level, *discussion groups* may be formed, focusing on problems pertaining to the immediate setting of the hospital, or on current relationships with family, or even on abstract topics such as politics and religion.

**4.** *Predischarge Groups.* Patients who have improved to the point of being able to leave the hospital, especially after having been there for a long time, usually face many difficulties and anxieties about re-entering the community. This type of group deals with these concerns, not only by talking about them, but also by actually visiting a boarding home, going out shopping, getting acquainted with local agencies, such as the the social service department, the mental health clinic, senior citizens organizations, and so on.

**5.** *Marital and Family Therapy Groups.* Marital and family conflicts are common problems among elderly patients. The stresses of chronic illness and hospitalization frequently have the unfortunate result of depleting the family's economic resources as well as its reservoir of good will. When it seems that the damage can still be repaired, joint meetings can be set up including the patient, the immediate family, and the therapist-counselor.

**6.** The concept of the *therapeutic community* has been applied to elderly, institutionalized patients.[5] The traditional hospital expects the patient to be good and cooperative in playing the sick role. However, an extended sick role fixates the patient in a regressed mold. To prevent such regression and to maintain optimal function of remaining assets, the therapeutic community provides the patient with meaningful tasks and demands: the role of worker, decision maker, or neighbor. The patient may be active in the hospital workshop receiving pay for his work. Patients retain individuality and dignity by wearing their own clothes, and by collaborating with the staff in decision making. The hospital ward is transformed into a homelike place, with opportunity for privacy and belonging.

**7.** The value of *recreational therapy* is the group context in which it takes place, the enjoyments of spectator entertainment, and in particular, the exercising of physical and mental functions. Such stimulating activities include "walk and talk" groups, rhythmic activities with dancing and singing, and games, picnics, parties, artwork, fishing, and gardening. Of special interest are programs bringing the aged closer to nature and living things, *e.g.*, working with flowers and vegetables in a garden, or plants indoors; having a pet; and being in touch with children or young people. In this context, foster grandparent programs may be mentioned, although here of course much more than recreation is involved.

**8.** *Occupational* and *industrial therapy* aim at maintaining or restoring specific skills. The rehabilitation of various functions and capacities involves programmed activities such as weaving, woodwork, and arts and crafts. In addition, occupational and industrial therapy provide opportunities for self-expression and enhanced self-esteem, and set the stage for socialization. The fact that elderly patients are often handicapped by psychomotor slowness, short attention span, forgetfulness, and sensory impairments, points up the need for occupational, recreational, and industrial therapists with special expertise in the field of aging.

**9.** *Reality orientation* refers to a planned program involving the reorientation of confused patients. During daily meetings the instructor presents, in a small group context, elementary information pertaining to time, place, person, and situation. Each patient is addressed individually, in a pleasant and unhurried manner. Patients may be asked about key items in their present perspective of time and space, *e.g.*, the weather, holidays, meals, and so on. The instructor rewards accurate responses by giving praise. Reality orientation can be extended beyond the group meeting through orientational devices, such as clocks, calendars, name tags, explanations of procedures, and bulletin boards.[6]

## SOME COMMENTS ON TECHNIQUES IN PSYCHOTHERAPY

### Nonverbal Communication

(a). Inherent in all techniques are two basic forms of communication: verbal language and *metacommunication*. The latter represents everything in the communication experience, other than actual words, that provides a clue for the correct interpretation of the verbal message. Metacommunication is reflected in the tonal qualities of the voice, the emotional significance of the word patterns, facial expression, and so on. This metalanguage is usually more meaningful than words themselves. Because variations of metalanguage are legion, a comprehensive discussion of them is beyond our scope; but a few abuses of metacommunication are worth mentioning.

1. Often, a question is phrased in such a way that instructions for the answer are given at the same time. People who are busy or in a position of authority may be especially prone to do this. If one enters a patient's room and asks with an air of cheerful determination, "Feeling pretty good today?", the implied message is "I am too busy to find out how you really feel, so be a good patient and tell me you feel fine." Such questions have built-in answers and few of them provide real information.

2. An aged patient is often seen in the presence of an adult offspring or a relative. It is then not uncommon to address oneself more and more to the relative who, after all, can communicate so much better. The patient himself is by passed. At the end of the session, the prescription may be handed to the relative. The patient will feel like a nonentity, who has no say-so about his own affairs.

3. Or, one might greet an elderly patient by saying "You really are looking good." The patient has no choice but to accept this as a compliment, even though he may think "I may look good, but I sure feel bad." Thus, the above greeting has the metacommunicative aspect of instructing the patient not to talk about his feelings. A better statement would be something like "You look good. I wonder if you feel as good as you look."

(b). *Empathy*, being a transient identification with the patient, should remain just that. An extended identification is a source of undue distress for oneself, and is of no help to the patient. Whereas overinvolvement is an occupational hazard in the treatment of children and younger adults, the other extreme, *i.e.*, defensive withdrawal from the patient, is more likely to occur in clinical work with old patients. Such a protective detachment on the part of the clinician would foster in the patient a sense of loneliness or rejection. An attitude of optimal empathy may be facilitated by keeping in mind that "this old person once had the same age I have now."

(c). In contrast to our professional contacts with younger adult patients, *physical touch* plays an important role in the therapeutic communication with older patients. Such physical contact between therapist and patient comes about in the most natural way. Very often, the patient will initiate it by making a gesture of reaching out. At other times, the therapist himself will become aware of a spontaneous impulse to touch his patient. The physical touch reflects a basic, natural way of getting in touch with the patient.

## Optimal Attitude

(a). For the purpose of therapeutic communication, it is necessary to view disturbed behavior as a malfunction of the total organism, just as one would regard physical symptomatology as a manifestation of malfunction of a particular organ. It is then easier to preserve an attitude of *detached concern*, and to remain both objective and helpful. This is especially useful when the patient's behavior is irritating, for example, when dealing with the communicative barriers encountered in aged patients.

(b). *Maintaining a Realistic Approach to Treatment.* Overenthusiasm on the physician's part sets the stage for a letdown for himself and the patient. While it is unethical, and therapeutically unwise to promise a patient too much, a pessimistic or fatalistic attitude may be even worse. A realistic approach is based on the recognition that, no matter what symptoms the patient presents, there is always something the physician can do to give relief. It is important that personnel involved with the care of the aged maintain an attitude that combines realism based on scientific knowledge with the humane desire to alleviate suffering. Only then is it possible to avoid extremes of detachment and overinvolvement.

(c). A *consistent approach* combines gentleness and firmness. Such an attitude makes it possible to set limits to undesirable behavior (*e.g.*, hyperactivity based on denial). Effective persuasion usually does not come about by forcing or commanding a patient to respond in certain ways. On the other hand, firm insistence may be effective, for example, in certain withdrawn and underactive patients.

(d). *Attitude therapy* involves the assuming of a specific behavioral attitude, on the part of the staff, toward a particular patient. These include kind firmness, active friendliness, passive friendliness, matter-of-fact approach, and no demand attitude.[7, 8]

(e). *Dual Roles.* There are several clinical settings and types of therapist-patient relationship which involve a set of dual roles on the part of both participants. This duality has nothing to do with the type of duality of feelings in ambivalence. Some examples of therapeutic relationships in which dual roles are important, include the following:

1. Sometimes, the patient may not only be older than the therapist, but he also may have had superior social or professional status. This may

pose a problem for both; the therapist may feel constrained by feelings of awe, and the patient hesitates to settle in an appropriately dependent position. In such cases, it is useful to remember that a patient's wish for support from a competent helper cuts across all ages and classes, and that one can make appropriate use of this universal tendency toward a spontaneous "positive transference." Yet, some of this should remain tacit. On the surface level of the interaction, social amenities can be carried on in keeping with the overt differences in status, class, and seniority. Thus, the therapist may comfortably assume a deferential attitude, especially at the beginning and the end of the contact, and as a junior may not challenge any pronouncements, but accept them with a mix of respect and matter-of-factness. And yet, somewhere during the interview he will shift his weight, easing both himself and the patient into the other dimension of their relationship, for example, by giving specific advice or changing medication.

**2.** In the therapeutic contacts with hypochondriacal patients, there can be an explicit, formal understanding to "do something" about the patient's physical complaints, while on a deeper level, there is a tacit, mutual understanding that things are not going to be that simple and that there is a lot more than meets the eye.

**3.** In the therapeutic management of patients with bitter, vindictive depressions, it is often necessary to be supportive without being obvious about it. Thus, the patient is given surreptitious support, and when he improves, he can allow himself to think that it was his own accomplishment, and that he is not beholden to anybody else for this. On a deeper level, of course, both he and the therapist know that there is more to it, but this knowledge remains tacit.

### Management of Maladaptive Defenses

**(a).** Maladaptive defenses aggravate the patient's suffering by exacerbating the very problem toward which they are directed. The aim of therapeutic intervention is to break up such vicious circles by removing or mitigating the maladaptive coping pattern. This can be accomplished by alleviating the underlying anxiety that prompted the particular defense, or by replacing that defense with a more appropriate coping technique. A patient's defenses should not be exposed or removed without first ascertaining what he is defending against. To remove defenses can be compared with taking away crutches from a paralyzed patient. When a particular defense is removed, another one is likely to take its place.

A 64-year-old withdrawn woman had not walked for several years. Neurological examinations showed no abnormalities. Through a concerted effort by the ward team, the patient was taken out of her wheelchair at regular intervals and taken for brief walks, supported by two attendants. After initial resistance, the patient began to go along with the walks. But soon she began to have outbursts of rage when anybody came close to her. Thus, both the "inability" to walk and the display of rage served to keep others away. When one behavior pattern was removed, another emerged to take its place. In this patient, the rage attacks were less maladaptive than the inability to walk because, after all, she had begun to interact with other people. After a few months, the rage attacks subsided while progress in walking continued.

(b). A specific form of correcting maladaptive behavior is *behavior modification*. Its theory and practice are based on the assumption that maladaptive behavior patterns are response habits which have been learned and have become part of the character. The therapeutic goal is to modify such behavior and reverse the learning process by selected techniques, including extinction procedures, counterconditioning, desensitization, negative reinforcement, and operant conditioning by token rewards. Clinical experience with these techniques in geropsychiatric management is still limited. It seems, however, that even in cases of moderate or severe organic brain syndrome the patient's behavior still can be modified, provided the reinforcement is specifically suited to the individual patient.[9, 10]

## Hope and Security

(a). *Reassurance.* The wish for reassurance reflects the universal human need for emotional security. The effectiveness of reassurance depends on whether it is true or false. False reassurance is not effective because it is prompted by the wrong motive, *e.g.*, the need to protect one's own self. False reassurance has a reactive quality; it is an automatic, reflexlike response, rather than consciously thought through. True reassurance, on the other hand, is deliberate and thought through. It acknowledges the personal meaning of a problem to the individual, the probability that emotional distress will arise, and his need for help in coping with it. True reassurance is also conveyed to a patient by emotional security and lack of alarm in the therapist. For example, discussing an emotionally charged topic in a tone that combines calm and lack of alarm can have a detoxifying effect on the patient's inner turmoil.

(b). *The Use of Regression.* Optimal regression permits the patient to accept his dependency, and therefore, care from others. When a positive transference (trust) exists, the patient looks forward to contacts with his physician, nurse, and so on. If possible, visits should be scheduled at regular intervals so that the patient has something definite to look forward to, and the element of uncertainty is removed. In a hospital setting, optimal regression can be quickly established by means of frequent, brief visits (*e.g.*, five minutes, three times a day, at the same appointed times).

(c). *Maintaining Hope.* An essential part of regression is an alteration in the time sense and temporal perspective. By taking on the different time scale, the patient does not look ahead as far into the future (*e.g.*, days instead of weeks or months). This may relieve anxiety and create a situation in which hope can be maintained or reactivated. Through living day by day, good prospects become real possibilities. When the future offers few, if any, good prospects, one may attempt to draw the patient's attention to what is presently at hand or immediately ahead. The same principle applies to patients dwelling on a past which contained few shares of happiness. A sense of disillusionment or despair may be prevented by focusing on whatever satisfactory experiences are available in the immediate here and now. On the other hand, when a person's past does contain many shares of happiness, it is useful to encourage the patient to reminisce about them. Through memory he has access to gratifying retrospects.

## Preserving Dignity

(a). Dignity involves a special type of self-esteem: to be regarded well in the eyes of others. This element of being regarded is also essential to its counterpart, shame. Dignity and shame are possible only when one is seen by another. One does not lose dignity in privacy, but in public. To protect dignity, it is necessary to provide the older person with the essentials of *privacy*: a space he can call his own, a place where he feels he belongs and can keep his belongings. In addition to lack of privacy, dignity can be lost in other ways and situations.

(b). The elderly patient—his body, his self, and self-image—often is in a fragile condition or a state of crisis. In view of this, it is all the more important to *foster his sense of identity*, his self-image as a person. Thus, it would be traumatic for a person who sees himself as courageous to break down with fear and trembling; for an optimist, to express pessimism; for a friendly person, to admit vindictiveness; for a generous person, to express envy. The risk to be avoided is that of loss of face. The injudicious puncturing of a social facade would leave the patient feeling helpless and embarrassed.

(c). Feelings of inadequacy and shame may occur for various reasons, *e.g.*, embarrassing disfigurements. To protect himself against possible ridicule and disgust from others, the patient withdraws. The price of intact dignity is isolation and loneliness. Also, once the patient himself feels ashamed, the people around him will feel embarrassed, too. The best management is to prevent such vicious circles from developing. In the case of a disfigurement, for example, we would do well to be especially aware of the need to show the patient respect, transcending the phenomenon of the pathologic alterations we are facing and relating to the whole person. Instilling in the patient a *foundation of self-respect* may enable him, in turn, to face others without shame.

(d). What may also be embarrassing, is a physical state of helplessness, a sense of loss of mastery, or the experience of being treated as a "case." It follows that all those efforts aimed at reducing helplessness and *promoting a sense of control* will also enhance the patient's dignity. In protecting the patient's dignity, we protect his person, his self-image, his image to others, and, in the final analysis, our own dignity. Our esteem for the old is based not only on how they appear to us now, but also on what they once were in the past, as a historically unique entity.

### REFERENCES

1. ZINBERG, N. E.: Special problems of gerontologic psychiatry. *In:* Geriatric Psychiatry: Grief, Loss, and Emotional Disorders in the Aging Process, M. A. Berezin and S. Cath, eds. International Universities Press, New York, 1965. pp. 147–149.

2. BUNZEL, J. H.: Recognition, relevance and de-activation of gerontophobia. *J. Am. Geriatr. Soc. 21:* 77-80, 1973.
3. WOLK, R. L., RUSTIN, S. L., AND SCOTTI, J.: The geriatric delinquent. *J. Am. Geriatr. Soc. 11:* 653, 1963.
4. LINDEN, M. E.: Group psychotherapy with institutitonalized senile women. II. Study in gerontologic human relations. *Int. J. Group Psychother. 3:* 150-170, 1953.
5. GOTTESMAN, L. E.: The response of long-hospitalized aged psychiatric patients to milieu treatment. *Gerontologist 7:* 47-48, 1967.
6. FOLSOM, J. C.: Reality orientation for the elderly mental patient. *J. Geriatr. Psychiatry 1:* 291-307, 1968.
7. Treatment Team, V. A. Hospital, Tuscaloosa, Alabama: Attitude therapy and the team approach. *Ment. Hosp. 16:* 307-323, 1965.
8. GINZBERG, R.: Attitude therapy in geriatric ward psychiatry. *J. Am. Geriatr. Soc. 3:* 445-462, 1952.
9. MUELLER, D. J. AND ATLAS, L.: Resocialization of regressed elderly residents: a behavioral management approach. *J. Gerontol. 27:* 390-392, 1972.
10. ANKUS, M. AND QUARRINGTON, B.: Operant behavior in the memory-disordered. *J. Gerontol. 27:* 500-510, 1972.

# 12

# management of anxiety

## INTRODUCTION

There are many obscurities in the clinical management of anxiety and the affective disorders. Witness the fact that some psychotropic drugs can have paradoxical effects; that some antidepressants and anti-psychotics are useful to treat anxiety; that most anxiety states have depressive features, and vice versa; etc. There are several reasons why certain drugs and psychotherapeutic interventions are often unpredictable. First, it is not always clear what the dominant affect is. One affect may cover another one, *e.g.*, defensive anger covering an underlying feeling of shame, guilt, or grief. Second, whereas some affects are free-floating and become clinically manifest, others may be latent, being held in check by specific defense mechanisms. In this case, the affect is not manifest, but covert. Its presence is in terms of a predisposition, or a potential to react emotionally in a certain way. Finally, a person does not have only one affect, but usually a spectrum of feelings, *e.g.*, the cluster of depression, envy, and vindictiveness.

An affect (or cluster of affects) is the result of at least two sets of factors: the psychobiological state of the interior; and, one's present perspective which encompasses prospects in the future and retrospective antecedents in the past. A position in the present implies a prospect, an outlook into the future. Anxiety results when a perspective in the present necessitates the anticipation of pain or danger, whereas hope prevails with the prospect of pleasure or joy. Thus, both anxiety and hope are affects oriented to the future. Any decrease of hope (any lessening of the probability of good prospects) results in anxiety. Thus, anxiety is the emotion being produced as one moves from a hopeful perspective toward a less hopeful one, along a line that eventually terminates in hopelessness. At this terminal point, where one no longer has anything to lose, anxiety ceases.

At the other extreme of the continuum, where hope is in a maximal configuration, the opportunity for anxiety is likewise the greatest: it is at this point, where I have everything to gain, that I can lose the most. When the perspective has actually changed in the direction from hope toward hopelessness, grief occurs as a response to this loss. The existence of grief does not mean that I cannot continue to feel anxiety about a subsequent, pending loss. Thus, at any given point, between the two extremes of the hope-despair continuum, anxiety (or fear) and depression (or grief) are merely two sides of the coin, being separated only by the difference of "not yet" and "no longer." Moving along the trajectory, then, anxiety will coexist with depression in varying proportions. At first, anxiety will be the dominating feature; at the midpoint, anxiety and depression will be about equal; during the last phase, depression will progressively eclipse anxiety, until the latter ceases at the end point of despair.

The position of hope being associated with high energy potential allows for the use of high energy coping mechanisms to brace against the slide toward less hopeful positions. (The effect of anxiety is activation and arousal; the physiological pathways involved are especially the pituitary-adrenal axis, and the endocrine systems. The metabolic effects are, by and large, catabolic). Adaptive coping mechanisms will restore the hopeful perspective. Maladaptive defenses will cause progressive deterioration of the position and increasing momentum in the downward slide. Somewhere, a point of no return may be reached which involves the realization that not enough energy is available to stop and reverse the downward course. When efforts to stop the slide are abandoned, surrender and giving up occur, and low energy defenses take over (regression, letting go, retreat). This change may subjectively be experienced as the "bottom dropping out." (The physiological state associated with depression, in contrast to anxiety is mostly one of retardation and suppression of neurovegetative and endocrine functions and may include anabolic processes).

## MANAGEMENT OF ANXIETY

Clinical management of anxiety, affective disorders, and other mental illness, especially in aged patients, does not rely on just one therapeutic modality, *e.g.*, drugs or psychotherapy. Rather, it involves a comprehensive approach in which drugs, psychotherapy, medical treatment, socioeconomic measures, and environmental manipulation are fitted into a therapeutic program which will suit the needs of the individual patient.

## PSYCHOPHARMACOLOGY

(a). The *antianxiety drugs* include the benzodiazepines, propanediols, and diphenylmethanes. There is clinical evidence that these drugs are safe and effective in treating anxiety in the elderly. They lessen anxiety and tension related to situational stresses or physical illness, but do not modify psychotic symptomatology.[1, 2, 3] Certain tricyclic antidepressants and phenothiazines are also occasionally used to treat anxiety and agitation in elderly patients.

1. The *benzodiazepines* include many popular drugs, such as diazepam (Valium), chlordiazepoxide (Librium), oxazepam (Serax), flurazepam (Dalmane), and chlorazepate (Tranxene). Chlordiazepoxide, diazepam, and oxazepam are similar in their sedative, muscle relaxant, and anticonvulsant properties. They differ with regard to dosage and

duration of action. Diazepam is somewhat more potent than chlordiazepoxide. Oxazepam, a metabolite of diazepam, is the shortest acting drug, while chlordiazepoxide is the longest acting. Oxazepam requires larger doses.[4] The benzodiazepines are primarily used for treatment of anxiety, and have replaced older drugs, *e.g.*, meprobamate and phenobarbital. Many physical symptoms associated with anxiety (*e.g.*, headaches, gastrointestinal distress, fatigue) respond well to the use of benzodiazepines.

**2.** *Glycerol derivatives* include meprobamate (Miltown, Equanil) and tybamate (Solacen). Although weaker and less effective, they have a useful role. Meprobamate is a mild tranquilizer with relaxant, sedative properties. Some of its action is subcortical; its sedative effect does not seriously impair mental functions. Meprobamate is useful in older people to control anxiety and mild agitation, because it does not cause muscular instability which may occur with the benzodiazepines. Tybamate, a slight chemical modification of meprobamate, is shorter acting and therefore, may be selected for daytime use. A combination of meprobamate (400 mg) and benactyzine (1 mg) (Deprol) combines the tranquilizing effect of the former with the antidepressant effect of the latter agent.

**3.** The *diphenylmethane derivatives* include diphenhydramine (Benadryl), and hydroxyzine (Atarax, Vistaril). Diphenhydramine is a widely used antihistamine, with sedative qualities. It is useful to induce sleep without side effects, has no addiction potential, but its value for treating anxiety is limited. Hydroxyzine, chiefly sedative, is also antihistaminic.

**4.** Other drugs used in the treatment of anxiety include certain *tricyclic antidepressants* and *phenothiazines*. Amitriptyline, doxepin, imipramine, desipramine, and nortriptyline can be anxiolytic, in addition to their antidepressant effect.[5] Some phenothiazines in small doses (*e.g.*, thioridazine) are useful for anxiety and tension, but have the disadvantage of lowering the blood pressure more often than the benzodiazepines. They may also cause feelings of lassitude or unreality.

**(b). Treatment Considerations.**

**1.** The minor tranquilizers are relatively *safe* in comparison to barbiturates. Unlike the latter, they do not seem to activate liver enzyme systems. Also, the benzodiazepines decrease the possibility of suicide in the depressed patient, since large amounts can be taken without fatal results, in contrast to barbiturates and meprobamate.

**2.** Some patients react to minor tranquilizers in a *paradoxical* way. They seem to resist the drug action, and become agitated rather than calm. Clearly, age-related pathology, *e.g.*, an O.B.S., may modify the clinical effects of these drugs in addition to the many other variables.

**3.** Individual susceptibility to the sedative effect of these drugs varies, so that it is difficult to set general standards for *dosage*. The side-effects of the antianxiety drugs are neither severe nor common. Some patients, however, even with small doses, experience drowsiness and unsteadiness of gait, but generally, few serious side-effects occur unless large doses are taken. Ataxia, nystagmus, and incoordination are clinical signs suggesting chronic overdosage. At very high dosage levels, benzodiazepines produce severe unsteadiness of gait, drowsiness, orthostatic hypotension, and coma.

4. *Addiction and habituation* can occur, usually when large doses have been taken for a long time. This is a greater risk than with the major tranquilizers, because the pleasure potential of minor tranquilizers can be similar to that of barbiturates and alcohol. Abrupt withdrawal from large doses of meprobamate, chlordiazepoxide, or diazepam results in a syndrome similar to barbiturate withdrawal.

5. While taking antianxiety drugs, the same *precautions* as for other psychotropic drugs are applicable: no alcohol, and special care in situations where drowsiness and impaired coordination would be hazardous.

6. It is advisable to *discontinue periodically* the minor tranquilizers, to avoid habituation and drug dependency, and to determine to what extent the placebo effect may play a role.

7. Patients often take minor tranquilizers, along with *other drugs* with sedative effects. Many alcoholics become habituated to minor tranquilizers without stopping drinking. On a short term basis, alcohol can potentiate the effect of tranquilizers and antidepressants, so that the dosage must be reduced to avoid toxic effects. Chronic alcohol use, however, induces changes in liver enzyme activity, resulting in more rapid metabolism which thus reduces the effect of drugs detoxified by the liver, *e.g.*, the benzodiazepines. The benzodiazepines are metabolized more rapidly by the alcoholic, so that larger doses are required for therapeutic effect.

**(c). Sedatives and Hypnotics.**

1. Old people tend to have less total sleep time than normal young adults, even though they may need more, rather than less, sleep.[6] The percentage of rapid eye movement (REM) sleep is slightly less; but Stage 4 sleep (deep sleep) tends to be considerably less, and sometimes is even absent. Stage 4 sleep is considered to be the most effective for fulfilling biological needs.[7] In addition, it takes longer for older people to fall asleep, and once they are asleep, tend to awaken more readily.[8] It is probably no exaggeration to state that of all signs, symptoms, and complaints in the field of medicine and psychiatry, disturbed sleep is the most common. It is important to keep in mind that, from a physiological point of view, sleep is not at all the passive state it once was thought to be; and that psychologically speaking, sleep is an art which many people never master. In conditions of anxiety, depression, and other mental illness, sleep disturbances are often first to appear and last to disappear.

2. In addition to the high frequency of sleep disorders, they also present complex problems in management. Some psychotropic agents, for example, are effective in inducing sleep, but happen to suppress REM sleep. Some tricyclic antidepressants have the effect of increasing REM latency, decreasing REM-sleep time, and increasing Stages 3 and 4 non-REM sleep. Certain CNS stimulants, such as phenmetrazine, tranylcypromine, and methylphenidate, also decrease REM time. Because dreaming activity is associated with REM sleep, one needs to

remain alert to the possible effects of such drug-induced dream deprivation.

Two other drugs deserve mention because of their widespread use: caffein and alcohol. It seems that caffein does not begin to exert its sleep-interfering effect until middle age. REM sleep is not appreciably affected by caffeine. Alcohol, as a CNS depressant, tends to facilitate the process of falling asleep, but not infrequently this is followed by waking earlier than usual. REM-sleep time is decreased by the use of alcohol.[4]

The ideal hypnotic would have the effect of rapid sleep induction, without changing the normal phases of sleep, and would insure a full night's sleep without a daytime hangover. It should present no risks of habituation, tolerance, or suicide if taken in overdosage. The currently available hypnotics meet all the above criteria in varying degrees, but none of them completely.[4]

3. Hypnotics should be used judiciously in the treatment of elderly patients. The most appropriate indication is for relief of *simple insomnia*, *i.e.*, insomnia not associated with depression, anxiety, or pain. Methyprylon (Noludar) is effective for simple insomnia in the elderly.[9] Commonly used hypnotics include secobarbital, pentobarbital, methyprylon, and ethchlorvynol (Placidyl). There is no general agreement about the relative efficacy of barbiturates, methyprylon, chloralhydrate, glutethimide (Doriden), and ethchlorvynol in terms of sleep induction and duration. Hence, it is necessary to use an empirical, individualized approach, in which the consideration of drug safety is a paramount factor. Paraldehyde is safe, but has the disadvantage of being highly distasteful. Chloralhydrate is a safe hypnotic: it does not significantly suppress REM sleep, it leaves little hangover or ataxia, and it has a low risk of habituation.

With regard to *barbiturates*, there seems to be no consensus as to their clinical usefulness for elderly patients. Although some authors recommend them, others state that barbiturates are not appropriate for the aged because delirium is a frequent side-effect. Because a consensus exists about the increased risk of untoward effects, it would follow that other types of hypnotics and sedatives are preferred.

*Bromides* are available in some over-the-counter hypnotics. Gradually increasing abuse of bromides results in bromide-intoxication which resembles an acute O.B.S. in its symptomatology. In suspected cases, the serum-bromide level should be tested. Treatment involves discontinuation of bromides, administering 2 to 4 g of sodium chloride every 4 hours, or ammonium chloride, which provides a chloride for displacing the bromide, and has a diuretic effect.

4. For insomnia resulting from *mild anxiety and tension* one may give: flurazepam (Dalmane), diazepam (Valium), hydroxyzine (Atarax; Vistaril), or doxepin (Sinequan). When insomnia is partly or mostly the result of the presence of a painful condition, administration of proper analgesics may prove to be necessary in addition to the hypnotic drugs.

5. Sedatives and hypnotics have little effect in cases of *severe anxiety or depression*. In the case of anxiety-depression of severe degree,

antidepressants and/or phenothiazines should be used, rather than sedatives or antianxiety drugs. In cases of mild to moderate severity, antianxiety drugs can be given, distributed throughout the day. This dosage pattern may eliminate the need for a hypnotic at bedtime.

**6.** For patients with organic brain syndrome, who are anxious and agitated, small doses of diazepam (Valium), chlordiazepoxide (Librium), thioridazine (Mellaril), or chlorpromazin (Thorazin) may be administered to relieve agitation and promote sleep.

## CLINICAL MANAGEMENT

Anxiety states in the elderly may be grouped depending on the origin of the anxiety. *Depletion anxiety* refers to insecurity about loss of external supplies, and the possibility of isolation and loneliness. *Helplessness* pertains to fears of loss of control and mastery, with feelings of shame. *Chronic neurotic anxiety* is usually a carry-over from earlier years, with physiological tension, motor agitation,and depressive admixtures. *Acute anxiety* may develop as an acute stress reaction or adjustment reaction of late life; or it may represent acute traumatic anxiety, resulting from a weakening of the ego's capacity to screen and ward off unwanted stimuli, as in catastrophic reactions of brain damaged patients, or informational overload. *Anxiety associated with psychoses* may be secondary to schizophrenic delusions, associated with paranoid states (persecutory anxiety); or it may be associated with chronic brain syndrome and senile dementia.

Generally speaking, to allay anxiety all the therapeutic principles underlying the optimal therapist-patient relationship must be observed. The promotion of appropriate dependency in the patient is therapeutically useful because it takes his attention away from anxiety-provoking concerns. Optimal regression, possible only in a firmly established therapist-patient relationship, is an effective antidote against anxiety; and when the motive of anxiety is absent, maladaptive defenses may be prevented from developing. An attempt should be made to prevent, eliminate, or treat anxiety-provoking factors which, in the aged, often pertain to loss of external supplies, role uncertainty, intrafamilial strife, borderline economic resources, relentless progress of physical disability, drastic changes in the body image, and so on. Antianxiety agents or sedatives should be employed promptly and decisively to interrupt any cycles of anxiety-depression, physical illness, and other stresses.

**(a). Depletion Anxiety.**

**1.** In elderly individuals, the nature of anxiety is not primarily in terms of a danger signal pertaining to unacceptable impulses from within but to object losses and loss of external supplies. Developmentally, this corresponds with separation anxiety; the apathetic depressions in old persons may be the clinical counterpart of anaclitic depressions in infants. Depressive anxiety may be precipitated or exacerbated by a loss or an environmental change. The patient himself may not always be aware of the source of his anxiety, and therefore a careful, thorough exploration of his life situation is in order. For example, it is possible that the patient's anxiety is based on the assumption that, when he will be in need of help, others will not be available or accessible. Frequently, this is expressed as anxiety about becoming a burden on others and as fears of abandonment.

**2.** The effect of anxiety is to increase the workload on a body whose homeostatic capacity is already diminished. In heart disease, for example, anxiety may make the difference between compensation and decompensation; the anxious patient overburdens his heart by becoming unduly restless. Hence there is the need for antianxiety drugs that will diminish the subjective experience of apprehension and protect the patient from the physiological stress associated with anxiety. Antianxiety agents, in the context of an optimal therapist-patient relationship, may also facilitate the process of gathering information about the patient's life situation. One should quickly explore the possible causes of the anxiety before it becomes chronic.

**3.** In addition to these immediate goals, there is the long-term therapeutic goal to re-establish the patient's equilibrium on a lasting basis. This will involve several procedures:

—One should make sure that necessary support is provided in the areas of concern, *e.g.*, financial assistance, homemaker services, legal aid, social contacts to prevent undue isolation, and so on.

—In some cases, it is necessary to establish a permanent relationship with the patient. At the very minimum, the patient should be told that he should feel free to return whenever he feels the need for this. If the patient is continued on antianxiety medications, this represents an implicit contract to follow him at regular intervals.

—If proper support has been provided, it may be useful to take the patient off the medications, and observe how he is doing. When he comes back still feeling anxious after the alleged deficiencies in his life situation have been corrected, there is obviously more than meets the eye. The probability rises then that the anxiety has multiple origins, and that the original complaint was only the tip of the iceberg.

**(b). Anxiety Associated with Helplessness.** Anxiety also may be generated by a move from a perspective of self-confidence in the direction of helplessness. Anxiety pertaining to loss of control and mastery may be acute (as in sudden physical illness) or slowly progressive (as the result of slowly accumulating losses in the area of personal competence and autonomy). The anxious feelings associated with this are in terms of loss of self-confidence and shame.

**1.** The initial goal in therapy is to develop an optimal physician-patient relationship, and to reduce some of the anxiety by way of medication. Once the patient has begun to feel more secure in the relationship with the therapist, specific concerns can be identified. Usually it is more difficult to obtain this type of information than in depletion anxiety (where the patient can simply point his finger to an external problem). In the case of helplessness, the deficiency is more personal, and may be embarrassing for the patient to verbalize. It may pertain to any neuromuscular, mental, and social capacities that represent basic instrumentalities in the areas of love, play, and work.

**2.** Under the protective aegis of the therapist-patient relationship, the patient is gently but firmly advised to get whatever medical examinations are in order. It is surprising how often elderly patients will resist having their alleged physical or mental defects examined. They may express fear about getting lost in the labyrinth of the modern hospital, or about finding out that theirs is a hopeless case. It may be necessary to provide arrangements to make sure that the patient, indeed, goes through channels and does not get lost in the maze of the hospital. After medical evaluation, it is also a frequent problem to get the patient to accept the recommended treatment. Here again, the positive transference in the relationship can serve its purpose.

**3.** In spite of appropriate medical evaluations and treatment, a residue of decreased physical, mental, or social competence may remain —enough to keep the anxiety going. In this case, supportive therapy should be maintained for an indefinite period of time. The goals of therapy include helping the patient adjust to the appropriate level of functioning, while simultaneously making efforts to provide for corresponding changes in the environment. These environmental changes are the reciprocal of the changes in the patient's status; the more helpless the patient, the more helpful the environment must become.

**4.** A few points with regard to psychotherapeutic techniques follow:

—Generally, for the purpose of reducing helplessness and enhancing a sense of control, an obsessive-compulsive behavioral style may be encouraged: preference for closure and predictability, avoidance of risks and uncertainty, and emphasis on schemas and schedules. One can emphasize the importance of regular routines and rhythmically patterning the patient's life activities.

—The relatives can be advised that feelings of helplessness in the aged family member can be alleviated by anticipating some of his needs. Such anticipation of needs before they arise fosters a subjective sense of control and thus may prevent angry frustration, depression, or shame. Patients who are handicapped by varying degrees of memory loss often have a relationship with one or more relatives, in which the latter serve as an extracorporeal, prosthetic memory device. In contacts with such patients and their relatives, one can observe that whenever the patient's memory fails him, he sends out a nonverbal signal (a quick look) toward the relative, who then responds by filling in the necessary details. Typically, neither the patient nor the relative are aware of the extent to which this goes on.

—It is essential, however, to remind the patient of remaining assets, and to encourage mobilization and diversions consistent with his remaining potential. Premature care, or an excessive amount of support has an adverse effect, by promoting regression. Thus, it is often difficult to stay on an intermediate course, avoiding, on the one hand, the extreme of insufficient support (which would create more anxiety), and, on the other hand, too much support (which would promote regression). The importance of sustaining patterns of activity is emphasized by the fact that decreased physical activity and bed rest can cause significant changes in the distribution, metabolism, and excretion of drugs.[10]

—Motivation for activity must include a goal that seems worth the

effort. A patient may learn to walk following a stroke, but, unless he has a
motive for walking, he may soon abandon the attempt. The milieu of the
average institution frequently offers little incentive to activity, thus
fostering regression and deterioration. Self care and independence have
appeal only to the extent that there is something to live for. Whether in
an out-patient or in-patient setting, the therapist and other members of
the treatment team can become sources of incentive, by appropriately
rewarding the patient's efforts.

(c). **Chronic Neurotic Anxiety.** This disorder may be a carry-over
from earlier adult years. By now, the psychodynamics of the anxiety
neurosis are less important than they might have been when the patient
was young. After a lifetime of behavioral patterns based on neurotic
anxiety, an etiologically-based therapy (insight therapy) is not indicated. The behavioral patterns and symptoms have become ingrained in
the character although they are usually not egosyntonic. The patient
suffers from tension and agitation, but is unable to explain why. Varying
degrees of depression are usually present as well.

1. The *physiological concomitants* of anxiety (muscular tension,
insomnia, cardiovascular distress, stomach upsets, urinary frequency,
etc.) are usually more prominent than the subjective feelings of anxiety.
Generally, such patients do not respond well to therapeutic attempts
aimed at insight, counseling, or guidance, without drug therapy. To most
of them, the physical symptoms or agitation are sufficiently real to
convince them that their problem is physical. They may intellectually
agree that their symptoms have an emotional origin, but this acknowl-
edgement usually comes about only after one has begun to aim therapy
at the physical symptoms.

2. Although antianxiety drugs can be used for the symptomatic
treatment of anxiety, agitation, insomnia, and tension, these symptoms
often can also be alleviated by *increasing the patient's level of activity.*
The expenditure of energy must be channeled toward constructive
activities; aimless agitation will aggravate the patient's anxiety because
of the lack of structure and meaningful fit. In drawing up a planned
program of activities, some basic points must be kept in mind.

—The need for an individualized approach to the elderly patient is
pointed up by the fact that for each individual, sick or healthy, the
pattern of age-related decrements is singular and the rate of decline varies
from one function to another.

—Activity is to be more than passive participation in time-filling work.
Therapeutic activity has purpose; the more completely it absorbs the
patient's energies, the more beneficial it will be. When activities bring
about contacts with other people, isolation is reduced.

—In designing an activity program for the patient, the following steps
are required: find out patient's interests; make a list of potential
activities (indoors, outdoors) appropriate for the season; determine
patient's attention span for each of the activities; note the preferred time
of the day and preferred sequence of activities; arrive at a mutually
agreed regimen of daily activities, which should cover about one month
at the time; have patient come back to report on regimen; review and

make changes as needed. These patients frequently like simple, mechanical work, which does not require problem solving or a deadline, *e.g.*, gardening.

—If insomnia remains significant, in spite of increased activities during the day, one may cluster the doses of antianxiety drugs toward the evening to obtain maximum benefit from them during the night. During a period of interruption of the minor tranquilizers, it will be necessary to use a sedative or hypnotic to insure adequate sleep. When the antianxiety drugs are started again, the sedatives should be discontinued. In this manner, the risk of habituation to either type of drug can be reduced.

3. In many cases, *maintenance drug therapy* is needed to alleviate the discomfort that could interfere with the patient's optimal participation in the therapeutic relationship: meprobamate for patients with mild muscle tension and agitation, whose ego strength is good; one of the benzodiazepines for moderate anxiety, associated with diffuse somatic complaints; phenothiazines (*e.g.*, chlorpromazine, thioridazine) for more severe cases.

4. *Depression with Agitation.* If tension continues, despite the use of minor tranquilizers, one should consider the diagnosis of depression instead of anxiety. Depression shares many symptoms with anxiety, but its pathogenesis and therapy are different. In mild depression, one can start with small doses of amitriptyline, especially if insomnia is present. If there is no improvement in 2 to 3 weeks, a larger dose (25 or even 50 mg q.i.d.) may be needed. Imipramine should be given earlier during the day, because it can cause insomnia. Tricyclic antidepressants may relieve the depression, but occasionally they cause agitation instead. Diazepam may control mild agitation, but more severe agitation requires a phenothiazine. Doxepin (Sinequan, Adapin) and thioridazine are antidepressant agents that do not cause as much agitation. The antianxiety effect of these drugs is prompt, but, as with other antidepressants, relief of the depression may not become manifest for 2 to 3 weeks. Other medications used for mixed anxiety-depression are the combination meprobamate and benactyzine (Deprol) for mild cases, and the combination of perphenazine and amitriptyline (Triavil) for moderately severe cases.

5. The restlessness and agitation resulting from chronic anxiety should be differentiated from akathisia, a side-effect of antipsychotic drugs; from the muscular quiverings, which can be a side effect of lithium; and from agitated depression. Therefore, before starting minor tranquilizers, it is useful to have a drug-free baseline.

**(d). Acute Anxiety Reactions.**

1. *Acute stress reactions* or *acute adjustment reactions of late life* are not uncommon. Such reactive anxiety may occur as a response to any stress or trauma, including retirement, acute physical illness, loss of a loved one, and so on. The treatment approach will depend on the patient's ego strength and general resources *vis-à-vis* the magnitude of the stress. It is in the nature of an adjustment reaction to be rather short in duration and responsive to counseling or guidance. Psychotherapy should focus on the patient's reactions to the precipitating event or on

resolving the environmental stress. Medication should be limited to a few weeks since chronic reliance on drugs may provide just enough relief to keep the patient from seeking a decisive solution. Nighttime sedation is often sufficient.

2. *Acute traumatic anxiety* may develop in older patients because of weakening of a specific ego function, the so-called stimulus barrier. Normally, the ego is able to screen and ward off unwanted stimuli through various mechanisms, *e.g.*, selective inattention; increased inner activity of the self; turning to external diversions, so as to create a white noise that drowns out unwanted stimuli. In conditions of moderate to severe regression (attributable to psychological factors or physical illness), the ego boundary becomes more penetrable, and the patient is more vulnerable to a barrage of unwanted stimuli. Such a barrage may attain the quality of a bombardment. Even minor stimuli, *e.g.*, a dripping faucet, are capable of producing such traumatic anxiety. This type of anxiety arises automatically when the psyche is overwhelmed by an influx of external or internal stimuli too great to be mastered. This state is characteristic of infancy, when the ego is immature, but may occur whenever the ego is relatively weak, as in old age. Clinically, it may be manifested not primarily in terms of anxiety in the usual sense of the word, but by a diffuse, primitive response of intense, painful displeasure. Milder cases show restlessness, tension, and irritability. More severe cases are characterized by outbursts of anger and rage, or defensive attempts to re-establish a stimulus barrier by way of withdrawal.

Clinical management is supportive and includes drug therapy and environmental procedures. For milder cases, the benzodiazepines can be used first; if the symptoms persist, or in more severe cases, phenothiazines or other antipsychotic agents should be tried.

Supportive measures pertaining to environmental structuring essentially involve the providing of an "ego prosthesis." When the combined impact of the illness and of regression breaks down ego organization, leading to diminished resistance to external stimuli (noise, procedures, and changes in the environment), a regimen can be provided that serves as an ego prosthesis. Such an artificial ego implies organizing the patient's environment for him, with the spatiotemporal relations of his milieu kept constant. The principle is that of sameness; by keeping the milieu constant, the sense of loss of mastery in the patient is minimized. Constancy can also be applied to arrangement of furniture, temperature, light, procedural methods, and so on. Temporal constancy pertains to times of visits by the physician, nurses, relatives, and so on.

(e). **Anxiety Associated with Psychoses.** Delusional phobias, persecutory anxieties, and paranoid fears may occur in the context of chronic paranoid schizophrenia, late life paraphrenia, paranoid states, or at some point along the final common path toward dementia. Clinical management includes the use of antipsychotic agents, in addition to whatever medical, social, and environmental intervention is indicated. In many such patients, the anxiety and helpless panic respond well to an approach which consists of: providing a structured relationship or environment; being generously supportive, while at the same time firmly insisting on suppression of psychotic thoughts, and focussing on the realities of the here and now.

## REFERENCES

1. CHESROW, E. J., KAPLITZ, S. E., BREME, J. T., MUSCI, J., and SABATINI, R.: Use of a new benxodiazepine derivative (Valium) in chronically ill and disturbed elderly patients. J. Am. Geriatr. Soc. 10: 667-670, 1962.

2. GERSHON, S.: Antianxiety Agents. In: Advances in Behavioral Biology, Vol. 6: Psychopharmacology and Aging, C. Eisdorfer and W. E. Fann, eds. Plenum Press, New York, 1973. pp. 183-187.

3. JONES, T. H.: Chloriazepoxide and the geriatric patient. J. Am. Geriat. Soc. 10: 259-263, 1962.

4. HOLLISTER, L. E.: Psychiatric and neurologic disorders. In: Clinical Pharmacology, Chap. 11, K. L. Melmon and H. F. Morrelli, eds. The MacMillan Company, New York, 1972. pp. 455-459.

5. PRANGE, A. J.: The use of antidepressant drugs in the elderly patient. In: Advances in Behavioral Biology, Vol. 6: Psychopharmacology and Aging. C. Eisdorfer and W. E. Fann, eds. Plenum Press, New York, 1973. pp. 225-237.

6. GOLDFARB, A. I.: Geriatric psychiatry. In: Comprehensive Textbook of Psychiatry, Chap. 47, A. M. Freedman and H. I. Kaplan, eds. Williams & Wilkins, Baltimore, 1967. pp. 1564-1587.

7. AGNEW, H. W., WEBB, W. W., and WILLIAMS, R. L.: Sleep patterns in late middle aged males: an EEG study. Electroencephalog. Clin. Neurophysiol. 23: 168-171, 1967.

8. KAHN, E. and FISHER, C.: The sleep characteristics of the normal aged male. J. Nerv. Ment. Dis 148: 477-494, 1969.

9. PATTISON, J. H. AND ALLEN, R. P.: Comparison of the hypnotic effectiveness of secobarbital, pentobarbital, methyprylon, and ethchlorvynol. J. Am. Geriatr. Soc. 20: 398-412, 1972.

10. LEVY, G.: Effect of bed rest on distribution and elimination of drugs. J. Pharm. Sci. 56: 928, 1967.

# 13

# management of affective disorders

## DEPRESSION

**Psychopharmacology**

(a). The *antidepressant drugs* include the monoamine oxidase (MAO) inhibitors, the tricyclic group, and other agents with occasional antidepressant effects (certain phenothiazines and antianxiety drugs).

1. *MAO inhibitors* inhibit the deamination of catecholamines and indoleamines which results in increased amounts of norepinephrine, dopamine, and serotonin at the central receptor sites in the brain. This group of drugs consists of the hydrazides, *e.g.*, phenelzine (Nardil); and the nonhydrazides, *e.g.*, tranylcypromine (Parnate). The MAO inhibitors preferably should not be used in the elderly. They have interactive toxicity with other drugs, and with certain foodstuffs.[1] The only indications for their use are a history of responding well to MAO inhibitors and a poor response to other antidepressants.[2] Of the hydrazide group, phenelzine has been recommended as the drug of choice, and of the nonhydrazide group, tranylcypromine.[3] These drugs should be given only in a hospital setting, because of the risk of serious side-effects (hallucinations, hyperreflexia, and sometimes, fatal hypertensive crises precipitated by the ingestion of foods containing pressor amines).

2. The *tricyclic antidepressants* are phenothiazine analogs, but they have a different pharmacologic action, being useful against depression. Their mode of action is thought to be in terms of increasing the amounts of biogenic amines at central receptor sites. The general effects of the tricyclics are adrenergic or anticholinergic, and may involve the cardiovascular, gastrointestinal, hematogenic, endocrine, and central nervous systems, as well as the liver. The tricyclics can be grouped according to their sedating properties. Nonsedating are imipramine (Tofranil), desipramine (Pertofran, Norpramin), nortriptyline (Aventyl), and protriptyline (Vivactil). Sedating tricyclics include amitriptyline (Elavil), and doxepin (Sinequan). Amitriptyline, doxepin, nortriptyline, imipramine, and desipramine also can relieve anxiety in the context of depression. Protriptyline, on the other hand, is a stimulating drug.[2]

—*Dosage.* Generally, the tricyclics are similar in potency of action and dosage range, except for nortriptyline (Aventyl) and protriptyline

(Vivactil) which are more potent than the others. The dosage level for out-patient maintenance usually is about one-half or two-thirds of that in the hospital setting. Dose levels for elderly patients are generally lower than for younger adults; the initial dose is smaller and increments are made at a slower rate. Using this approach, with regular monitoring for side-effects, the dosage ceiling for an individual elderly patient is established.

—Tricyclics have more *side-effects* in old patients than in younger patients (Table 1). *Psychological-behavioral* side-effects include mild hypomanic excitement, exacerbation of schizophrenic symptoms, and exacerbation of manic conditions. Adding a phenothiazine helps in manic shifts or when a latent schizophrenic reaction is activated by the antidepressant. *Physical* side-effects are related to anticholinergic action, *e.g.*, dry mouth, lowered threshold for toxic confusion, glaucoma, urinary retention, constipation, and cardiovascular problems. Some of these can be potentially serious.[4] The central anticholinergic syndrome, in combination with the peripheral signs of anticholinergic toxicity, resembles the symptomatology of atropine or scopolamine toxicity.[5] The exact mechanism of another side-effect, *i.e.*, parkinsonism, is obscure. It should not be treated with antiparkinson drugs, because they can cause toxic confusion, like the tricyclics. When this side-effect occurs, it is best to lower the dose of the tricyclic drug.

### 3. Other Antidepressants.

—*Phenothiazines* have been used with success in treatment of agitated depression. When anxiety and agitation coexist with depression, phenothiazines (*e.g.*, thioridazine) can be combined with tricyclics. A combination of perphenazine and amitriptyline (Triavil) is frequently used for treatment of agitated depressions of mild or moderate degree.

—*Antianxiety drugs* are sometimes beneficial in reducing mild or moderate depression associated with anxiety. The combination meprobamate and benactyzine (Deprol) has also been used for this purpose.

—*Gerovital H3* has been studied with regard to its antidepressant effects.[6, 7, 8] The evidence so far suggests that Gerovital H3 has antidepressant qualities and can be effective and safe in treating depression in the elderly. GH3 is a weak, reversible, and competitive inhibitor of MAO, which selectively inhibits the deamination of certain important brain monoamines. There is no risk of the hypertensive crisis so typical of other MAO inhibitors.

### (b). Treatment Considerations.

1. It is advisable to get pretreatment baseline medical data, and during drug therapy, to monitor the following physiological functions: heart (EKG); neurological (sensory and motor functions; coordination); eyes (intraocular pressure); GU (prostate; libido); metabolism (blood sugar); and liver.

2. Drug therapy should begin with the tricyclics, amitriptyline (Elavil), and imipramine (Tofranil) being the drugs of choice. The patient should be free from all antidepressant medication for at least 1 week. With amitriptyline, the initial daily dose of 75 mg should be raised

TABLE 1. *Important Side-effects of Tricyclic Antidepressants*

| | Clinical Signs | Causative Factors | Prevention and Treatment |
|---|---|---|---|
| Behavioral | excitement; "manic shift" | stimulating effect | lower dose or change drug |
| | exacerbation of psychotic symptoms | underlying paranoid or schizophrenic disorder | use antipsychotics in combination or alone |
| Central Nervous System | EEG changes | large doses, parenteral admin. family history of epilepsy | lower dose, avoid parenteral admin. do not combine with MAOI |
| | seizures | history of CNS injury, combination with MAOI or phenothiazines | wait 1–2 weeks after one drug before starting another |
| | Parkinsonism; tremors | unclear; rare | lower dose or change drug; don't use antiparkinson drugs |
| | Central anticholinergic syndrome: acute confusion, hallucinations, agitation, short term memory loss | anticholinergic effects, combination with antipsychotics or antiparkinson drugs | differential diagnosis: Korsakov, transient ischemic attacks, etc.; check peripheral anticholinergic signs treatment: physostigmine |
| Neurological | hypertonus hyper-reflexia ataxia neuropathies tremors, fasciculations | anticholinergic or adrenergic effects; combination with MAOI; old age; vitamin deficiency | lower dose or stop drug avoid polypharmacy give vitamins |
| Cardiovascular | EKG changes; hypotension myocardial infarcts (→ CVA) increased blood pressure in hypertensive patients | pre-existing CVD adrenergic & anticholinergic effects blocking of guanethedine | do pretreatment EKG monitor cardiovascular indices stop drug or use other antihypertensive, *e.g.,* hydralazine |
| Ocular | glaucoma, blurred vision, accomodation paralysis | anticholinergic effects | lower dose or stop drug |
| Genitourinary | urinary retention; delayed ejaculation | prostate hypertrophy | lower dose or stop drug |
| Gastrointestinal | dry mouth, constipation fecal impaction | | lower dose or stop drug stop drug |

gradually to 150 or 200 mg until a therapeutic effect occurs. Because multiple factors play a role in producing therapeutic or toxic effects, there is considerable variability among patients with regard to optimal dose and maximum dose tolerated. Improvement may become apparent within 2 to 3 days and should appear at least by the third week of treatment. Reduction of the dosage to a maintenance level should be gradual. If no improvement occurs in 2 or 3 weeks, hospitalization is advisable. The medication should be stopped, and the use of ECT or MAO inhibitors should then be considered. MAO inhibitors must not be given in combination with other antidepressants or initiated on an out-patient basis.

3. In *acute* depressions, drug therapy is continued for 4 to 6 weeks beyond the point of maximum therapeutic benefit, then in gradually diminishing doses. The patient needs to be followed up for at least several months, depending on the duration of the episode, and the speed of recovery. In patients with *recurrent* or *chronic* depression, antidepressant drugs may need to be continued indefinitely.

4. *Side-effects*, like *placebo effects*, may become part of the overall symptomatology. The best means to prevent such a complication is a good therapist-patient relationship; the latter will have the effect of detoxifying or neutralizing many unwanted drug effects. The patient may be advised to consider mild side-effects, *e.g.*, dry mouth as evidence of favorable drug action.[3] Drowsiness usually disappears soon in patients who will favorably respond to tricyclic drugs; if it continues, another drug may be tried. Blurred vision and dry mouth often persist.

5. Despite close chemical resemblance to the phenothiazines, the tricyclics are not as safe when taken in high doses. *Overdosage* of imipramine or amitriptyline produces coma, clonic movements or seizures, respiratory depression, hyperpyrexia, and disturbances of cardiac rhythm.

6. It is not sound clinical practice to treat every depression with drugs. When there is marked loss of weight, serious risk of suicide, or other self-destructive behavior, *ECT* is indicated and can be lifesaving. Delay for trial of drugs leads to greater risk of suicide or chronicity, and more expense and socioeconomic disruption.

7. Tricyclics should not be combined with MAO inhibitors. Such a combination may lead to a *synergistic* effect manifested by intense CNS sympathetic stimulation: restlessness, muscle twitching, convulsions and hyperpyrexia, followed by death. There must be a waiting period of at least two weeks between one type of drug and the other.

8. Assessment of *treatment effectiveness* and *clinical improvement* may be hampered by several factors. First, there is no clear cut nosology of depression. Second, affective disorders are usually self-limited in duration, with remissions being followed by recurrent episodes. Third, many depressed patients hate to admit that they feel better. Consequently, it is essential to evaluate improvement (or lack there of), as much as possible, by way of objective criteria. These criteria pertain mostly to the physiological concomitants. Thus, clinical improvement can be assessed by observing the degree to which patterns of sleep,

appetite, weight, bowel function, psychomotor activity, and sexual activities are being restored to normal. Subjective criteria include the patient's mood statement, reports about decreasing physical malaise, the ability to concentrate, and the return of initiative and interests.

**9.** The danger of *suicide* should always be kept in mind, particularly when the depressed patient seems to be getting better. During an intermediate phase of recovery from depression, the patient may have regained enough energy to carry out an earlier plan for suicide.

**10.** As the depression improves, the patient may begin to show more *anger and hostility*. Usually, these negative feelings were present all along, but were suppressed by the patient. The development of *paranoid features*, however, indicates that the depression is worsening. It is therefore, important to differentiate between anger, irascibility, querulousness, and so on, on the one hand, and suspiciousness, ideas of reference, and paranoid ideation, on the other hand.

### Clinical Management

**(a).** *Reactive depressions* in which a specific event is the precipitating factor last for one to three months. Such a grief reaction, with its lowered mood, sense of emptiness, and physical distress is a natural response to the loss of a loved one. Grief of more than a year's duration, however, is pathological suggesting an ambivalent relationship with the lost object, or circumstances which otherwise inhibited emotional expression. Psychotherapy of a prolonged grief reaction should focus on mobilizing and expressing the emotions and exploring the role of ambivalence. Medication should be limited to nighttime sedation. Antidepressants are usually ineffective and, in fact, may obfuscate the process of working through the loss.

Management of *acute grief reactions* involves promoting a realistic awareness on the part of the patient of the loss which he suffered, and encouraging open expression of his bereavement. Ventilation of grief and sadness not only affords the patient a sense of relief that is both physiologic and psychologic, but also makes him feel closer to the therapist who is present to share the experience. Sometimes an individual needs the reassurance that grief and sadness are natural and that mourning represents a period which must be entered, traversed, and completed. But at the same time he can be advised that, although thoughts concerning the lost object will be frequently on his mind, it is wise to seek new activities and contacts to avoid excessive preoccupation with the loss. Thus, one attempts to guide the patient down an intermediate path which, on the one hand, avoids premature closure (suppression of grief) and, on the other, steers away from excessive melancholic involvement by venturing into new activities which will eventually engage the energy previously invested in the lost object. Frequently, simple counseling techniques are sufficient.

A 67-year-old unmarried woman continued to mourn her mother's death for many months. She had lived with her mother for many years, and filled her time by taking care of her. Since the mother had had a serious heart condition, the patient had been well aware that death could come at any time. Yet, in spite of this anticipatory grief work, she remained painfully preoccupied with the loss. Her unresolved grief was illustrated by an unrealistic plan to become a nurse's aid—an attempt to perpetuate the role she had played *vis-à-vis* her mother. She said she was not even able to go into the room which her mother had occupied for so many years. ("There would be too many painful memories if I go in that room.") The suggestion was made that she rearrange the furniture in her house, remove her mother's bed, and buy some new furniture. The patient expressed surprise that she herself had not thought of this solution.

Defenses aimed at avoiding awareness of grief and loss (denial, suppression, rationalization) can become maladaptive and require clinical intervention for several reasons. First, hyperactivity, inherent in being diversion-prone, may exhaust the patient. Second, although mild forms of denial can be conducive to good adjustment, extreme denial (often coupled with rebellious protest) is self-destructive, because the patient tends to reject appropriate assistance. Finally, the longer one holds onto an illusion, the more painful the disillusionment will be.

When dealing with denial, it is necessary to preceed with caution. One should never try to break through the denial, by forcefully uncovering the underlying emotions and confronting the patient with them. Ventilation of concerns is useful for specific therapeutic goals. Certain emotions lying just below the surface (grief about loss of an organ, anger at medical personnel, guilt about dependency imposed by illness) can be alleviated by expressing them. It is also useful to bring out into the open unrealistic assumptions or magical notions, such as guilt feelings about having done something wrong in the past, or even having lived the wrong kind of life, and now being punished for that by having a physical affliction or having suffered other losses.

In many aged persons, however, the self is in a state of transition or crisis. Therefore, it is not always prudent to probe for deeper thoughts and emotions, especially those which do not contribute to the patient's sense of closure, such as past disillusionments. The tendency of many older people to make the best of it, to count one's blessings, to retouch life's pictures stored in the memory by highlighting the bright and obscuring the dark—all this is not just a denial of some piece of reality. Rather, the attempt to seek out the sunny side of things in the here and now and, in retrospect, to beautify the past is nothing more than the work of that vital principle, hope.

(b). *Chronic neurotic depressions* are quite common and may be manifested by a diversity of clinical symptomatology. Frequently, anxiety is a relatively prominent feature. Clinical management of these conditions can be most difficult. It is often easier to deal with a frankly psychotic depression, in which ECT or other antidepressant treatment is quickly effective. In contrast, chronic neurotic depressions may drag on, with minor ups and downs—not unlike the fate of Sisyphus. The vexing problem with many neurotic depressions at any age is the masochistic core of needing to suffer, and often for an ulterior (*i.e.*, vindictive) purpose. This tendency is clinically demonstrated by the so-called negative therapeutic reaction; that is, at the very moment we have every reason to believe that the patient should improve, the opposite happens and he gets worse. This also presents problems for the therapist who must come to grips with his own frustration and countertransference. Not infrequently the combination of a few negative therapeutic reactions on the patient's part and a steady build up of countertransference feelings in the therapist adds up to a termination of the relationship after a few months or a few years.

By the time a patient with a history of chronic depression has reached middle age and moved into senescence, the emotional and behavioral patterns are usually well established. Depending on multiple factors (see Chaps. 3 and 6), these patients may hold their own, gradually change for the better, or slowly decompensate. For some individuals, a chronic depression becomes a way of life.

A chronically depressed woman had managed to remain the center of the family, by her stubborn silence, withdrawal, and asceticism. She found the energy to maintain this painful existence in one source: she cherished, with a vengeance, the memory of a thoughtless remark from her husband, twenty years ago. Even though he and their three children cared a good deal for her, she had become increasingly withdrawn and depressed. More and more often, she found herself at the edge of suicide. In the therapeutic contacts with this patient, she first would adamantly refuse any medications. After she had finally, in desperation, agreed to take antidepressant drugs, she indicated there was "a most important problem," but stubbornly declined to talk about it. Likewise, various suggestions and recommendations in the course of therapy were dismissed. Yet, she would continuously complain of the agony she was in. After she had eventually verbalized her "most important problem" (*i.e.*, her husband's slighting her), there was no letup in her savage depression. After several years of psychotherapy and numerous antidepressants, she still was not willing or able to let go of the depression; the secondary gains (controlling her family) were of such a magnitude that she was willing to pay the high price of continuous suffering. This case also illustrates the role of narcissism and vindictiveness in depression and her inability to forgive and forget.

(c). Depressions of a *mild* degree and relatively *recent* onset can be treated with guidance type of psychotherapy, often in combination with antidepressant drugs. The psychotherapy focuses on exploring the factors that produce the lowered self-esteem, which is central to the depression, and on clarifying environmental influences. Quite often such depressions occur in the beginning of the *involutional* period, which again points out that most depressions of the involutional type are not psychotic.

1. Many of these patients are female, in their late 40's and 50's. One of the major goals in therapy is to prevent decompensation toward hypochondriasis or a fixation of the patient's withdrawal. It will be necessary to focus on the need for developing new interests, contacts, and activities. Amitriptyline and imipramine are useful adjuncts for the

treatment of menopausal depressions. The benzodiazepines are effective when anxiety and mild agitation are present.

Occasionally, the patient's spouse will be seen as well, in conjoint sessions. Marital counseling and sexual advice is probably more often needed than carried out. Handling sexual and other highly personal matters in joint sessions requires special discretion and judgment to prevent further disruption of an interpersonal balance, which is often already tenuous.

In the case of female patients, the past history often reveals gynecological problems and surgery, including hysterectomy. Surprisingly, some patients are not certain whether the ovaries were removed or left in. At any rate, endocrinological factors may play a role in these depressions, and estrogen replacement therapy should be considered for possible inclusion in the management of postmenopausal depressions.[9, 10, 11]

**2.** The involutional depressions in men tend to occur at a later age than those in women, and are less distinct in symptomatology. When sexual involution coincides with retirement, it may be difficult to sort out which factor is more important. Some men develop an involutional depression in their 50's; and when the depressive episode is rather prolonged and includes many physical complaints, early retirement is a risk. This may permanently lower their self-esteem. The depression is complicated by increased anxiety which may require indefinite supportive psychotherapy and drug therapy (antidepressants and antianxiety drugs in milder cases; combinations of antidepressants and phenothiazines in more serious cases). Again, the focus in therapy is on utilizing the patient's remaining assets; one should limit one's commiseration with the patient in favor of an attitude of firm insistence, while directing him toward new interests. A program of activities may need to be developed as described above.

**(d).** *Depressive equivalents* are common, in both female and male patients, during senescence. The first problem one has to deal with may be the patient's resentment toward the medical profession. Such patients may have seen many physicians for their physical complaints, some of whom may already have informed them that the underlying cause is "psychological." Thus, some patients seek psychiatric help only as a last resort. During the initial contacts, it is important to tune in on the patient's feelings of resentment and futility, and to convey, through empathetic responses, a sense of understanding. Having established rapport with the patient, the next goal is to get the patient in touch with his real feelings. This means one has to get behind the surface layer of physical symptoms, and explore, together with the patient, what feelings might exist on that deeper level. At this stage in therapy, it would theoretically be better to withhold antidepressant drugs, and this is possible in cases of mild to moderate severity.

An attractive, middle-aged woman had complained for years of a swollen sensation in her arms, constant sleepiness, a feeling that other people seemed to be far away, and a persistent craving for chocolate. Her mood was one of mild tension and apprehension about the physical sensations. In psychotherapy, it was possible to interpret these as a defense against her becoming aware of an underlying depression. Only after she had stopped focusing on the physical sensations, did the depression emerge, and was the patient in a position to explore why she was depressed. Although she had been taking various antidepressant drugs before psychotherapy, none of these seemed to be effective. On the other hand, once she realized what the source of her misery was, she was able to go ahead with appropriate, corrective action. This, in turn, resulted in a disappearance of the depression.

Because insight alone is not always enough to bring about corrective action and improvement of the depression, antidepressants or anxiolytics may need to be used, depending on the patient's reactions to various life events. In the case of antianxiety drugs, the patient himself can often decide when he needs them and then they can be prescribed on a PRN basis; one does need to indicate what the maximum daily dose is. With antidepressants the patient should not be the judge of when or how much to take; these are taken regularly, in specified amounts, until the physician decides to change the regimen.

**(e). Further Comments on Psychotherapy.**

**1.** When unconscious hostility seems to play a major role in the development of guilt feelings, the therapist may carefully probe for such negative feelings. The hostile, vengeful thoughts and feelings may have been thoroughly walled off, and caution is needed when inserting one's probe through this defensive wall into the interior of the emotional abscess. The evacuation of its contents, *i.e.*, the expression of hostile feelings, must be done in a low key manner and only after a positive relationship has been established. The therapeutic quality of the procedure depends on the suppressed hostility being brought out in the open, where in the light of reality there usually is a way for its detoxification.

**2.** Also important in the psychotherapeutic management of guilt feelings is the removal of fantasies, views, or conclusions which the patient has developed on the basis of magical thinking. One type of patient may hold himself responsible for something that, in fact, was beyond his control. Another patient ascribes his current misery, or its cause, to alleged misdeeds or failures in the past. A third type of situation involves the guilt feelings in persons who have been taking care of a chronically ill relative. After the latter's death, the survivor is painfully preoccupied with the question, "Did I do all that I could or should have done?" In most cases, one can reassure the patient with a statement to the effect that "from what we know about you and what you have done, it is clear that you did everything you were capable of—to give the best you have is all that can be humanly expected."

**3.** Other psychotherapeutic techniques which may be useful in dealing with neurotic guilt include the following:

—Encourage the patient to suppress self-depreciating fantasies, and to abandon excessive introspection in favor of an orientation toward present realities.

—Try to liberate the depressed patient from the prison of the past (where he dwells on his sins, transgressions, shortcomings), by siding with him as he faces the discomforting openness of the future.

—Demonstrate to the patient that such gratifications as affection, approval, and so on do not require prepayment in the form of self-derogation, guilt feelings or other misery—that it is alright to receive gifts without strings attached.

—Unmask the patient's continuous preoccupation with his shortcomings, guilt feelings, or sense of rejection as a means of coercion or expression of hostility. (This is especially necessary for patients who obtain sizeable fringe benefits from their depression in terms of making their family miserable, or coercing them into giving special favors by effective display of depressive misery).

—Point out to the patient who constantly complains about his worthlessness and sinfulness the existence of an underlying layer of self-aggrandizement. In effect, such patients are playing God, inasmuch as they have set themselves up as the sole judge, as if the judgement of others no longer matters.

(f). *Psychotic depressions* may be an involutional melancholia, the depressive phase of manic-depressive illness, a retarded psychotic depression, or an agitated depression. Hospitalization is indicated to insure vigorous treatment. Antidepressant therapy is usually started with drugs rather than ECT. But there are exceptions, especially psychotic depressions in elderly male patients, because of the high suicidal risk. Patients who are going to get good responses to antidepressants will achieve them within two to three weeks. If there is no response within this time, electroconvulsive therapy should be considered. Properly given, ECT remains the safest, most effective treatment for depressive psychoses.

**(g). Electroconclusive Therapy (ECT).**

**1.** In general, old age is not a contraindication against ECT. If properly administered, ECT tends to be safer than many psychotropic drugs because it does not have their many side-effects. The *indications* for ECT include the affective disorders: psychotic depression (including depressive equivalents); involutional melancholia; and manic-depressive illness (depressed, manic, and circular types). ECT is effective in more than three-fourths of patients with such disorders.[12] In patients with an involutional paranoid state or psychotic manic reaction, it is advisable to try antipsychotic drugs first. Although ECT can be given in conjunction with antianxiety, antipsychotic, and antidepressant drugs, it is wise to give only one type of treatment at the time in order to be able to assess the efficacy of each form of treatment.

**2.** ECT may be used for the treatment of moderate to severe depression, in the presence of mild organic brain syndrome. In view of the frequently difficult differential diagnosis between depression and organicity, the administration of ECT in these cases will have the element of a therapeutic trial. If the patient improves, the diagnosis of depression is justified in retrospect.

**3.** The risk of serious *complications* can be reduced by hospitalization (out-patient ECT for elderly patients is contraindicated); ruling out serious systemic illnesses (recent myocardial infarct; cardio-respiratory decompensation; uremia, hepatic failure; severe O.B.S.); use of muscle relaxants (succinylcholine) to avoid bone fractures; adequate oxygenation before each ECT to counteract the interference with respiration caused by muscle relaxants; and omission of short-acting barbiturates, as may be used for younger patients.

**4.** ECT is given at a *frequency* of once or twice weekly. When signs of clinical improvement appear, the frequency can be gradually diminished. One complete course of ECT usually includes 10 to 12 treatments, given over a period of 5 to 6 weeks. If the patient is going to respond favorably at all, improvement usually becomes manifest after the first few treatments. But even then, it is prudent to add a few additional treatments to be sure of consolidating the therapeutic benefits.

**5.** Some depressed patients may show cognitive deficits, incontinence, and confusion, rather than overt depression. When they are successfully treated with antidepressants or ECT, these symptoms disappear. If not properly treated, however, these *pseudosenile* patients may remain institutionalized until they die.[5] Older patients who seem confused and depressed may respond well to tricyclic antidepressants, with an improvement of cognitive function, and in mood, but ECT remains the most effective form of treatment for severe depression.

**6.** A *quick response* to ECT should be viewed with some reservation. The improvement of the affective disorder may be related to the effect of ECT on memory function, rather than on the basis of a real alleviation of the underlying disorder. Because of the effect on memory, and as part of the post-ECT confusion, the patient becomes less alert and less capable of emotional expression. Thus, premature interruption of ECT may cause a relapse, upon recovery of memory function. Because many elderly patients have marginal cerebral resources and tend to become confused by ECT, early improvement is not always genuine.[3]

**7.** *Post-ECT confusion* usually becomes detectable after two or three treatments. If confusion is relatively severe, the frequency of the treatments should be diminished in proportion (*e.g.*, 1 treatment per week instead of 2 treatments per week). The confusion itself is not a serious side-effect provided the patient receives adequate supervision and protection during this time. After several weeks it usually clears up, and the patient's mental capacities return to the pre-ECT level of functioning.

## APATHY

Apathy (literally, absence of emotion) refers to a condition of emotional exhaustion (as in severe physical illness) or a state of profound emotional withdrawal (as in schizophrenia and senility).

**(a).** In the *depressions of late life* the affective manifestations may not be as prominent, and the patient may appear to be apathetic. Such types of depression are often comparable to the so-called anaclitic depressions. The primary etiological factor in these is object loss and depletion of narcissistic supplies. In addition, some late life depressions involve the psychodynamics of withdrawal and regression, rather than the typical depressive mechanisms of introjection, hostile identification, and so on. Clinical management will be aimed at correcting the factor of depletion and insufficiency of narcissistic supplies (*e.g.*, supportive measures such as increasing social contacts, decreasing relative sensory deprivation, re-establishing a hopeful perspective, etc.). In addition, antidepressant drugs may be given but their role is secondary to the importance of a broad, comprehensive supportive approach.

**(b).** Apathy, in the sense of *emotional exhaustion*, should not be treated by an approach of stimulation but by intensive supportive treatment. The principle involved is to nurture and restore an organism whose inner resources and adaptive capacity are critically diminished. This involves adequate treatment of any physiologic disturbance; insuring adequate sleep, rest, food intake, and promotion of anabolic-metabolic processes in general; and elimination of emotional insecurity by establishing a firm rapport and permitting the patient to become dependent on the parental figure of the therapist (anaclitic therapy). Upon return of emotional responsiveness and interest in the external world, one should not withdraw his support, but maintain contact with the patient allowing him to set his own tempo of emotional recovery. Withdrawal from the patient when he improves encourages relapse in apathy. It is important, during this recovery phase, to explore with the patient toward which persons and activities his reawakened interests can be directed.

**(c).** Apathy, in the sense of *withdrawal and seclusiveness*, may respond to an approach of appropriate stimulation. Many such patients are apathetic, not because of exhaustion, but because they prefer the gratifications of their inner fantasy world over those provided by the real world. The treatment approach includes elimination of possible iatrogenic apathy (*e.g.*, a chemical straight-jacket of excessive tranquilization); elimination of undue social isolation and relative sensory deprivation; remotivation, resocialization, and other group experiences; auxiliary therapies (OT, RT, IT, and PT); and appropriate stimulation involving a clinical trial of antipsychotics or antidepressants. In the apathy of some chronic, "burned out" schizophrenics, there may be a depressive element. In view of this possibility, tricyclic antidepressants may be given a trial, perhaps in combination with the antipsychotic drugs which the patient is already receiving. However, if the apathy is attributable to prolonged withdrawal and seclusiveness, antidepressant drugs are not likely to be effective.

**(d).** Apathy, in the sense of hopelessness, involves the mechanism of *giving up*. Regression, carried to its extreme, ends in surrender to the threat. Clinically, a pattern of giving up may manifest itself in apathy. When apathy is a reflection of underlying anxiety of overwhelming intensity, antianxiety medications may produce what seems to be a paradoxical response, *i.e.*, instead of becoming more tranquil, the patient becomes more active, more alive.

## MANIC CONDITIONS

Manic grandiosity and hyperactivity require treatment, especially when the patient's behavior is self-destructive, causes serious disruptions in his milieu, or when his overconfidence and lack of judgement prompt him to make unwise decisions or engage in inappropriate actions. ECT may be considered when psychotropic drugs fail to produce clinical improvement, or when the patient's manic behavior has resulted in physiological exhaustion.

## Lithium.

Lithium is effective in the treatment and prevention of manic-depressive illness, including the manic and the depressive types. In contrast to its effectiveness in bipolar affective disorders, lithium does not seem to be useful in unipolar affective disorders.[13] Lithium inhibits the enzyme, tyrosine-hydroxylase, and increases the deamination of norepinephrine which results in decreased amounts of norepinephrine at the receptor sites in the brain. It also has a marked effect on sodium and potassium metabolism. In view of the toxicity and frequent complications of this drug, lithium therapy should be initiated in the hospital.

(a). In a *severe manic attack*, it is useful to combine lithium with an antipsychotic drug, *e.g.*, haloperidol. The therapeutic action of lithium generally becomes effective after two or three weeks, and because antipsychotic drugs act more rapidly, it is beneficial to treat patients with the combination. After several weeks, when lithium has become effective, the antipsychotic drugs can be discontinued. When there is no urgent need to achieve quick remission, as for example, in *hypomanic* conditions, lithium can be given without the antipsychotics. Because lithium is useful in *preventing recurrence* of manic-depressive illness, many patients are continued on it. Generally, phenothiazines and antidepressant drugs may be used in combination with lithium. For agitation, excitement, and hypomanic and manic disorders, chlorpromazine, thioridazine, and promethazine (Phenergan) can be effective.

In hypomanic and manic patients, the prognosis for remission is good, but occasionally such patients present a clinical picture of pseudosenility (see page 60). A thorough mental status examination will show that the cognitive deficits are, in fact, attributable to deficits in concentration, attention span, distractibility, and so on. Thus, the differential diagnosis is crucial, because if these (essentially manic) patients do not receive specific treatment, their condition may quickly worsen as a result of physical exhaustion, and by then the patients will appear more senile—a self-fulfilling prophecy.

(b). *Dosage Schedule.* Start with 300 mg of lithium carbonate daily and do serum levels 2 or 3 times a week. Increase dose slowly after serum level has become stable. and until therapeutic effects are achieved. Continue to monitor for side-effects and toxicity. Whereas, the half-life of lithium is about 24 hours in younger patients, it is more prolonged in elderly patients. Hence, smaller doses of lithium will result in a therapeutic blood level. Because elderly patients excrete lithium more slowly, they can build up the desired blood level with lower doses. For example, to achieve a therapeutic level of 1.2 to 1.5 meq/l, one might give a younger patient a daily dose of 1500 mg, but an elderly patient 600 to 900 mg.[5]

(c). *Side-effects*. Lithium produces CNS, gastrointestinal, and neuro-muscular toxicity, and aged patients are more susceptible to these, especially confusion. Side-effects may develop at lower blood levels (*e.g.*, at 1.5 meq/l, with a therapeutic response at 1.2 meq/l), and this necessitates close monitoring of the blood levels. Mild side-effects are anorexia, nausea, vomiting, diarrhea, and mild tremors. Serious side-effects include dystonia and dysarthria, polydyspsia and polyuria, ataxia, hyperreflexia, and muscle spasms, confusion and coma.[4] Un-supervised use of lithium may cause electrolyte imbalance, especially low salt and potassium levels. Discontinuation of lithium, urging fluids, and supplementary NaCl and KCl will correct the toxic state. Special caution is required in the presence of cardiac or renal disease.

(d). Increasing confusion, a major sign of lithium *toxicity*, usually occurs when an out-patient is maintained on lithium without close medical supervision. The family may ascribe this to senility and delay medical help until the patient is near coma. Therefore, patients and relatives should be instructed about side-effects and toxicity. Lithium toxicity may develop insidiously. It is manifested by a worsening of the tremor, fasciculations, slurred speech, drowsiness and confusion, ataxia and choreoathetoid movements, and a diabetes insipiduslike syndrome (increased water intake and urine output).[5]

## Expansive Behavior.

Expansive behavior occurs not only in manic disorders, but also in certain paranoid conditions, and some cases of organic brain syndrome.

(a). In *paranoid* conditions, the patient's thought contents may be grandiose, and his behavior expansive or aggressive, but the affect of euphoria or elation is lacking. On the other hand, superficial cheerfulness may be present in certain *organic brain syndromes*, such as Korsakov's syndrome and presbyophrenia. Paranoid grandiosity preferably is treated with antipsychotic drugs, ECT rarely being indicated. The same holds true for grandiose and expansive behavior associated with chronic brain syndrome. Hyperactivity in patients with chronic brain syndrome may be treated with one of the benzodiazepines or an antipsychotic agent.

(b). Hyperactive or expansive behavior in *acute brain syndrome*, such as caused by alcoholism, requires that primary attention be given to eliminating the cause of the O.B.S., along with symptomatic treatment with benzodiazepine derivatives. Phenothiazines (*e.g.*, chlorpromazine, promazine, perphenazine, or prochlorperazine) also control agitation and gastrointestinal disturbances in the alcoholic.

(c). When the manic disorder is not part of a manic-depressive illness, but appears to be an isolated instance, the diagnosis *psychotic manic reaction* is appropriate. Treatment of such cases would involve the use of antipsychotics or ECT rather than lithium. All of these patients should be suspected of having an early serious systemic illness; medical and neurological evaluation and treatment is an essential part of the clinical management of psychotic manic reactions. When the psychodynamic configuration in these patients is what one would expect for a psychotic depression, antidepressant drugs may be given a therapeutic trial.

## REFERENCES

1. GOLDBERG, L. I.: Monoamine oxidase inhibitors. *J. Am. Med. Assoc. 190*: 456–462, 1964.
2. PRANGE, A. J.: The use of antidepressant drugs in the elderly patient. *In*: Advances in Behavioral Biology, Vol. 6: Psychopharmacology and Aging, C. Eisdorfer and W. E. Fann, eds. Plenum Press, New York, 1973. pp. 225–237.
3. GOLDFARB, A. I.: Geriatric psychiatry. *In:* Comprehensive Textbook of Psychiatry, Chap. 47, A. M. Freedman and H. I. Kaplan, eds. Williams & Wilkins, Baltimore, 1967. pp. 1564–1587.
4. JANOWSKY, D., EL-YOUSEF, M. K., AND DAVIS, J. M.: Side effects associated with psychotropic drugs. *In:* Drug Issues in Geropsychiatry, W. E. Fann and G. L. Maddox, eds. Williams & Wilkins, Baltimore, 1974. pp. 19–28.
5. DAVIS, J. M., FANN, W. E., EL-YOUSEF, M. K., AND JANOWSKY, D. S.: Clinical problems in treating the aged with psychotropic drugs. *In:* Advances in Behavioral Biology, Vol. 6: Psychopharmacology and Aging, C. Eisdorfer and W. E. Fann, eds. Plenum Press, New York, 1973. pp. 111–125.
6. MACFARLANE, M. D.: Possible rationale for Procaine (Gerovital H3) therapy in geriatrics: inhibition of monoamine oxidase. *J. Am. Geriatr. Soc. 21:* 414–418, 1973.
7. ZUNG, W. W. K, GIANTURCO, D., PFEIFFER, E., WANG, H. S., WHANGER, A., BRIDGE, T. P., AND POTKIN, S. G.: Evaluation of Gerovital H3 as an antidepressant drug. *Psychosomatics 15*: 127–131, 1974.
8. COHEN, S. AND DITMAN, K.: "Gerovital H3 in the treatment of the depressed aging patient. *Psychosomatics 15*: 15–19, 1974.
9. WILSON, R. A. AND WILSON, T. A.: The basic philosophy of estrogen maintenance. *J. Am. Geriatr. Soc. 20*: 521–523, 1972.
10. MEEMA, H. E. AND MEEMA, S.: Involutional bone loss in women and the feasibility of preventing structural failure. *J. Am. Geriatr. Soc. 22*: 443–451, 1974.
11. RHOADS, F. P.: Continuous cyclic hormonal therapy. *J. Am. Geriatr. Soc. 22*: 183–185, 1974.
12. WILSON, W. P. AND MAJOR, L. F.: Electroshock and the aged patient. *In*: Advances in Behavioral Biology, Vol. 6: Psychopharmacology and Aging, C. Eisdorfer and W. E. Fann, eds. Plenum Press, New York, 1973. pp. 239–244.
13. COPPEN, A., NOGUERA, R., BAILEY, J., BURNS, B. H., SWANI, M. S., HARE, E. H., GARDNER, R., AND MAGGS, R.: Prophylactic lithium in affective disorders. *Lancet 2*: 275, 1971.

# 14

# hypochondriasis and related states

## INTRODUCTION

The clinical management of hypochondriasis depends on the degree of self-absorption and the context in which it has developed. We can distinguish between types that are relatively mild, transitory, benign and those that are of a chronic, progressive, malignant nature. The degree of self-absorption corresponds with the extent of withdrawal, and depends on whether the patient considers his state of stagnation as still reversible or a permanent impasse.

In the early, milder forms, the echoes of the disillusionment and depression that anteceded the hypochondriasis can still be heard. Because withdrawal from others has not extended over a long distance, the process is still reversible; external objects have not suffered significant depreciation.

During the intermediate phase, a greater distance separates the patient from others; there has been more devaluation of external objects by the patient. He has not yet reached the point of no return and his perspective still permits him to believe that the process is reversible. Along with his increased alienation, however, he views life with more skepticism and bitterness. Feelings of ambivalence toward others are prominent. Three sets of wishes are in a tug of war: to move back toward people, to move further away from them, or to move against them. In the wake of bitterness follows envy toward those who appear to be more fortunate; increased disappointments in those who did not try to entice him back and convince him that his skepticism was not justified; and hostility toward those who did not help him when he came to them in his search for hope. The patient may stagnate in bitter resignation, or decide to do something about it.

When such a psychodynamic constellation receives a charge of energy, the result may be aggressive vindictiveness. Part of the patient's goal is to vindicate himself, as if he has a score to settle. But the struggle is often futile, or even conducive to further deterioration of his position. His vindictiveness (manifested by chronic complaints, fault finding, obstinate refusal to collaborate with others, subtle, vengeful sabotage of therapeutic programs, etc.) has the effect of confirming what the patient suspected all along: that people are no good. At this point, ideas of refer-

ence, feelings of being singled out for neglect or mistreatment, and related paranoid elements may enter the picture.

It is also possible that, rather than taking vindictive action, the patient
continues in his move away from others. Along this pathway, a point of
no return is reached, when the distance to go back has become too great;
the patient feels that the process is irreversible. External objects become
less visible, then out of sight, and finally, out of mind. Other people do
not matter anymore, and the patient does not care anymore. His anger
and hate being replaced by indifference, there is no more ambivalence.
Resignation makes place for fatalism, a perspective closely related to
that of hopelessness.

## MANAGEMENT OF HYPOCHONDRIASIS

The hypochondriacal patient presents many difficulties in therapeutic
management. The enthusiastic therapist who sets out actively to do
something about the patient's complaint may find to his surprise that
the symptoms do not respond; or that when they do respond they are
replaced by other symptoms; or even that the patient may get more
depressed as the physical symptoms improve. The first requirement in
management is a formulation of the specific psychodynamic factors
playing a role. The physician's understanding and formulation, however,
are not to be communicated to the patient, as in insight-oriented
therapy. Any interpretation of the dynamics tends to be dismissed by the
patient, and may in fact cause an exacerbation of the symptoms. To
explain to the patient, in more general terms, that he has no real physical
illness and that the symptoms are related to emotional conflict is of no
help either. Sometimes, the patient may intellectually agree that the
mind can affect the body, but he is sure this does not apply to his case.
Nor would it do any good to advise him to stop worrying. At first sight,
this may seem quite rational and reassuring, but it fails because to the
patient such reassurance is false. The patient's reaction to such advice is
usually paradoxical: an increase in his complaints. Because he needs to
maintain his only defense, he must now convince the therapist that the
latter was wrong in his diagnosis.

Rather, it would be wise to treat the symptoms without expecting that
they will disappear. This is not therapeutic hypocrisy or cynicism, but
involves a communication on two levels. On the superficial level, the
patient and therapist are engaged in a traditional contract: to do
something about the complaint. On a deeper level, however, there is a
tacit understanding that in order to function the patient needs his
symptoms; that they are a form of coping with personal problems and life
situations, perhaps the only coping technique available right now; and
that the therapist is prepared to do the best he can to treat these
symptoms, no matter how long it will take.

### Giving a Particular Diagnosis

Some clinicians may decide to go along with the patient's contention
that he is physically ill, by giving him a particular diagnosis and a
specific medication. Again, from a rational point of view, one would

expect that such an accepting approach (taking the patient on his word, recognizing the legitimacy of his symptoms) would give the patient what he wants. And, indeed, there now may follow a period of quiescence of complaints. But sooner or later the patient returns, either with the old symptoms or with new complaints. The patient's first triumph was a pseudovictory. Winning the therapist over to his side was only a victory-in-defeat. The real winner was the physician who had maneuvered to set the stage for a traditional medical contract (*i.e.*, the patient has an "illness", he gets medicine and is "supposed to get better"). But meanwhile the physician had gotten the patient out of his office, so he was the winner in this game. He had responded to the patient by implying, "O.K., we will do it your way, so you will be satisfied—and if not, don't blame me."

The patient's symptoms will return, because the hypochondriasis represents his only major defense.[1] From this point on, several vicissitudes may develop in the doctor-patient relationship. The patient may go back to the same physician for round two, with a new set of complaints or with the original symptoms. (The fact that he returns to the same physician is prognostically a good sign that should not be overlooked.)

If the patient comes back with a *new set of complaints*, there are several risks and traps. One would be to give a new diagnosis, thereby sending the patient on his way to becoming an ambulatory nomenclature. He'll collect one diagnosis after another using them as needed in his contacts with physicians and other caretaking personnel to explain his behavior, to justify his requests for medications, and so on.

One "professional" hypochondriac, a postmenopausal woman, had been making rounds on innumerable physicians. In the course of a decade, she had developed an awesome collection of diagnoses, each of which symbolized an injustice done to her. She was capable of nonstop talkathons, using all the diagnoses and treatments given to her as points of departure into righteous indignation. The monologue would start off as a quiet lament, then become a litany with the ever-recurring refrain of nobody caring, ending in a crescendo of accusations.

By presenting new complaints, the patient (usually without consciously realizing this) puts the physician on the spot. The patient is implying that the first medication he received was not good enough to prevent new symptoms, or that the initial diagnosis was not accurate. During round two of the relationship, the physician has the option of changing the medication or the diagnosis. If only the medication is changed, the patient will wonder how the old diagnosis can be maintained *vis-à-vis* the new symptoms, or how the new medication can be justified *vis-à-vis* the old diagnosis. If the physician maintains his original diagnosis, he is put on the spot in terms of explaining the failure of the treatment, searching for a justification to continue its use, or having to decide on another medicine. If the physician changes the diagnosis, he has little choice but to change the medication as well. By changing the diagnosis, however, he has simply added a new one to the patient's nomenclature. The first diagnosis is kept in reserve by the patient, as a standby, for handy reference or p.r.n. manipulation.

In this manner, round two seems to end in the same way as in the first contact. But the fact that the patient has a new diagnosis will only reinforce his hypochondriacal self-image. In addition, he has probably lost some confidence in the physician, whom he can bend to his will. Moreover, with the new diagnosis and new medication, the patient is now again supposed to be a good patient, in terms of responding favorably to the doctor's diagnosis and therapeutic skills. It is obvious that such an approach eventually ends in failure and in termination of the doctor-patient relationship. Thus, a second round may be followed by several more rounds, but after some time both participants begin to see the futility of their efforts.

If the patient returns with the *same complaints* as in round one, he is coming on more strongly. In effect, he gives the physician a "dare"; the refractory symptoms acquire an element of obstinacy or defiance. The physician has now the option of changing the diagnosis or the treatment. A change in diagnosis is tantamount to the physician's admission that he no longer has a grasp on the situation. The patient may achieve a small victory in the context of his coercion and gamesmanship, but his confidence in the physician will be diminished. The risk of adding more diagnoses is compounded by the danger of having to give medication for each of these "illnesses."

What also frequently happens, somewhere along the line, is that the patient has succeeded in convincing a surgeon that an operation is indicated. The irrevocable fact of a surgical procedure and the visible trophy of a surgical scar can be used by the hypochondriac to prove that the problem was really physical or that he was mistreated (because of the surgical attack).

One way or the other, the therapist's tact and patience are sorely tried. The temptation is strong to fall into one of the patient's traps, and surrender to a coercive ploy, for example, by saying something like, "Well, since my treatment was no success, maybe you'd prefer to see someone else. I'll be glad to give you a good referral."

The timid patient who prefers to shy away from confrontation may go to a *different physician* with his original complaints. The first physician may never know it, and may conclude that the patient had been treated successfully. In reality, however, our patient is making rounds on the physicians in the area.

### Vicissitudes

The vicissitudes, then, that may develop after one has given the hypochondriac a real diagnosis, make it clear that this approach is not effective.

The first step toward effective management is the recognition that the hypochondriac needs his physical complaints to maintain adequate self esteem and object relationships. When a physician tells his patient that his symptoms are not real but emotional or imaginary, he merely increases the patient's adjustment problems.[1] Even more damaging would be to give such information to the relatives. This is tantamount to pulling the rug from underneath the patient. The relatives will inform the hypochondriac that the doctor has told them he has no basis for his complaints. The hypochondriac then is forced to become more defensive and prove he is really sick. He also feels he has been betrayed by the physician, who has now become an enemy. This is one of the ways in which hypochondriacal patients develop a sense of being treated unfairly or victimized. This may even proceed to the point where feelings of persecution and paranoid ideas develop.

The therapist who accepts the fact that the patient needs his hypochondriacal defense, thereby accepts the patient as well. If he listens attentively and avoids confronting the patient with medical facts, the latter will feel secure rather than threatened by somebody intent on taking his defense away.

When the patient asks for a diagnosis, it is prudent to circumvent this ploy, and respond to the effect that "it is obvious that you have trouble; there is a problem. At this point I am not certain about the real cause, but I am glad to do whatever I can to help you." Usually, the hypochondriac will accept such a statement, which at face value seems noncommittal but at a deeper level is actually a statement of the physician's commitment.

Meanwhile the therapist has to do something. Without some form of treatment the patient may feel rejected because his symptoms are not taken seriously, or because his illness is not real enough to necessitate medication. Of course, many hypochondriacs do have actual somatic symptomatology that would respond to appropriate medication. Drugs may be prescribed provided one does not further contribute to polypharmacy, and provided the drug has not already been used and become contaminated by the patient's negative fantasies. It is better not to convey that this drug will be 100 percent effective, but that "it will help take the edge off the problem, and we'll have to see how much relief you'll get from it." The latter phrase implies that the patient is to come back to tell the physician how he is doing. By following this approach, one creates a no lose situation: neither the doctor nor the patient will be forced into a position of defeat. The element of no lose is essential to prevent the manipulative ploys and coercive games which would otherwise destroy the therapeutic alliance.

During the next phase, the patient will test out the therapist's truthfulness. He will do so in several ways. He may ask "When do you want me to come back?" The answer depends on several variables, such as the therapist's schedule, the amount of support needed by the patient, and so on. A practical compromise is that return visits be scheduled no more than once a week, and no less than once a month; that each visit last from 20 to 30 minutes; and that the patient be told that "if anything comes up before the next visit, be sure to call me."

The next test may be the patient's question, "How long will it take? How long will I need to take this medication? How long will I need to see you?" Giving an optimistic answer, to the effect that the patient may soon recover or improve, is tantamount to failing the patient's tests. The patient knows full well that things won't happen this way—he can't see himself without the security of his illness that soon. Giving a pessimistic answer, to the effect that the patient's condition is permanent, is also wrong, because the patient will wonder about the physician's professional motives of having him come back for follow-up visits. If the situation is that bleak, why bother with any treatment? The correct response to the question is based on the recognition that the patient is not trying to find an objective piece of truth from the physician, but rather some evidence that the physician is true to him. The patient frequently makes the test of truthfulness even more difficult, e.g., by complaining that the time schedule for the follow-up visit is inconvenient. (The patient's thoughts would run something like: "Doctor, I am giving you a chance to get out of this appointment with me; all you have to say to me now is, 'Gee, that is too bad. Why don't you give me a call when you have some convenient time.' And if that's what you are going to say, I'll know you are like all the rest, the other ones who did not care, and were just polite, going through the motions to make me think they cared.") So, to avoid this trap, the therapist needs to face the situation with honesty, decide on the trueness of his commitment to the patient, and reiterate with firmness, "It is important for you to come, and I expect to see you even if it is inconvenient." The tacit message here is: "Look, in this relationship, you aren't going to duck inconveniences, and you can expect the same on my part." The point is implicitly made that the importance of the relationship transcends the magnitude of inconvenience. Thus, one introduces a basic therapeutic ingredient: for the patient to carry on in spite of his problems.

When the hypochondriacal patients returns for follow-up appointments, he finds that the physician's attitude has not changed. When he expresses hostility against previous physicians, one must refrain from defending one's colleagues, confining one's remarks to recognition of the patient's previous experiences as disappointing. Again, no diagnosis or prognosis is ventured. During the interview the therapist does not try to select the topics but there may be opportunities to guide the patient toward areas of conflict.[1]

When the patient begins to improve, this should not become a basis for declaring him to be "cured," or to have had "maximum benefits" from the treatment—and then terminating the treatment program. Rather the opposite view should be taken: the patient's improvement indicates that the treatment regime is sound and must be continued. By the same token, one would not stop giving insulin to a diabetic because he is responding well. Thus, the fact that the patient improves on a particular treatment regime may be a reason for continuing, rather than stopping it.

(Incidentally, the same applies to another situation, i.e., some cases in which a patient improves during hospitalization. Many patients with chronic physical or mental problems improve once they are in the supportive setting of a hospital. The hospital staff may then decide to discharge the patient back into the community. Soon after release from the hospital, we find this same patient being readmitted. The point is that the decision to discharge the patient did not consider the fact that the improvement was attributable precisely to his being in the hospital.)

As the patient returns for future appointments, the physician will easily detect any tendency on the patient's part to shift away from his self-absorption. More emphasis may be directed toward problems related to people, external interests, or outward-oriented activities. Thus, the patient may gradually become less preoccupied with his imaginary ills. He may have an exacerbation of his symptoms when his problems increase but at least he is able to return to reasonable efficiency in his living habits. Having established a secure relationship with the physician, he knows he will not be attacked, and the energy which he has been using to ward off such attacks can be directed toward more rewarding endeavors. He has gained some confidence because, even if he falters in some way, he can return to this one person who will not accuse him of being a failure, but will accept him without the need for an alibi.

### Some Comments on Placebos and Drugs.

The placebo effect can be defined as any effect from a substance or procedure not caused by its pharmacodynamic properties. The placebo effect is derived from the meaning to the patient of the whole situation surrounding the therapeutic effort. Placebo effects are not imaginary but can actually cause measurable physiological changes. The type of medication given to the hypochondriac may come close to being a placebo, e.g., vitamins. Such a placebo-like drug is justifiable if it does not interfere with the primary goal in treatment. The Latin derivation of placebo (I will please) implies getting involved with the patient rather than getting rid of him. Thus, giving placebos is not a simple procedure, but presupposes an optimal doctor-patient relationship; the placebo effect is an effect of the doctor-patient relationship. The patient takes his prescription with the feeling of "he is taking care of me." This is the meaning of the therapeutic effort to him.

It is also important to keep in mind that placebo effects can be either negative or positive, a phenomenon related to positive and negative transference. Thus, the existence of positive and negative placebo effects will be a source of information to the physician, about the degree of ambivalence in the relationship. Some patients with a high degree of ambivalence toward the therapist may lose the prescription on their way home; others just keep it and don't have it filled; again, other patients will disregard the prescription and secretly buy their own favorite patent drugs. In some cases, the negative placebo effect consists of an alleged inability to swallow the drug; or the drug may cause nausea and vomiting; or if the drug remains inside, it causes various types of idiosyncratic discomfort.

A rare type of placebo effect was seen in a patient who had longstanding physical symptoms but refused to take medications. She finally was persuaded that it would be safe to take the medication (an antidepressant). At the next visit, she looked much better. The therapist remarked on her improved appearance, the reduction of physical symptoms, and so on, and the patient was in full agreement. So it seemed that both therapist and patient were resonating on the same wave length, until, by the end of the interview, she casually remarked, "By the way, I did not take any of the medication you prescribed." Essentially, this illustrates a negative transference, manifested in terms of a flight into health. The patient was in effect saying, "Look, I do not really need you; I can do it on my own."

The other extreme is illustrated by the case of an obese, elderly woman who used to frequent the hospital emergency room complaining of pain "all over" in her stomach. The E.R. nurse had become well acquainted with her and had, by way of serendipity, arrived at an effective treatment: injecting a few cc's of saline subcutaneously in the abdominal region. Within a few minutes, the patient would get up, state how much better she felt, and leave contentedly. The patient had become emotionally dependent on the accessibility of the nurse whenever she was in distress. The availability of the procedure had become a symbol for the availability of a person.

Management of pain in the hypochondriacal patient should involve a consideration of the intimate connections between anxiety, depression, tension, and pain. Organic pain conforms in a characteristic manner to what one would expect on the basis of anatomic lesions. The fact that perception of pain and reaction to pain-inducing stimuli decrease with age may be a complicating factor. Compared with younger people, the aged person may not readily perceive the early onset of pathological changes and this presents a handicap in diagnosis and treatment. Pain which is more or less psychogenic, however, is related to anxious fantasies about an illness, mental conceptions of progression of pathology, and to body image disturbances. Painful distress which has significant psychogenic components is usually reported by way of idiosyncratic phrases that do not conform to anatomical facts but are related to the body image. The regressed or hypochondriacal patient may be so preoccupied with bodily overconcern, that almost any sensation or distress can be perceived as painful.[2]

It should not be forgotten, however, that many older persons do suffer from one or more chronic illnesses, which may cause a variety of distressing symptoms. A longstanding pattern of psychogenic pain should not tempt the clinician to be less alert to the development of an authentic organic illness; even a hypochondriac can get physically sick.

Persistent physical complaints are common in many psychiatric disorders, such as schizophrenia and organic brain syndrome. The often strange or bizarre physical complaints of the schizophrenic patient may represent his attempt to give expression to his chaotic inner world. To some extent, the same is true of the patient with O.B.S. Psychiatric treatment of these cases usually involves antipsychotic drugs.

Although it is usually true that idiosyncratic descriptions of pain suggest a "psychic signature,"[2] in the case of patients with O.B.S. or dementia, this rule does not apply. The complaint of physical pain may be expressed by these patients in a highly idiosyncratic form, involving delusions, hallucinations, or bizarre behavior. The mechanism responsible for this was described earlier, and revolves around the loss of abstract thinking (see case of patient whose feces were stones, p. 57, and the case of patient complaining of ants crawling over her skin, p. 43). In cases of fecal impaction, for example, patients may express their distress nonverbally, through changes in posture and gait.

Pain may give rise to fear and disorganization of thought and behavior. In addition to specific treatment, relief from pain is indicated as a means of controlling the emergence of florid psychopathology in frightened persons with reduced or marginal cerebral competence.[3]

## MANAGEMENT OF RELATED STATES

### Vindictive Behavior

Psychotherapeutic management can be more complex and demanding in cases of hypochondriasis in which the patient has become chronically embittered, and acts this out by way of vindictive behavior. These hostile behavior patterns are frequent problems in nursing homes and rest homes. Characteristically, the pattern of hostility has become more prominent over a period of several years. The clinical phenomena correspond with a regression to an oral-sadistic or anal-sadistic phase of development, in which ambivalence is a prominent feature.

The clinical *manifestations* include refusal to accept assistance deemed appropriate by concerned others; being mean, ugly, cantankerous, obstreperous; excessive complaining about medical, social, or material needs, but recalcitrance in cooperating with corrective intervention; nearly total lack of appreciation for what is done in their behalf; blaming others for their plight; cursing, fussing, and arguing; hitting persons (relatives, roommates in a rest home, hospital attendants); spiteful acts (*e.g.*, soiling themselves, just after having been cleaned up); refusing to tend to personal hygiene (occasionally to scare others away and create a no man's land around them); and so on.

*Management* of these behavior patterns requires an exploration of the role played by the premorbid personality and recent stresses, and a recognition that the hostile behavior patterns are clinical manifestations of regression to an early ambivalent phase of development. The orally aggressive patient "bites the hand that feeds him," but yet feels dependent on that same person. In cases of anal-sadistic regression, the typical features are stubbornness, obstructionism, oppositional behavior, and making a mess out of things. Such a patient does not seem to be as dependent. In both categories, the common denominator is the patient's ambivalence toward the significant persons around him, with the negative, hateful feelings in the foreground. It is essential to recognize that one is dealing with the behavioral expressions of ambivalence and to keep reminding oneself of the psychodynamic forces producing the patient's disagreeable behavior, in order to avoid countertransference feelings.

The next step is, from a position of neutral objectivity and with an attitude of detached concern, to address oneself to the underlying concern and to try to alleviate the stress. This may be a feeling of exasperating helplessness, shameful loss of dignity, bitterness about having been betrayed, fighting against letting go for fear of being let down, and so on. In offering the needed support, it is often necessary to use a special form of tact. The supplies are given to the patient in a surreptitious manner—they are being slipped over to him, as it were. The giving is not done openly, not explicitly or formally, but tacitly and casually. This matter-of-fact method makes it possible for the patient to have his cake and eat it: he is receiving the needed narcissistic supplies, and can still have his kicks by indulging in various protestations.

Once the patient has accepted the supplies, the stage for a collaborative relationship has been set. For a period of time, the main focus is on getting the patient to accept, digest, and assimilate what is being offered to him; and the hostile behavior is left alone, for the time being. This phase reaches its goal when the patient appears to have a sense of certainty that the provider (the feeding hand) is reliable; that his own hostility will not destroy the giver, and that his own ill will cannot contaminate the other's goodwill. Essentially, the patient learns during this phase that there is indeed love with no strings attached, the gift is not a bait—and if he swallowed it, he'd be painfully hooked.

During the last phase, one may attempt to deal with the regression and the associated disagreeable behavior by setting limits. One method would be simply to convey to the patient one's own disapproval for the way he sometimes acts, but without the threat of shape up or ship out. More effective probably is the approach of conveying to the patient the recognition that he is making some good progress, and that this attests to his strength or courage—an admirable achievement. Again, the fact that the patient's strength, so to say, has been borrowed from the therapist is left unspoken, covered by the tacit pact. At this point, one might bring up a question to the effect of: Would the patient now be strong or courageous enough to do something that goes against his grain, like showing some appreciation to this person, or kindness to that one? In this manner, one might try to change the patient's false pride into authentic pride. But even during a moment of warmth, or an act of kindness, the patient may still show his barbs, *e.g.*, in the form of the rationalization: "I am only nice and kind for your benefit—because you want me to."

## Reversal of Autism

Although in most cases, hypochondriasis is the consequence of disengagement, in some instances the reverse is true. Hypochondriasis then represents a favorable development which actually may be encouraged. This happens when a very withdrawn, autistic, or schizophrenic patient begins to turn his attention toward the real world. The first object encountered in his own body, which is, as mentioned before, something like a bridge between the inner self and the outer world. Two cases were presented earlier (See page 101 and page 117) illustrating the appearance of somatic self-absorption in schizophrenic patients as a favorable development. The presence of physical complaints sets the stage for contact and interaction between the patient and another person.

## Maintaining Closeness

Hypochondriacal complaints may also represent a primitive, nonverbal cry for help, or a means of maintaining closeness. This happens in situations in which isolation has been imposed from without, rather than developed from within. In some children, we see that the very anticipation of loneliness can set in motion a hypochondriacal process which serves the purpose of preventing the possibility of isolation from becoming a reality. Such a child may complain of aches and pains when they face relative loneliness at bedtime. The physical complaint serves as an expedient medium to express a nameless dread and to keep in touch with the protective parental figure. The element of vagueness in these physical complaints provides a useful clue. If a parent consistently disregards such clues, but responds to the physical complaints at face value, the foundations for hypochondriacal reaction patterns are being laid. Such responses to anxiety situations, especially separation anxiety, may persist from childhood through the adult years into late life.

An elderly female patient had been for many years on the geropsychiatric unit of a mental hospital because of senile dementia. Her ability to communicate had progressively deteriorated, but she still was agile in her walking and daily living activities. During ward rounds, this patient would come to the physician and express a vague complaint about her neck. When asked to repeat the complaint, the second version would differ from the first. While the patient's hands would be gesticulating all over the afflicted zone, there was an intent gaze in her eyes, trying to lock into the physician's eyes. After a brief on-the-spot examination, the physician would tell what seemed to be the trouble, and promise something would be done about it. The effect of this on the patient was rather striking: her complaint seemed gone, and she appeared pleased, as though this was all there was to it, with nothing further to be expected. This state of closure lasted until the next ward round, when the interaction would be repeated.

## REFERENCES

1. Busse, E. W. and Pfeiffer, E.: Functional psychiatric disorders in old age. *In:* Behavior and Adaptation in Late Life, Chap. 10, E. W. Busse and E. Pfeiffer, eds. Little, Brown and Company, Boston, 1970. pp. 183–235.
2. Engel, G. L.: Psychogenic pain and the pain-prone patient. *Am. J. Med. 26:* 899, 1959.
3. Goldfarb, A. I.: Geriatric psychiatry. *In:* Comprehensive Textbook of Psychiatry, Chap. 47, A. M. Freedman and H. I. Kaplan, eds. Williams & Wilkins, Baltimore, 1967. pp. 1564–1587.

# 15

# schizophrenic and senile disorders

## THE FINAL COMMON PATHWAY

Although chronic schizophrenia and senile dementia are two separate, distinct syndromes, the clinical symptomatology of the two entities frequently shows some resemblance and overlap. Schizophrenia has been conceptualized as a *functional dysencephalization* (in other words, a functional brain syndrome) as the result of overwhelming anxiety.[1] This process of functional disintegration of neuronal patterns, or disharmony of microscopic spatiotemporal patterns of activity in the neuronal network, presumably affects specific areas of the cortex (portions of the temporal, occipital, and parietal lobes). These cortical areas apparently are the last to appear in phylogeny, and to myelinize in ontogeny. Amongst their functions are the mediation of abstract thinking and symbolism. *Encephalization* refers to the process by which functions that in lower species are mediated by more caudal centers shift toward higher centers.[1] In the brain as well as in mental function, *centralization* and *hierarchic order* are achieved by stratification, by superimposition of higher layers that take the role of leading parts. Three major layers, or evolutionary steps, can be distinguished. In the brain these are (1) the paleencephalon, in lower vertebrates, (2) the neencephalon (cortex), evolving from reptiles to mammals, and (3) certain "highest" centers, especially the motoric speech (Broca's) region and the large association areas which are found only in man. Concurrently there is an anterior shift of controlling centers[2].

Dysencephalization, then, may be viewed as a process in the opposite direction. In schizophrenia, this may take place in a functional way. In senile dementia, the process has a predominantly organic origin, although functional aspects may be present and contribute to the symptomatology. The *final common pathway* of dysencephalization (either functional, organic, or mixed) is a psychotic behavior characterized primarily by regressive phenomena.

The psychotic state is sometimes said to be a regression to older and more infantile forms of behavior. This is not accurate. The psychotic patient regresses to, but does not integrate at, a lower level; he will remain disorganized. Regression is essentially disintegration of personality, *i.e.*, dedifferentiation and decentralization. Dedifferentiation does

185

not mean loss of part functions, but a reappearance of primitive states (syncretism, synesthesia, paleologic thinking, and so forth). Decentralization is, in the extreme, functional dysencephalization in the schizophrenic.[2]

## PSYCHOPHARMACOLOGY

### Antipsychotic Drugs

This group of drugs includes the phenothiazines, butyrophenones, and thioxanthene derivatives. Their mode of action involves an inhibition of critical noradrenergic and dopaminergic receptor sites in the CNS; possibly, desensitization of the reticular activating system to impulses transmitted from the primary sensory pathway collaterals; and an anticholinergic effect. Much of the emotional response to external or internal stimuli would be reduced by such actions.[3] The development of extrapyramidal reactions, a frequent and unique concomitant effect of antipsychotics, may be mediated by the dopaminergic blockade.

In contrast to sedatives, these agents calm the excited or agitated patient without induction of sleep. Their main characteristic effects are: the relief of agitation, violent and irrational behavior, and perceptual disturbances; and the extrapyramidal side-effects. They tend to increase muscle tone, lower the convulsive threshold, and have a negligible risk of drug dependence. Many pyschotic manifestations, such as disturbed thinking, paranoid symptoms, delusions, emotional and social withdrawal, and personal neglect may improve. Amelioration of such psychotic symptoms justifies the name antipsychotic.

(a). *Phenothiazines*, the most frequently used antipsychotic agents, comprise three subgroups: aliphatics, piperidyls, and piperazines. The piperazine congeners, with a halogen (especially fluorine) attached to the main nucleus, have an increased potency, but extrapyramidal syndromes are more common and dosage control is more difficult. Compounds with an *aliphatic* side chain (*e.g.*, chlorpromazine) are relatively low in potency and high in sedative effects. The *piperadine* group includes thioridazine (Mellaril). Variants of the *piperazine* side chain, along with variations of the ring substituent, create a large class of piperazinyl phenothiazines, *e.g.*, prochlorperazine (Compazine), perphenazine (Trilafon), trifluoperazine (Stelazine), fluphenazine (Prolixin, Permitil). These compounds are more potent than the aliphatic series. They possess less sedative effects than the other two classes, but are more likely to produce extrapyramidal reactions at equivalent therapeutic doses.

(b). Substitution of a carbon atom for the nitrogen in the central ring of the phenothiazine nucleus produces the *thioxanthene* nucleus. Chlorprothixene (Taractan) and thiothixene (Navane) are thioxanthene derivatives. They should not be used in patients with convulsive disorders or abnormal electroencephalograms.

(c). *Haloperidol* (Haldol), a butyrophenone derivative, resembles the phenothiazines in antipsychotic action and in evoking extrapyramidal syndromes. It is an effective antipsychotic, but can produce muscular rigidity and extrapyramidal symptoms at dosages of more than 1.5 mg daily.

## Treatment Considerations

(a). **Indications.** Phenothiazines and other antipsychotics can be used to treat schizophrenia, organic pyschoses, agitated depressions, or severe anxiety states in the elderly. *Contraindications* include CNS depression as a result of drugs (alcohol, barbiturates, etc.), Parkinson's disease, organic brain syndrome with lethargy and clouded sensorium, hypertensive patients taking guanethidine, and glaucoma.

(b). **Selection of Drug.** The number of drugs available creates practical problems in choosing drugs. It is probably best, on the whole, to start with one of the less sedative, less hypotensive drugs (*e.g.*, haloperidol). If undue extrapyramidal signs develop, change to thioridazine or chlorpromazine. The rationale is to avoid extrapyramidal symptoms, since these symptoms would require an additional drug, *i.e.*, antiparkinson drugs.[4] The choice of the proper drug involves an individualized approach, because there is much overlap of side-effects among drugs, and aged patients usually require smaller doses. Most antipsychotic drugs are equally efficacious, although individual patients respond differently to different drugs. Therefore, the choice of drug is often empirical. A rational way to narrow the choice of antipsychotics is to master the pharmacology and use one of each of the three types of phenothiazines, one of the two thioxanthenes, and a butyrophenone.[5]

(c). **Dosage.** In contrast to younger patients, massive doses of antipsychotic drugs are not indicated for geropsychiatric patients. This is particularly relevant in view of the risk of long-term toxicity of a permanent nature, *e.g.*, tardive dyskinesia, an extrapyramidal syndrome involving various dystonic movements, especially of the face and tongue. By avoiding unduly prolonged use of antipsychotics whenever clinically feasible, the risk of tardive dyskinesia is reduced. Likewise, other side-effects (*e.g.*, postural hypotension which, in turn, may cause strokes, heart attacks, falls, and fractures) may be prevented by maintaining patients on a low dosage or, if possible, stopping the drug altogether.

Phenothiazines in liquid preparations are useful for patients who cannot or will not swallow tablets. Extended-release capsules reduce the frequency of administration. Many drugs are available for intramuscular administration, but this increases the risk of hypotensive reactions. Oral medications should be substituted as soon as possible.

(d). Antipsychotic drugs have been used effectively and safely in conjunction with most other psychiatric therapies. Electroconvulsive therapy can be used simultaneously with phenothiazines, so long as the lowered convulsive threshold produced by the drugs is kept in mind.

(e). **Side Effects.** (Tables 1 and 2)

1. *Hypotension* may manifest itself as progressive confusion or transient ischemic attacks. Every aged patient should have his blood

TABLE 1. *Side-effects of Antipsychotics*

| | Clinical Signs | Causative Factors | Prevention & Treatment |
|---|---|---|---|
| Behavioral phenomena | overseduation | dose, age; especially aliphatics & thioridazine | avoid other CNS depressants; lower dose or change drug |
| | aggravation of psychiatric symptoms | premorbid personality; patients with insight; depersonalization | lower dose or change drug; use antianxiety drug |
| Cardiovascular System | postural hypotension → syncope, CVA, or heart attack | adrenergic blocking & anticholinergic effect (especially chlorpromazine & thioridazine) | lower dose or change drug; check electrolytes; do not use epinephrine |
| | cardiac arrhythmia, palpitations, tachycardia | age, dose; parenteral administration; drug-drug toxicity; existing cardiovascular disease | lower dose; avoid I.V. administration & polypharmacy; pretreatment cardiac evaluation; monitor cardiovascular factors |
| | EKG changes (Q and T wave distortions) | especially with thioridazine | do pretreatment baseline EKG |
| EEG | EEG slowing, lowered seizure threshold, convulsions | dose level; individual susceptibility; O.B.S. | lower dose; consider anticonvulsants (after proper evaluation) |
| Autonomic Nervous System | nasal congestion, dry mouth, constipation, urinary retention, inhibition of ejaculation | adrenergic-blocking & anticholinergic effects; combination of tricyclics & antiparkinson drugs | explanation & reassurance; lower dose, or stop drug if symptoms are severe or continue; review need for tricyclics and antiparkinson drugs |
| | weight gain, edema | hypothalamic effect (especially thioridazine) | lower dose or change drug if symptoms are severe |
| Eye | blurred vision, pigmentary retinopathy | anticholinergic effects; prolonged high dose | keep thioridazine under 800 mg daily; |
| | melanin pigmentation, corneal and lens deposits | long-term treatment; high doses | switch to low dose piperazine derivative |
| Skin | dermatoses, photosensitivity | allergic or toxic reaction | stop or change drug; avoid exposure to sun |
| Blood | agranulocytosis, purpura, hemolytic anemia, pancytopenia | rare; elderly women; usually first 3 months | stop drug; medical treatment |

TABLE 2. *Extrapyramidal Side-effects of Antipsychotics*

| | | | Dyskinesias: Early or Tardive | | |
|---|---|---|---|---|---|
| | Parkinsonism | Akathisia | Dystonia | Facial-buccolingual Dyskinesias | |
| Clinical Manifestations | rigidity, bradykinesia, pillrolling tremors, resting tremors, salivation and seborrhea, shuffling gait | uncontrollable restlessness, feelings of muscular quivering | posturing of face, neck, and tongue: retrocollis and torticollis; oculogyric crises | chewing & mouthing movements, aimless writhing of tongue, lipsmacking | choreiform and athetoid movements of neck, trunk, and extremities |
| | early in treatment | days-months after treatment | early or late in treatment | early or late in treatment | late (tardive) |
| | generally reversible | usually reversible | acute = reversible | usually irreversible | |
| Causative or Predisposing Factors | more in old age and women | middle-age; more in women | younger; more in men | older patients; more in women | |
| | current dose level | | current dose level in acute dystonia | sum total of drug amount over the years | |
| | individual susceptibility to DA blocking effects | | individual susceptibility to anticholinergic effects | | |
| | decreased activity of Dopamine or increased activity of cholinergic system in striatum | increased activity of dopamine system or decreased activity of cholinergic system in striatum (relative imbalance) | | | |
| Prevention or Treatment | differential diagnosis: agitated depession | differential diagnosis: early Huntington | differential diagnosis: dystonia due to lithium | differential diagnosis: spontaneous F.B.L. dyskinesia | |
| | antihistamines antiparkinson drugs | lower dose or change drug; no L-Dopa | avoid long term use of antipsychotics (esp. piperazines) use lowest possible doses periodic drug-free intervals don't use antiparkinson drugs routinely | | |
| | | try thioridazine | Benadryl for acute dystonia | | increasing doses of antipsychotics give transient relief, but probably worsen basic neuropathology |

pressure taken supine and sitting or standing. Postural hypotension can last for a few weeks and may require bed rest to prevent stressing the vascular system.[6]

2. *Extrapyramidal* effects apparently are produced because of the blocking of dopaminergic receptor sites in the corpus striatum. Haloperidol, in daily amounts of more than 1.5 to 2.0 mg tends to cause extrapyramidal symptoms and muscular rigidity. Extrapyramidal signs, the most common effects of antipsychotics, respond well to antiparkinson drugs. *Anticholinergic* agents for treating parkinsonism resulting from antipsychotics include benztropin mesylate (Cogentin), trihexyphenidyl (Artane), biperiden (Akineton), and procyclidine (Kemadrin). Their side-effects are essentially similar to those of the tricyclic antidepressants. These drugs should not be given routinely, because some patients will not develop significant extrapyramidal side-effects to begin with. Because antiparkinson drugs have anticholinergic effects, they may contribute to the risks of polypharmacy and drug-drug toxicity.

3. *Tardive dyskinesia* is associated with long-term use of phenothiazines and appears in many older patients, particularly women. It is associated with buccal-facial-lingual movements and involuntary movements of the limbs and trunk. Although an increase in the amount of phenothiazine can reverse the signs, this is only a temporary effect and the pattern reappears. Therefore, authorities recommend the use of drug-free intervals, reduced dosages, and drug withdrawal, with the rationale that a reduction in the total amount given over the years will lessen the risk of dyskinesia.[7]

4. *Akathisia* appears after rather short periods of treatment with antipsychotics. It consists of uncontrollable restlessness and agitation which are not typical of the original psychotic disorder. The differentiation from severe anxiety states and agitated depression may be difficult, especially when a reliable record or past history is not available. Akathisia may respond well to diphenhydramine (Benadryl) and other antihistamines.

5. Other side effects secondary to the *anticholinergic* action include constipation, urinary retention and an increased risk of glaucoma, alterations in the electrocardiograms, and other changes such as reduced drive and libido.

## Other Compounds and Drugs

A number of other compounds, which are not psychotropic in the strict sense of the word, need to be briefly reviewed because of their effects on cerebral functioning. Included here are certain vitamins and hormones, vasorelaxants and anticoagulants, and hydergine.

(a). **Vitamins.** According to Libow[8] more than 10 percent of the elderly have deficiencies of several important vitamins. Deficiency of *vitamin B₁* (Thiamine) causes beriberi, part of which is the Wernicke-Korsakov syndrome. Thiamine is a mild appetite stimulant, and under stress it tends to be depleted in the adrenal cortex, where it has essential metabolic action. *Ascorbic acid* also seems to be essential to adrenal cortical function. It is rapidly depleted with stress and poor nutrition.

Since toxicity of vitamin B and C is very low, the use of these vitamins in large amounts is frequently recommended. However, the usefulness of preventive vitamin therapy in the aged has not been sufficiently verified by double-blind studies. *Niacin* (nicotinic acid) deficiency produces pellagra, which may be manifested by various CNS disturbances such as impaired memory and orientation, confabulations, cogwheel rigidity, and primitive grasping and sucking reflexes. *Vitamin $B_{12}$* is used for the treatment of pernicious anemia, a chronic macrocytic anemia, in which CNS symptoms occur in 40 percent of the patients.[8] Deficiencies in *folic acid* may be attributable to inadequate diet, chronic alcoholism, intestinal malabsorption, or antagonism between folic acid and di-phenylhydantoin. A deficiency in folic acid results in a macrocytic anemia. Folic acid is contraindicated in the treatment of pernicious anemia because it may aggravate the neurocerebral symptomatology.

**(b). Hormones.**

**1.** *Estrogen* replacement therapy for postmenopausal women may be effective in preventing or slowing down the development of osteoporosis. In some postmenopausal depressions in which headaches, generalized aches and pain (because of osteoporosis), and chronic fatigue are major complaints, estrogen therapy can be effective. Such therapy is not routinely indicated for postmenopausal women, but only on the basis of proven or probable estrogen deficiency.

As an anabolic agent, *testosterone* may be useful in terms of improving appetite and weight. There has been some suggestion that androgen therapy may improve memory function, but it may also produce liver toxicity.[9] There seems to be no beneficial effects from the use of estrogen on the mental functions of elderly male patients with cerebral arterio-sclerosis or senile psychosis.[10]

**2.** *Hypothyroidism* can be mistakenly diagnosed as senile dementia. (see page 42). There is probably no justification for the practice, occasionally encountered, of giving thyroid preparations to older persons who complain of apathy, weakness, or fatigue. The proper indication for thyroid preparation is hypothyroidism verified by laboratory tests. *Hyperthyroidism* may cause a thyrotoxic psychosis, but in the elderly it may be manifested by apathy and depression. This condition has been termed "apathetic hyperthyroidism."[8]

**3.** Changes in the blood sugar level also may cause CNS symptoms. The more easily detectable *hyperglycemia* is the ketoacidotic state. Less common is the lactic acidosis syndrome seen in diabetic patients taking phenformin (DBI). Less easily detectable, but more common, is the nonketotic hyperosmolarity syndrome (hyperglycemia and confusion without ketosis). This syndrome and hypoinsulinemia may also be induced by drugs such as diphenylhydantoin. *Hypoglycemia* may occur during treatment with insulin or the sulfonylureas (tolbutamide, chlor-propamide). Predisposing factors include diminished caloric intake, with physical or mental illness, and reduced hepatic or renal function.[8]

**4.** *Corticosteroid hormones* suppress the body's immune defenses. Their usual psychological effect is an initial euphoria, and then depression.

(c). The many claims that *vasodilating* and related agents are useful have generally not been supported by well-controlled studies. On the other hand, it may be wise to give some of these drugs the benefit of the doubt, for the time being. *Nicotinic acid* is supposedly a vasodilator, but its value for producing lasting therapeutic benefits in elderly patients is probably negligible. *Cyclandelate* has been shown to produce small, but significant, improvement of several mental functions.[11] Traditionally, stimulants such as pentylenetetrazol and vasomotor dilators (*e.g.*, papaverine) have been used to treat the elderly. Some authors report good results, whereas others are skeptical. However, there is enough evidence that vasodilators may be useful to warrant further research.

(d). *Hydergine*, a combination of the hydrogenated derivatives of three alkaloids of ergotoxin, has been tried in the treatment of geropsychiatric patients. Various authors report beneficial effects, such as lessening of emotional withdrawal, conceptual disorganization, depressive mood, motor retardation, and blunted affect and disorientation.[12, 13]

## CLINICAL MANAGEMENT

### Confusion and Disorientation

(a). The presence of confusion and disorientation, especially when acute, requires first a search for *physical etiological* factors (Table 3).

TABLE 3. *Causes of Pseudosenility**

---

*Medications:* errors in self-administration; L-dopa, steroids; diuretics; drugs with CNS action, *e.g.*, phenothiazines, barbiturates.

*Metabolic Factors:*

1. *Hypercalcemia* resulting from lung or breast cancer; multiple myeloma; hyperparathyroidism; Paget's disease; thiazide.

2. *Hyperglycemia* involving ketoacidosis or lactic acidosis.

3. *Hypoglycemia* secondary to insulin or sulfonylureas.

4. *Hypothyroidism* and *hyperthyroidism*.

5. *Hypernatremia* as a result of inadequate fluid intake; I.V. hypertonic saline; tube feeding of high protein mixtures.

6. *Hyponatremia* caused by bronchogenic carcinoma; C.V.A.; postoperative.

7. *Azotemia* caused by nephritis; dehydration; prostatic hypertrophy; neurogenic uropathy (diabetes, anticholinergics, adrenergics); potent diuretics causing bladder overload *e.g.*, furosemide.

8. *Febrile Conditions.*

*Nutrition:* deficiencies in vitamin C, $B_{12}$, thiamine, riboflavin.

*CNS Tumors:* gliomas (50–60%); metastatic (20–50%).

*Hepatic:* cirrhosis, hepatitis.

*Cardiac failure:* caused by arrhythmia, congestive heart failure, pulmonary emboli, or acute myocardial infarction.

*Cerebrovascular:* transient ischemic attacks; C.V.A.; subdural hematoma (20% of all intracranial masses).

*Pulmonary:* emphysema with hypoxia or hypercapnea.

*Acute emotional stress* or *depression.*

---

* From Libow.[8]

Effective treatment of such factors causing an acute secondary organic brain syndrome is of paramount importance.

**(b).** In addition to the treatment of somatic factors, the following measures should be considered concerning *medications*.

**1.** Eliminate unnecessary medications; prevent poly-pharmacy. Drugs that are slow acting or metabolized slowly are contraindicated.

**2.** Remain alert to CNS side-effects of lithium (causing confusion) and the possibility of a central anticholinergic syndrome (see page 126).

**3.** If the patient is already receiving other medications (for pre-existing physical illness), be aware of possible interactional effects between these drugs, and also between the present medication and the drug to be selected for sedating the confused patient.

**4.** In acute confusion and disorientation, the following drugs can be considered: hydroxyzine (Vistaril), haloperidol (Haldol), chloralhydrate, or promazine (Sparine).

**(c).** Therapeutic measures that are not pharmacodynamic are primarily *environmental* in nature and are aimed at preventing decompensation of a brain which has marginal reserve. Cerebral decompensation resulting from environmental factors has been reviewed in terms of a functional brain syndrome (see page 38).

**1.** Maintain spatial and temporal constancy, by keeping the external environment the same, reducing the frequency of strangers and new personnel, and avoiding transfers and alterations in routine.

**2.** Regularly explain procedures in simple terms mentioning one's name and function at regular intervals.

**3.** Alleviate nocturnal confusion by preventing the relative isolation and sensory deprivation which may occur during the night.

**4.** Alleviate psychogenic factors which may contribute to confusion and disorientation, *e.g.*, extreme withdrawal (as in depressive stupor), severe agitation, panic, and so on.

**5.** Promote contact with reality by means of visitors, familiar newspapers, calendars, and clocks, pictures of spouse, children, and so on (reality orientation).

**6.** Structure a time perspective. Within each day, meaningful events should be arranged, and the days of the week should become distinguishable from each other by virtue of noticeable day to day differences in the routine. Otherwise, the hours and days become undifferentiated time, and it would be useless to try to reorient the patient with clocks and calendars: they would only indicate empty, meaningless time.

**7.** Provide opportunities for specific group experiences, such as remotivation and resocialization. This category of therapeutic measures becomes more relevant as the acute confusion subsides and the patient is reaching the base-line level of his cerebral status, *e.g.*, a chronic brain syndrome of mild to moderate degree.

**(d).** *Nocturnal confusion* is common in O.B.S., and is frequently a major complaint on the part of the family. Nocturnal restlessness also may occur after an environmental change such as hospitalization or an intrahospital transfer; it may take from several days up to a few weeks for the patient to readjust himself to the new environment. These types of nocturnal restlessness and disorientation can sometimes be alleviated by leaving a nightlight on in the patient's room. Physical restraints should be avoided if at all possible.

An example illustrating the multifaceted aspects of confusion and disorientation is the following case.

An 82-year-old widow arrived by bus at the local bus terminal. She drew attention from the bus station personnel because she kept aimlessly wandering around. When questioned, she stated that she did not know where she was, or where she had come from. She was then taken to a local hospital. Physical and mental status examinations revealed an organic brain syndrome, arteriosclerotic cardiovascular disease, and nutritional anemia, all of mild degree. The history, as it unfolded over a period of weeks, revealed that the patient had been moving, for many years, between the homes of her five children. They lived in different states, so the patient did a good bit of traveling. Reportedly, she never stayed with one child for more than a few months, and she would unexpectedly leave. Significantly, the patient would not get along well with the family, during a particular stay. Most likely, the patient received subtle messages to the effect that she was not all that welcome. Thus, soon after arrival in one of her children's homes, she would more and more "draw away" until she "unexpectedly" left. In the more remote history, it is of interest that the patient was the youngest of ten children. She had not been "planned" by her parents. One of the basic themes of her existence had been that there was "no place for her". She married, had five children, and after her husband died (when she was 36 years old) she raised them by herself in the home where the children had been born. After the last child left home, the patient did likewise.

Thus, her caring for the children had represented an attempt to establish the home she never had herself when young. In the light of this past history, the original presenting symptom ("I don't know where I am, and where I came from") is not just the concrete manifestation of an O.B.S. It is overdetermined in that it also is the figurative expression of an existential theme. This patient was placed in a rest home. She has been taking thioridazine (Mellaril) 25 mg, t.i.d., and there have been no more confusional episodes.

## Deterioration of Neuromuscular Skills

Deterioration of neuromuscular skills includes regressive changes in coordination, locomotion, and control of the urinary and anal sphincters. Locomotor skills and sphincter control are acquired during the anal development phase. The equivalent term, autonomy, points up that sphincter control is not the only developmental issue, but that the act of standing up and moving about vertically in a gravitational field is also important.

(a). During the process of senile regression, a point may be reached at which the patient no longer seems to have the energy to push himself up against the force of gravity. He prefers to give in to the pull of gravity and seeks the horizontal position, in bed or anywhere. This is a milestone in the path of regression, because the *loss of locomotor skills* sets the stage for loss of sphincter control, for decubitus, and flexion contractures. In view of this, efforts should be made to maintain the patient's locomotor skills as long as possible, by means of physical therapy and other activity programs. Oversedation and chemical straightjackets should be avoided. Walking can be done by the patient himself with the help of a cane or a walker, or with the assistance of relatives, ward personnel, or other patients.

1. *Physical therapy*, in general, has an important place in the spectrum of comprehensive management. Specific rehabilitation is indicated for neuromuscular malfunctions following a stroke or hip fracture, for preventing regressed patients from becoming bedridden and incontinent, and for preventing decubitus and contractures when patients are relatively immobilized in wheelchair or bed. Almost all patients benefit from appropriate physical exercise programs (passive or active). Needless to say, these physical procedures cannot fail to have a beneficial effect on the entire person.

2. *Geriatric Prosthetics*. The increasing array of prosthetic devices is one of the exciting developments of modern medicine. We already take for granted prosthetics such as glasses, hearing aids, dentures, crutches, canes, and walkers, artificial limbs, cardiac pacemakers, and so on. Less known are other prosthetics such as the artificial hip joint and devices compensating for loss of sphincter control. Obviously, there are limits to the extent that prostheses can be used, particularly the constraints of the "host" characteristics. There comes a point at which even an ideal prosthesis can no longer fit, because the infirmity of the prospective recipient does not provide a support basis for the prosthesis. Nevertheless, it is hoped that further research will produce more prosthetic devices, refine the quality of those already in use, and that timely application of these devices will permit them to be utilized effectively by aging individuals. For example, it should be possible to develop safe and effective mechanical devices which would enable the patient to maintain and exercise his locomotor skills. From a utopian point of view, it is conceivable that almost all organs and parts of the body can be replaced by a prosthetic device, the one exception being the brain.

(b). *Incontinence* is a problem of major concern, one reason being that cleaning up requires so much personnel time.

1. Causes of *fecal incontinence* include:

—Local pathology (infections; prolapse of rectum, weakness of the pelvic floor; malignancies; etc.).

—Neuromuscular incoordination of central origin (O.B.S.).

—Acute confusional states, *e.g.*, resulting from "transplantation shock" or massive regression.

—Intentional incontinence may be a symptom of spiteful behavior, or a result of conditioning (*e.g.*, when the person has learned to get attention by soiling himself).

—Constipation may lead to fecal impaction, and this in turn to incontinence. Fecal impaction may be attributable to decreased activity and the anticholinergic effects of psychotropic drugs. Fecal impaction should be suspected if the patient is vomiting, bending over to one side, and if there is any increasing agitation, lethargy, or confusion.[6] In such cases, a careful rectal examination should be done forthwith. Apparently there can be an age-related decline of rectal sensitivity to distention which may play a role in the development of constipation patterns.[14]

**2.** Causes of *urinary incontinence* include:

—In women, stress incontinence, uterine prolapse, or weakness of the pelvic floor; in men, prostate hypertrophy.

—Infections and neoplasms.

—Urinary retention with overflow incontinence because of bladder outlet obstruction, or neurogenic bladder.

—Neurogenic incontinence, *e.g.*, as a result of spinal cord lesions or O.B.S.

—In confusional states, the bladder and its neuronal connections are essentially intact, but the patient may be confused about the purpose of a toilet, or he may keep forgetting where the bathroom is.

—Environmental factors: the patient may be pulled into a regressive drift because of the constant proximity of other patients who are incontinent.

Most cases of incontinence can be treated with some degree of success. An evaluation of etiologic factors is the first step, with proper medical and surgical treatment, as indicated. Transient incontinence, attributable to acute confusion, will improve with the clearing of the confusion itself. In chronic incontinence, it is important to establish the specific pattern of incontinence. An incontinence chart consists of the systematic recording by the nursing personnel of all instances of urinary and fecal incontinence for individual patients. Such a chart has both diagnostic and therapeutic value. By recording the type of incontinence, and the time and context, it may be possible to detect a pattern. Knowledge about the incontinence pattern typical for an individual patient is essential in retraining efforts. Retraining may be effective when senility or regression is not advanced. Maintaining locomotion may be essential in preventing incontinence. The use of drugs is restricted to those necessary to treat local pathology. The use of drugs affecting the physiology of bladder and rectum is controversial. Psychotropic drugs with anticholinergic side effects may need to be discontinued. Specific prosthetic devices are available for patients with permanent incontinence.[15]

Having the toilet doors marked by a bright color, by name, and a silhouette of a man or woman help some confused patients find the right facility more quickly. Taking the patient to the toilet at regular intervals also may be useful, especially when his pattern of incontinence is known. In cases with a functional (psychogenic) component, there is often improvement as the patient begins to participate in an active therapeutic milieu.

## Phases of Senile Regression

Senile dementia involves regression through a series of backward steps through the phases of personality development.[16] The early phase is marked by reliving of past experiences, but when the patient becomes a participant in the events recalled, he is living in the past. Subsequently, there is an inability to place events in their proper time frame, associated with memory defects. Reality testing begins to fail, objects are misplaced or lost, and then thought to be stolen. But the condition is not yet irreversible, depending on physical illness, lack of support, and other stresses.

During the next phase, there is increasing withdrawal into fantasy life, with weakening of behavioral controls. Primitive drives may be acted upon or acted out. Logical thought and the ability to cope with novel situations progressively decline. The combination of decreased impulse control and the awareness of failure results in periodic rage. Those mental functions learned late in development, disappear first, whereas those acquired early, are retained the longest (e.g., responsiveness to rhythm). People who used to be familiar are no longer recognized. With the increased need for care, come accusations of neglect. The environment is interpreted as hostile or protective depending on intrapsychic processes rather than on reality testing.[16]

All of this evokes considerable feeling in those responsible for his care.

An 83-year-old woman had resided in a rest home for several years, and was regularly taken to an outpatient clinic by the manager of the home. The patient was in a fairly advanced stage of senile regression. She stated she was 63 years old and was still grieving about the recent death of her husband—"but at least I can talk to my mother every few days. She cannot visit me because she lives in another town and has no transportation. So I call her up over the phone. Talking with her makes me feel better." (The patient's mother had been dead for at least 30 years). At the end of the brief interview, the manager of the rest home turned to the physician asking him, "Could you find out if she knows me?" The physician asked the patient along this line. She blandly looked at the rest home manager and said, "She? I do not know her. I have never seen her before."

The journey back into the past varies in terms of its duration and the extent of reversibility. During the early phases, the episodes of living in the past are transient and reversible. Such episodes are characterized by the onset of acute confusion and hallucinatory experiences. The voices and visions often pertain to people in the patient's past, usually people who are now dead. But through the patient's living in the past, there is a resurrection of the dead. By observing which particular people are resurrected, we are able to estimate the depth of the patient's regression into the past. For example, it is one thing for a female patient to hear the voice of her father who died when she was 30 years old, but another thing if she hears her mother who died when the patient was 13.

During the early phases of senile regression, it is possible to retrieve the patient from his drift into the past, *e.g.*, by appropriate sensory stimulation, and alleviation of undue social isolation. During the intermediate stage, the episodes of living in the past (with concomitant disorientation *vis-à-vis* the present) become more frequent and extended. During the final phase, the episodes coalesce into a continuous existence of living in the past, and this is usually irreversible.

To predict the outcome of organic and functional illness for an individual patient on the basis of the clinical diagnosis is extremely difficult. The prognosis for each elderly patient with whatever psychiatric disorder cannot be based on his age, the diagnostic classification, or any one single variable. Rather, it must be based on the patient's total condition, including his sociocultural background, premorbid personality, current environmental, psychological and physical stresses, and the structural and functional status of his brain. Among aged institutionalized patients, predictions that death would occur within a certain time after admission were correct in only one-third of the cases; usually the prediction was more pessimistic than the actual outcome.[17]

## REFERENCES

1. ARIETI, S.: Schizophrenia. *In*: American Handbook of Psychiatry, Vol. 1, Chap. 24, S. Arieti, ed. Basic Books, Inc., New York, 1959. pp. 491–493.
2. BERTALANFFY, L.: General system theory and psychiatry. *In:* American Handbook of Psychiatry, Vol. 3, Chap. 43, S. Arieti, ed. Basic Books Inc., New York, 1966. pp. 705–721.
3. FRIEDEL, R. O.: Biochemical basis of psychopharmacology. *In:* Drug Issues in Geropsychiatry, W. E. Fann and G. L. Maddox, eds. Williams & Wilkins, Baltimore, 1974. pp. 9–17.
4. JANOWSKY, D., EL-YOUSEF, M. K., AND DAVIS, J. M.: Side effects associated with psychotropic drugs. *In:* Drug Issues in Geropsychiatry, W. E. Fann and G. L. Maddox, eds. Williams & Wilkins, Baltimore, 1974. pp. 19–28.
5. HOLLISTER, L. E.: Psychiatric and neurologic disorders. *In:* Clinical Pharmacology, Chap. 11, K. L. Melmon and H. F. Morrell, eds. The MacMillan Company, New York, 1972. pp. 463–467.
6. WHANGER, A. D. AND BUSSE, E. W.: Care in hospital. *In:* Modern Perspectives in the Psychiatry of Old Age, Chap. 21, J. G. Howells, ed. Brunner-Mazel, New York, 1975. pp. 450–485.
7. FANN, W. E. AND LAKE, C R.: Drug induced movement disorders in the elderly: an appraisal of treatment. *In:* Drug Issues in Geropsychiatry, W. E. Fann and G. L. Maddox, eds. Williams & Wilkins, Baltimore, 1974. pp. 41–48.
8. LIBOW, L. S.: Pseudo-senility: acute and reversible organic brain syndromes. *J. Am. Geriatr. Soc. 21:* 112–120, 1973.
9. SILVER, D., LEHMANN, H. E., KRAL, V. A., AND BAN, T. A.: Experimental geriatrics—selection and prediction of therapeutic responsiveness in geriatric patients. *Can. Psychiat. Assoc. J. 13:* 561, 1968.
10. LIFSHITZ, K. AND KLINE, N. S.: Use of an estrogen in the treatment of psychosis with cerebral atherosclerosis. *J. Am. Med. Assoc. 177:* 501, 1961.
11. FINE, G. W., LEWIS, D., VILLA-LANDE, I., AND BLAKEMORE, C. G.: The effect of cyclandelate on mental function in patients with arteriosclerotic brain disease. *Br. J. Psychiatry 117:* 157–161, 1970.
12. DITCH, M., KELLY, F. J., AND RESNICK, O.: An ergot preparation (Hydergine) in the treatment of cerebrovascular disorders in the geriatric patient, double blind study. *J. Am. Geriatr. Soc. 19:* 208–217, 1971.
13. ROUBICEK, J., GEIGE, C. H., AND ABT, K.: An ergot alkaloid preparation (Hydergine) in geriatric therapy. *J. Am. Geriatr. Soc. 20:* 222–229, 1972.
14. NEWMAN, H. F. AND FREEMAN, J.: Physiologic factors affecting defecatory sensation: relation to aging. *J. Am. Geriatr. Soc. 22:* 553–554, 1974.

15. BROCKLEHURST, J. C.: The treatment of incontinence. *In:* Intensive Course in Geriatrics for General Practitioners, E. Woodford-Williams and A. N. Exton-Smith, eds. S. Karger, Basel, 1967. pp. 298–308.
16. LEEDS, M.: "Senile recession —a clinical entity. *J. Am. Geriatr. Soc.* 8: 122–131, 1960.
17. GOLDFARB, A. I., FISCH, M., AND GERBER, I. E.: Predictors of mortality in the institutionalized aged. *Dis. Nerv. Syst.* 27: 21–29, 1966.

# 16

# an old man with dementia

The following case is presented in detail to illustrate the diagnostic complexities of dementia, the influence of premorbid personality characteristics on the clinical symptomatology, and to offer recommendations for a comprehensive therapeutic regime.

Mr. Joseph K., a 79-year-old man of great wealth was admitted as an emergency to a local hospital. Earlier that day he had become agitated, confused, and suspicious of what was going on at home. He ordered his secretary to drive him to the City Hall. On the way over there, he changed his mind and ordered the secretary to go to the County Court House. Having arrived there, he gave instructions to go to the railroad station. Meanwhile, some concerned relatives were following from afar, not daring to interfere, because Mr. K. had always been an awe-inspiring figure. In the course of his life he had built up a vast business empire (oil, cattle, etc.). His many philanthropic activities and substantial donations to community projects had given him an almost legendary stature. No one had ever told him what to do, or had the audacity to stand up to him. When Mr. K. had arrived at the railroad station, however, got out of his car and proceeded to walk by himself along the railroad tracks, the relatives decided to intervene. He was rushed to a nearby hospital for emergency admission.

### Recent Illness

Mr. K. had been in fairly good health until three years ago, when he began to complain of recurrent, brief spells of dizziness. This was treated by the family physician with anticoagulants, in an attempt to counteract cerebrovascular ischemia, but without significant relief. There also had been a noticeable decrement in recent memory, manifested by difficulties in recalling names, recent events and dates, or sudden inability to remember what he was about to say.

Reportedly Mr. K. was aware of these changes in his intellectual faculties but apparently was able to continue functioning in his usual work pattern. At least, he would go to his office every day and engage in decisions about business transactions involving huge amounts of money. Any suggestions made by his family, business associates, and physician to slow down, and to delegate more responsibility to others, were summarily dismissed. His obstinate refusal to let go, combined with the manifest deterioration of his judgement, caused much apprehension among his family, friends, and business associates.

A few months before admission, the patient had fallen on the street and fractured one of the small bones in his left foot. Presumably, the fall was a result of an attack of dizziness. (During later psychiatric examination, Mr. K. denied there had been anything like a fracture, maintaining that "it was just a bruise.")

The relatives further reported that Mr. K. had become much more irascible during the last few weeks. On the day of hospitalization, in fact, he had used "some very strong language" toward his accountant and his secretary.

## Physical and Mental Examination on Admission

Physical examination was essentially within normal limits, except for a moderate hearing loss. Blood pressure was 145/85. The admission note stated that he had visual hallucinations and delusional ideas of a paranoid nature. He felt persecuted by members of an "underground organization, left wing radicals or communists, who were trying to kidnap him and hold him hostage, so they would get a huge ransom." During the acute confusional state, the patient actually believed he had been kidnapped and now was "underground." The mental confusion, hallucinations, and delusions cleared up within several days after admission to the hospital. The EEG was abnormal, characterized by generalized slowing and dysrhythmia. No definite focal changes were noted.

## Medical History

Mr. K. had been in good health until the age of 72, when he developed coronary insufficiency as indicated by EKG. Since then, there had been no significant cardiac or respiratory problems, and his blood pressure had always been within normal limits. The most recent EKG was normal. There was no evidence of orthostatic hypotension, or major fluctuations in the pulse pressure. There was no past history of episodes of paralysis, aphasia, or other neurological signs that would suggest a major cerebrovascular accident. There was no evidence of any major psychiatric disorder in the history before the present episode.

## Family History

Family history was obtained from Mr. K.'s brother. Mr. K.'s wife died 10 years ago, from cancer of the uterus. Reportedly, Mr. K. "grieved for only a short while about her death. He lost himself again in his work; in fact, he never stopped working." Significantly, there was never any overt talk between Mr. K. and his wife that she had a terminal illness and was about to die. The brother feels certain, though, that Mr. K. knew about the nature of his wife's illness.

The same type of reaction was observed after the death of his only child, a son. He died of leukemia when Mr. K. was in his late fifites.

Although he knew about his son's terminal illness, he reportedly "went on with business as usual. He would never sit down and grieve about a loss. In fact, he actually scolded his son for not working hard enough."

**Comments.** These observations point to a central feature of Mr. K.'s personality. He has always seen himself as a winner, and in a way, he has never experienced defeat. He has reacted to losses (death of son and wife) in terms of denial. He has been able to avoid the working through of these losses by concentrating more intensely on his work. The significant point is that he has not learned to cope with the inevitable losses of late life. Now that his own physical and mental capacities are declining, he finds himself equally unprepared to deal with these personal losses and to accept them. The behavior patterns which, in the past, served him so well in building up a vast business empire have now become maladaptive.

### Psychiatric Examination

Mr. K.'s general behavior was characterized by attempts to maintain control. It was he who decided which persons would be present during the interview, what topics to talk about and in what manner. *Orientation* for time, place, person, and situation was intact. The sensorium was clear, but the capacity for attention and concentration was decreased to a mild-moderate extent. (The impression was gained that this decreased attentiveness resulted from a combination of impaired cognition and general defensiveness.) With regard to his *perception*, there was no evidence that impaired vision or hearing interfered with the interview. Illusions, perceptual distortions, or hallucinations were not noted. Concerning his *affect*, suspiciousness and irritability were overtly manifest. The patient questioned the motives of the examiner and other persons present. He quickly expressed annoyance when some wishes were not immediately carried out, *e.g.*, getting his attorney to sit in during the interview. He seemed to be unaware of the unreasonable nature of some of his demands. (This implies lack of good judgement.) Interestingly, he would smile whenever he had difficulty answering a particular question. (This is in keeping with his tendency to deny and rationalize his losses. Behind the facade of suspiciousness and irritability, there would seem to be a great deal of anxiety. Under certain stress, *e.g.*, interference with his defenses, this anxiety may increase to the point of overt panic. The suspiciousness and irritability serve to keep his attention focused externally. His occasional jocular behavior has a similar aim, *i.e.*, diversion away from his own problems.)

*Thought Processes.* No delusions were observed, but there were several ideas of reference, *e.g.*, asking suspiciously what people were talking about before coming in his room. To some extent, this is understandable in view of his present situation, but the intensity of his response was not appropriate. Likewise, he became suspicious and defensive when asked about retirement, the aging process, future plans, and so on. He dealt with the issue of retirement by questioning the interviewer's motives; he talked about the question of how old age had affected him by presenting a detached semi-intellectual description of the process of arteriosclerosis. When it came to his future plans, he became defiant, explaining that he had rejected previous medical advice to slow down in his work, and that he would continue working as before.

There is evidence of some loss of the capacity for abstract thought and conceptual thinking. For example, when asked about the year of his son's death, he knew that this was twenty years ago. But after repeated questions about what year it actually had been, and after establishing what the present year was, he was not able to subtract 20 years from that. Instead, he added them on to the present year, which brought him close to the end of the 20th century. At this point, he revealed perplexion and profound anxiety. His next statement was spoken in a mumbled way: "or 2000?" (This illustrates the catastrophic reaction[1] of brain damaged individuals: the patient gives a wrong answer, is aware of his inability to perform accurately, develops profound anxiety, and becomes totally unable to perform at all.) The patient's wrong answer does not illustrate an inability to calculate, but conceptual confusion about the difference between two fundamental arithmetical procedures, *i.e.*, subtraction *versus* addition.

The history provides other examples of such conceptual confusion. A few weeks ago, he called one of the nurses a waitress. Likewise, his search for the city hall, the court house, and the railroad station was a manifestation of conceptual confusion: he knew he had to go somewhere for help, but was unable to assess the nature of his troubles, and accurately match this need with the proper place for help, a hospital. The fact that he sought out the city hall and court house is in keeping with the observation that he felt persecuted by the "underground" organization. This conceptual misinterpretation is primarily the result of the organic brain syndrome, but from a psychodynamic point of view, this delusion served to reinforce the tendencies of denial of the real problem, and represented a last desperate effort to maintain the intactness of the self and self-image.

*Memory.* There was considerable difficulty remembering names of persons he had known for some time. Interestingly, he turns to his relatives immediately, who then supply the correct name. The same is true with regard to dates and recent events. (Because Mr. K. has been, and still is getting this type of support from his environment, he has not had to come to grips with the real extent of his memory loss. The implication for management is that he should continue to have, as much as possible, such external agents who can serve as a memory prosthesis for him. A stranger would not be able to function in this role.)

*Judgement.* It is clear from the above that the capacity for judgement is impaired. The impairment is evident with regard to his physical and mental abilities (their nature, extent, and prognosis) and to the action implications and consequences resulting from whatever disabilities he admits.

## Diagnostic Impression

The clinical data indicate the coexistence of two types of organic brain syndrome: cerebral arteriosclerosis and senile dementia. *Arteriosclerotic* organic brain syndrome is suggested by the longstanding history of dizziness and the occasional fainting spells; the recent occurence of acute, transient episodes of confusion and excitement; the EEG findings ("generalized slowing and dysrhythmia, consistent with cerebral arteriosclerosis"); and the fluctuations in the course of the illness. *Senile dementia* (*i.e.*, senile brain atrophy) is indicated by significant memory impairment, especially for names, and recent dates and events; impaired cognitive abilities, especially a deficit in the capacity for abstract thought and concept formation; gradual personality changes, including increased suspiciousness, irritability, self-centeredness, and the emergence of pathological defense mechanisms (marked denial; projection); and the patient's age and gender inasmuch as organic brain syndrome in a male octogenarian is usually attributable to senile brain atrophy.

The signs and symptoms of O.B.S. depend not only on the structural, pathological changes in the brain, but also on characteristics of the premorbid personality. Some reference to significant personality factors was already made: his aggressive ambitiousness; his tendency to see himself as strong and undefeated; the rigid pattern of being absorbed in work, at the expense of leisure and recreational activities; his inability to adequately work through personal losses to the point of resolution of the grief and acceptance of loss; his tendency to continue patterns of coping that used to be adaptive (with the emphasis on aggressive mastery) but have now become obsolete. In fact, what appears to emerge now is an intensification of these earlier patterns, rather than attempts to accommodate himself to the realities of late life.

The diagnosis includes: chronic brain syndrome resulting from arteriosclerosis and senile dementia, manifested by dizziness, memory deficit, impaired cognitive capacities, and changes in personality; and history of acute brain syndrome, manifested by acute episodes of disorientation, hallucinations, and paranoid delusions.

## Prognosis

Prognosis for chronic brain syndrome is poor. Chances for reversal of basic pathology or symptomatology are practically nil. The chances for arresting the progress of the disease process are very small. However, prognosis with regard to the acute brain syndrome is fair. With proper medical, psychiatric, and nursing care management, the risks of further episodes of acute brain syndrome may be greatly diminished.

## Recommendations

(a). Rule out the possibility of occlusive disease of the extracranial cerebrovascular supply, *e.g.*, atherosclerosis of the carotid arteries. Special studies, such as cerebral blood flow determination, may be indicated. Rule out possible episodes of hypotension or decreased pulse pressure, from whatever sources, because these would interfere with adequate brain oxygenation or would aggravate an already existing deficiency in cerebral oxygenation.

(b). Maintain optimal *physical health*, with special attention to cardiovascular, renal, and respiratory functions. Maintain adequate nutrition and dental care. Administer regular high potency multiple vitamins. Try to reduce hearing impairment by providing suitable hearing aid.

(c). Specific medications and procedures aimed at *improving cerebral oxygenation* and functioning generally have doubtful value. In no instance is there a significant chance of clinical benefit, but some medications reportedly have been useful.

1. Medications that are *possibly helpful* should be given a trial: hydergine, vasorelaxants, anticoagulants, and high potency multiple vitamins.

2. Medications or procedures that are *experimental or controversial* include hyperbaric oxygenation;[2] metrazol (alone or in combinations); procaine therapy; anabolic steroid hormones; special diets, such as low cholesterol or low fat; choline or inositol.

3. Medications that appear to be *useless* are monosodium glutamate and RNA therapy.

*Hydergine* (dihydrogenated alkaloids of ergotoxine, DHAE) has been found to be useful for the treatment of cerebrovascular insufficiency, associated with cerebral arteriosclerosis. Apparently, it is a safe drug which may improve important aspects of cognitive function, mood, behavior, and the ability to perform daily living tasks.[3]

The effectiveness of *vasorelaxant agents* such as papaverine is less certain. In one double-blind study, hydergine was superior to papaverine in improving mental alertness, confusion, depression, and inertia.[4] Nicotinic acid, which supposedly is a vasodilator, does not seem to produce therapeutic benefits for patients with cerebrovascular ischemia.[5] Cyclandelate is another vasodilator, which may have possible usefulness, but its therapeutic efficacy has not been clearly demonstrated.[6]

*Anticoagulants, e.g.*, Dicumarol, have been used in the treatment of cerebrovascular ischemia and senile dementia, on the assumption that anticoagulant therapy will improve the cerebral blood flow or prevent further impairment. Several reports in the literature suggest that anticoagulant therapy can be beneficial, especially in elderly patients who have arteriosclerosis with thromboembolic complications. Although there may be some uncertainty about the degree of their therapeutic or preventive usefulness, there is general agreement that if anticoagulants are administered, careful control and follow-up is essential, in view of the risk of hemorrhages.[7, 8]

The role of *nutritional* deficiencies in geropsychiatric disorders is still uncertain. Whanger and Wang found that more than 70% of elderly hospitalized patients had been on inadequate diets. Of these, 50% had borderline or low levels of folic acid, and 12% had borderline or low levels of vitamin $B_{12}$, both of which may be associated with dementia and other psychiatric disorders.[9] Classical vitamin deficiencies are rare nowadays, but when vitamin deficiencies exist, multiple deficiencies are the rule. It is not always easy to determine whether such deficiencies are the cause of the mental disorder, or the result. In view of the frequent malnutrition in aged patients, it is prudent to administer a daily multivitamin preparation. It may take up to one year of therapy to reverse deficiency problems in the elderly. Even in the hospital or nursing home, aged patients may maintain nutritional deficiencies because of deficient food habits, *e.g.*, eating mostly carbohydrates; loss of vitamins (especially vitamin C and folic acid) in institutional food; failure to eat the food served; and factors interfering with vitamin utilization (decrease in digestive enzymes, altered intestinal flora, and the use of mineral oil and antivitamin drugs like phenobarbital).

**(d).** Medications recommended for *psychiatric disturbances* are the following:

**1.** For *acute episodes* of restlessness, excitement, confusion or agressive behavior: haloperidol (Haldol), 0.5 mg t.i.d.; or one of the phenothiazines, such as trifluoperazine (Stelazine), 2 mg b.i.d., or thioridazine (Mellaril), 50 mg t.i.d.; or hydroxyzine (Vistaril, Atarax), 25 mg t.i.d. Try these medications in the sequence indicated. Each drug should be given long enough to be sure of its effectiveness, or lack thereof (a test period of at least 3 weeks). Avoid overmedication; do not give more than one major tranquilizer at the same time, if at all possible. Start with relatively small doses and increase the dosage gradually.

**2.** For *chronic tension*, anxiety, or mild agitation: diazepam (Valium) 2 mg t.i.d.; or hydroxyzine (Vistaril, Atarax) 25 mg t.i.d.; or doxepin (Sinequan) 25 mg b.i.d.

**3.** For *insomnia*: chloralhydrate (Noctec) 500 mg h.s.; or flurazepam (Dalmane) 15 mg h.s.

**(e). Social and Environmental Management.**

**1.** *Homecare*, with adequate nursing help available as needed, should be provided if possible. Prevent admissions to hospital or other institutions whenever circumstances allow.

**2.** Structure *daily activities* according to a regimen that is consistent, predictable, and sufficiently diversified. A consistent repertoire of daily activities is essential in fostering the patient's sense of self-confidence and minimizing the risk of loss of control. The activity spectrum should provide diversions and stimulations in keeping with the patient's personal wishes and his remaining potentials. Avoid the extreme of excessive involvements and overstimulation, on the one hand, and that of social isolation and sensory deprivation, on the other, since each will exacerbate the symptomatology.

**3.** Recognize that attempts to alter longstanding character patterns are not only futile, but possibly harmful. The patient's behavior should be met with an attitude of *matter-of-fact acceptance*. Support must be given without the physician being overbearing; helpful assistance should never be accompanied by undue efforts to correct him, or by pointing out to him (explicitly or tacitly) his deficiencies. The manifestations of anger, irritability, aggressive behavior, and so on may gradually get worse, as the dementia itself becomes worse in time. It is helpful for persons having contact with the patient, especially those providing care, to remember that such negative emotions are not meant to be personally directed against them; they are, by and large, the specific manifestations of an illness, senile dementia.

4. Recognize his need to *maintain self-esteem* and a self-image of strength. The latter will require a certain amount of denial mechanisms on the part of the patient. This denial should be left intact, as long as it does not provide a serious risk to himself, others, or vital business matters. Interference with the denial mechanisms may lead to more serious and maladaptive defenses, such as paranoid projections.

5. The patient's *dependency* on others, for providing him with basic support in the areas of memory and conceptual thinking, sets the stage for several possible undesirable developments. Because he has an obvious problem admitting weakness or dependency, he may react to increased dependency by becoming more controlling, angry, and defiant, and by insisting he can do without help from others. If, for whatever reason, the supporting people in the environment happen to be absent or unresponsive, he will tend to feel lost, confused, and quite anxious. If the supporting persons try to point out that he was wrong, or try to correct him, he may react with anger; this can intensify to the point where he might feel that others are against him.

6. The fact that he must rely on others for support in the area of *memory, abstract thought, and judgement* has the important implication that these persons, in order to be able to give support, need to be well acquainted with the patient. This type of support cannot be expected, for example, from a nurse who has known the patient only briefly. Although this support needs to come from relatives and close acquaintances, these persons are advised not to get involved in manifestations that are the expression of psychopathology and matters that would require medical-psychiatric expertise.

7. Although it is important to convey respect to the patient, and allow him to continue in roles in keeping with his self-image, it is also necessary to provide him with the *protection* that his condition requires. This protection can be given in tacit ways or in direct ways. Tacit protection is called for when it is clear that the inherent demands of a situation would exceed the patient's capacities; *e.g.*, tasks requiring the use of abstract thought, independent initiative, innovative problem solving, or decisions involving complex issues with far-reaching consequences. Protective support can be given by letting others have the information available and provide this to the patient in a matter-of-fact, casual (perhaps even surreptitious) manner. The patient may well accept such help and information without openly acknowledging it, as if he himself accomplished something important. If such tacit, subtle approaches of protecting the patient against the risks of his illness prove to be inadequate, a more direct, open approach is necessary. The element of firmness will then be essential. It is recommended that, if firm intervention is needed, this not be carried out by relatives, friends, or business associates, but by a physician, nurse, or other representative of the medical profession.

## REFERENCES

1. GOLDSTEIN, K.: Functional disturbances in brain damage. *In:* American Handbook of Psychiatry, Vo. 1, S. Arieti, ed. Basic Books, Inc., New York, 1959. pp. 770–793.

2. EDWARDS, A. E. AND HART, G. M.: Hyperbaric oxygenation and the cognitive functioning of the aged. *J. Am. Geriatr. Soc. 22:* 376–379, 1974.

3. RAO, D. B. AND NORRIS, J. R.: A double-blind investigation of hydergine in the treatment of cerebrovascular insufficiency in the elderly. *Johns Hopkins Med. J. 130:* 317–324, 1972.

4. BAZO, A. J.: An ergot alkaloid preparation (Hydergine) versus papaverine in treating common complaints of the aged: double-blind study. *J. Am. Geriatr. Soc. 21:* 63, 1973.

5. SMITH, C. M.: Nicotinic acid therapy in old age. *J. Am. Geriatr. Sqc. 11:* 580, 1963.

6. ADERMAN, M., GIARDINA, W. J., AND KORENIOWSKI, S.: Effect on cyclandelate on perception, memory, and cognition in a group of geriatric subjects. *J. Am. Geriatr. Soc. 6:* 268–271, 1972.

7. WRIGHT, I. S.: Comments on the use of anticoagulants in geriatric patients. *J. Am. Geriatr. Soc. 21:* 1–3, 1973.

8. RATNER, J., ROSENBERG, G., KRAL, V. A., AND ENGELSMANN, F.: Anticoagulant therapy for senile dementia. *J. Am. Geriatr. Soc. 20:* 556, 1972.

9. WHANGER, A. D. AND WANG, H. S.: Vitamin $B_{12}$ deficiency in normal aged and elderly psychiatric patients. *In:* Normal aging, Vol. 2, E. Palmore, ed. Duke University Press, Durham, N. C., 1974. pp. 63–73.

# 17

# contact with the family

The structure and dynamics of the family unit depends on intrinsic factors (the characteristics of its individual members) and extrinsic factors (societal influences). In this chapter, our focus will be primarily on the first set of determinants.

## THE DYNAMICS OF FAMILY CHANGE

The family, like other organisms, is not a static structure, but a dynamic entity that continuously evolves. From a structural point of view, the relationships between family members can be described as horizontal (*e.g.*, marital, or between siblings), or vertical (*e.g.*, parent-child). The family structure may be nuclear or extended. The former involves the smallest societal unit: husband-wife-child. The extended family includes members of more than two generations.

## Roles

From a functional point of view, family relationships can be described in terms of the roles of the individual members *vis-à-vis* each other. The role of one individual is complemented by the counter-role of one or more other family members, *e.g.*, husband-wife, parent-child. If role and counter-role represent a good fit, the relationship tends to be harmonious. The concept of role is a social one; it refers to behavior carried out for and with others. It is clear that intrapsychic phenomena do not necessarily correspond to the social role: private thoughts and subjective feelings may or may not be in tune with one's social role. If they are in tune, there will be a state of relative harmony and absence of tension in the individual. If, however, social role and intrapsychic forces are in conflict, the former or the latter (or both) will feel the impact. Thus, a man may faithfully continue in various roles (husband, father, provider, disciplinarian) although inwardly he is aware of wishes incompatible with those roles. Chronic conflicts usually have a neurotic origin. In personality disorders, the conflict between social role obligations and intrapersonal tendencies typically does not last very long because individual drives tend to win out over social responsibilities.

## Phases and Changes

(a). In the course of the years, the family undergoes modifications in structure and function, *e.g.*, when children are born, when they leave home, and so on. The family passes through the following *phases*: preparental, parental, postparental, and the phase of the aging family (following retirement). Thus the relationships of the family members and the repertoire of roles change continuously. This may even happen within the span of a particular phase. During the parental phase, for example, the parents need to grow up along with their children. The behavior appropriate in the parent-infant relationship is very different from that between parent and teenager. The changing developmental tasks with which the child is confronted require concomitant, appropriate changes on the part of the parents.

**(b).** The family may change, not only as the result of its own intrinsic developmental factors, but also because of broad *societal alterations* in the way the concept of family is viewed. In previous times (until the early 1900's), it was a common experience that one parent had died before the last child was grown up. Typically, the wife/mother would succumb to the risks attending pregnancy and childbirth. Medical progress has changed all that, so nowadays the average marital couple still has many years together after their children have departed from home. The concept of the family as a basic societal unit has also been modified by the changing role of contemporary woman, which has led to a reappraisal of many roles that were considered traditional, or were taken for granted. Society's impact on the family is further reflected by the increasing attention on children's rights. Finally, experiments with alternative family organizations (*e.g.*, solo parents, multifamily living arrangements) have become more common and accepted.

Of special interest are the opportunities and constraints regarding living-together arrangements for old persons. Two major factors play a role in setting the stage for alternative arrangements. First, the number of old women exceeds that of old men, which has provoked some considerations with regard to polygyny as a possible solution.[1] Secondly, the economic facts of life may prompt older men and women, each of whom receives individual social security income, to cohabitate without formally legalizing this arrangement.

**(c).** Experimentation with alternative types of family organization does not bewilder the thoughtful observer, because the basic themes are few and simple. They include the essential needs of belonging and self-actualization. There is a natural tension between these two motives. The sense of belonging evokes the image of the individual as part of an interpersonal network within which he fits and finds shelter, as a nodal point in a larger nexus that encompasses him. On the other hand, in the creative act of becoming a self, the individual stands out and stands alone. In becoming a person (a being that never was before, and never will return, a once-and-for-all kind of existence), the individual transcends the network he belongs to. Ideally, the tension between the two basic drives (to belong *versus* to stand out) is one of a healthy equilibrium. Thus, the sense of belonging would facilitate one's self-actualization; and conversely, self-actualization enables one to carve out a private niche of one's own in an alien world.

The motive of attaining a sense of belonging is reflected in the extended family organization. The emotional or spatial vicinity of three or more generations suggests ongoingness: the reassuring sense that one belongs to a family tree, whose survival does not depend on the fate of its individual branches. On the other hand, the drive toward self-actualization seems to correspond to the emphasis on the nuclear family unit. In this smaller type of family, it allegedly is easier to live a life that allows one "to be just yourself." The tension of having to subordinate (part of) oneself to the rules and roles of the extended family system may cause one to break away; the new, separate subsystem may be more free, but also more alienated. Conversely, the tensions inherent in the smaller nuclear family unit may prompt a search to join, or merge with, a larger, extended family.

In everyday life, we see both processes at work. It is not uncommon nowadays for persons, who have reached middle age and fulfilled their obligations to their parents and children, to break away from it all and start a new life. The search is then for a new identity, to find out who one was all along, or to do what one always had wanted to. However, any breaking away from established ties (people and places) represents, according to definition, a loss. The loss may be a calculated gamble to attain a long-term gain, like taking a few steps back to make a long jump forward.

Then, there are those who are more or less isolated or alienated in search of a sense of belonging. The larger system which they eventually join may be the (extended) family group; but often, by way of mental processes of abstraction and generalization, this new, larger family system is a conceptual one: a belief, ideology, a group of people espousing a cause, and so on. Considering the human life cycle in its entirety, it appears that the motive for a sense of belonging is relatively more prominent at either extreme of the continuum, i.e., in childhood and in old age.

## Role Reversal and Filial Role

It is often assumed that once the children are grown up and on their own, the relationship between them and their parents is pretty well finalized. In many instances, this is an oversimplification because even between adult offspring and aging parents the relationship may continue to change. The very fact that the parents are aging is a major factor responsible for this. The adult offspring need to recognize that no longer can they look to their parents for the support they used to get. No longer are the parents strong or omnipotent, qualities ascribed to them by younger children. If the relationship between adult progeny and their parents has been mature, the role transition can be made without difficulties. The ability to relate to one's parents as a mature adult involves a genuine emancipation from them, and viewing them as persons in their own right, with their own unique identity. Such a mature, objective view cannot be clouded by remnants of conflict drifting over from the past. Such psychological changes, reflected in specific changes of role, are part of a developmental process which leads to *filial maturity*. The filial crisis of this stage occurs when one realizes that the aging parents are no longer the pillars of support they used to be, but that they themselves begin to need the support of their children.

This transition involves, therefore, a reversal of roles, which to some individuals may cause considerable problems. The adult child does not assume a parental role to his own parents; rather, the filial role involves being depended upon and being dependable. The performance of the filial role leads to filial maturity which has characteristic gratifications of its own. The clarification of one's filial role and the delineation of one's obligations toward an aging parent may not come about, until after considerable upheaval.[2, 3]

A 40-year-old man was hospitalized because of a stomach ulcer. He had been working under high pressure, one reason being that he had to support his aged mother who had been living in with him and his wife. Also, there had been chronic strife with his fussy wife. After two weeks in the hospital, the ulcer symptoms had improved and he returned home. Shortly thereafter, his wife packed her belongings, moved out, and announced her intentions to separate. This left the patient and his mother together at home, neither one feeling happy with the way things developed. The next happening was the hospitalization of the elderly mother, for ill-defined symptoms. While she was in the hospital, the wife returned and moved back in the home. Eventually, a living arrangement evolved with the aged mother residing in a rest home, and her son and his wife continuing to live together. Thus, in the course of a few months, these three people had tried out three types of living arrangements. First, the adult son removed himself from the home leaving his mother and his wife together. Then, the wife departed, leaving her husband and his mother together. Finally, the mother went, leaving the home to her son and his wife. This last arrangement was arrived at by trial and error, which had caused undue hardship for all. What they had been trying to decide was an answer to the question, "Who is responsible for whom?"

Individuals who have remained immature, overly dependent, or neurotic frequently have problems in this area. The immature person has a strong need to depend on somebody who is strong and supportive. Thus, it may happen that the aging parent is not permitted to become more dependent on the adult offspring. Because the latter continues to regard his parent as (unrealistically) capable and self-reliant, the aging parent is subjected to multiple burdens: he has to play a role which he does not want and is not capable of.[4]

The source of the problem may also originate with the aging parent; for example, when he tenaciously adheres to an outdated set of roles or obsolete self-concept. Such a person may continue to see himself as head of the family, or as somebody who should have the final word in family decisions, being unaware that what once was an appropriate role is no longer so. In most instances, the difficulties in the process of role reversal are attributable to psychological factors in both the aging parent and the adult child.

### The Aging Family

A wide range of stresses affects the aging family (postretirement phase). Mentioned already was the potential stress inherent in reversal of roles between aging parents and their adult children. Other stressful factors are the effects of biological aging, retirement, economic deprivation, loss of spouse, loss of home, and so on.

(a). Townsend examined three-generation relationships in low income families and found that the social and family circumstances determined the capacity for adjustment and self-care in later life.[5] For aged persons, especially women, the vertical family relationships become more meaningful than the horizontal ones. Nonfamily activities diminish; mates may pull apart with regard to their interests and activities. The first-generation woman is busy with her grandchildren and her daughters with whom she maintains frequent contact as a family helper. The sons visit the mother but usually come alone. The first-generation man is isolated from many friends through retirement, and from his wife by her relative independence. When a woman is ill or disabled, she tends to depend first on a daughter, then on close female relatives, and last on her husband. When the aged man is ill, the most common source of aid is his wife, then female relatives, and the daughter. Thus, the most isolated person was the first-generation man. When this isolation is complicated by loss of spouse or close friends and by changes in environment, the chances for survival are slim.

According to other authorities, the role of the older man in the multigenerational family is more significant.[6, 7] Compared with the maternal relationship, the paternal one would become more important in later years. The final task of becoming an adult may involve more of a coming to terms with "the old man" than with the mother. Undoubtedly, cultural factors and differences in socioeconomic status play a major role in determining the importance and significance of the aged man *vis-à-vis* the aged woman in the extended family.

(b). The reaction to the *loss of spouse* through death or illness depends among other things on predisposing factors, particularly lifelong character patterns. For example, the pseudoindependent person may be stripped of his facade, and overt manifestations of dependency may appear for the first time, much to the concern or dismay of children and friends. The stress factor of loss of spouse is illustrated by the fact that suicide rates are highest after divorce or separation, and next highest after widowhood. The rate of suicide after divorce (both for men and women) is about two and a half times greater than that of the general population. The risk of suicide is highest in the first year after the loss of spouse, but it remains higher than average for at least five years.[8, 9]

Women seem to adjust better to the loss of spouse than men do. There are several possible reasons for this. First, the loss of spouse often is a stress experienced by women at a younger age than in the case of men, when there is relatively still more potential and energy for coping available. In addition, women seem to prepare themselves for the possibility of widowhood by way of anticipatory rehearsal for the role of widow. Such a mental process is set in motion by the deaths of married men in the circle of friends, the loss of the woman's father, and the departure of her children. This anticipatory grief can be useful, and may represent adaptive coping. The husband may react to loss of wife in several ways. He may remarry, for any number of reasons (*e.g.*, a healthy sexual drive, or strong dependency needs). The family's involvement in this decision can precipitate another crisis. A less adaptive coping response to the loss of the wife is withdrawal from the family, while making demands indirectly by various complaints. The reaction to the loss of a spouse is not always easy to predict or understand, even in the light of overt lifelong character patterns.

A man, in his mid-70's, died after a long bout with lung cancer. He had always been a strong, strong-willed person whose role as patriarch and ruler of the three-generational family was never disputed. In contrast to his dominance (maintained until his death), his wife was meek and mousy. Before his death, the man, as well as his three adult offspring worried about "what would become of mother" if she should lose her pillar of strength. What happened was somewhat of a surprise. Even on the very day of her husband's death, this presumably helpless woman took charge of all necessary arrangements. She turned out to have financial expertise, social leadership, and personal stamina that more than matched those of her late husband. It just so happened that, given his dominant personality, there could not have been "two skippers on the ship." It was her particular strength that for so many years she could stay in the background and accommodate him.

(c). Another crisis of the aging family is *loss of the home* or moving to a new environment. In younger years, moves are considered an expanding event, but to the aged, a move is usually a constricting, isolating event. The same loss occurs when members of the family move away. Aged persons who are on the waiting list for a home for the aged undergo special types of stress, because of their status in limbo. After admission to the home, anxiety usually decreases.[10]

## CONFLICTS IN THE FAMILY

Family pathology comprises disorders of the family as a whole and disturbed relationships between two or more individuals within the family. The former usually represent longstanding, habitual patterns, whereas the latter may be more acute and reactive in nature. Many varieties of disturbances occur in both of these categories, and some of the more common types will now be reviewed.

### Family as a Whole

Pathology of the family as a whole refers to ingrained patterns, behavioral styles, and ways of doing things, of which the family members themselves are hardly aware.

(a). *Problems in perceptiveness* and *deficiencies in communication* among family members may have been present for decades. The aging parents, or other elderly relatives, may become the victim of such patterns. Insufficient perception and awareness of what is happening to the elderly family members may be caused by denial, selective inattention, or rationalization. Accurate perception of age-related changes in the parents may be too threatening, as for example, in the case of an unmarried child—chronologically an adult but emotionally still dependent and childlike—who lives with an aging parent. Such a state of affairs may be a great burden on the aging parent who is forced to continue playing a role for which he or she is no longer suited. In other cases, selective inattention is expedient because it enables one to avoid confrontation with certain filial responsibilities—and some people do not want to be bothered. It is interesting that professional attempts to deal with such patterns of denial and disturbed communication in families with an aged, disabled member frequently are not successful.[3, 4]

(b). *Attraction of Neurotic Opposites.* Marital partners normally are attracted to each other on the basis of differences in sex (gender), but similarities and a shared outlook in nonsexual matters. Of course, there are some apparent exceptions; *e.g.*, a man who is the silent, serious type may do well in marrying a vivacious, cheerful woman. Such complementarity does not contradict the general rule because this couple may share a common outlook, *i.e.*, that seriousness and cheerfulness are neither good nor bad in themselves, but that their value is relative, depending on factors in the situation. In the case of neurotic opposites, however, there is no true complementarity and stability because within the partners there exist specific neurotic conflicts. The conflict in one individual may be the reverse, or mirror image as it were, of that in the other. Typical of the conflict is that one part of it is beyond awareness. An example may clarify this.

Let us assume that a man has strong dependency needs which are kept unconscious for whatever reasons. What is outwardly manifest is excessive independence (a reaction formation). Such a man is likely to attract a dependent woman because role and counter-role form a good fit. This couple will get along reasonably well as long as the man's independent facade remains intact. If, however, the reaction formation crumbles because of aging or illness, the underlying dependency comes to the fore. Now there are two dependent partners in the relationship, which is a very unstable situation (see case on page 93).

Other examples of such neurotic opposites are the following: one partner has cruel (sadistic) characteristics, the other is the suffering martyr (masochistic); one partner is chronically depressive and the other hypomanic (unduly optimistic and cheerful). In all these instances we may find that the outwardly visible behavior has an invisible counterpart which is the opposite of the former. The masochist may be a sadist in disguise, the hypomanic defends himself against depressive feelings, and so on.

(c). For some families, stress and crisis is a way of life. The family members may complain about their burdens, *e.g.*, the presence of elderly parents in their home, but in fact it is precisely this stress that holds the family intact. There may be many reasons for this, only two of which will be mentioned here. First, some families are close only during times of stress and crisis because the only thing they are good at is the business of providing support. Second, some families may, secretly or unconsciously, welcome stressful circumstances because the external crises prevent them from having to face their inner conflicts. Thus, when relatives complain about the presence of aging parents in their home, it is wise to try to ascertain to what extent these relatives are *crisis prone*. This can be done by taking a brief history of their past. If their past is a succession of crises or near-crises, then one should suspect that the external turmoil serves a defensive purpose.

(d). Few entities are more intriguing than *folie à deux*, the "psychosis of association," in which the same delusions are shared by two. Folie à deux in the aged is similar to folie à deux in the population as a whole, both with regard to incidence and nature of psychopathology. Among the factors common to folie à deux in patients of all ages are isolation and poverty; a very high proportion of blood relationships, particularly sister-sister combinations; a high level of dependency; and a high rate of persecutory delusions (Table 1).[11, 12]

The two theories most commonly presented to explain folie à deux suggest that either the delusion is imposed on a weaker member by a stronger person, or that two people simply become psychotic at the same time and one borrows the delusion from the other. Dependency is felt to be of importance in the development of the syndrome. It is probably more accurate to regard the need to preserve intimacy as the most important factor leading to a unitary delusional system. This view of the etiology of folie à deux would de-emphasize the role of contagion and emphasize the adaptive function of a unitary delusion, *i.e.*, how both partners can project interpersonal and other frustrations outward while at the same time joining forces against a common enemy. If one of them assumes a dominant role in the relationship and the other a submissive role, then the chance for disagreement between them is further reduced and even greater closeness might result. Gralnick found persecutory delusions in nearly all cases in which relationships had been of extended duration.[11] Hostility was projected outward against a common enemy.

It must be kept in mind that folie à deux represents the extreme, at one end of a continuum. Along this continuum, we find instances of dyadic pathology of varying degrees. Thus, it is not unusual to encounter relationships between two relatives (either old-old, or old-young) that are characterized by intense dependency as well as mutual exploitation. A fairly typical example is the situation of an aged, widowed, infirm parent, living with an adult offspring who has one or more handicaps (*e.g.*, mental retardation, alcoholism, physical disabilities). One cannot help but suspect that such a child was selected to stay at home, while the others were permitted to leave (*c.f.* case on page 91).

## Conflicts within the Family

Conflicts within the family may revolve around an aged parent, or develop between the aged husband and wife. Many of these maladaptive patterns are precipitated by the vicissitudes of the aging process, and are therefore relatively recent and acute.

(a). The aged person may react by becoming unduly helpless and turning to others in the family for assistance in almost all of his life activities. This *regressive behavior* may become an excessive burden on the other family members, not only because they provide so much support but also because the regressed person frequently feels angry and guilty about his childlike dependency. His dependency is often a hostile clinging, which is self-defeating, and it may become impossible to do anything that satisfies him. Depression may color the clinical picture, in which case the depressive symptoms may have the purpose of communicating to the other family members, "Look how miserable you make me feel."

In some instances regressive behavior in one family member may be unconsciously encouraged by one or several other family members. To the latter, the burdens imposed by the regressive behavior of the former are the lesser of two evils. They are willing to pay a price, sometimes a very high one, to achieve an important gain. This gain often pertains to a power maneuver, *e.g.*, the attempt to keep the other person (the helpless one) dependent, to keep him under control, or in line. Such power plays designed to keep another person attached to oneself are security operations (albeit maladaptive) to prevent the risk of object loss. The situation can get truly complicated if both marital partners are equally involved in such neurotic interactions, and if each one simultaneously is active instigator and passive recipient.

A 63-year-old chronically disabled woman was referred for psychiatric consultation by a community agency. Her chief complaint was "I can't afford to pay for my medications anymore." She took 13 types of medication every day. Especially significant was what her husband said during the interview. He considered himself almost as disabled as his wife. The medication count in his case came to seven. He stated that, if he no longer could take care of his wife, he would feel like killing himself. Underlying this neurotic interaction was the dual need in both partners to be at once the helpless, passive recipient and the helpful, concerned caretaker. This pattern of vicarious dependency gratifications had begun after the children had left and sexual intimacies had stopped. The ensuing vacuum had been filled by regressive activities, *i.e.*, hypochondriacal concerns. Both partners needed each other for consensual validation of their new (regressive) identity. Only in the realm of physical symptoms could they still relate to each other. The maladaptive nature of the interaction is pointed up by the continuous escalation of medications, and increasing despair ("I'll kill myself if I can't take care of her anymore").

Management consisted of allowing them to view each other and themselves as physically sick; reducing the medications by 75 percent, enough to eliminate financial stress but not so much to cast doubt on the authenticity of their physical symptoms; and introducing a set of caretakers, one for each partner. If the new caretaker had been one and the same for both partners, there would have been a

TABLE 1. *Psychosis by Association in Patients Aged 65 or Over, Reported in English Literature**

| Case Report | | Patients Involved | | | | Characteristics of Illness | | | |
|---|---|---|---|---|---|---|---|---|---|
| Date | Author | Relationship | Age | D or S† | Assoc. (yrs.) | Diagnosis | Nature of Delusions | Hallucinations | Type |
| 1877 | Lasegue and Falret | Mother and | 66 | S | 28 | Par.schiz. | Grandiose | ? | FI |
|  |  | daughter | 28 | D |  | Par.schiz. | Grandiose | ? |  |
| 1888 | Tuke | Husband | 70 | ? | 26 | Par.schiz. | P & A | ? | FS |
|  |  | and wife | 60 | ? |  | Par.schiz. | P & A | ? |  |
| 1897 | Elliot | Sister and | 75 | ? | 25 | Par.schiz. | P & A | Aud. | FS |
|  |  | sister | 65 | ? |  | Par.schiz. | P & A | Aud. |  |
| 1917 | Clark | Father and | 68 | D | life | Par.schiz. | P & A | ? | FI |
|  |  | son | ? | S |  | ? | P & A | ? |  |
| 1934 | Gotten | Father and | 73 | D | life | Par.schiz. | Religious | Yes | FC |
|  |  | daughter | 33 | S |  | Par.schiz. | Rel. S & P | Yes |  |
| 1936 | Grover | Sister and | 65 | D | 46 | Par.schiz. | P & A | Aud. | FC |
|  |  | sister | 67 | S |  | Par.schiz. | P & A | ? |  |
|  |  | Mother and | 70 | S | 7 | Par.schiz. | ? | Aud. | FS |
|  |  | daughter | 29 | S |  | Par.schiz. | ? | Aud. |  |
|  |  | and daughter | 26 | D |  | Par.schiz. | ? | Aud. |  |
| 1940 | Postle | Mother and | 81 | D | 25 | Par.schiz. | P & A | None | FS |
|  |  | daughter | 48 | S |  | Par.schiz. | P & A | ? |  |
| 1942 | Gralnick | Mother and | 66 | D | life | Par.schiz. | P | Yes | FC |
|  |  | daughter | 46 | S |  | Par.schiz. | P | No |  |
|  |  | Twin sis. and | 66 | D | life | Paranoia | P | No | FC |
|  |  | twin sis. | 66 | S |  | Par.schiz. | P | No |  |
| 1943 | Kibzey | Father and | 70 | S | life | Paranoia | P & S | No | FC |
|  |  | daughter | 33 | S |  | Par.schiz. | P & S | ? |  |
|  |  | and daughter | 27 | D |  | Par.schiz. | P & S | Aud. |  |

| Year | Author | Relationship | Age | | Duration | Diagnosis | | Hallucination | Type |
|---|---|---|---|---|---|---|---|---|---|
| 1949 | Schmidt | Husband | 66 | S | 40 | Simple schiz. | P & A | No | FI |
|  |  | and wife | 63 | D |  | Par.schiz. | P & A | Aud. & tactile | FI |
| 1956 | Dewhurst | Sister and | 74 | D | 34 | Sen.Par.Psy. | P & S | ? | FS |
|  |  | sister | 64 | S |  | Sen.Par.Psy. | P & S | Visual | FS |
|  |  | Sister and | 78 | D | ? | Senile Psy. | P & S | ? | FS |
|  |  | sister | 71 | S |  | Senile Psy. | P & S | Aud. | FS |
|  |  | Mother and | 80 | D | 42 | Par.schiz. | P & A | Aud. | FI |
|  |  | daughter | 42 | S |  | Par.schiz. | P & A | Aud. | FI |
| 1963 | Waltzer | Father and | 72 | D | 17 | Par.schiz. | P & A | ? | FS |
|  |  | mother and | 37 |  |  | Par.schiz. | P & A | ? | FS |
|  |  | 9 children | 4–15 |  |  | Par.schiz. & emotional | P & A | Not stated | FS |
| 1970 | McNiel | Sister and | 72 | D-S | life | Par.schiz. | P & A | No | FS |
|  |  | sister | 77 | S-D |  | Par.schiz. | P & A | No | FS |

* Reprinted from McNiel et al.[12] by permission of the editor of the Journal of the American Geriatric Society.

† D: dominant; S: submissive; P: persecutory; A: aggressive; S: sexual; FS: folie simultanée; FI: folie imposée; FC: folie communiquée.

risk of negative transferences, in the form of a destructive sibling rivalry between husband and wife.[13]

**(b).** In the case of regression, interpersonal relationships have changed but they are not broken off. In *withdrawal* there is a moving away from other people, not primarily physically, but emotionally. Withdrawal of this kind threatens to disrupt interpersonal relations, a fact of great importance because maintaining contacts with others is a crucial need for aging persons. The pattern of withdrawal may lead to isolation with its risks of self-absorption, hypochondriasis, disuse atrophy of social skills, or progressive loss of contact with reality.

**(c).** Regression and withdrawal represent flight responses (moving away from). It is also possible that the aging family member *moves against* others. This happens when he perceives them to be responsible for his plight (through projection). This pattern is usually associated with aggressive behavior, ideas of being neglected or maltreated, and angry accusations. Such a paranoid reaction is maladaptive because others in the family will respond with a counterattack. The response confirms the paranoid person's idea that his suspicions were correct after all.

**(d).** Another type of aggressive reaction to stress is the attempt to *control* others. The individual may feel that others are capable of providing satisfaction, but he is uncertain that they are willing to provide it. The efforts to gain control are security and power operations manifested in several possible ways. One may manipulate others by trying to make them feel guilty, by flattery, by physical force, by depressive or self-destructive behavior. Or, one may attain a dominating position by making the other person dependent on oneself, by keeping him childlike, sick, or incompetent. If this control is directed at a submissive person, there may be no conflict; most people, however, resent being manipulated and will respond with various countermaneuvers. As a result, family members may spend tremendous amounts of time and energy in this tug-of-war. The effects of such excessive security operations can be harmful not only to the aging person himself, but also to younger members of the family. A (rather tragicomical) example of this is the following case.

A 50-year-old man was hospitalized because of recurrent depressions. He had been living with an uncle for the last twenty years. The circumstances which brought the patient and his uncle (then 62 years old) together were as follows. The aging uncle had no immediate family, but did have a big estate. The patient, then 30 years old, was asked by the uncle to live with him on his farm and to take care of him. As a reward the uncle would, upon his death, leave the patient all his material possessions. The patient had figured that this was a winning proposition. He admitted having had the thought that his uncle, being sickly, would not live but a few more years, whereupon all his uncle's wealth would be his. But the uncle did not die at his appointed time. In his own mind, the patient had given him five to ten years of additional life when he had moved in with the uncle. When ten years had passed, however, the uncle was still living, and the expenses incurred in providing medical and nursing care inexorably nibbled away at the estate. About this time the patient suffered his first depression. But he stayed on the farm with his uncle: since he already had invested ten years of his life in this gamble, he felt that he could not afford to back out. During the next ten years, the uncle continued to be alive, the estate continued to shrink, and the patient became more depressed.

**(e).** Instead of moving against others, a person may turn against himself and become *depressed*. This also involves a shift from primarily interpersonal to primarily intrapsychic pathology. In fact, the family may often be quite unaware that one of them is actually suffering from a depression. This is of great practical importance in view of the fact that suicide is a serious risk of depression in elderly men.

The case example, described above illustrates not only the attempt to control others, but also the turning of hostility against the self. The patient clearly had had death wishes toward his beneficent uncle. As the uncle overstayed his welcome, the intensity of the patient's death wishes increased proportionately. In this instance, it was difficult for the patient to face the death wishes and realistically come to grips with them, because he had solemnly resolved to give his uncle the best of care.

**(f).** In some families we can observe a complex interaction involving regression, hypochondriasis, and competition. This transaction may be described by the phrase, *"Who can be the sickest?"* Characteristically, this involves two persons, *e.g.*, an aged marital couple, who have become progressively more dependent because of age-related loss of autonomy. They have begun to relate to each other in the manner of sibling rivalry, competing for the attention and support of a relative or parent figure, *e.g.*, social workers.[13] The intervention needed here is to arrange adequate support for both partners individually, and to convey the idea that support of one of them is not at the expense of the other. Only then will they feel secure enough to give up using physical symptoms in the service of competition and attention getting.

An aging couple was referred for psychiatric consultation, because of their constant bickering and arguing. Each had a number of chronic illnesses. The husband, now 83, used to be a mild mannered, easy going man. But since the onset of arthritis and heart disease, which limited his activities and made him more dependent on his wife (76 years old), his friendliness had been eclipsed by more and more irascibility. His wife, never having seen this side of him, had felt taken aback but tried to accomodate him. Her efforts along this line began to falter when her own health began to fail while her husband's regressive behavior (the irascibility) continued to worsen. At this point, a social case worker had entered the scene, but the more she tried to help out, the more antagonism developed between her two clients. It was a baffling situation, because "both these people used to be so nice." Then, an exacerbation of the husband's heart disease required his hospitalization. During this time, both husband and wife reverted to their habitual friendliness. After the husband's release from the hospital, the bickering began again, with a crescendo at each visit by the case worker. Then the wife needed to be hospitalized, and again both were more peaceful during the separation. But once she was back home, the dissonance returned as well. And so it went, on and on, for two years. Eventually it became clear that the hospitalizations were breathing spells for the two combatants. Both husband and wife showed regressive behavior which had a potentiating effect on each other; each had developed a strong transference toward the case worker. They competed for attention by putting each other down and playing up their own symptoms. The caseworker, the family physician, and the psychiatrist reached a consensus that it would be best to place the couple together in a rest home, and provide each one with an individual case worker. The security of the rest home and the reassuring knowledge of "having my own caseworker" acted in combination to decrease their anxiety, hypochondriacal games, and destructive sibling rivalry. A follow-up revealed that, once again, they had become the nice persons they used to be.

## REFERENCES

1. KASSEL, V.: Polygyny after 60. *Geriatrics 21:* 214–218, 1966.
2. SHEPS, J.: New developments in family diagnosis in emotional disorders of old age. *Geriatris 14:* 443–449, 1959.
3. SAVITSKY, E. AND SHARKEY, H.: The geriatric patient and his family—study of family interaction in the aged. *J. Geriatr. Psychiatry 5:* 3–19, 1972.
4. MILLER, M. B., BERNSTEIN, H., and SHARKEY, H.: Denial of parental illness and maintenance of familial homeostasis. *J. Am. Geriatr. Soc. 21:* 278–285, 1973.
5. TOWNSEND, P.: The Family Life of Old People. Penguin Books, London, 1957.
6. BIRREN, J. E.: Life review, reconciliation and termination. *In :* The Psychology of Aging, Chap. 12. Prentice Hall, Inc., Englewood Cliffs, N. J., 1964.
7. BUTLER, R. N.: The life review: an interpretation of reminiscence in the aged. *Psychiatry 26:* 109–114, 1963.
8. PAYNE, E. C.: Depression and suicide. *In:* Modern Perspectives in the Psychiatry of Old Age, Chap. 13, J. G. Howells, ed. Brunner-Mazel, New York, 1975. pp. 290–312.
9. BUNCH, J.: Recent bereavement and suicide. *J. Psychosom. Res. 163:* 361, 1972.
10. LIEBERMAN, M. A., PROCK, V. N., and TOBIN, S. S.: Psychological effects of institutionalization. *J. Gerontol. 23:* 343, 1968.
11. GRALNICK, A.: Folie à deux—the psychosis of association. *Psychiatr. Q. 16:* 230–263, 1942.
12. MCNIEL, J., VERWOERDT, A., and PEAK, D. T.: Folie à deux in the aged: review and case report of a role reversal. *J. Am. Geriatr. Soc. 20:* 316–323, 1972.
13. LAVERTY, R.: Reactivation of sibling rivalry in older people. *Soc. Work 7:* 23–30, 1962.

# 18

# environmental planning

With advancing age, the capacity for homeostasis gradually declines; the range of adjustment and adaptation becomes smaller and narrower. This aspect of aging, the *decreased effectiveness of homeostasis*, deserves to be emphasized because it implies an important principle: in environmental planning one should not attempt primarily to adjust the aged person to the demands of the environment, but to adapt the environment to the needs and limitations of the aged person. When the environment (both in its physical and social aspects) has been adjusted to meet the needs of the aging individual, a state of equilibrium and health prevails. On the other hand, discrepancy between environmental stresses and capacity to cope with them leads to a state of disequilibrium and disease. For effective environmental planning, it is necessary to have a working knowledge of the specific needs and limitations resulting from the aging process.

## PRINCIPLES AND PRACTICAL IMPLEMENTATION

Biological, age-related alterations occur in all of the organ systems. Changes in anatomic structure include decrease in size (atrophy), degeneration (*e.g.*, arteriosclerosis), changes in the connective tissue (*e.g.*, arthritis), and so on. Associated with these are physiological changes which are of interest from a practical point of view.

### Neuropsychological Changes

(a). Complaints about *impaired vision* are extremely common and may pertain to cataracts, glaucoma, and macular degeneration resulting from arteriosclerosis. Cataract surgery can be performed regardless of age and with few risks of complications. If macular degeneration is also present, however, the surgery will be less beneficial.[1] Generally, because of diminished visual acuity, there is need for greater illumination. In twilight and in the dark, visual impairment is especially prominent; hence the frequent occurrence of confusion and the risk of accidents during nighttime.

(b). *Hearing losses* are practically universal, especially for high tones and sounds. For this reason an elderly person may comprehend the spoken words of a man but not those of a woman. It is important to speak

223

slowly, enunciate clearly, and to face the person to facilitate lip reading. A person who is continually unable to comprehend what others are saying frequently becomes suspicious. As with so many other prosthetic devices, the aged person frequently has problems in accepting a hearing aid and making effective use of it.

(c). The *brain* serves mental functions and neuropsychological capacities, such as thinking, perception, intelligence, memory, learning, and coordination of motor behavior. With aging, most of these functions occur at a slower tempo; but these changes are by no means uniform, and they vary from person to person. Individual personality factors and past life experiences have a significant influence on the final outcome.

Life long practices and habits are not likely to change easily in the later years, and in planning *activity programs* for the aged, it is well to remember this. The program should be in keeping with the individual's habits and his potentials. The capacity for learning is not lost, although more time is needed to acquire new habits, ideas, or skills. An important principle is that functions which have been used regularly throughout life, and continue to be exercised in later years, tend to remain relatively more intact; this principle applies not only to intellectual functions, but also to neuromuscular skills, exercise tolerance, sexual capabilities, social competence, and so on.

General *intelligence*, once it reaches its peak, may maintain this level in old age, especially if people continue to be active and if they suffer no deterioration through extensive physical and neurological changes. Education fosters maintenance of intellectual ability; continued learning throughout life probably has a similar effect. Older people may compensate for a decline in intelligence by modifying their behavior or by adopting alternative responses (emphasis on accuracy rather than speed of performance). A high level of intelligence, a good education, and a continuous practice in exercising the capacity to learn may delay the onset of intellectual decline. Therefore, it is useful to develop continuing education programs for the aged. Some may want to complete high school or college education; others may want to pursue special interests and talents. Older citizens may be encouraged to participate actively in community affairs, especially organizations for and of the elderly themselves. Aged persons could be trained to function as "friendly visitors." The stimulation involved in such activities is likely to have a beneficial effect on overall intellectual alertness.

General loss in *speed of function* affects many complex psychological processes. This slowing of response is largely related to altered brain function rather than the result of changes in the peripheral organs. The organization of behavior becomes progressively more difficult and accuracy is stressed above speed. The psychomotor skills involved in driving are also affected.[2] Healthy people in their sixties and seventies are more frequently involved in highway accidents than middle-aged persons, but they are safer drivers than teen-agers and many people in their twenties. Although reflexes are often slower, the elderly driver tends to exercise greater caution and better judgment than the younger driver.

*Accident prevention* is an important aspect of environmental planning for the aged. The triad of loss of touch sensations in the feet, loss of visual and auditory acuity, and psychomotor slowness predisposes the aged person to disorientation in the dark, and falling becomes a hazard. To counteract the decrements in sensory acuity, it may be useful to magnify textural and visual contrasts and to intensify auditory cues from floors and surroundings. Accidents are the third most frequent cause of death among aged males, the fifth among aged females. For every fatal accident, there are many nonfatal but disabling accidents. Accidents are caused most frequently by cars hitting the aged pedestrian; by falls, the majority of which occurs at home; and by burns.

## Musculoskeletal Changes

(a). Atrophic changes in bone structure and stiffened joints may cause reduction in height, a stooped posture, and limitation in mobility. There is loss of muscular power and a decrease in the ability to perform rapid movements at will. Lack of activity aggravates these changes, and can lead to actual disability (*e.g.*, the permanent contractions of joints of aged people who are bedridden). Although joints and ligaments become progressively stiffer, there is often good preservation of motion. Changes in the muscular system make routine tasks more difficult and, more important, tend to impair the efficiency of such vital functions as breathing, urination, and defecation. Stiffening of the rib joints may also add to respiratory difficulties.

(b). *Skeletal pain* is a frequent complaint, and may be caused by osteoporosis, osteoarthritis, or less common conditions such as gout, rheumatoid arthritis, or bone metastases. Osteoporosis is a specifically age-related, disabling condition which occurs much more frequently in women. There is need for additional research to establish the usefulness of estrogen replacement therapy in postmenopausal women, as a means to prevent the development of osteoporosis, or to treat it once it exists.

(c). *Hip fractures*, as a result of falls, occur frequently and illustrate the interaction of multiple pathogenic factors. The fact that a fall causes the fracture illustrates the effect of aging on bone structure. The accident of the fall itself can be precipitated by many factors: sensory deficits and deficient psychomotor coordination; lack of adequate safety precautions and accident prevention; dizziness caused by transient ischemic attacks; hypotensive episodes caused by cardiac illness or drugs (antidepressants, antipsychotics); and so on. Once a hip fracture has occurred, many new complications may develop. The immobility in bed facilitates psychological regression, which leads to more immobility and proneness to accident. Also, contractures may develop during the state of immobilization. Once a contracture exists, it is nearly impossible to correct it. Contractures develop under the same conditions as decubitus (pressure sores). They are prevented by not allowing the individual to remain immobilized in the same position, by encouraging as much activity as he is capable of, or by providing passive exercises, *i.e.*, moving the individual's arms and legs for him. Prevention of contractures and decubitus is a major nursing problem in many aged institutionalized patients. Restoring and sustaining the ability to walk is the best protection. If the patient is confined to the bed or chair, it is necessary to change his position at regular intervals. Inspection of the skin may reveal the development of anemic areas, requiring meticulous hygiene and careful massage to promote local blood flow. Once the skin has broken down and a decubitus sore has developed, the wound tends to become larger and permanent. In short, a fall causing a hip fracture, which in turn produces physical immobilization, psychological regression, and possibly decubitus and contractures, can represent a milestone on the pathway toward senile regression.

## Nutrition

(a). Aged-related changes that affect *eating habits* and *nutritional status*, include loss of teeth, and mandibular atrophy; atrophic changes in the tongue, tastebuds, and gastric glands; decreased gastrointestinal motility; decreased need for caloric intake; and so on. Changes in eating patterns include a decreased fluid intake, increased liking for sweets, and a preference for meals that are easy to fix and food that requires minimal chewing efforts. Associated with these, there is a greater risk of malnutrition, vitamin deficiencies, anemias, painful conditions in the mouth because of ill-fitting dentures, constipation, and so on. The loss of teeth is a serious narcissistic trauma and physical loss. The subsequent mandibular atrophy makes it difficult to develop fitting dentures. Because dentures tend to be painful, older persons often disregard or "lose" them.

(b). The *psychological aspects* of food and eating are also important. Food may symbolize affection or pleasure, security or strength. For many persons, eating is not only a matter of intake of calories, but also a social experience. Thus, people who live alone may begin to neglect their meals. Poor eating habits result in decreased physical and mental vigor which, in turn, aggravates the poor eating syndrome. On the other hand, social isolation may create a constellation in which eating is the only pleasant experience in a bleak existence. When food replaces company, overeating or regressive food cravings may be the result.

(c). In advising *specific regimes* of nutrition for various medical illnesses, it is useful to weigh the pros (of improving physical aspects of the illness) and the cons (of depriving the patient from psychologically satisfying experiences). It is possible that any physical gains are outweighed by the development of emotional distress. A cardiac patient, for example, may be told to go on a low calorie, low fat, low cholesterol, low salt diet, and to stop smoking and drinking alcoholic beverages. His cardiac status may improve on this regime, but the patient may develop a depression that cripples him more than his heart disease did. The important point is to treat the whole patient, to evaluate physical and psychological aspects, to assess their relative importance and mutual effects on each other, and to treat both of them simultaneously.

Because the psychological and social aspects of food and eating are so important, special booklets describing attractive and adequate menus for older people could be prepared and made available to community agencies for distribution. Such pamphlets could also be sent to the medical practitioners in the community. Perhaps even local restaurants and cafeterias might be interested along this line. Specific attention in the area of nutrition should be directed toward aged people who live alone or who require special diets because of illness. With regard to the institutionalized aged, it would be useful for a "geriatric dietitian" to have periodic consultation with managers of boarding homes, nursing homes, and other extended care facilities to discuss nutritional, psychological and social aspects of meals.

## ENVIRONMENTAL CHANGES

### The Elderly Person and His Family

(a). The move to an institution, e.g., a boarding home, nursing home, or mental hospital, usually is the final outcome of a long difficult series of events. When the elderly person has been living at home with relatives, some degree of psychological stress and friction is the rule rather than the exception.[3] Although these problems in the family are not necessarily abnormal, it is useful to be alert to their existence. The psychological stress may arise from several sources, such as the children's inability to accept age changes in the parent; the family's frustration about the aged person's inability to cope with the physical or mental problems; irritation because of the lack of improvement in the elderly person; and guilt about increasingly strong wishes to be freed of the burden of caring for one's disabled parent. Usually, a mixture of these emotions and attitudes is present in family members. The aged parent himself may vacillate between a wish to be close to and dependent on his children, and feelings of guilt or resentment about this dependency. Such ambivalence, a mixture of positive and negative feelings, may have a significant effect on the *making of decisions*. Effective decision making, e.g., concerning a possible move to a boarding home, requires a clear comprehension of the issues at stake. When positive and negative attitudes are both present (ambivalence), it becomes more difficult to have an undistorted view of the overall situation. This is particularly true when one set of feelings is being suppressed. The suppressed thoughts and feelings, however, continue to exert influence. The opposing sets of attitudes lead to impaired decision making, or persistent doubts about decisions that have been made. A relative's guilt feelings, for example, may prompt him to interpret the move to the boarding home as a rejection. If the decision amounts to a postponement of effective action, this will only aggravate the problem.

(b). Timely *counseling* and *guidance* concerning the issues at stake, with clarification of interfering emotional factors and support in carrying out a rational plan, represents the best intervention in such situations. In determining what course of action is best, each case should be evaluated individually, with consideration of the following factors:

—*Patient:* his disability for usual life activities; the extent to which he is harmful to himself or to others, or is a social nuisance.

—*Family:* economic resources (financial resources, available space in the home, etc.); attitudes toward the aged family member (hostility, rejection, ambivalence, ratio of ill will *versus* goodwill).[4]

—*Community:* availability of mental hospital, nursing homes, boarding homes; various programs of service for the aged.

Only by taking these factors into consideration, can one arrive at a plan satisfactory to the patient and his family. It may seem rather obvious that the relatives need professional assistance in decisions involving placement of a psychiatrically ill aged family member. Yet one gets the impression that such professional assistance is often not available; or if it is, that the relatives are not aware of it and do not seek it. In many instances, counseling or guidance, or the services of information and referral agencies, may actually be more useful to the family than to the patient himself. The presence in the home of an aged person with psychiatric illness is a stressful burden on the entire family, and may even precipitate psychopathology in the other family members.

## Moving to a Boarding or Nursing Home

(a). Whenever feasible, it is good practice to enlist the cooperation of the aged person himself. He should not as a rule, be moved to a boarding home without his prior knowledge and approval. He should not be "taken for a ride." Ideally, the transfer to an institution or chronic care facility involves a consensus between the aged individual, the significant family members, and a third party (social worker, physician, and the operator of the boarding or nursing home). A move should not be carried out suddenly, without the necessary preparation, because this may lead to a "transplantation shock" in the aged person.[5, 6] In preparing him, one could arrange a series of preliminary visits to the boarding home before the move. When the move takes place, the individual should be encouraged to take some of his (most personal) possessions with him.

The *traumatic effects* of environmental changes on the aged person are generally well known. Essentially, a relocation can amount to a dislocation.

A 74-year-old man had lived alone for years in a dilapidated shack. Holes in the walls permitted wind, rain, and cold to come in. Rats were visitors of all seasons. The man lived in filth and constant danger of being burned (he used a wood stove to prepare meals). For years, the social service department had tried to improve the habitat of this recluse, but in vain. None of the suggested changes or the material assistance was accepted. Finally, a solution seemed to present itself. A well-to-do farmer nearby had a cabin and offered it to our hermit. The cabin was a fine little building with conveniences such as plumbing and electricity. The old man was persuaded to make the move, and a long-standing problem (which had been a concern throughout the small community) appeared to have been solved in a humane fashion. A few days after the move, however, the social worker received an urgent call from the farmer in whose cabin the old man was now living. Upon her arrival, the social worker found the man in a state of acute confusion; he was lying in his bed, with the evidence of fecal incontinence all around him. (Neither disorientation nor fecal incontinence had been a problem, before then.)

The significance of this episode lies in the fact that, to the old man, home was the old shack where he had lived for decades. It was there that he felt he belonged, not in the nice, new cabin. But those around him felt exactly the other way around. What mattered in the end, was that the physical relocation became a psychological dislocation. In the unfamiliar environment, the old man lost his grip on the world, and this loss of control was reflected in the function of his sphincters: they too lost their grip. The loss of sphincter control was part of a general loss of control.

(b). Such untoward reactions to unfamiliar environments can be prevented by allowing the older person to make the change in a more gradual way. A comparison can be made with the mechanisms of immunity. A foreign element introduced into the organism elicits different reactions depending on quantitative factors. A large amount of an alien substance (virus, toxin, etc.) may overwhelm the organism's defense mechanisms. A smaller amount, however, stimulates some kind of defense or resistance. Repeated administration of small amounts can build up a solid immunity against the invasion of large amounts of alien elements. What is true on the physiological level, applies also to the mental apparatus and the psychological level.

## The Concept of a Home

Some psychological and interpersonal aspects of the boarding or nursing home deserve further discussion, with special emphasis on the concept of home. We will define a home as a place where one belongs and where one has one's belongings; to feel at home is to belong. And, usually, a home is a place where a family lives. How does this apply to such facilities as a rest home, boarding home, nursing home, or even the chronic geriatric wards in mental hospitals?

(a). First, inasmuch as the home is a place of belonging, it is our goal to promote in the elderly person residing in the institution a sense of belonging, and to make him feel at home. Efforts in this direction include the following:

1. The amount and type of space allocated to the elderly resident should be in keeping with the need for *privacy* and the principle of territoriality. This principle involves the delineation of a space which the person can regard as "my own." The boundaries of this space can be compared to what, on a psychological level, is the ego boundary. It is that space around me, in the center of which I myself am located—extending from me to its boundaries. Everything within the perimeter of that space is felt to be my own, while the space beyond it is felt to be that of the "other." My private space can be invested, filled as it were, with my psychic energy or interest. The concept of privacy includes the sense of private ownership, and the opportunity to be on my own and to have visual privacy. Without being shielded from the eyes of others, there is a loss of personal dignity.

There are several ways to allocate space in such a way that the above requirements are met. Boundaries between the respective spaces belonging to the various residents are no problem when there is a one-person-per-room situation. With two persons in one room, a curtain in the middle can be a boundary that also insures visual privacy. On wards with several patients, it is useful (but not easy) to arrange beds, chairs, nightstands, and so on in clusters and configurations that suggest and delineate individual life spaces.

2. Within the boundaries of this private space, the person is to have subspaces for his *personal belongings*. The location and characteristics of these spaces (*e.g.*, individualized color schemes, type of furniture, pictures, plants, etc.) may facilitate in the aged person an experience of recognition that this is "my own," of remembering that "this belonging of mine is here, and that one over there."

A 67-year-old woman belonged to that category of patients designated as having grown old in the institution. It was no longer possible to determine whether her intellectual and emotional deficiencies were the long-term consequences of simple schizophrenia or the manifestations of mental retardation (a differential diagnosis which is not always easy to make). The patient shared her room with three other elderly females. Her only furniture was a bed and a nightstand. Generally, she seemed mildly content and never displayed much emotion. During the routine ward rounds, we discovered that she was using the lower compartment of her nightstand as a crib for a doll. The crib was a primitive thing, consisting of pieces and remnants of towels. The doll had been assigned a permanent berth in this make-believe crib. When we expressed our pleasure at the sight of this touching scene, the patient responded with a smile. In fact, the only times she would smile at all were in connection with the doll. The doll in the nightstand represented a transitional object, which the patient treated as she herself wished to be taken care of (vicarious gratification). Also, the nightstand (something "out there") had become a part of herself. The boundaries of herself (her ego, her body image) had extended so as to incorporate that dark, intimate enclosure with its precious contents. Whether or not this is the acting out of a pregnancy fantasy is a matter of speculation. This same patient would regularly feed a patient in the bed across from her, who was blind.

3. People differ greatly with regard to the amount of personal space, and the distance or closeness to the other (their neighbor) which they consider optimal. Part of the sense of belonging is the feeling of being part of a neighborhood. Some persons like (or don't mind) being close up against each other, whereas others need to have a good bit of distance between themselves and their neighbor. Some of these differences are socioculturally determined; at other times they are manifestations of specific psychopathology. Chronic patients on the wards of mental hospitals tend to distribute themselves in characteristic patterns across the ward space: most seem to feel crowded, and try to maintain maximum

distance so that they are evenly distributed across the ward space. At the other extreme are those patients in search of closeness, physical touch, or togetherness. Such a patient may get in bed with another one, or is always following another patient around. Although the final outcomes of chronic schizophrenia and senile dementia have much in common, it is our impression that one of the differences is that the chronic schizophrenic retains his distance, whereas senile patients often reach out for contact as if starved for a personal touch. This reaching out for physical touch is also emotionally touching: it has a basic quality of urgency conveying the wish, "Be with me." This physical reaching out has its corollary in the verbal question often asked, "When can I go home?" If one then asks where home is, one is surprised to discover that the patient has no idea where his home is. Or, he may talk about a home he once had in the remote past. One can't help but feel that the question "When can I go home?" is a primitive, concrete way of expressing something more abstract, like, "This place is not like home. I wish I could be at home, or feel at home. Is there anything you can do to make me feel at home here?"

An elderly male patient on the geriatric ward always had a small travel bag, containing his belongings, placed right in the center of his bed. The patient, who was profoundly confused, never was able to give a verbal explanation of his behavior. When asked about it, he just smiled. For that matter, he never tried to pick up his bag and leave. Yet his actions signalled that he was ready to go home.

**4.** Part of the concept of neighborhood is *communal space* where I can be in touch with others. This being in touch is not first of all physical, but represents contacts involving the experiences of seeing, hearing, and sharing things. This communal space ideally should contain activity centers that provide opportunities for a wide spectrum of human interests.

**5.** It is also necessary to pay attention to the *dimension of time*. The sense of time comes about as one moves through space. In the same manner that allocated space is to be made private and personal, and filled with my belongings, so time should be filled with activities that are meaningful. The experience of the flow of time is an essential ingredient of optimal mental functioning. When time ceases to flow, a state of stagnation, of timelessness, results. This will exert a powerful regressive pull upon the patient. When he succumbs to it, he will be sliding into a state of regression, autistic withdrawal, or irreversible senility.

**(b).** Now what about the home as a place where a family lives? Obviously it is not possible to replicate family life in the usual sense of the word. Upon entering the home, however, the elderly person takes with him characteristic attitudes and ways of relating to others. To a large extent these feelings and attitudes are derived from past life experiences, including those which the individual had with his parents, siblings, and children. These feelings, expectations, attitudes—ways of looking at the world and others—are transferred from one situation to another. Thus, emotions, ideas, and expectations may be detached from the people in one situation, transferred, and attached onto persons in the new situation. This phenomenon of *transference* is universal in human relations.

When transference phenomena occur in an institutional setting, they will vary depending on the type of home and the personality of the resident. Because a boarding home is a home with an operator (manager, director) in charge, the operator may be seen as a parental figure and the other residents as siblings. This may happen regardless of any age differences. Thus, an elderly resident may (unconsciously) view a home manager 30 years his junior as a maternal figure. He may begin to relate to her in ways similar to the relationship he once had with his real mother. The concept of transference is not only of theoretical interest, but frequently there are important practical implications. This is especially true when negative feelings (hostility, guilt, envy) are being transferred. An individual who, at one time, had a troublesome relationship with his real mother may (again, unconsciously) expect the same kind of difficulties with a rest home operator. If one is alert to the possibility of such transference distortions and tries to understand their underlying meaning, one is in a better position to tolerate unusually difficult behavior and to find the proper means to handle the real problem. In this connection, special attention may be needed for the home operator as well as the resident or patient. Possibly helpful would be information exchange sessions specifically aimed at consulting with the supervisory staff of boarding homes, nursing homes, and other long-term care facilities.

## THE SPECTRUM OF COMPREHENSIVE SERVICES

Comprehensive services are based on the recognition that a person's condition is determined by physical, psychological, interpersonal, cultural, economic, and environmental factors. Because these factors interact in a complex manner, comprehensive services must be flexible. To implement comprehensiveness, as well as individualization, of services, rigidity in organization should be avoided. A person with an economic catastrophe should receive assistance just as quickly as a patient with a serious illness. Aged persons in need should receive appropriate help without having to go through unnecessary channels. To attain comprehensiveness, flexibility, and speediness of services, two sets of community resources are needed: a central agency that gathers and distributes information, and a spectrum of service facilities and programs concerned with medical care, health maintenance, economic and vocational assistance, and so on.

### The Information and Referral Agency

The central facility that collects and distributes information relevant to aging is essentially an information and referral service.[7] Its basic functions include the following:

(a). *Information.* The information and referral service aims at the distribution of pertinent information. It needs to make itself highly visible and well known to the community, especially to the aged. This can be done with the aid of local news media and by distributing special brochures and pamphlets. Efforts must be made to inform aged persons how to take advantage of community resources, and find their way through the system.

**(b).** *Evaluation and Planning.* This includes periodic review of existing services, and the conceptualization and initiation of new services. In these efforts, the central facility (or the information and referral service) can make specific contributions in terms of organizing meetings on the local level, and disseminating pertinent information regarding policies and programs on the higher levels (regional, state, and federal). The planning and implementation of local developments are facilitated when they are attuned to, and fit in with, larger trends and currents. Program development is a "construction job" involving two phases of activity that differ with regard to their direction. The first, that of building from below upward, requires local initiative (in our case, it would be optimal to include a representative cross-section of the elderly population). The second phase is the process of building, from above downward; this involves governmental initiative. Both types of processes are essential for program development. The risk to be avoided is that "the twain never shall meet"—that halfway, the tracks do not meet, and that the two components of program development fail to interlock with each other.[8]

**(c).** *Facilitation and Coordination.* The objective here is to initiate appropriate channels of contact and communication between important local services and facilities. For example, the moving of aged persons from their home to a boarding home, nursing home, general hospital or mental hospital (and subsequent moves between these places) usually is not well regulated. This is largely attributable to lack of coordination between these institutions. What needs to be avoided in the development of multiple programs and services is the risk that everyone begins to assume that the problems will be solved by somebody else. With increasing numbers of service programs, the amount of buck passing can increase in geometric terms. The elderly patient is passed from one agency (facility, program) to the next. The danger in a community network of multiple programs is that the staff of the respective agencies begins to believe that they have solved the problem by referring the patient elsewhere. In fact, they only solved their own problem, *i.e.*, they got rid of the patient. Meanwhile, the patient himself falls down in the gaps of the network; he falls between the slats. Eventually, the patient may show up again at the initial agency after he has made the rounds. When he returns at the starting point (the initial agency), it would be part of the pattern of the self-deception to view his return as a readmission. On the contrary, the patient is not readmitted for a recurrence of his problem or illness, but he returns because his problem was never ameliorated in the first place.[9, 10]

**(d).** *Central Clearinghouse.* To reduce the frequency of such unfortunate malfunctions, the central facility (information and referral service) might explore the use of a special system of data collection and retrieval. This would involve a kind of central registry on elderly persons who, at any point, have entered the network of community service programs. The information to be recorded would include routine identifying data, data pertaining to the presenting problems (type, severity, cause), data on proposed problem solving or treatment plan, and follow-up data. The appropriate agency records the data, and transmits them to the information and referral facility for data storage and further processing. The processing involves, among other things, the transmission of data to agencies (facilities, programs) that are nodal points in the network of services. The transmission and distribution of data could be routinized or automated so that relatively little additional expenditures of time and money are required. The objective is to have pertinent agencies share available information on elderly clients who have entered the system, and to keep this information up to date. Such a clearinghouse or registry would prevent unnecessary expenditures of professional effort (*e.g.*, repetitive history taking), the pitfalls of the patient's falling between the slats, and so on. It would also provide a valuable repository of data for research activities. The automation of data collection, retrieval, and distribution could be done by means of computers.

The advantages of data sharing need to be weighed against the disadvantages, *viz.*, the risks of loss of privacy and confidentiality. The constraints of interagency data sharing are set by ethical principles and legal guidelines aimed at the protection of individual privacy and privileged information.

(e). *Case detection* involves special efforts aimed at locating aged persons who have problems. Such individual case identification is facilitated by periodic local publicity about the existence of an information and referral service. It also requires the active interest and participation of key people in the community, such as physicians, the clergy, social case workers, department of public health, and so on. Other services can be added depending on specific local needs and conditions. Thus, if an information and referral service is located in the outpatient clinic of a hospital, certain medical services may be incorporated into the basic structure. Be that as it may, there should be clear channels of communication with all other agencies and services relevant to the aged; actual physical proximity to other facilities is desirable from a practical point of view.

## Comprehensive Service and Community Care

(a). *Diagnostic centers* or "well-aging clinics" can be located in the out-patient clinic of a general hospital, in local departments of public health or social service, or they could be associated with a day care center or highrise apartment building for the aged. Timely detection of disease in the aged is always a problem. All too often patients come to medical attention at a relatively advanced stage of their illness. The assessment center would place primary emphasis on health maintenance since anxiety is not an optimal motivator. Some individuals avoid physicians for fear that a serious condition will be diagnosed, that hospitalization or surgery will be recommended, and so on. A well-aging clinic could take initiative in getting aged persons regularly to the clinic for routine checkups. Attention should be given to the problems of transportation to the clinic. Some aged persons have trouble driving, whereas others have no car or live far away. Transportation can be organized by community groups, churches, department of social services, senior citizens groups, and so on. Perhaps there is merit in the idea of using buses (of the school bus variety) for transporting aged persons to such facilities as diagnostic center, hospital clinic, or day care center. The transportation expenses need to be solved by the community as a whole.[11]

**(b).** *Extended care facilities* include nursing homes and the geriatric units of mental hospitals.[12] Some general hospitals have facilities for chronically ill patients. Relatively large homes for the aged may have the capability to develop an adjoining infirmary. It is difficult to make general statements about which type of facility is most desirable. The answer depends frequently on local conditions. This caution about generalizing also applies to the statement frequently heard nowadays that elderly patients in a mental institution should return to the community as soon as possible. Indiscriminate application of such generalizations facilitates the pattern of passing the buck from one institution to another, or from the institution to the community. Again, the patient is passed from pillar to post. Frequently such moves only represent administrative (pseudo) solutions and the aged patient is the victim of the resulting confusion. Mutual collaboration between local institutions concerning each other's goals and methods would prevent much of this confusion.[13] (See Scheme 1.)

The drive to get patients back into the community may result in good or bad consequences. An example of a good result is the case of a 73-year-old man who had spent more than 40 years in a mental hospital. Having existed in almost total isolation from the rest of the world, he was unfamiliar with modern society. Reportedly, he had never seen an airplane except on T.V. It was the steady effort of one case worker who, in two years, succeeded in preparing this man for living on the outside. The two of them made frequent, regular trips into the community so that the patient could discover what life on the outside was all about, and prepare himself for the transition to a rest home.

**(c).** The success of such efforts depends on a multitude of factors: the patient's assets, the availability of health care personnel with both mature judgement and a sense of commitment, the quality of available boarding homes, and so on.[14] There is no question that the operators of many boarding homes are quite capable and responsible, and provide a living environment superior to that of the mental hospital. On the other hand, other boarding homes are inadequate, certainly when compared with the renovated geropsychiatric facilities that have begun to emerge in some mental hospitals.[12]

**(d).** *Home care programs* developed by local hospitals, the public health department, and so on are aimed at keeping selected patients at home, thus preventing the need for more expensive hospitalization. The home care team consists of a physician, visiting nurse, and other therapists (physical therapy, dietitian, social worker). Such programs

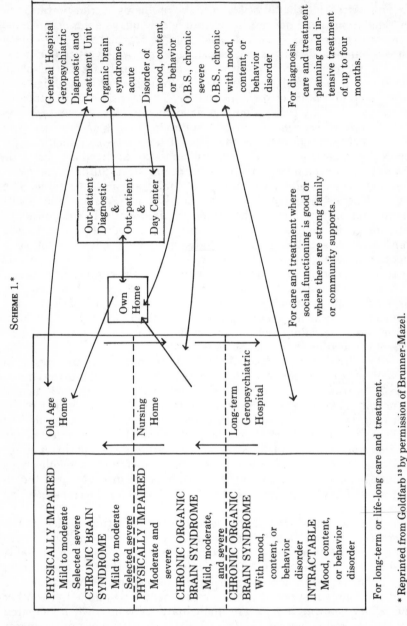

SCHEME 1.*

**Own Home**

**Out-patient Diagnostic & Out-patient & Day Center**

General Hospital Geropsychiatric Diagnostic and Treatment Unit

Organic brain syndrome, acute

Disorder of mood, content, or behavior

O.B.S., chronic severe

O.B.S., chronic with mood, content, or behavior disorder

For diagnosis, care and treatment planning and intensive treatment of up to four months.

For care and treatment where social functioning is good or where there are strong family or community supports.

Old Age Home

PHYSICALLY IMPAIRED
Mild to moderate
Selected severe

CHRONIC BRAIN SYNDROME
Mild to moderate
Selected severe

Nursing Home

PHYSICALLY IMPAIRED
Moderate and severe

CHRONIC ORGANIC BRAIN SYNDROME
Mild, moderate, and severe

Long-term Geropsychiatric Hospital

CHRONIC ORGANIC BRAIN SYNDROME
With mood, content, or behavior disorder

INTRACTABLE
Mood, content, or behavior disorder

For long-term or life-long care and treatment.

* Reprinted from Goldfarb[13] by permission of Brunner-Mazel.

can be combined with other services such as meals on wheels, friendly visitors, and so on. Again this points up the need for a central agency that can coordinate the various services and determine what package of services is indicated. The cooperation of the family members is essential in implementing home care programs.[15]

**(e).** *Homemakers* can provide some basic assistance to the aged in their own home. Some aged persons have limitations in specific areas which make it impossible for them to carry out basic activities. For example, an arthritic patient may be able to care for himself at home, but may be unable to go shopping, to do the laundry, and wash dishes. In such a case, a homemaker may make the difference between the individual staying at home and being institutionalized. Companions may live in with an older person or couple, or spend only part of the day. They may be recruited from the aged person's relatives, neighbors, and so on. The companion may receive free lodging and some compensation for her services in the home. The total expenditures are likely to be less than in the case of admission to an institution.

(f). *Friendly visitors* are volunteers who visit the aged in their homes or in the institution. Aged individuals in reasonably good health may be encouraged to become friendly visitors themselves. Some friendly visitors can get caught up, unwittingly or unwillingly, in complicated family conflicts. They may rush in where angels fear to tread. When caught in the quicksand of a family conflict, a friendly visitor will soon become a frustrated visitor. This risk implies that friendly visitors should receive preliminary training for this type work, or work under supervision.

(g). *Meals on Wheels.* The service of bringing meals to the home, is especially useful for aged persons who are isolated, require special diets, or are incapable of preparing meals. These programs also aim at preventing or breaking up any vicious circles leading to progressive undereating or overeating. Likewise, homemakers, friendly visitors, visiting nurses, and others can play an important role in altering deficient eating habits.

(h). *The day care center*, a facility where an aged person can remain during the day, may offer a variety of services and opportunities. Group activities, games, hobbies, and so on can be carried out with the help of a recreational expert, or independently. Associated with the center may be a physician, psychologist, or social worker who could provide counseling and guidance, or conduct group therapy sessions. Limited medical-geriatric services may be offered as well. In planning a day care center, attention should be given to the types of services needed in view of the local conditions in the community. Ideally, there should be enough space around the center to make gardening possible, to keep pets on the premises, to go outside for walks on the grounds, and so on. Recreational activities (e.g., music, films, discussion groups) can be organized by interested volunteers or by recreational therapists.[16]

(i). *Mental health services* can be made available through the local mental health clinic, a nearby hospital, the out-patient clinic of a general hospital, the day care center, and so on. These services are important in view of the frequent emotional disorders associated with physical illness, social isolation, or other deprivation. Effective mental health services can be offered only by a team of professionally trained individuals; the psychiatrist, the psychiatric nurse practitioner, and the psychiatric social worker represent the core of such a team. The community mental health programs would aim at methods of identifying and treating acute situational problems; counseling and guidance with regard to such problems as retirement, social role change, altered family relationships and leisure time activities; assistance to families caring for disabled or emotionally disturbed aged relatives; consultation with other community agencies, e.g., with regard to release planning for institutionalized aged patients; and organizing educational experiences for other professionals about normal and geropsychiatric aspects of aging.

(j). Other services and programs included in a comprehensive spectrum are protective services; legal aid; vocational projects; sheltered workshop; continuing education; and foster grandparents program.

## REFERENCES

1. ECKSTEIN, D.: Common symptoms and complaints of the elderly. *J. Am. Geriatr. Soc. 21:* 440–443, 1973.
2. GIANTURCO, D. T., RAMM, D., AND ERWIN, C. W.: The elderly driver and ex-driver. *In:* Normal Aging, Vol. 2, E. Palmore, ed. Duke University Press, Durham, N. C., 1974. pp. 173–179.
3. LA BARRE, M. B., JESSNER, L., AND USSERY, L.: The significance of grandmothers in the psychopathology of children. *Am. J. Orthopsychiatry 30:* 175–185, 1960.
4. GRAUER, H., BETTS, D., AND BIRNBOM, F.: Welfare emotions and family therapy in geriatrics. *J. Am. Geriatr. Soc. 21:* 21–24, 1973.
5. ALDRICH, C. K., AND MENDKOFF, E.: Relocation of the aged and disabled: a mortality study. *J. Am. Geriatr. Soc. 11:* 185–194, 1963.
6. LIEBERMAN, M. A.: Relationship of mortality rates to entrance to a home for the aged. *Geriatrics 16:* 575–579, 1961.
7. Guidelines for an Information and Counseling Service for Older Persons. Center for the Study of Aging and Human Development, Duke University, Durham, N. C., 1970.
8. SHANAS, E.: Factors affecting care of the patient: clients, government policy, role of the family and social attitudes. *J. Am. Geriatr. Soc. 21:* 394–397, 1973.
9. FRIEDMAN, J. H.: Misassignment of geriatric patients to a state mental hospital. *J. Am. Geriatr. Soc. 19:* 172, 1971.
10. State Policy and the Long Term Mentally Ill: A Shuffle to Despair. City of New York Commission on State-City Relations. 1972.
11. ROBINSON, R. A.: The assessment center. *In:* Modern Perspectives in the Psychiatry of Old Age, Chap. 18, J. G. Howells, ed. Brunner-Mazel, New York, 1975. pp. 379–396.
12. WHANGER, A. D. AND BUSSE, E. W.: Care in hospital. *In:* Modern Perspectives in the Psychiatry of Old Age, Chap. 21, J. G. Howells, ed. Brunner-Mazel, New York, 1975. pp. 450–485.
13. GOLDFARB, A. I.: Integrated services. *In:* Modern Perspectives in the Psychiatry of Old Age, Chap. 26, J. G. Howells, ed. Brunner-Mazel, New York, 1975. pp. 540–569.
14. GLADUE, J. R.: The role of the physician in the nursing home: past, present, and future. *J. Am. Geriatr. Soc. 21:* 444–449, 1973.
15. RESDORFER, E. N., PRIMANIS, G., AND DOZORETZ, L.: Family care as a useful alternative to the long term hospital confinement of geropsychiatric patients. *J. Am. Geriatr. Soc. 19:* 150, 1971.
16. McDONALD, R. D., NEULANDER, A., HALOD, O., AND HOLCOMB, N. S.: Description of a nonresidential psychogeriatric day care facility. *Gerontologist 11:* 322, 1971.

# 19

# protective
# intervention

## PROTECTIVE SERVICES: LEGAL AND PSYCHIATRIC ASPECTS

### Legal Aspects

The term protective services essentially could be used for any medical, psychiatric, or social treatment modality, but in the course of the years it has acquired a specific meaning. Nowadays, protective services pertain to those services required to protect an individual from abuse, neglect, safety hazards, mistreatment, or exploitation. They are undertaken with or on behalf of elderly persons who are unable or unwilling to secure these services for themselves, or who are without able and responsible persons acting in their behalf.

In keeping with the contemporary concern about patient's rights, laws are now being enacted to protect specifically the rights of elderly individuals. A Reporting Law for Protection of the Elderly became effective in 1974 in North Carolina.[1] The law defines an elderly person in need of protective services as any one over age 65 who is unable to perform or obtain services essential to his physical and mental health. Anyone who has reasonable cause to believe that a person over age 65 is in need of protective services must report this to the county director of social services. The county director must make a prompt and thorough evaluation, which includes a visit to the elderly person and consultation with individuals familiar with the case. After completing his evaluation, the director of social services indicates whether or not protective services are needed.

The law defines protective services in terms of measures necessary to prevent abuse or neglect. *Abuse* includes the willful infliction of physical injury or mental anguish and the deprivation by a caretaker of essential services. A *neglected* elderly person is one who lives alone and is unable to provide for himself or is not receiving the services from his *caretaker*. The latter is defined as a person responsible for the care of the elderly person as a result of family relationship or who has assumed such responsibility for the care of the elderly person voluntarily or by contract. If an elderly person consents to protective services but his caretaker objects, the director of social services may petition the district court for an order enjoining the caretaker from interfering. This petition is required to allege facts showing that the elderly person needs protective services, that he has consented to receive them, and that the caretaker refuses them to be provided. The judge may issue an order to enjoin the caretaker from interference.

The law gives the elderly person *the right to decide* whether he will consent. The county director of social services has the legal responsibility to provide protective services if the elderly person consents. If the latter does not consent, services may not be provided unless the director of social services determines that the elderly person lacks capacity to consent, in which case he may seek authority from the court to provide protective services under the procedures prescribed by the reporting law. If the elderly person consents but later withdraws his consent, the services must be terminated unless the director secures court authority to provide protective services on the grounds that the elderly person lacks the capacity to consent.

If an elderly person is abused or neglected and *lacks the capacity to consent*, the director can petition the court for an order authorizing protective services. The law requires that the district court have a hearing within 14 days after the petition is filed if sufficiently specific facts are alleged. The elderly person must receive at least five days' notice of the hearing. He has the right to be present and the right to counsel at the hearing. If the court finds that the elderly person needs protective services but lacks the capacity to consent, the judge may order that the services be provided, and designate an individual or organization to be responsible for the welfare of the elderly person and to have the right to consent to protective services in his behalf.

### Psychiatric Aspects

From the above, it has become clear that the central issue is not the contents or substance of the protective services to be rendered, but the manner in which this is done. This implies the existence of any number of factors in the situation which function as obstacles and barriers. The successful implementation of a program of protective services depends on effectively removing these obstacles, by way of skillful and effective *intervention*. Under the heading of protective intervention, our concern here is with the following questions:

What kinds of conditions in old people would cause us to depart from our usual methods of making services available?

In what way do these methods differ from the usual ones?

Are there specific conditions which require the use of certain new techniques of making services available?

### CONDITIONS REQUIRING MODIFICATION IN METHOD

Sooner or later anyone who has been working with elderly individuals in need of assistance discovers that certain problems arise in the implementation of a particular plan. There may be clear awareness that a problem exists, that a service is needed, and various services may indeed be available. But yet, obstacles begin to develop, and somehow one finds oneself unable to implement a program of action. There may be two reasons for this. First, the difficulty may rest with the clinician or practitioner himself. He may have arrived at an inaccurate evaluation of the client's problem, the service required, or both. It is also possible that, although correct with regard to the diagnosis and treatment plan, the practitioner is incapable of effective implementation because of inadequate training, or special problems such as "blind spots," personal idiosyncrasies, and sensitivities. A second set of obstacles are those presented by the client or his family who, for whatever reasons, resist efforts aimed at alleviating their distress. A review of these obstacles will be presented, with brief mention of some psychiatric conditions in which they may occur.

## Danger to Self

This category refers to self-destructiveness in general. The various patterns can be relatively involuntary and unintentional, or they can be more or less voluntary, deliberate, and willful.

**(a). Involuntary Patterns of Self-destructiveness.**

**1.** *Inability to care for self* may be attributable to physical or psychological infirmity and may involve varying degrees of disability for basic daily living activities (eating, locomotion, personal hygiene, etc.). Serious problems may develop if there is lack of adequate assistance from family or neighbors. This category occurs frequently and calls for protective services in the sense of making routine supportive care available.

**2.** *Inability to make use of available resources* may be attributable to physical isolation, *e.g.*, an aged person who lives alone, is far from neighbors, and has no means of transportation. This, too, is not an uncommon situation and does not necessarily create unusual obstacles, as long as the prospective recipient is cooperative.

In the following categories however, the obstacles are harder to overcome because the impediments are related to the individual's behavior and personality instead of external contingencies.

**3.** *Denial of Illness, Disability, or Need for Assistance.* In these cases, the aged person communicates, explicitly through verbal statements or implicitly through actions, his disagreement with, or resistance to, the opinion of others stating he needs assistance. The individual may deny the fact that he is sick or disabled; or while acknowledging the illness and disability, he may deny its seriousness or the necessity to do anything about it. Patients with severe physical illness (*e.g.*, cardiac illness or cancer) frequently deny the existence of their illness, or that the illness has serious implications. In manic patients, there may be an elated mood and grandiose behavior involving denial of underlying problems. The patient with organic brain syndrome may be unaware of many of his problems because he has lost the capacity to comprehend the real significance of what is happening to him.

**4.** *Poor judgment* is a manifestation of many psychiatric disorders. Inasmuch as good judgment is a function of intact ego functioning, the extent of poor judgment reflects impaired ego functioning. When good judgment is lost, the individual becomes accordingly more helpless and is at the mercy of forces over which he has no control. Such a person cannot protect himself adequately. Furthermore, he may inadvertently cause problems for others (*e.g.*, a senile person who squanders his savings). Judgment is affected most severely in psychotic reactions and in O.B.S.

**5.** *Faulty living habits* involve behavioral patterns which in the long run become deleterious to physical or psychological health, *e.g.*, poor eating habits, alcoholism and other addictions, poor personal hygiene, and so on. Such faulty living habits occur in many conditions, especially schizophrenia, O.B.S., mental retardation, and certain personality disorders.

**6.** *Regressive behavior* includes phenomena related to loss of mastery and control, resulting in deterioration of the personal milieu, personal hygiene, neuromuscular capacities, and sphincter control.

—Deterioration of the *personal milieu* is a common complaint. Usually, these complaints are not made by these old people themselves, but by relatives, neighbors, or case workers. There are several ways in which such problems may develop and manifest themselves. The milieu in which a person lives, the space he calls his own, is a territorial extension of the self. The maintenance of a life space requires the expenditure of energy. When the energy required to create and maintain order is unavailable, the life space becomes a microslum. An imbalance between intake and output may result in congested clutter. Diminished ability to rid the personal milieu of excess or waste materials produces conditions of hoarding and filth. Typically, the elderly individual himself is not fully aware of the extent of decay, and this may present a problem in persuading him to accept protective services (*e.g.*, home help).

—Deterioration of *personal hygiene* frequently coexists with the decay of the personal milieu. The old person becomes neglectful in bathing, grooming, and personal appearance; clothes are not cleaned or repaired, and the same old clothes may be worn constantly. Sometimes, idiosyncratic combinations are fashioned (one dress on top of another; special items such as a hat, a cane, briefcase, may become a permanent fixture of the appearance). There may be some last attempt to control the regressive drift. The individual may retreat into one room of the house, relinquishing control over the rest of his lifespace. Some individuals, oblivious to the disarray around them, become proportionately more concerned (sometimes obsessed) with personal cleanliness. A variant of the principle of sweeping dirt under the rug can be seen in some elderly women whose efforts consist of applying more and more makeup on their face. Isolated phenomena of an obsessive-compulsive nature further include increased preoccupation with housecleaning, with the purity of food, water, and utensils, and so on. One elderly male had developed the compulsive habit of washing his walking cane every day. The concerns about dirt may acquire phobic qualities; the patient becomes afraid of specific types of dirt, especially contamination of food. Various community agencies may get involved because the elderly person begins to call on them, complaining about the dangers he thinks he is exposed to, and asking for help.

**7.** *Accident proneness* may occur on the basis of unconscious guilt, or it may be attributable to sensory and motor deficits. The latter are more commonly found among the aged; impaired vision and hearing combined with motor weakness and poor coordination predispose individuals to accidents.

**(b). Voluntary Self-destructiveness.** Behavior patterns of this type appear to occur less frequently than involuntary self-destruction. When these patterns occur, they present greater problems in management, because the tendency toward self-destruction is no longer a simple drift with the individual being a helpless victim, but the tendency involves an active urge. Or again, it may manifest itself as an active resistance against any therapeutic intervention. We will mention three forms in which this self-destructive tendency may be manifested.

**1.** *Refusal of medical care* sometimes occurs in aged persons who suffer from a treatable illness but who believe that any treatment is useless. They may feel that life is over for them, preferring to be left alone to die in peace; or they may fear the discomfort and expenses associated with medical care and hospitalization. The patient with a severe depression feels that he does not deserve to get well. The paranoid patient may refuse help because he is suspicious that others try to frame him, trick him, or gang up on him.

**2.** *Extreme social isolation*, as seen in the aged recluse, usually indicates serious psychopathology. These withdrawn individuals often are quite suspicious of others, and are possibly paranoid. Because their isolation signifies a thorough insulation, it is difficult to reach out toward them; the withdrawn person misinterprets a stretched out hand as a move with hostile intent.

**3.** *Suicide* is the clearest example of active self-destructiveness. It occurs most frequently in elderly males. Suicide prevention is a crucial aspect of protective intervention, and one should be especially alert to the danger of suicide in aging white men.

## Danger to Others

**(a).** *Involuntary dangers and stresses to others* refer to situations in which the aged individual, by virtue of his specific age-related impairments, causes undue burdens on others. Neither the aged person himself, nor his family contribute to the problem by way of deliberate intent. Instead, the problem has come about from without, gradually encroaching on the patient and his family so that they tend to feel they are helpless victims of external circumstances or forces beyond their control. The aged person may be an excessive burden on his family in terms of depleting the family's financial resources, or exhausting their physical and psychological reserves. The family may continue in their attempts to care for the aged family member because of a sense of duty and loyalty, or because they do not know where to turn for help.

An aged person becomes a source of social nuisance when he is mentally so impaired that he continuously wanders away, exposes himself, is incontinent, is very boisterous, hoards a multitude of senseless items, and so on.

**(b).** *Voluntary stresses or active threats* posed by an aged individual may acquire the characteristic of deliberateness. Such an element of active initiative occurs in conditions involving "geriatric delinquency." [2, 3]

**1.** *Combativeness* can reach the point of serious physical attack on others. A patient suffering from paranoid schizophrenic delusions, or a brain damaged patient with impaired grasp of reality may feel that his relative or the fellow in the next bed is a mortal enemy, and may then proceed to attack him. With suspicious, hostile, or paranoid patients, one should try to solve the problem within a medical-psychiatric framework rather than by resorting to legal intervention. These patients are already inclined toward litigation to begin with, and the use of legal interventions (police intervention, legal commitment, warrants, etc.) tends to solidify their combative stand.

**2.** Geriatric delinquency includes, beside combativeness, behavior considered to be *sexually deviant* (*e.g.*, making sexual advances to children, exhibitionism). [4]

**3.** One particular form of combativeness is not physical, but verbal, *i.e.*, the malicious gossip that may occur in some paranoid or senile patients (presbyophrenia). Frequently this concerns relatives or neighbors, and the contents of the harmful rumors and gossip often has an erotic flavor.

## Mixed Situations

An aged person and his spouse, or other family member, may be involved in pathological interactions in which all partners contribute to the destructive pattern. Uusually what happens in such situations is that not only do all the family members suffer subjectively, but they also inflict suffering upon each other. These interactions may gather momentum in the manner of a vicious circle, and if outside intervention does not break up this circle, the weakest link in the chain will give way—which may be the vulnerable aged family member. Such pathological family interaction can be seen, par excellence, in the relatively rare condition of folie à deux (see page 216).

> Two elderly sisters were legally committed to the mental hospital. This followed a lawsuit instituted by neighbors, who charged that the sisters had made "unrestrained, vile, and untrue statements about them and that they were public nuisance." On admission, the sisters were cooperative and friendly but insisted that their niece and nephew were after their property and that the niece, in fact, had destroyed it. They alluded to certain "whiskey people" who had antagonized them by throwing stones at them and placing dynamite in the basement. They complained that the neighbors ("whiskey people") had poisoned their chickens. Eventually the sisters boarded the windows and put up a fence. The difficulties came to a head when they began shooting at the neighbor's clothespins.

## DIFFERENCES IN APPROACH AND METHODS

In what way do the above conditions require a different methodology and approach? The traditional approach is usually based on the assumption that people who need help are willing, if not eager, to get it. This is the rational viewpoint and certainly would apply to most cases. But humans are not always rational, and some are never rational. Unfortunately, these not-always-rational or always-irrational people often need help the most.

Rationality involves an element of freedom. Conversely, the more irrational and the more impaired a person is, the more he has lost his freedom to act, and the more he is compelled to behave under the influence of impulses beyond his control. With this in mind, two principles can be formulated. First, the more a person is under the influence of irrational tendencies and the less rational control he has, the more he will be in need of a controlling agent or agency other than himself. Second, since there are degrees of rational control and loss thereof, the need for external controls will vary accordingly. This is not an either-or situation in which control and reason are either present or absent, but a continuum of varying degrees.[5]

It is doubtful that among humans any really free and totally rational relations ever occur. In contacts with the aged there is ample opportunity to observe that freedom to choose, as well as rational control of self and environment, are significantly reduced. Usually there seems to be no problem: the aged person "freely" accepts the inevitable, and the practitioner accordingly feels that no force or coercion needs to be used. But how often is it necessary to resort to some form of coercion, force, persuasion, limit setting, reinforcing of rules, suggestions, guiding, or decision making? This is impossible to tell. There is no problem as long as the patient or client more or less voluntarily endows the professional worker with authority. In such a case there is a fit between the role of the client and the counterrole of the professional worker.

With increasing loss of rational control on the part of the client, there is increasing need for a substitute authority to step in and take over. The entry of the external authority should take place on a graded scale, with the amount and type of authority and control being attuned to the specific needs and deficiencies of the individual. The schema below presents various degrees and techniques of taking over control and suggests three stages or types of relationships (Scheme 1).

In Stage I, there may be no real relationship between practitioner and client at first (for example, when simple information is being given), or a relationship may just begin to develop. Either way, the client remains relatively free and on his own in this stage.

In Stage II, there is a definite relationship, in the course of which the client becomes less free, inasmuch as the professional worker assumes more and more control and authority. All this occurs within the setting of a structured relationship.

In Stage III, the relationship in terms of mutual cooperative action is beginning to be dissolved as a result of the increasing loss of autonomy and freedom on the part of the patient, and the concomitant increase of authority and control on the part of the clinician. Initially, or as long as the two participants agree on the transfer of authority, the structure of the professional relationship may still remain intact. When, however,

SCHEME 1

| Degrees of Freedom | Function and Role Characteristics | |
| --- | --- | --- |
| | Clinician-practitioner | Patient-client |

|  |  |  |
| --- | --- | --- |
| | | *CLIENT* |
| Stage I | a.— *information* | —on his own; free. |
| | no strings attached | —no cooperation or relationship |
| | ("take it or leave it") | necessary |
| | b.— *counseling* | —cooperative relationship |
| | no strings attached | |
| | c.— *guidance* | —more involved in collaboration |
| | more expectations regarding | reciprocity; equal partners |
| | client; joint decisions | |
| | | *PATIENT* |
| Stage II | a.— *suggestions & persuasion* | —more passive, less on his own |
| | active ("Do") and authoritative | |
| | b.— *reinforcing rules & limit setting* | —beginning transfer of control |
| | more active ("Do"); | and responsibility |
| | also prohibitive ("Don't") | |
| | c.— *decision making, manipulation* | —increasing transfer of control |
| | commands & coercion | and responsibility |
| | ("Do this or else." | —freedom not yet totally lost |
| | "Don't do that or else.") | because cooperation may remain |
| Stage III | a.—items a, b, c of Stage II, in greater | —passive within the doctor- |
| | quantity | patient relationship |
| | b.—items a, b, c of Stage II, with additional backing (legal) | —totally passive, but usually no longer within doctor-patient relationship |

this transfer becomes a matter of dispute, auxiliary reinforments tend to becalled into action, such as the family, the family physician, a consultant-specialist, the minister, or the court. By this time the element of mutuality or reciprocity in the relationship has usually been considerably reduced because the client has become, so to say, an object that is being manipulated. In some cases, a skillful clinician-practitioner may call in auxiliary forces while still maintaining an intact relationship with his patient.

## INDICATIONS FOR SPECIFIC TECHNIQUES

It is logical that the more authoritative, forceful, and controlling approaches are to be reserved for those conditions described above as being the most serious. Conversely, those conditions that are relatively mild and tractable require only a minimum of intervention and control. The involuntary patterns of danger to the self or others would require lesser amounts of authoritative intervention than patterns that are voluntary, active, self-initiated, or intentful. The reason is that a person caught in some involuntary pattern has already abandoned control and lost his own authority. The outsider who steps in to take over is likely to be welcomed as a liberator, rather than seen as an intruder. Freedom, rather than being lost, is regained.

The question of how much pressure, force, or persuasion to bring to bear on the intervention depends also on the degree or severity of the problem. For example, when a patient uses denial to avoid specific feelings about his being physically ill, then only Stage I type of intervention is indicated. If the patient acknowledges the existence of his illness, but denies the action implications (*i.e.*, the need for medical help), then Stage II intervention is called for. And, if the patient denies the very fact of his illness, we would need to resort to Stage III. Likewise, poor judgment, faulty living habits, and accident proneness may differ in terms of their seriousness. Voluntary self-destructiveness and active, deliberate danger to others call for forceful application of protective services (Type III).

Family situations that involve pathological interactions and harmful vicious circles should, in principle, be approached with an attempt to reduce the pathological interaction by pulling the sparring partners apart. The clinical practitioner is, as it were, a referee who stops the boxing match when one fighter is getting too many blows. This may require Type II techniques appropriately "titrated" in strength and concentration so as to fit the occasion. The specific techniques should be employed with a degree of force or intensity that is just sufficient to have the desired effect.

Practical know-how and clinical skills are acquired through experience; a thorough discussion of this falls beyond the scope of this review. It may be useful to keep in mind one last point. As clinicians and practitioners, we have authority, whether we want it or not. This authority, inherent in the professional role, should be used with discrimination, not for its own sake but for protective intervention, and in a manner that is rational and well thought through. Legal means sometimes are necessary, but the court is to be reserved as a last resource.

## REFERENCES

1. Protection of the Abused or Neglected Elderly Act; Article 6 of General Statutes Chapter 108 (Social Services); Charter 1378 of the 1974 North Carolina General Assembly.
2. HAYS, D. S. AND WISOTSKY, M.: The aged offender: a review of the literature and two current studies from the New York State Division of Parole. *J. Am. Geriatr. Soc. 17:* 1064–1073, 1969.
3. WOLK, R. L., RUSTIN, S. L., AND SCOTTI, J.: The geriatric delinquent. *J. Am. Geriatr. Soc. 11:* 653–659, 1963.
4. WILSON, J. G.: Signs of sexual aberration in old men. *J. Am. Geriatr. Soc. 4:* 1105–1107, 1956.
5. REGAN, J. J.: Protective services for the elderly: commitment, guardianship, and alternatives. *William and Mary Law Review, 13:* 569–622, 1972.

# 20

# work and retirement

## ENGAGEMENT AND DISENGAGEMENT

### Personal and Interpersonal Aspects

Senescence is characterized by a reduction in physical activities and social interaction, and by a constriction of lifespace. Some withdrawal from life activities by the aged is probably a normal developmental process of the later years. The change from striving to withdrawing has been described as disengagement.[1] The theory of disengagement proposes that there is a mutual withdrawal between the aging person and others in the social system. The equilibrium that existed in middle life between the individual and society now evolves into a new equilibrium characterized by greater distance. The depth and extent of a person's engagement can be estimated by the degree of potential disruption that would follow his sudden death. However, the death of someone who has an important symbolic engagement with his society (scientists, artists, political leaders, etc.) can result in simultaneous loss and gain because the survivors can rally around the symbols he represented, thereby reaffirming their universal and timeless value.

The notion of disengagement is complicated by the tendency to equate activity and engagement on the one hand, and withdrawal (or passivity) and disengagement on the other hand. To avoid confusion between these concepts, it must be kept in mind that activity is a more encompassing concept than engagement. That is, the latter refers specifically to the social aspects, whereas the former includes any and all activities of the human organism. It seems there are several types of combinations of being (in)active and (dis)engaged, as indicated below.

**(a).** *Engaged and Active.* This type would refer to those persons who are socially engaged in an active manner. In this constellation, we would also expect active use of somatic and psychological functions.

**(b).** *Engaged and Inactive.* This type is socially engaged, but in a passive, inactive way. The individual needs the closeness or company of others, but does not necessarily actively reach out for this, or make active contributions to the social interaction. An example would be persons who are introverted and reticent, or individuals who are regressed but not withdrawn. In fact, in the case of regression, interpersonal closeness is intensified inasmuch as the regressed person has become more dependent; and it is this very closeness which eventually may become stifling.

248

**(c).** *Disengaged and Active.* This combination is illustrated by a well-adjusted hermit. Such a socially isolated person has few, if any, social contacts but may remain quite active in other respects.

**(d).** *Disengaged and Inactive.* If a person is socially disengaged, and also passive or underactive with regard to the use of his somatic and psychological functions, his survival may be at risk. It would seem that, for the sake of survival of the organism, the disadvantage implied in social disengagement needs to be compensated for by an actual increase of nonsocial activities. Hence, of the four possible combinations, this one seems to be most maladaptive and conducive to psychopathology. Examples include cases of isolation and introversion that progress to the point of autism; or withdrawal decompensating into a state of apathy.

It would seem, then, that there is no sound basis for any conflict between proponents of activism and disengagement. Of course, the disengagement theory should not be used as a pretext to acquiesce in all of the aspects of loneliness and withdrawal. But for some individuals, the isolation which accompanies introspection may be more like a freely chosen retreat than an exile. An emphasis on introspection and reminiscence does not necessarily preclude the need for optimal engagement in various activities. Introspection can serve as an active, if not manifestly expressive, effort to find oneself. The point is that the emphasis on one or the other should be a differential emphasis based upon knowledge of all relevant clinical data and the life style of the older person.

The various features of disengagement *versus* engagement, and activity *versus* passivity are vividly illustrated by the example of a 65-year-old professional man who decided to embark on a journey into the self. His plan had been carefully thought through and involved a self-chosen retreat in the mountains for one year. During this time, he would have no contacts with other people, and would concentrate his energies on writing down his thoughts and impressions as they emerged from day to day. Before beginning his solo venture, he discussed the plan with various physicians, including a psychiatrist, and had physical, psychological, and psychiatric checkups. The data indicated that he was in good physical and mental health and that his plan for the retreat was not a manifestation of psychopathology.

During the twelve months of his retreat, he was in isolation, not only as far as people were concerned, but also in terms of having himself cut off from telecommunications (radio, T.V., newspapers). The journey into the self produced a monumental volume of writings (illustrating a high degree of activity and productivity, as well as the ability to maintain contact with reality, under the stress of prolonged social isolation).

Basically, there were two dimensions to the quality and contents of his thoughts as they were entrusted to paper, day after day. The first one was vertical, reaching back in time toward the beginnings of his existence; this dimension was essentially autobiographical.

The second type of mental activity was horizontal and impressionistic, in response to momentary observations. While the autobiographical process involved a great deal of mental effort, *e.g.*, concentration, memory, and logical thought, the second (horizontal) thought processes required less effort, were more playful, and frequently employed free association. Significantly, the autobiographical thoughts were more frequent during the first half of the retreat, whereas the other type was more dominant during the second portion.

After successfully completing the entire twelve months period of retreat, he re-entered the human world, and re-engaged himself without difficulties. Medical and psychiatric examinations did not show significant differences between preretreat and postretreat data.

### Old Age as a Consummatory Phase

Let us return once more to the notion of goal in senescence, the final phase of human development: in view of so much deline, how can old age be called the golden years? Is this a deceptive euphemism or does the phrase contain an element of truth? Talcott Parsons suggests that, as a kind of counterpoint to the basic instrumental emphasis of our culture, old age should come to be viewed as a consummatory phase.[2] It should be the period of harvest when the fruits of previous instrumental commitments are gathered in. The tendency has been to think of the enjoyments of youth as the prototypes of consummation (the pleasures of exhibiting physical prowess, of sexual gratification, etc.) and to think of old age as entailing a renunciation of the best things. In contrast, the last phase of life could be viewed as a reward for a life well lived. What is needed is a reward system offered by society, which makes it clear that for most persons it is good to be old. A reward system would need to be delicately tailored to the highly differentiated and specific styles of life which it is to reward. In addition, there is the task for older people themselves to learn to interpret their own life situations in appropriate terms, and to view old age as an opportunity for the sheer enjoyment of the consummatory phase of life.

These notions lead us to the concept of leisure time activities. *Leisure* refers to private time, the time one has for oneself and during which one is free to engage in private activities. These activities can be described in terms of hobby, recreation, or private work (in contrast to the occupational work role). Education toward leisure time activities would seem to be an essential part of retirement counseling, either pre- or postretirement. Certain programs can be developed to acquaint aging persons with a variety of recreational activities and to provide educational experiences in the area of their interest.[3]

### PSYCHOPATHOLOGY OF WORK AND RETIREMENT

### Personal Work and Vocational Work

(a). *Energy* is the capacity for doing work. The human organism is an open system which is capable of producing free energy. The human being is at work, in the most general sense of the word, from the moment of conception until death. In any system undergoing senescence, there is a steady decrease in the energy yields of that system. As energy production decreases, there is a negative change in the rate at which usable energy is produced. Power can be defined as work per unit of time. Senescence may be conceptualized as a decline in free energy production with time.[4]

The transfer and application of energy onto specific functions produce various types of work activities. During the early developmental phases (e.g., autonomy, initiative, industry), energy is transferred (cathected) into basic neuromuscular and psychomotor skills. Later on, energy is used for the acquisition of highly specific, individual skills which prepare the individual for vocational work. Thus, vocational work patterns and skills are among the last to appear, developmentally speaking; and later on in life, they will be among the first to disappear. The disappearance of work skills corresponds, to some extent, with the social phenomenon of retirement.

**(b).** Being at work, then, includes the vocational work role and the private work patterns. The *vocational work role* (occupational work) involves the following properties: expenditure of energy, financial remuneration, production of goods and services, social interaction, and social status.

*Private work* refers to other forms of energy expenditure, such as leisure activities, sports, hobbies, and so on. Leisure and hobby activities do not necessarily have properties of vocational work, with the exception of expenditure of energy. Both types of work have also in common that they play a role in the economy of the mind: they pose challenges for mastery, offer satisfactions, or may become involved in psychological conflict. *Retirement* signifies the end of the vocational work role thus leaving the individual with the opportunity for private work only. Retirement, therefore, is a transition that involves both a loss and a gain. What is lost is the occupational work role; what is gained is the opportunity for private work.

Any period of change and transition in life may lead to psychological difficulties. In the case of retirement, these can usually be traced back to specific psychological problems that existed earlier in life. In other words, the psychological aspects of retirement depend on the psychology of work; and conversely, the *psychopathology of work* tends to become the *psychopathology of retirement*.

### Individual Patterns

**(a).** The optimal expenditure of energy and the very exercise of bodily and mental functions are usually enjoyable experiences. This *functional pleasure* also applies to the exercise of skills in work and productivity, and can make work an enjoyable necessity.[5] Functional pleasure in work activities may decline because of loss of energy, or because of loss of specific work activities, *e.g.*, retirement. In the case of retirement, that quantum of energy invested in occupational work is freed, as it were, and will seek new outlets. This state of affairs is basically similar to a grief reaction. The loss of the work role usually represents a significant loss, because we have invested much of our time, interest, and energy into our occupation.[6] A successful resolution of the grief reaction may be more difficult or become impossible because of the interference by specific emotional factors and attitudes, *e.g.*, ambivalence. Thus, ambivalent and conflicting attitudes toward work that existed during the working years may, at the time of retirement, interfere with the resolution of the loss and become obstacles in the process of role transition. In such cases, the individual may have considerable difficulty in directing his available energy toward new activities, or in using it to reactivate old interests and hobbies.

(b). We shall now briefly review some patterns and constellations encountered in individuals whose work was *in the service of conflict*. Of course, some people never appear to invest any interest or energy at all in their work. Some lack basic drive or talent; others, during their formative years, did not invest the time or energy needed to develop skills. People who never learned or developed skills will have a steady but colorless work career at best, and an erratic career at worst. Because work has not meant very much to them, neither will retirement.

1. The *lonely, inwardly isolated* person tends to view the world as a cold, inhospitable place. Work serves defensively as a way to avoid close contact with others and to build his own personal bastion of strength from which he can deal safely at a distance with other people. Upon retirement such a person will again face the original conflict, and thus become more lonely. The longstanding interpersonal conflicts, that work has been taking care of for almost a lifetime, now come out in the open.

A man in his late 60's, who had been a sea captain, had always preferred to be alone at sea, pitting his own strength against the elements. When he was about to retire, he divorced his wife and went to a small town which was "a village that is dying." The dying village was an outward representation of his inner sense of isolation.

2. Other individuals used work to *regain a lost paradise*. They may have a vague memory of some idyllic state in their early life which they attempt to regain through hard work. Their aim is to earn their place in the sun, and in some instances, within the shortest time possible. There may be wishes or fantasies of retiring very early in life. Sooner or later, such people become aware that the lost paradise cannot be regained in reality. Feeling that their activities proved to be futile, they are overtaken by nostalgic depression and a sense of having missed the boat.

A 48-year-old man, who had been a driving, hard-working business executive, had climbed to the top in the firm where he was employed. As his circumstances improved, his wife became more interested in material comforts, which in turn made it necessary for him to work even harder. When, at the age of 41, he had reached the peak of his career, he and his wife went separate ways. By this time, he had accumulated enough wealth that he could afford to retire. Soon, however, he was hospitalized for a nervous breakdown. Against the advice of his doctors, he married the nurse who had cared for him during his emotional illness. The couple moved to a sunny climate, bought a ranch, and settled down in what promised to be a happy existence. Instead, there were frequent quarrels during which he experienced chest pains which turned out to be angina. In addition, his depression returned. By age 48, this man had gone through two marriages, seven years of retirement, and a series of depressions. He continued to be materially wealthy, but he was vexed by the problem that his life was basically empty, and that he had pursued something in life that turned out to be a mirage.

**3.** A third type is the *overly independent* person. Such an individual may be excessively self-reliant because he cannot accept dependency gratifications. Perhaps he perceives his dependency wishes to be so strong that he is afraid to give in to them or he was taught in his younger years that dependency was tantamount to weakness and was rewarded for presenting a facade of strength. When such a person retires, he may find it difficult to alter his lifelong pattern. Because his self-esteem depends on a self-image of activity and independence there is a tendency to remain overly active.

A man in his mid-50's had opened his own restaurant. His one and only concern was to serve others. He slaved from the early morning to the late evening to provide the best for his customers, completely neglecting his own welfare. In spite of these considerable personal sacrifices, the restaurant did not do well. Nevertheless, he bought his wife expensive gifts. In short, it was all important for him to have a self-image of being generous and self-reliant. Finally, he began to suffer from chest pains. His wife called in a physician but the patient ignored the warnings, continued his excessive pace, and soon collapsed due to a myocardial infarct.

**4.** Again another group is composed of the *perfectionists*—those who pay more attention to the detail than the overall pattern. The compulsive or perfectionistic person works in order to do the right things, at the right time, in the right place. How he does something is more important than what he does. He usually works with great energy, as long as he can do it the right way. When, however, the details can no longer be attended to, or when perfection cannot be attained, he tends to feel at a loss and his productivity may come to a halt. In senescence, there may occur a critical decline in the energy required to live up to his high standards. Feelings of helplessness and shame and a sense of inadequacy may be the result.

A 60-year-old man had, over a period of three years, gradually become unable to do any productive work. He spent his time drinking and making unrealistic plans to get back in business. In the past he had been in the realty business but had never been really successful, because of his tendency to be overly precise and to present his clients with so many pros and cons that he hardly ever closed a deal. As he became increasingly aware of his lack of success, he began to enroll in a number of business courses to improve his skills and knowledge. However, he failed these courses, and then he withdrew from work altogether.

**5.** Some people have, for a lifetime, struggled with extremely *aggressive* and *competitive* feelings. Important in this particular psychological constellation is the fact that these impulses exist primarily on the fantasy level, and that the capacity to channel them through socially acceptable outlets is somehow lacking. Consequently, there is a kind of accumulation of these competitive drives with a resulting proliferation of them in fantasy life. Because such persons never learn to distinguish clearly between hostility and normal self-assertion, they become overly fearful of asserting themselves. Every time success comes within their reach, they shrink back; success may connote to them that it was at someone else's expense that they succeeded. Their life is a succession of near successes, or actual failures; their work career will be substandard. The end of the work career may be perceived as a final failure or defeat which provokes guilt and anger.

**6.** When a person has a problem in the area of *personal identity*, he may be unable to decide which goals in life to pursue or which course of action to choose. As a way out, he may choose a career or occupation which will serve as an identity, a name tag as it were, or as a way of becoming somebody. The danger inherent in the loss of the occupation is a feeling of anonymity or a sense of identity diffusion.

Needless to say, there are many overlaps among these personality constellations, and none of them exists in pure culture. Generally, most individuals appear to handle the transition from the work role into retirement reasonably well. The elements of anticipation, foresight, and preparation probably play an essential role in a successful transition and may have two important implications. First, foresight may lead to appropriate planning, well ahead of time, for the future event (*e.g.*, financial and economic planning). Thus, retirement will not find the individual totally unprepared from the economic point of view. Of course, the existence of retirement provisions tends to facilitate effective planning. Second, the imaginative anticipation of a future event may evoke specific emotional feelings associated with the event. In the case of an anticipated loss, a person may experience anticipatory grief. This has psychological value because when the loss finally occurs, a certain amount of the grief work will have already been done. Conversely, if anticipatory grief is absent, the person will have to absorb the full impact of the loss all at once. Frequently, interference with preparation for retirement is attributable to denial mechanisms. In those instances where work functions in the service of psychological conflict, denial mechanisms and lack of foresight are relatively prominent.

## REFERENCES

1. CUMMINGS, E. AND HENRY, W.: Growing Old: The Process of Disengagement. Basic Books, New York, 1961.
2. PARSONS, T.: Old age as a consummatory phase. *Gerontologist 3:* 53, 1963.
3. PFEIFFER, E. AND DAVIS, G. C.: The use of leisure time in middle life. *In:* Normal Aging, Vol. 2, E. Palmore, ed. Duke University Press, Durham, N. C., 1974. pp. 232–243.
4. CALLOWAY, N. O.: A general theory of senescence. *J. Am. Geriatr. Soc. 12:* 856, 1964.
5. VON BERTALANFFY, L.: General system theory and psychiatry. *In:* American Handbook of Psychiatry, Vol. 3, Chap. 43, S. Arieti, ed. Basic Books, New York, 1966. pp. 705–721.
6. COBB, S.: Physiologic changes in men whose jobs were abolished. *J. Psychosom. Res. 18:* 245–258, 1974.

# 21

# intimacy, loneliness, and sex in senescence

## THE CONCEPT OF INTIMACY

Human development is a process of becoming that encompasses the entire life cycle. During each one of the developmental phases of the life cycle, the sense of intimacy (and its counterpart, loneliness) differs with regard to some basic dimensions, such as the type of partners, the nature of sharing, the objects that are shared, and the way in which intimacy is subjectively experienced.

Typical for the first year of life is the intimacy between child and mother. Because this relationship is so close, and the sharing involves feeding and nurturing, we speak of a symbiosis. Later on, the child may have intimacy with the father, and in this relationship the child wishes to share the father's strength. Through intimate relationships with peers, such as siblings and friends, the child learns to play. It is through play activities that the child masters many insecurities and challenges.

During adolescence, there usually are intimate friendships with peers. Through these close relationships the adolescent learns much about himself. By the end of this developmental phase, the young person has a unique identity. Only then, after a personal sense of identity has been formed, intimacy with the opposite sex becomes possible.

When one becomes a parent oneself, the intimacy of the parent-child relationship is again experienced, but now one is on the other side of the fence, as it were. Still, many young, perceptive parents may sense a peculiar familiarity about it all. This familiarity is a direct carry-over from the intimacy one had long ago with one's own parents.

Thus, in the course of time, many types of intimacy evolve and the new forms build on previous ones, thereby including rather than replacing them. During the middle years of life, a person can have many intimate relationships: with one's parents, one's friends and co-workers, one's spouse, children, grandchildren, and so on. On the other hand, middle aged individuals may be so involved in many activities and relationships, that they are too busy to take time out for moments of intimacy.

Old age brings inevitable losses. Each loss represents the disappearance of an intimate relationship, and increases the likelihood of loneliness. Thus, one of the main psychological tasks in old age is to accept the inevitable losses, and to learn to be more alone without feeling too lonely. The more an old person has become capable, through mental processes of abstraction and sublimation, of extending his interests to encompass phenomena that are not bound by time and space (*e.g.*, art, science, religion, society, nature), the greater his psychic immunity against the risk of loneliness.

In the usual sense of the word, though, intimacy involves the contact with another person. Of course, we can be intimate with our own self: our body, our thoughts, feelings, and memories. In fact, this intimacy with oneself is enriching, and the self can be a source of creativity and a wealth of experiences. But the self being a "lonely fortress," the sense of intimacy is fulfilled most in the contact with another person. Now, what are some of the basic *qualities of intimacy* with another person, as for example between a man and a woman?

First, there is a *sense of belonging*, in terms of "I belong to you; you belong to me; we belong to each other." This implies a sense of fit and harmony. The fact that this or that experience is intimate means that I can fit it into my life, into what is already there, and harmonize it with my past, present, and future self. The sense of fit and harmony is preceived as something that could not be any other way. Thus, one person will say to the other, "We are made for each other"; or, they marvel that the forces of destiny directed their paths so as to meet each other, as if such a harmony of feelings could only be the work of a higher providence—"It had to be."

Second, there is the element of *familiarity*. One cannot be intimate with what is new or unfamiliar, strange or alien. In fact, the counterpart of intimacy is referred to as alienation. Thus, nothing that is new is intimate. And, everything intimate fits in with a previous experience. It follows that the mental process of recognition is essential. Now, recognition is repeated cognition, as is also true in the case of remembering (memory).

We can now add a third characteristic of intimacy: the fact that *repetition* is built into the experience. On the one hand, intimacy is experienced as a repetition of a previous experience; on the other hand, one wishes it to be repeated in the future. Intimacy is not a brief encounter.

The idea that the past is repeated in the present, and the present in the future, points up the next characteristic, that of *sameness*, and permanence. Such notions as change and transience are alien to the experience of intimacy. Through sameness one attains a kind of transcendence, a transcending of time. There is a process of time binding, *i.e.*, the tying together of past, present, and future into one cohesive perspective. But there also is an element of timelessness in this transcendence, as if one has risen above the flow of time. Such transcendence of time is a sort of eternity. In the experience of intimacy, we see this illustrated when one says to a loved one: "It is as if I have always known you" (transcending time backward into the past)—or "our love will last forever" (transcending time forward into the future). There is nothing new or strange about this timelessness. It is our unconscious that is timeless and knows nothing about clocks and calendars. Time, in the sense of objective calendar time, is learned over a period of years. A true appreciation of time and a mature time sense do not occur until early adolescence. The timelessness of intimacy corresponds to mental processes that can be traced back to the early origins of our existence, and that continue to be present in the deeper, unconscious layers of the mind.

Finally, the activity of intimacy is *sharing*. What may be shared is something material and external (possessions, money, etc.), or time and space (as in a home), or the phenomenon called "each other." In sharing each other, the I and the you create the we. The we encompasses something bigger than I and you added together by way of simple arithmetic. In the language of systems theory, the system as a whole (we) is larger, greater, more than the sum of its parts (I + you). As people sometimes describe love, "It's bigger than me." Christian doctrine, systems theory and psychoanalysis converge at this point: the religious emphasis on love corresponds to the above mentioned principle of systems theory as well as to the psychoanalytic principle of sublimation. Sublimation refers to the mental process of becoming less self-centered and more selfless, of subordinating the wishes of the self to the interests of a larger entity. This larger entity that transcends the narrow self can be concretely human (the we, or a family), or this entity can be an abstraction (art, science, humanity, mankind).

It might be noted here that one measure of the success of one's life is the measure of one's *sublimations*. (The submerging of the self in the service of a higher cause is the religious theme of losing oneself in order to find it). Corresponding to sublimation, there is the simultaneous process of desexualization. By this we mean that one learns to transform sexual energy so that it can be used for selfless aims, for the higher things in life, as it were. In summary, sublimation involves an orientation away from the self toward a larger, transcendent phenomenon, and an orientation away from sexual pleasure toward nonsexual satisfaction and achievements. Ideally, the way intimacy would change, in the course of life, is along these same lines; that is, an increasing amount of sublimation (or love, if you wish). The outcome of this would be two-fold: to belong intimately to something that is larger than I am, that transcends me and, in fact, will outlive me; and to transform sufficient amounts of sexual drive into non-sexual energy for the purpose of achieving something that lasts and endures.

## THE CONCEPT OF SEXUALITY

In the broad sense of the word, sexuality refers to wishes, drives, and feelings that have a somatic-physiological origin and have the aim of attaining pleasure.

### Somatic Origin

Feelings or drives of a sexual nature originate from multiple sources in the body, such as the mouth and gastrointestinal tract, the sense organs, the skin, the muscles, and so on. In each case, the sexual drive or energy that originates from that organ system has a specific quality. At different stages of human development, different body parts or organs assume relative importance. For example, during the first year of life the dominant erogenous zones are the mouth, upper gastrointestinal tract, and the skin. Later, the lower intestinal tract, the neuromuscular system, and sense organs also become important. The emergence of a particular organ system as a significant source of pleasure (*i.e.*, sexual stimulation and satisfaction) depends on processes of somatic and psychological maturation. For example, by age five or six, parts of the genital organs begin to mature, and the strength of sensations originating from them increases significantly. Hence, this is called the phallic phase of development.

## The Striving for Pleasure

The nature of sexual drives is the attainment of pleasure. In our present framework, pleasure is defined as the release of tension, or the removal of excitations originating in a particular organ system; and organ pleasure is defined as "sexual." When the organ system from which pleasurable excitations originate is the genital apparatus, we speak of genital-sexual wishes or satisfactions. The genital apparatus is relatively late in its maturation; other parts of the body, in the course of development, emerge sooner as an important source of sensations. For this reason, these nongenital sexual excitations are called *pregenital*. In this context, the term pregenital connotes something that happened before something else; the sexuality that precedes genital sex is called pregenital. But, there is a second reason for the term pregenital: the sexual feelings originating from within the genital system are stronger than those from other organ systems. We speak of the dominance or primacy of genital sexuality. In this context, pregenital refers to the quality of being a forerunner of genital sex; and, in that sense, pregenital is equivalent to being *subordinated* to genital sexuality. To put it differently, pregenital sex drives are like a prelude or foreplay *vis-à-vis* genital sexuality. In the case of normal adult sexuality, the former culminate in the latter.

The *primacy* of genital sexuality depends on the maturation of the genital apparatus as a result of hormonal, anatomic, and physiological factors. The dominance of the genital system comes into being during early adulthood (puberty) and lasts until some indefinite point in late life. Thus, genital sexuality is only one form of sexuality, albeit the dominant one. It appears last, developmentally speaking; and generally, what developed last is most likely to disappear first. That means pregenital sexuality not only precedes (antedates) genital sex, but also will outlast it.

Between *intimacy and sex*, there is no one-to-one relationship. One can have intimacy without sex, and sex without intimacy. Intimacy can be sexually neutral; and sex can be lonely. But often intimacy is sexual and sex is intimate. By the same token, sexual intimacy may involve genital sexuality (in terms of specific consummation), or pregenital sexuality.

No statistics are known about this, but probably people spend considerably more time being together in sexual intimacy that is pregenital in nature.

## SEX IN SENESCENCE

Research in sex in old age is a relatively recent phenomenon. Publications on adult sexuality began to appear in the late 19th century. Publications on adolescent and child sexuality appeared 20 to 30 years later (1920's), and those on sex in senescence again some 20 to 30 years later (1950's). This development may be related to several factors. First, social attitudes used to be characterized by the notion that older people are sexless, or at least that they should be. Second, the increase in the number of older people and the emergence of gerontology and geriatrics have focused attention on the problems of living in old age, including those of sex. Finally, although many older people live in conditions that are less favorable than those of other age groups, there have been positive changes, such as social security, medicare, and improved retirement provisions. This has focused attention on old age as a phase with its own opportunities for leisure and recreation. As time goes on, more healthy individuals who are still vigorous and look forward to leisure, including the recreation of sex, will reach old age.[1]

### The Effects of Aging on Sex

Sexual capacities and functions show definite age-related changes; in this respect, sex is not different from other biological and psychological functions that show a decline with increasing age.[2, 3] To the extent that we speak of "normal" aging phenomena, these age-related changes in sex can also be viewed as a normal process. In our research at Duke, we studied 254 men and women, ranging from 60 to 94 years of age.[4, 5] Some of the relevant findings are presented below.

(a). In the overall group, the incidence of sexual *activity* declined from a level of more than 50 percent during the early 60's, to a level of between 10 and 20 percent after age 80.

(b). The incidence of sexual *interest* does not show an age-related decline: mild-to-moderate degrees of interest may persist into the 80's.

(c). In general, the incidence of sexual interest is higher than that of activity, and this discrepancy is more prominent in men.

(d). *Marital status* has little effect on the sexual activity and interest of aging men. Unmarried women have only a negligible amount of sexual intercourse, but about 20 percent of this group report sexual interest. The sexual activity and interest of men is greater than that of women, regardless of marital status.

(e). *The Influence of the Past*. Living patterns of the earlier years set the stage for those of the later years. This also holds true for sexual behavior patterns. The sexual drives and activities of older people correlate with those of the younger years. Men and women who used to enjoy sex when they were young are likely to still enjoy it when old. This finding disposes of the (superstitious) notion that one only has a limited amount of sexual energy, or that by keeping some in reserve one may have more sexual energy later on in life. Actually, the reverse is true: active and regular use of sexual capacities is likely to maintain them in old age. In this respect, sex is no different from other functional capacities (*e.g.*, intelligence) that benefit from active and regular use.

(f). *Individual Variability*. The final common path of human sexual behavior is under the influence of a great variety of factors, including biological endowment, developmental and age-related changes, psychodynamic forces, interpersonal relationships, and sociocultural factors. It is no surprise, therefore, to find a great deal of variability among aging individuals with regard to their sexual behavior. Some of these individual variations include the following:

1. Although, in general, elderly men are sexually more active than women, in the course of time the differences become smaller.

2. Among men surviving into the 80's and 90's, continued sexual activity is no great rarity; about one-fifth of these men are still sexually active.

3. Although sexual interest declines with age, about one-half of the subjects surviving into the 80's and 90's report they still have sexual interest of mild to moderate degree.

4. Unmarried men have about the same level of sexual activity and interest as married men. In fact, unmarried men report not infrequently a pattern of increasing activity and interest.

5. About one-fourth of the men, regardless of age, report an increase in the degree of activity or interest, over a period of time covering several years.

## The Effects of Sex on Aging

With regard to the influence of sexual activity on aging, there is some evidence from animal experiments suggesting that continued sexual activity may contribute to, or is associated with, longevity. In male rats, for example, regular mating improves their condition and increases longevity. It has been pointed out that married persons live longer than unmarried ones, but this does not prove the beneficial effects of continued sexual activity.[6] The Duke research data suggest that continued sexual activity may be a characteristic of vigorous individuals who may represent a *biological elite*. These aged people tend to be still married, even if quite old; to retain physical and psychological health; and to remain socially, as well as sexually, active. Continued sexual activity is a correlate of continued vigor.[7]

The notion of a life-prolonging or vigor-restoring benefit from sexual contact is very old, and encountered in several cultures. The alleged beneficial effect on old males from the proximity of a young woman is called gerocomy, or *Shunamitism*, a phrase derived from the story of King David (1 Kings 1:1–5). Reportedly, the famous 18th century Dutch physician Boerhaave advised the elderly mayor of Amsterdam to lie between two young girls to recover his strength and spirits. The influence allegedly responsible was the heat or breath of a young virgin, coitus being excluded as dangerous. The terms spirit and breath bring to mind the physiological processes of inspiration and their deeper figurative meaning: to inspire is to create life; to be inspired is to be creative.

Apart from any magical or superstitious elements, we wonder to what extent we see something like Shunamitism in settings where nursing care is given to geriatric patients. Often we are impressed by the enthusiasm of youthful nurses whose warmth restores the spirits of elderly patients. The close proximity and intimacy, expressed in so many ways (*e.g.*, touch, voice, feeding) is an expression of sublimation, which means that the relationship has been desexualized and thus has become sexually neutral. The stimuli transmitted in such contact, far from having a sexual significance, have the much broader aim of restoration and of regenerating a sense of well being.

## Qualitative Aspects

Sexual behavior changes continually during the life span. The various phases of human development have their own psychosocial characteristics which are reflected in sexual behavior. Through the years the sexual drives change with regard to their physiological sources of origin, their purpose, and the human context in which the sexual needs are satisfied. The postmature years—those following middle age—may cover a period of 20 to 30 years, or about one third of the lifespan. Pfeiffer and Davis[8] studied the determinants of sexual behavior in men and women aged 46 to 71 years. Their findings indicate that the sexual behavior in these individuals (between middle and old age) depends on multiple factors, including the level of sexual functioning in younger years, the age and sex of the subject, and the subjective and objective health ratings. The sexual behavior of men was influenced by a much greater number of variables than that of women. In the latter, the most important determinants are age, degree of past sexual enjoyment, and marital status. This again emphasizes the fact that for women the availability of a sexually capable and socially sanctioned partner is a crucial factor.[8, 9] This point has particular relevance to the multifaceted issue of widowhood. Because the life expectancy of women exceeds that of men, there is in later life, a discrepancy in the number of men and women. This problem has even prompted consideration of polygyny as a possible solution.[10]

Generally speaking, if sex is to continue playing an important role, then its quality is a pertinent issue. The subjective quality of sexual experience is more relevant than the quantity. Our attempt to understand some of the qualitative aspects is facilitated by keeping in mind a few points and considerations.

(a). Because sex usually is no longer procreative, there may be more emphasis on its recreative aspects. In spite of the anatomic and functional decline of the genital apparatus, interest in sexual activity tends to persist.

(b). Because of involution of the genital organs, there may be a shift of interest, away from traditional sex (sexual intercourse with orgasm), in the direction of other types of sexual activity, *i.e.*, sexual drives and behavior that are not primarily aimed at discharging genital excitation through orgasm. These pregenital needs and activities include sexual excitations from many parts of the body and a great variety of stimuli (oral, touch, and temperature stimulation, etc.).

(c). Such a relative predominance of pregenital drives in an older person cannot be simply compared with the sexual immaturity of children or adolescents. Old age is not a second childhood. A lifetime of experience makes the difference.

(d). The aim of sexual activity may not be primarily orgastic release of sexual tension, but rather the developing or maintaining of excitation. In this context, sexual activity may also serve more general aims, e.g., the need for intimacy and warmth, or a sense of being alive.

## Sexual Problems in Old Age

Sexual problems may occur at any age, and old age is no exception. We do not know if the incidence of sexual problems in old age is higher or lower than in other phases of life, or whether they are similar in nature. Sexual problems may begin with the aging process; they may ameliorate in old age; or, as a life-long problem they may be carried over into later years. Individuals with a background of life-long sexual adjustment or personality maturity tend to have few, if any, sexual problems in old age.

Loss of any capacity, including sexual functions, may give rise to a grief reaction. In men, sexual potency usually declines gradually, and this makes it possible to work through the grief little by little, and to accept the loss without severe emotional upsets. Sexual involution in women, the menopause, usually takes place at a more rapid rate than the climacteric in men. Consequently, in women the psychological reactions to the change of life are often stronger or more visible than the corresponding reactions in men. But the intensity of the grief reaction does not necessarily have a bearing on the final outcome. It is important to note that because women usually cope with involutional problems at a younger age than men do, they may have greater adaptational capacity when they really need it.

To a large extent, sexual drives can be understood in terms of their role in human relationships. Eros tends to bring people together, and the loss of sexual capacity may lead to anxious concerns about possible disruptions of intimate relations (e.g., fear of loneliness). Also, the loss of an important function can be perceived as a narcissistic injury resulting in lower self-esteem. In order to maintain or restore self-esteem, several psychological techniques may be employed (denial, projection, regression, and withdrawal). Whether these mechanisms are adaptive or maladaptive depends mainly on the degree of the particular mechanism.

(a). The individual who tries to deny his sexual decline may appear to be hypersexual. True hypersexuality, however, is very rare and usually it is "pseudo," in the sense of a hypersexual facade. Such persons may seek out a great number of sexual experiences or variations, and this activity has an urgent, compulsive quality. The person does not act his age, but behaves as a younger adult. Again, whether or not such behavior is normal (adaptive) depends on the degree of these traits. In fact, a certain amount of denial or compensation can be useful. Some ingredients of romanticism and role playing add spice to life. As long as fantasy and make-believe do not get to the point of actual self-deception, no problem exists. Along with romantic make-believe comes the search for beautification; and again, as long as the beautification measures are aesthetically appropriate, and consistent with the individual's age and life style, we are dealing with normal and adaptive behavior.

(b). Decline of sexual function may lead to fears concerning loss of love. Some persons are bothered by a nagging fear that they will lose their hold on the spouse. *Possessiveness*, the attempt to have a permanent hold on the other person, is based on insecurity or dependency. The possessive person suffers from jealousy, a pathological apprehension about the possibility of alienation of affection. (Clinically, pathological jealousy and suspiciousness may occur in involutional depressions, or in paranoid states). The individual uses projection to find a scapegoat, often blaming the spouse for the trouble. What is ironic and tragic, is that this becomes a self-fulfilling prophecy: suspiciousness alienates others, and the alienation then becomes proof of the original suspicion.

(c). When a person feels that, with regard to some important activity, he is less capable than he would like to be, he may protect himself by way of a *retreat*. He may retreat from those situations that provide opportunities for that particular activity. Such a protective retreat may also occur as a response to feelings of sexual inadequacy and manifest itself as a regression into hypochondriasis. The physical symptoms provide an alibi for the alleged inadequacy.

(d). Avoidance of sexual opportunities (because of the fear of failure) may lead to another risk, *viz.*, *withdrawal* from the other person. After some time, a new relationship becomes solidified, with the two partners now being further away from each other. The fear of failure often is the result of an all-or-none view. If sex is viewed as an all-or-none business, without a place for intermediate sexual activities (sex short of orgasm through intercourse), then the options are limited. The husband, for example, may feel that to enjoy sex he is obliged to go all the way. Perhaps his wife feels likewise; more likely she does not. Of course, some women interpret any failure on the part of their husband as rejection. Instead of viewing sexual involution as a fact of life, they take it personally. Their sense of rejection or loneliness is not based on actual, but imagined, rejection.

(e). *Embarrassment and shame* are troublesome feelings that may originate in several ways. First, most people feel that aging does not enhance beauty, and that the aged body is less beautiful to see. Whereas in earlier years, looking at one partner's body was a source of sexual stimulation, this is no longer so. By the same token, being looked at by one's partner may evoke feelings of embarrassment or shame. No longer is the emphasis on showing and showing off, but more on the need to cover and have privacy, from one's own eyes and those of one's partner. The ideal of dignity has as its counterpart the risk of shame. Loss of face may be the result of acting inappropriately, *i.e.*, not acting one's age. A third source of shame or guilt is related to the relative predominance of pregenital strivings. It is interesting that the experts may advise older persons to relax and not worry about guilt and inhibitions regarding sex. One gets the impression that older persons are being encouraged to enjoy the kind of sex that younger people do, as if age made no difference at all. Thus, a new (false) stereotype may develop, replacing the previous one of the sexlessness of old age. This new stereotype—that older persons can have sex lives comparable to younger persons—might be more damaging than the old one, because it tends to set a standard of behavior beyond the reach of the majority of old people. Such a development only would increase fears of failure and reinforce the view that anything short of heterosexual intercourse with orgasm is something to feel embarrassed about.

(f). Personal identity is closely related to one's self-concept as a man or woman. Therefore, decline or loss of sexual functions may pose a threat to an individual's sense of identity, in particular sexual identity, *i.e.*, being a man, being a woman. The resulting *identity crisis of late life* may be quite disruptive. Frequently, we find that earlier psychological problems (dating back to adolescence and childhood) are reactivated.

## Sex and Chronic Illness

(a). Many patients suffering from a variety of chronic *physical conditions* continue to have sexual interest, and maintain sexual activity. Chronic conditions such as heart disease, stroke, neurological diseases (*e.g.*, multiple sclerosis, hemiparesis), and urogenital diseases interfere to some extent with sexual interest and activity. But this interference is not necessarily a total one. In the case of men, for example, who have had a coronary attack or a prostatectomy, approximately three-fourths are able to continue sexual activity.[11, 12, 13]

Certain problems, however, may arise in these situations, and these apply particularly to male patients. The disability resulting from the chronic illness may specifically interfere with the capacity to take sexual initiative and to perform in an active and sustained manner. It becomes, therefore, necessary for such patients (and their wives) to seek *new ways of sexual intimacy*. This requires, in both partners, open-mindedness and cooperation which in turn permit experimentation with new sexual techniques. An example of what might be a rather difficult readjustment is the change from an active mode to a less active or passive mode. Such a transition would be difficult for highly aggressive, independent, or self-assertive men.

The patient with a chronic illness (or the spouse) may come to feel that sex no longer has, or should have, a place in their life. For example, many women used to believe that a hysterectomy would signify the end of enjoyable sex. Or, a man may be convinced that prostate surgery will render him impotent. Unfortunately, such convictions may be self-fulfilling prophecies. Disfiguring and mutilative surgical procedures (mastectomy, colostomy, etc.) can be especially a problem for women. Women are generally more vulnerable to the trauma of disfigurement with the resulting loss of attractiveness, whereas men are more vulnerable to loss of power.

**(b).** Patients with *organic brain damage* often present sexual problems of a specific nature. Because of the brain damage, there may be psychological impairments such as poor judgment and poor impulse control. Such elderly patients may show sexual behavior that is inappropriate with regard to time, place, and social context. Examples of such behavioral disturbances are exhibitionism, masturbation in public, pedophilia, and so on. Such behavioral manifestations of dementia may occur among geriatric patients in chronic care facilities. This can be upsetting to both the personnel and the other patients.

**(c).** Geriatric patients in institutions may also present problems in terms of *sexual acting out*. What is acted out, through sexual behavior, can be a variety of impulses or psychological conflicts. For example, a patient may express hostile, defiant, or rebellious tendencies through provocative sexual acts. Another patient has discovered that exhibitionism is a guaranteed attention-getting device. Again another type of patient seems to have learned, through some sort of conditioning, that the only opportunity to be touched by human hands is the forceful restraint that follows his attack on somebody else, or being cleaned up after soiling himself. In the therapeutic management of these disturbances it is helpful to have some understanding of the psychological problem that underlies the overt behavior. The knowledge that a patient's disturbed sexual behavior is a manifestation of his confusion, or is prompted by anger, loneliness, or boredom, enables us to see the disturbing behavior in the proper perspective, to maintain our professional attitude of detached concern, and to follow a plan of rational therapy that is aimed, not at the symptom, but at the cause.

## REFERENCES

1. GREENBLATT, R. B.: The psychogenic and endocrine aspects of sexual behavior. *J. Am. Geriatr. Soc. 22:* 393–396, 1974.
2. KINSEY, A. C., POMEROY, W. B., AND MARTIN, C. E.: Sexual Behavior in the Human Male. W. B. Saunders Company, Philadelphia, 1948.
3. KINSEY, A. C., POMEROY, W. B., MARTIN, C. E., AND GEBHARD, P. H.: Sexual Behavior in the Human Female. W. B. Saunders Company, Philadelphia, 1953.
4. VERWOERDT, A., PFEIFFER, E., AND WANG, H. S.: Sexual behavior in senescence. I. Changes in sexual activity and interest of aging men and women. *J. Geriatr. Psychiatry 2:* 163–180, 1969.
5. VERWOERDT, A., PFEIFFER, E., AND WANG, H. S.: Sexual behavior in senescence. II. Patterns of change in sexual activity and interest. *Geriatrics 24:* 137–154, 1969.
6. SHEPS, M. C.: Marriage and mortality. *Am. J. Public Health 51:* 547–555, 1961.
7. PFEIFFER, E., VERWOERDT, A., AND WANG, H. S.: The natural history of sexual behavior in a biologically advantaged group of aged individuals. *J. Gerontol. 24:* 193–198, 1969.
8. PFEIFFER, E. AND DAVIS, G. C.: Determinants of sexual behavior in middle and old age. *J. Am. Geriatr. Soc. 20:* 151–158, 1972.
9. CHRISTENSON, C. V. AND GAGNON, J. H.: Sexual behavior in a group of older women. *J. Gerontol. 20:* 351–356, 1965.
10. KASSEL, V.: Polygyny after 60. *Geriatrics 21:* 214–218, 1966.
11. FORD, A. B. AND ORFIRER, A. P.: Sexual Behavior and the chronically ill patient. *Med. Aspects Hum. Sexuality 1:* 51–61, 1967.
12. HELLERSTEIN, H. K. AND FRIEDMAN, E. H.: Sexual activity and the postcoronary patient. *Med. Aspects Hum. Sexuality 3:* 70–96, 1969.
13. FINKLE A. L.: Sex after prostatectomy. *Med. Aspects Hum. Sexuality 2:* 40–41, 1968.

# 22
# the golden age

The term golden age suggests that old age is a period in life which has prestige, high value, or great satisfaction. Related to this is the optimistic belief that continued progress in medicine, science, and social conditions will eventually enable man to live the full length of his life span, "adding years to life and life to the years." Whether or not this utopian prospect will ever come about is a matter of speculation.

Or, maybe this view of old age as a golden age is a cover-up. Could it be an invention, or an unconscious expression of our own pessimistic, gerophobic attitudes? By creating the mirage of a golden age at the horizon of life, we may comfort ourselves and feel relieved from doing anything about the stark realities of old age. Then, the phrase would be a hypocritical euphemism and a form of self-deception.

Notions which younger people have about old age, *e.g.*, gerophobia, must be in the nature of prejudice because they have not had first hand experience with being old. These prejudices are carried along by these people, through adult years, into old age. By this time, the prejudice boomerangs against its carrier: the old person has become what he used to be afraid of. Thus, preconceived, unfavorable notions about old age are self-defeating not only to the aged of today, but also to people who are still young but will be old someday.

Between the overly optimistic and overly pessimistic points of view, there may be a more realistic position.

The aging person does have a decline in physical functioning, and it is particularly these physical changes that underly our gerophobic tendencies. Nevertheless, it is important not to forget that many functions hold up reasonably well with aging; that aging is not synonomous with illness; that only a small minority of the aged (5%) is so disabled that they have to be institutionalized; that some of the chronic illnesses and disabilities occurring in old age may become more treatable in the nearby future; and so on. And it must be kept in mind that aging, physiologically and psychologically, is an individual matter: different organ systems in the same individual may age with different times of onset and at different rates of speed. Also, time of onset and tempo varies from one individual to another.

With regard to social aspects, there is, of course, little doubt that the aged are less involved and engaged than, say, middle-aged persons. Nevertheless, social functions appear to be relatively age-resistant, be-

266

ing interpersonal in nature and not quite as dependent on physical factors.

Most of the aged are not alone or do not feel lonely; most of them wish to retain some degree of independence and they seem to succeed reasonably well in this. Aging persons are as individual in their preference with regard to closeness *versus* distance to relatives as younger people are.

Retirement is not just the loss of one's occupational work role; it is also an opportunity for more private work. General progress in education in the younger years, and proper attention to preretirement planning will enable retired persons to make optimal use of their free time for recreation or even creative purposes.

Psychological capacities decline in effectiveness. There is a common notion that old people are more conservative and less flexible. By and large, productivity and creativity, following a peak in the 30's and 40's, decline gradually thereafter. Nevertheless, personality does not drastically change with aging. This does not mean that people do not change at all in the course of time, but in the midst of change, an individual's identity can remain the same. Rather than describing old people in terms of being rigid, conservative, or cautious, we should wonder about the totality of their life style. Certain functions are more apt to stand out in late life, such as historical perspective, wisdom, and judgment. The historical perspective that comes from accumulated life experiences involves also a perspective on one's own life. The life review is a creative mental process through which the aged person reflects on the meaning of his own life and sometimes life in general. Besides the subjective goal of recalling personal historical events, reminiscing can be useful for others by communicating historical and cultural values to members of younger generations. Productivity and creativity do not necessarily come to a standstill in late life, but their quality may change. Creative interests may have a different focus (*e.g.*, interest in history, nature, etc.).

All of this has a familiar ring. Somehow it still lacks power of persuasion. The nevertheless element in all of the above considerations reminds me of a letter of recommendation which I had requested concerning somebody, many years ago. The respondent's letter started off with, "I have known Dr. X for eight years. Nevertheless, I can recommend him very highly." I am also reminded of what a well-known geriatrician said after almost a lifetime of work in the field of aging, "Old age *is* a depression."

There are innumerable ways of being happy or miserable. In fact, it is hard to know what happiness is; it is ephemeral and evanescent. In order to see it one needs to have astigmatic vision, because by directly focusing at happiness, it seems to disappear. The pursuit of happiness is probably a self-defeating method. Happiness is also elusive, because at the very moment of experiencing it, I become aware of its transience.

Be that as it may, there seem to be three principal ways of happiness. First, one can be happy in anticipation of something. Implicit in this happiness is the hope, trust, or certainty that the happy prospect will become reality. This happiness has a temporal quality of the "not yet." Second, there is the pleasure of actual gratification and the joy of attainment in the present. This is the happiness of the "now," a transient moment between the "not yet" and the "no longer." Third, there is the happy contentment of having had pleasure and happiness and knowing and remembering it. The temporal quality is that of "no longer," but the past experience can be retained as mental images and memories and they can be recalled at will.

Each of the three modes of happiness has its own specific risk of misery. The happiness of the hopeful anticipation may shift toward anxiety, *i.e.*, doubt about the probability of the hoped-for prospect. The happiness of the actual satisfaction in the here and now may be mixed with a nostalgic awareness of the transient nature of pleasure and its evanescence. The happiness of contentment and fulfillment may be replaced by depression or despair, when the person believes that his past was empty and that it is now too late to do anything about it.

A 75-year-old man, for example, stated that "Since I was 15 years old, when I got started on my own, I have had 100 hours of happiness." Over a 60 year period, that comes to approximately two minutes of happiness per week.

People in general differ in regard to their preference for these modes of happiness. Eager anticipation is more typical for young people. Involvement in the present is more characteristic for the middle years. And ideally, late life is the time for a sense of completeness: the certainty that what was once a promise has been fulfilled. The retrospective access through one's memories to the shares of happiness may result in a sense of gratitude. All of this may add up to a perspective in old age which could be a strong counterforce against cynicism or despair.

The key is the attainment of a sense of a fulfillment. A young patient, 20 years of age, who was on a path toward schizophrenia, once said during an interview, "I wish that I were old." At first, I did not quite understand his point. He did not sound depressed, or tired, but one thing was beyond a doubt: the depth of his anxiety. Facing the openness of his future terrified him. What his statement implied was something to the effect of, "I wish that I were old. Then I would have completed all the living ahead of me; then I could at least say that all the experiences of a lifetime would be unalienably mine. Nobody could take them away. Nobody could touch me. I would have made it to the other side, without dying before my time."

Anxiety in younger years often reflects fears of missing out on life's opportunities, or of dying before one's time. Having lived a full life places one beyond anxiety, in a sphere of serenity.

Related to the concept of fulfillment is the idea of coming home. The theme of "home" or "going home" is a leitmotiv in old age. The senile patient goes back home, to where he was born. The religious person looks forward to going home in a very different sense. A pervasive nostalgia is all around. But regardless of what home and where, aren't we also talking about being at home with myself, a special sense of belonging between me and myself? Being at one with myself is not a place, but an inner quality of being.

Up to this point, we have evaded the most difficult question, *viz.*, what about people whose lives were empty? Are they victims to be abandoned to despair? Erikson defines integrity as the acceptance of life and the people in it, as something that had to be and that, by necessity, permitted no substitutions; and as the acceptance of one's life and what happened in it, as one's own responsibility. Something that has to be "by necessity" is in accordance with the laws of determinism, fate, or Necessity (Ananke). On the other hand, my responsibility is based on freedom and choice. The transcendence of fate and the transformation of Necessity into Providence is ultimately possible only because of the sovereignty of the self. Man creates his own world, makes his own history, and is his own historian. History is not mechanical copying of facts, but selective choosing of relevant events. And who is the one to decide what is relevant? What judge is there to go to? Even the choice of a judge would be my decision. In the end, there is no one else to go to for the final answers except oneself.

## CONCLUDING REMARKS

The emphasis in this last chapter has been on finding the positive elements and accounting for the goal in the golden age. Those of us who are in regular contact with the aged do not have to be convinced of the need of presenting the aged themselves with a message of hope. If it should become a habit to bring them messages of decline and depression, we would soon be without an audience, if not without work. On the other hand, it is equally difficult to hand out false reassurances and to deceive our aged clients and ourselves with Pollyannish pronouncements. All of this, far from being philosophical, is an urgently practical matter.

The various points presented above as positive elements have to be thought of as goals and ideals. Few people reach all of their goals and few reach any one goal as completely as they had wished. Goals and ideals are guideposts; they point the way. Old people vary greatly with regard to the progress they have made toward the end goals. It is safe to say that the overall situation of the aged nowadays, in spite of many recent improvements, is still not conducive toward assisting the aged to attain their goals. We hope improvements will continue to occur so that many ideals will be more closely approximated.

Apart from any and all such improvements, we must keep in mind that the golden values of the golden age do not come without work, conflict, and struggle. The value of gold lies precisely in the fact that it is rare and that one has to work hard at getting it. Finding it makes all the hardships worthwhile; knowing there is indeed gold present makes it possible to continue working with confidence.

# index